2017 Annual Competitiveness Analysis and Impact of Exchange Rates on Foreign Direct Investment Inflows to ASEAN Economies

NUS National University of Singapore

LKY Lee Kuan Yew School of Public Policy
ASIA COMPETITIVENESS INSTITUTE

In 2016 and 2017, ACI was ranked 13th globally, 2nd in Asia and 1st in Singapore amongst 90 think tanks worldwide under the "Best University Affiliated Think Tank" category by the Think Tanks and Civil Societies Program at the University of Pennsylvania, USA.

About ACI

The Asia Competitiveness Institute (ACI) was established in August 2006 as a research centre at the Lee Kuan Yew School of Public Policy (LKYSPP), National University of Singapore (NUS). It aims to build the intellectual leadership and network for understanding and developing competitiveness in the Asia region. ACI seeks to contribute to the enhancement of inclusive growth, living standards and institutional governance through competitiveness research on sub-national economies in Asia. It identifies mitigating issues and challenges for potential public policy interventions through close collaboration with regional governments, business corporations, policy think-tanks and academics. ACI's three key research pillars include (i) sub-national economies level competitiveness analysis and city-level liveability analysis, (ii) firm-level competitiveness analysis in 16 Asia economies, and (iii) Singapore's long-term growth strategies and public policy analysis.

ACI's value propositions may be encapsulated in its acronym:
Analytical inputs to initiate policies for policy-makers and business leaders in Asia
Capacity building to enable others through improvement in productivity and efficiency
Intellectual leadership to create pragmatic models of competitiveness and inclusive growth

The institute's core research competencies can also be encapsulated in this acronym describing our evidence-based assessments conducted on public policies for **A**SEAN in the context of the rise of **C**hina and **I**ndia.

Vision and Mission

- ACI's over-arching vision is to build up its research credibility with policy impact, contributing as a professional, world-class think-tank.
- ACI's mission is to establish our niche as a leading policy think-tank by identifying competitiveness trends, opportunities and challenges, as well as promoting competition and synergising complementarities amongst Asian economies and business corporations.
- ACI endeavours to articulate sound recommendations, entice discourse, and shape agenda in the arena of public policy amongst Asian governments.
- ACI undertakes evidence-based analysis of public policy issues and decisions, in order to provide assessment of their effectiveness as well as economic and societal impact.

Research Initiatives and Collaborations

I. Identify trends of competitiveness and policy analysis on trade and investment of ASEAN, within the regional context of competition and complementarities with China and India.
II. Identify competitive strengths and conduct policy analysis on Singapore within the context of regional economies with international benchmarking.
III. We are regularly releasing three indices on liveability ranking including 64 Global Cities, 100 Greater China Cities and 17 Shandong Cities.
IV. We have established an Ease of Doing Business Index on Attractiveness to Investors, Business Friendliness and Competitive Policies for 21 sub-national economies of India and 33 sub-national economies of Indonesia.
V. We have signed Memoranda of Understanding with The World Bank (2015), SPRING Singapore (2014) and European Central Bank (2014). The Memorandum of Understanding between The World Bank and National University of Singapore, coordinated through ACI, was signed in 2016.

VI. We have signed Memoranda of Understanding with various institutions in Greater China economies, including Shanghai Academy of Social Sciences (2016), Shandong Academy of Social Sciences (2015), Chongqing Municipal People's Government (2015), China Institute for Reform and Development, Haikou (2015), Counsellors' Office of the People's Government of Guangdong Province (LOI, 2014) and Chung-Hua Institution for Economic Research, Taiwan (2015).

VII. We have signed Memoranda of Understanding with six Chief Ministers' Offices in Andhra Pradesh (2015 & 2017), Bihar (2015), Chhattisgarh (2015), Madhya Pradesh (2015), Odisha (2015) and Punjab (2015).

VIII. We have signed Memoranda of Understanding with Committee for Acceleration of Priority Infrastructure Delivery at Coordinating Ministry for Economic Affairs, Indonesia (2016), Indonesia Investment Coordinating Board (2014), Indonesian Agency for Agricultural Research and Development at Ministry of Agriculture (2014), Indonesian President's Delivery Unit for Developing Monitoring and Oversight (2013) and Employer's Association of Indonesia (2013).

IX. We have signed Memoranda of Understanding with ASEAN think-tanks and institutions, including Vietnam Chamber of Commerce and Industry (2016), Centre for Strategic and International Studies, Indonesia (2015), Institute of Strategic & International Studies, Malaysia (2015), Philippine Institute for Development Studies (2015), Thailand Development Research Institute (2015) and Central Institute for Economic Management, Vietnam (2015).

About ACI's Research Pillars

ACI has consciously engaged in economic research that has significant relevance to Singapore and the Asian region. Over the years, ACI has focused on our expertise in quantitative competitiveness analysis and simulation, spinning off volumes of research output in the applications of our methodology and regional insight. At this stage, ACI has identified three core research pillars that will guide and define its research efforts moving forward. The three research pillars are as follows:

Pillar I. Sub-national Economies Competitiveness Analysis

ACI engages in systematic and methodical competitiveness analyses of the *sub-national economies* by using an evidence-based, empirical approach involving a comprehensive list of relevant indicators, which are categorised under multiple layers called the 'environments'. A number of our projects, including competitiveness analyses of Greater China, ASEAN-10, India, and Indonesia, as well as other thematic research projects, were conducted by adopting this common methodology, with potential variations in the specific environments and indicators. ACI's competitiveness analysis of Asian economies goes beyond the usual ranking to offer constructive policy recommendations on how individual member states can improve their rankings vis-à-vis their sub-national or regional peers through the application of the 'what-if' simulation, which provides the projected improvements of each state's ranking whereby the bottom one-fifth of its indicators are enhanced.

Pillar II. Micro-based Firm Level Competitiveness Analysis

Micro-based firm level competitiveness analysis is ACI's second research pillar that has been developed in view of the intrinsic importance of firm-level competitiveness in terms of productivity, efficiency, and governance. In the context of globalisation, mobility of economic activities, and blurring of borders, an understanding of the determinants and dynamics of firm-level competitiveness is paramount, in order for policy makers to make adjustments and prepare their industries for an increasingly competitive economic landscape. To this end, ACI has partnered with the European Central Bank to carry out research in this area, possessing a solid foundation in firm-level productivity research in the form of European Competitiveness Network database and methodology. ACI envisaged the expansion of CompNet into Asia, thereby pioneering the Asia CompNet research network encompassing 16 economies in Asia.

Pillar III. Singapore's Long-term Economic Growth Strategies and Public Policies Analysis

The third and imminent research pillar focuses on Singapore's long-term economic growth strategies in the context of changing circumstances, future trends, and emerging opportunities for Singapore in the decades ahead. In particular, ACI will take on the task of critically examining Singapore's public policy strengths and areas of improvement by assessing policy successes of the past, identifying new issues to address and the current policy gaps, through a systematic and evidence-based research inquiry using quantitative methodology and empirical data, leveraging on our network of policy experts.

Founding Patron and International Advisory Panel

Asia Competitiveness Institute

Asia Competitiveness Institute - World Scientific Series

(ISSN: 2424-9912)

Series Editor: Tan Khee Giap (*Lee Kuan Yew School of Public Policy, NUS, Singapore*)

In the tradition of the Asia Competitiveness Institute (ACI) at the Lee Kuan Yew School of Public Policy, National University of Singapore (NUS), our research publications make a distinctive contribution to the understanding of economic development in Asia. These books, first published in 2013, in the Asia Competitiveness Institute - World Scientific Series evaluate and track competitiveness for the sub-national economies of China, India, Indonesia and ASEAN annually through combining leading-edge methodologies with an extensive dataset. The study covers four environments of competitiveness: (1) Macroeconomic Stability, (2) Government and Institutional Setting, (3) Financial, Businesses and Manpower Conditions, and (4) Quality of Life and Infrastructure Development. It also conducts "what-if" policy simulations to propose policy suggestions.

2017

2017 Annual Competitiveness Analysis and Impact of Exchange Rates on Foreign Direct Investment Inflows to ASEAN Economies
by Tan Khee Giap, Luu Nguyen Trieu Duong, Chuah Hui Yin & Nguyen Duy (Lee Kuan Yew School of Public Policy, NUS, Singapore)

Balanced, Sustainable and Competitiveness Enhancement Study for Vietnam: A Critical Evaluation with Development Potentials
by Vu Tien Loc (Vietnam Chamber of Commerce and Industry, Vietnam), Tan Khee Giap, Luu Nguyen Trieu Duong & Nguyen Duy (Lee Kuan Yew School of Public Policy, NUS, Singapore)

2017 Impact Estimation of Exchange Rate on Foreign Direct Investment Inflows and Annual Update of Competitiveness Analysis for 34 Greater China Economies
by Tan Khee Giap, Zhang Xuyao, Leong Puey Ei & Tan Yang En Isaac (Lee Kuan Yew School of Public Policy, NUS, Singapore)

2017 Annual Competitiveness Analysis and Impact of Exchange Rates on Foreign Direct Investment Inflows to Sub-National Economies of India
by Tan Khee Giap, Sasidaran Gopalan, Jigyasa Sharma & Leong Puey Ei (Lee Kuan Yew School of Public Policy, NUS, Singapore)

2017 Annual Competitiveness Analysis and Impact of Exchange Rates on Foreign Direct Investment Inflows to Sub-National Economies of Indonesia
by Tan Khee Giap, Mulya Amri, Nursyahida Ahmad & Diamanta Vania Lavi (Lee Kuan Yew School of Public Policy, NUS, Singapore)

2016

2016 Annual Competitiveness Analysis and Growth Slowdown Analysis for ASEAN-10
by Tan Khee Giap, Nguyen Le Phuong Anh & Luu Nguyen Trieu Duong (Lee Kuan Yew School of Public Policy, NUS, Singapore)

*More information on this series can also be found at http://www.worldscientific.com/series/aciwss

(Continued at end of book)

2017 Annual Competitiveness Analysis and Impact of Exchange Rates on Foreign Direct Investment Inflows to ASEAN Economies

Tan Khee Giap

Co-Director, Asia Competitiveness Institute
Lee Kuan Yew School of Public Policy, National University of Singapore

Luu Nguyen Trieu Duong

Research Associate, Asia Competitiveness Institute
Lee Kuan Yew School of Public Policy, National University of Singapore

Chuah Hui Yin

Research Assistant, Asia Competitiveness Institute
Lee Kuan Yew School of Public Policy, National University of Singapore

Nguyen Duy

Research Assistant, Asia Competitiveness Institute
Lee Kuan Yew School of Public Policy, National University of Singapore

Special Remarks

K Shanmugam
Minister for Home Affairs and
Minister for Law, Singapore

Tommy Koh
Ambassador-At-Large
at the Ministry of
Foreign Affairs, Singapore

Liew Mun Leong
Chairman of Changi Airport Group and
Surbana Jurong; Provost Chair
and Professor of National University
of Singapore, Singapore

Reviewers

Lee Jae Young
Group Head and Lead Economist,
ASEAN+3 Macroeconomic Research Office
(AMRO), Singapore

Tham Siew Yean
Adjunct Professor, Institute of Malaysian and
International Studies (IKMAS), Malaysia and
Senior Fellow, ISEAS-Yusof Ishak Institute,
National University of Singapore, Singapore

Darius Tirtosuharto
Economist, Economic and
Monetary Policy Department,
Macroeconomic Division,
Central Bank of Indonesia, Indonesia

Sin Chor-Yiu
Professor, Department of Economics,
College of Technology Management,
National Tsing Hua University, Taiwan,
Republic of China (ROC)

Wang Lee-Rong
Research Fellow, International Division,
Chung-Hua Institution for Economic Research,
Taiwan, Republic of China (ROC)

Lee Kuan Yew School of Public Policy
Asia Competitiveness Institute
NUS National University of Singapore
World Scientific

Published by

World Scientific Publishing Co. Pte. Ltd.

5 Toh Tuck Link, Singapore 596224

USA office: 27 Warren Street, Suite 401-402, Hackensack, NJ 07601

UK office: 57 Shelton Street, Covent Garden, London WC2H 9HE

British Library Cataloguing-in-Publication Data
A catalogue record for this book is available from the British Library.

Asia Competitiveness Institute – World Scientific Series
2017 ANNUAL COMPETITIVENESS ANALYSIS AND IMPACT OF EXCHANGE RATES ON FOREIGN DIRECT INVESTMENT INFLOWS TO ASEAN ECONOMIES

ISBN 978-981-3273-05-4

Desk Editor: Jiang Yulin

Typeset by Stallion Press
Email: enquiries@stallionpress.com

Printed in Singapore

Contents

About Asia Competitiveness Institute (ACI) iii
Foreword xiii
Preface xv
Acknowledgements xvii
About the Authors xix
List of Abbreviations xxi
List of Figures and Tables xxv

Chapter 1 Economic Development in ASEAN: Past, Present and Future 1

1.1 Introduction 1
1.2 Regional Integration and Economic Development in ASEAN since 1967 2
1.3 Opportunities and Challenges for ASEAN's Future Development 8
1.3.1 Development Divide in ASEAN 8
1.3.2 Demographic Transition 10
1.3.3 The Fourth Industrial Revolution 14
1.3.4 The Rise of Protectionist Sentiments 16
1.3.5 Gaps in ASEAN's Regional Integration Agenda 18
1.4 Development Vision and Strategies for ASEAN-10 18
1.5 Roadmap of the Book 26
References 27

Chapter 2 The ASEAN Charter at 10: Prospects and Retrospect 33

2.1 Introductory Notes 33
2.2 The ASEAN Charter at 10: Prospects and Retrospect* 34
2.2.1 Introduction 34
2.2.2 The Making of the ASEAN Charter 35
2.2.3 ASEAN Charter: A Revolutionary Document 36
2.2.4 Reviewing and Amending the Charter 38
2.2.5 Conclusion 39
References 39

* Based on the ASEAN Lecture delivered by Professor Tommy Koh, Ambassador-At-Large at the Ministry of Foreign Affairs of Singapore, at the ISEAS–Yusof Ishak Institute on 3 August 2017.

Chapter 3 2017 Update on Annual Competitiveness Analysis for ASEAN-10 **41**

3.1 Introduction 41
3.2 ACI Competitiveness Framework and Methodology 42
3.2.1 Literature Review on Competitiveness 42
3.2.2 ACI Competitiveness Framework 43
3.2.3 Data Sources 44
3.2.4 Computation of Standardised Scores Using Equal Weights 45
3.2.5 *What-if* Competitiveness Simulation Analysis 45
3.3 Competitiveness Analysis of ASEAN-10 Economies, 2000–2014 46
3.3.1 Overall Competitiveness 46
3.3.2 Macroeconomic Stability 48
3.3.3 Government and Institutional Setting 51
3.3.4 Financial, Businesses and Manpower Conditions 54
3.3.5 Quality of Life and Infrastructure Development 57
3.3.6 Competitiveness over Time Analysis 60
3.3.7 Maximising Strengths and Minimising Weaknesses 68
3.3.7.1 Top 20 Percent Strongest and Weakest Indicators 68
3.3.7.2 Median Competitiveness Web Analysis 78
3.3.7.3 Maximum Competitiveness Web Analysis 85
3.3.8 Upgrading Competitiveness through *What-if* Simulation Analysis 92
3.4 Shapley Weightage Methodology as Robustness Check 95
3.4.1 Shapley Value 95
3.4.2 Shapley Weightage — The "Bottom-up" Approach 96
3.4.3 Comparison between the Shapley Method and the Entropy Method 96
3.4.4 Findings Based on the Shapley Weightage Methodology 98
3.5 Concluding Notes 101
References 103

Discussant Notes 3.1 Dr Lee Jae Young
Group Head and Lead Economist, ASEAN+3 Macroeconomic Research Office (AMRO) 104

Discussant Notes 3.2 Dr Tham Siew Yean
Adjunct Professor, Institute of Malaysian and International Studies (IKMAS) and Senior Fellow, ISEAS-Yusof Ishak Institute, National University of Singapore 106

Chapter 4 Impact of Real Effective Exchange Rates on Foreign Direct Investment Inflows to ASEAN Economies **109**

4.1 Introduction and Motivation 109
4.2 Importance of Foreign Direct Investment (FDI) Inflows as a Source of External Financing: Trends and Patterns 115

4.3 Literature Review 124
4.3.1 General Empirical Literature 124
4.3.2 Empirical Literature on ASEAN Economies 126
4.4 Data Description, Statistical Computation and Sources 145
4.5 Empirical Methodology 150
4.5.1 Baseline Model: Panel Fixed-effects Regression 150
4.5.2 Augmented Model 151
4.6 Empirical Results 154
4.7 Robustness Checks 156
4.8 Concluding Notes and Policy Implications 161
References 162

Discussant Notes 4.1 Dr Darius Tirtosuharto
Economist, Economic and Monetary Policy Department, Macroeconomic Division, Central Bank of Indonesia 165

Discussant Notes 4.2 Professor Sin Chor-Yiu
Department of Economics, College of Technology Management, National Tsing Hua University, Taiwan, Republic of China (ROC) 167

Discussant Notes 4.3 Dr Wang Lee-Rong
Research Fellow, International Division, Chung-Hua Institution for Economic Research, Taiwan, Republic of China (ROC) 171

Chapter 5 One Belt One Road Initiative: Global and Geo-economic Perspectives 175

5.1 Introductory Notes 175
5.2 One Belt One Road Initiative: A Global Perspective** 176
5.3 Belt and Road Initiative (BRI) from a Geo-economic Perspective*** 200
References 215

**Based on opening remarks by Minister K Shanmugam, Minister for Home Affairs and Minister for Law of Singapore, delivered at the 2017 Asia Economic Forum at Lee Kuan Yew School of Public Policy, National University of Singapore on 28 August 2017.

***Based on keynote speech by Professor Liew Mun Leong, Chairman of Changi Airport Group and Surbana Jurong, as well as Provost Chair and Professor of National University of Singapore delivered at 2017 Asia Economic Forum at Lee Kuan Yew School of Public Policy, National University of Singapore on 28 August 2017.

Chapter 6 Concluding Remarks and Future Research Agenda 217

6.1 Summary of Key Findings 217
6.2 Policy Implications 222
6.2.1 Positioning ASEAN in the One Belt One Road Initiative 222
6.2.2 Stimulating Foreign Direct Investment 227

6.3 Future Research Agenda: Impacts of Exchange Rate Movements and Volatility on Exports in the Global Value Chain Context in ASEAN 228
References 229

Appendices

Appendix 1 Competitiveness Analysis of ASEAN-10 Economies, 2000–2014 — List of Indicators 233
Appendix 2 Competitiveness Analysis — The Algorithm 239
Appendix 3 The Shapley Value Methodology 243

Foreword

This book entitled *2017 Annual Competitiveness Analysis and Impact of Exchange Rates on Foreign Direct Investment Inflows to ASEAN Economies* is the fifth annual update of the analysis of economic competitiveness covering the 10 member countries of the Association of Southeast Asian Nations (ASEAN) by the Asia Competitiveness Institute (ACI) at the Lee Kuan Yew School of Public Policy (LKYSPP), National University of Singapore (NUS). ACI's study brings a unique dimension to the research literature on competitiveness as it does not stop short at providing competitiveness ranking but also provides concrete policy suggestions for individual economy through the *What-if* simulation. The Asian Infrastructure Investment Bank finds the competitiveness index highly relevant as two of the major environments comprising the ASEAN Economic Competitiveness Index are Infrastructure Development and Fiscal Sustainability. The methodology of the index renders the comprehensive range of indicators comparable and tracks infrastructure development and fiscal sustainability across time, thus facilitating decision making.

In this year's book, I see three important value additions compared to the previous editions. First, there is a methodological innovation in the ACI's annual competitiveness analysis. By now, it has been established that ACI's approach to competitiveness differs quite distinctly from other international indices put together by organisations such as the World Economic Forum and the International Institute for Management Development. In this annual update, they have gone one step further by introducing a novel approach for assignment of weights to the various indicators that constitute competitiveness. Using the Shapley values — a tool used in game theory — ACI's analysis has introduced an element of objectivity in terms of the distribution of weights. The findings using the Shapley values tend to validate the robustness of results obtained from ACI competitiveness index over the past years. This methodological innovation holds a lot of promise and potential in terms of its application to construction of similar indices that ACI's research involves.

The second value-addition is the thematic chapter on foreign direct investment (FDI) inflows to ASEAN economies. ACI provides a rigorous empirical analysis on the drivers of FDI inflows to ASEAN, with a specific focus on the role of exchange rate movements. For a group of economies looking to leverage on FDI and trade to transform themselves into the fourth-largest economy in the world, it is important for ASEAN to achieve high external competitiveness, especially in terms of the member states' real effective exchange rates (REER). Thus, the research findings in this book make important academic and policy contributions by teasing out the relationship between REER levels, volatility and FDI in the ASEAN context.

Third, this book collates speeches by academics and policy-makers on issues of key interests to the future development of ASEAN. It contains the reflection on the ASEAN Charter by

Professor Tommy Koh, Ambassador-at-Large at the Ministry of Foreign Affairs of Singapore. I also read with great interests the discussions on the One Belt One Road initiative and its implication for the region by Mr K Shanmugam, Minister for Home Affairs and Minister for Law of Singapore; and Professor Liew Mun Leong, Chairman of Surbana Jurong and Changi Airport Group as well as Provost Chair and Professor of NUS. Taken together with ACI's cutting-edge research, the insights from these luminaries make this book a valuable compendium for policymakers, thinkers, and anyone who has an interest in Southeast Asia and the Asia-Pacific.

To sum up, I extend my congratulation to the ACI team for this excellent volume. I look forward to ACI future research projects which will undoubtedly add immense value to our understanding of competitiveness and illuminate issues of great policy-relevance in Asia.

Luky Eko Wuryanto

Chief Administration Officer and Vice President
Asian Infrastructure Investment Bank

Preface

The celebration of ASEAN's 50th anniversary in 2017 is a toast to the diversity of regional cooperation which has brought us together rather than driving us apart. Over the past five decades, ASEAN has emerged as one of the most enduring regional associations in the developing world today, with a strong economic development record. As a single entity, ASEAN has risen to become the seventh largest economy in the world, with the potentials to become the fourth largest economy by 2030. Nevertheless, ASEAN's continued development predicates on the ability of the bloc to cope with structural issues and disruptive mega-trends which range from persistent development divides within ASEAN to rapid demographic transition and technological disruptions arising from the Fourth Industrial Revolution. On the world stage, the implementation of China's ambitious transcontinental infrastructure development plan, the One Belt One Road (OBOR) initiative, brings about both opportunities for ASEAN economies to plug their infrastructure financing gaps and challenges as OBOR will decisively alter the regional geo-economic and geopolitical dynamics in Asia.

This book presents the latest findings on the relative competitiveness of ASEAN-10 economies. The framework adopted by the Asia Competitiveness Institute (ACI) at the Lee Kuan Yew School of Public Policy (LKYSPP), National University of Singapore (NUS) is one of a kind, going beyond ranking to incorporate a *What-if* policy simulation on how each economy can improve its competitiveness. In this edition, ACI has also supplemented their analytical framework with an objective method to assign weights to indicators, sub-environments and environments in their competitiveness index based on the Shapley values. This adds another layer of robustness to ACI's analysis. Furthermore, in light of the importance of foreign direct investment (FDI) for economic growth in ASEAN, the book provides an empirical study on the relationship between exchange rate and its volatility on FDI inflows to ASEAN economies which yields important implications for regional exchange rate policy-making.

At the same time, this book is an excellent compendium of insights from public intellectuals and policy-makers on key issues faced by ASEAN. In Chapter 2, Profcssor Tommy Koh, Ambassador-at-Large at the Ministry of Foreign Affairs of Singapore, reflects on the ASEAN Charter, ASEAN institutional arrangements and ways to take ASEAN forward. Meanwhile, Chapter 5 is devoted to thoughtful discussions by Mr K Shanmugam, Minister for Home Affairs and Minister for Law of Singapore, and Professor Liew Mun Leong, Chairman of Surbana Jurong and Changi Airport Group as well as Provost Chair and Professor of NUS, on the OBOR initiative. Policy-makers, academics and observers who are interested in Southeast Asia will benefit from the valuable information contained in the following pages.

With this publication on ASEAN, as well as similar companion volumes on Greater China, India and Indonesia, ACI has proven to be a leading institute in understanding and developing economic competitiveness in Asia. We hope this study will augment the policy dialogue in ASEAN and help the region navigate an increasingly complex external environment to achieve greater heights.

Ramkishen Sundara Rajan
Vice Dean (Research) and Professor
Lee Kuan Yew School of Public Policy
National University of Singapore

Acknowledgements

We from the Asia Competitiveness Institute (ACI) at the Lee Kuan Yew School of Public Policy (LKYSPP), National University of Singapore (NUS) have combined leading-edge research methodologies with extensive data collection efforts to evaluate and track economic competitiveness since 2000 at both national and sub-national levels for over 100 Asian economies including Greater China, India, Indonesia and the 10 members of the Association of Southeast Asian Nations (ASEAN).

In this book on *2017 Annual Competitiveness Analysis and Impact of Exchange Rates on Foreign Direct Investment Inflows to ASEAN Economies*, we recount the development experience of ASEAN over the past 50 years, describe the long-term mega-trends which will shape ASEAN's development trajectory and propose a development vision with actionable policy recommendations for ASEAN to become the fourth largest economy in the world by 2030. In terms of recommendations for effective community-building in ASEAN, the book benefits from the insights of Professor Tommy Koh, Ambassador-at-Large at the Ministry of Foreign Affairs of Singapore, on the ASEAN Charter and how ASEAN as an organisation can evolve in the coming decades.

In addition, the book updates the annual economic competitive analysis for ASEAN-10. In this year's edition, we introduce an innovation to our methodological framework, which is the use of Shapley values to come up with objective weights for indicators, sub-environments and environments in our competitiveness index. Recognising the importance of foreign direct investment (FDI) to growth and development in the region, we conduct an empirical investigation of the drivers of FDI inflows, with specific focus on the effects of exchange rate and its volatility. Finally, as the One Belt One Road (OBOR) is shaping up to the most ambitious and perhaps the most transformative economic initiative of the 21st century, we present speeches by Mr K. Shanmugam, Minister for Home Affairs and Minister for Law of Singapore, and Professor Liew Mun Leong, Chairman of Surbana Jurong and Changi Airport Group as well as Provost Chair and Professor of NUS, which shed light on the far-reaching geo-economic and geopolitical implications of OBOR for Asia and the world.

We would like to place on record our heartfelt gratitude to Minister Shanmugam, Professor Tommy Koh and Professor Liew Mun Leong for their contributions to Chapters 2 and 5 of this book. Moreover, the publication of the book would not have been possible without the tremendous support from various country experts who attended the ACI–World Bank Asia Economic Forum jointly organised by ACI and the World Bank at LKYSPP. We wish to thank the following reviewers who gave their constructive comments and offered instructive insights on the respective chapters as incorporated in this book:

Dr Lee Jae Young
Group Head and Lead Economist, ASEAN+3 Macroeconomic Research Office (AMRO)

Dr Tham Siew Yean
Adjunct Professor, Institute of Malaysian and International Studies (IKMAS) and Senior Fellow, ISEAS-Yusof Ishak Institute, National University of Singapore

Dr Darius Tirtosuharto
Economist, Economic and Monetary Policy Department, Macroeconomic Division, Central Bank of Indonesia

Professor Sin Chor-Yiu
Department of Economics, College of Technology Management, National Tsing Hua University, Taiwan, ROC

Dr Lee-Rong Wang
Research Fellow, International Division, Chung-Hua Institution for Economic Research, Taiwan, Republic of China (ROC)

We would also like to place on record our appreciation for the support and encouragement from Acting Dean Danny Quah; Professor Ramkishen Rajan, Vice Dean (Research); Mr Donald Low, Associate Dean (Research and Executive Education); Mr Thomas Chan Hean Boon (Associate Director, Research Support Unit) and other colleagues at LKYSPP. Finally, this book would not have been possible without the dedicated effort of all research and administrative staff at ACI. Thus, we note with tremendous appreciation the high team spirit of all ACI staff including Yap Xin Yi, Tracy Cai Jiao and Nurliyana Binte Yusoff.

Tan Khee Giap
Luu Nguyen Trieu Duong
Chuah Hui Yin
Nguyen Duy
Asia Competitiveness Institute
Lee Kuan Yew School of Public Policy
National University of Singapore

About the Authors

Tan Khee Giap is a Co-Director of the Asia Competitiveness Institute (ACI) and Associate Professor at the Lee Kuan Yew School of Public Policy, National University of Singapore. He is also the Chairman of the Singapore National Committee for Pacific Economic Cooperation. Upon graduating with a PhD from University of East Anglia, England, in 1987 under the Overseas Research Scheme awarded by the Committee of Vice-Chancellors and Principals of the Universities of the United Kingdom, he joined the banking sector as a treasury manager and served as secretary to the Assets and Liabilities Committee for three years, thereafter he taught at the Department of Economics and Statistics, National University of Singapore, 1990–1993. Dr Tan joined Nanyang Technological University in 1993 and was Associate Dean, Graduate Studies Office, 2007–2009.

Dr Tan has consulted extensively with the various government ministries, statutory boards and government-linked companies of Singapore government including Ministry of Finance, Ministry of Trade & Industry, Ministry of Manpower, Housing & Development Board, Civil Aviation Authority of Singapore, Singapore Tourism Board, Trade Development Board, Maritime Port Authority, Ministry of Information, Culture & Arts, Economic Development Board, Ministry of National Development, Media Development Authority, Ministry of Environment and Water Resources, Singapore Design Council, Ministry of Community Development, Youth & Sports, Singapore Press Holdings, Yayasan Mendaki, StarHub, CapitaLand and Great Eastern Life. He has also served as a consultant to international agencies such as the Asian Development Bank, Asian Development Bank Institute, United Nations Industrial Development Group, World Bank Group, World Gold Council, ASEAN Secretariat, Central Policy Unit of Hong Kong, Kerzner International, Las Vegas Sands and Marina Bay Sands.

Dr Tan is the lead author for more than 20 books, serving as journals editor and published widely in international refereed journals. He is the associate editor of the journal *Review of Pacific Basin Financial Markets and Policies* (US) and is on the editorial advisory board of the journal *Competitiveness Review* (UK). His current research interests include Cost of Living and Purchasing Power Index for World's 105 Cities, Global Liveable Cities Index, Ease of Doing Business Index and competitiveness analysis on sub-national economies of China, India, Indonesia and Association of South East Asian Nations.

Dr Tan was Deputy President of the Singapore Economic Society, 2004. He served in the 2002 Economic Review Committee (ERC), served as Chairman of the Task Force on Portable Medical Benefits (PMB), served as the Deputy Chairman of the IPS Forum for Economic Restructuring (IFER) in 2003 and served as a member of the Resource Panel of the Government Parliamentary Committee for Transport, Government Parliamentary Committee for Finance and Trade & Industry and Government Parliamentary Committee for Defence and Foreign Affairs since 2007. Dr Tan is currently an Independent Director of the publicly listed BreadTalk Group, Boustead Projects, TEE Land and Chengdu Rural Commercial Bank.

Luu Nguyen Trieu Duong is a Research Associate at the Asia Competitiveness Institute (ACI), Lee Kuan Yew School of Public Policy (LKYSPP), National University of Singapore (NUS). Luu graduated from NUS with a Second Upper Class Honours Bachelor of Social Sciences in Economics. A recipient of the ASEAN Undergraduate Scholarship, Luu was placed on the Dean's List and Dean's Scholar List on multiple occasions during his course of study. Luu's research interests include international economics, growth and development, applied econometrics and public economics. At ACI, Luu is the coordinator of research projects on econometric modelling of domestic and external engines of growth; the effects of exchange rate movements and volatility on exports as well as growth slowdown analysis by income thresholds for ASEAN economies. Furthermore, he coordinates ACI's research on city-level cost of living, wages and purchasing power for expatriates and ordinary residents. He also helps to oversee the ASEAN research cluster. Throughout the course of his work at ACI, he has co-authored journal articles, books and editorial-opinions on growth dynamics, cost of living and ASEAN economic development.

Chuah Hui Yin is a Research Assistant at the Asia Competitiveness Institute (ACI), Lee Kuan Yew of Public Policy (LKYSPP), National University of Singapore (NUS). Hui Yin holds a Master's Degree in Development Studies from London School of Economics (LSE). She was a recipient of Commonwealth Scholarship nominated by LSE. Prior to that, Hui Yin graduated with a first-class honours Bachelor degree in Economics from University of Malaya. At ACI, Hui Yin works on research related to international trade, ASEAN economies and small and medium enterprises. Her research interests include development studies and public policy.

Nguyen Duy is a Research Assistant at the Asia Competitiveness Institute (ACI), Lee Kuan Yew School of Public Policy (LKYSPP), National University of Singapore (NUS). Duy received his Bachelor (Honours) degree in Biology with first class honours from NUS and was also a recipient of the ASEAN Undergraduate Scholarship. His most recent publications are: "How Do Exchange Rates Affect Foreign Direct Investment Inflows?" and "Impact of Real Effective Exchange Rate Movements and Volatility on Foreign Direct Investment Inflows into Indonesia: An Empirical Assessment". His research interests and current research tasks being assigned in ACI are quantitative estimations such as Vector Error Correction Model and competitiveness ranking and Simulation Studies for ASEAN-10. He is also being involved in building and computing survey data for small and medium enterprises in Singapore and maintaining the data matrix for Cost of Living, Wages and Purchasing Power Index for expatriates and ordinary residents in 105 cities across the world.

List of Abbreviations

ABMI	Asian Bond Markets Initiative
ACI	Asia Competitiveness Institute
ACIA	ASEAN Comprehensive Investment Agreement
ADB	Asian Development Bank
ADBI	Asian Development Bank Institute
AEC	ASEAN Economic Community
AECV	Asia Economic Connectivity Vision
AFAS	ASEAN Framework Agreement on Services
AFC	Asian Financial Crisis
AFTA	ASEAN Free Trade Area
AIA	ASEAN Investment Area
AICHR	ASEAN Intergovernmental Commission on Human Rights
AIIB	Asian Infrastructure Investment Bank
AMAF	ASEAN Ministers for Agriculture and Forestry
AMRO	ASEAN+3 Macroeconomic Research Office
APEC	Asia-Pacific Economic Cooperation
APTA	ASEAN Preferential Trading Agreement
ARDL	Autoregressive Distributed Lag
ASEAN	Association of Southeast Asian Nations
ASTFI	ASEAN Seamless Trade Facilitation Indicators
ASW	ASEAN Single Window
ATIGA	ASEAN Trade in Goods Agreement
ATISA	ASEAN Trade in Services Agreement
BIS	Bank for International Settlements
BRI	Belt and Road Initiative
CEPT	Common Effective Preferential Tariff
CLMV	Cambodia, Laos, Myanmar and Vietnam
CMI	ASEAN+3 Chiang Mai Initiative
COT	Competitiveness Over Time
CPI	Consumer Price Index

CPTPP	Comprehensive and Progressive Trans-Pacific Partnership
DVA	Domestic Value Added
EAS	East Asia Summit
ECM	Error Correction Model
EDB Index ABC	Ease of Doing Business Index on Attractiveness to Investors, Business Friendliness and Competitive Policies
EIU	Economist Intelligence Unit
EPG	Eminent Persons Group
ERIA	Economic Research Institute for ASEAN and East Asia
EU	European Union
FAI	Fixed Asset Investment
FBMC	Financial, Businesses and Manpower Conditions
FDI	Foreign Direct Investment
FTAAP	Free Trade Area of the Asia-Pacific
FTAs	Free Trade Agreements
FVA	Foreign Value-Added
FXR	Foreign Exchange Reserves
GARCH	Generalized Autoregressive Conditional Heteroskedasticity
GATS	General Agreement on Trade in Services
GCR	World Economic Forum's Global Competitiveness Report
GDP	Gross Domestic Product
GFC	Global Financial Crisis
GFCF	Gross Fixed Capital Formation
GIS	Government and Institutional Setting
GMID	Global Market Information Database
GNP	Gross National Product
GRDP	Gross Region Domestic Products
GSDP	Gross State Domestic Products
GVCs	Global Value Chains
HDI	Human Development Index
HLTF	High-level Task Force
IAI	Initiative for ASEAN Integration
ICT	Information and Communications Technology
IFC	International Finance Corporation
IKMAS	Institute of Malaysian and International Studies

ILO	International Labour Organisation
IMF	International Monetary Fund
IT	Information Technology
IV	Instrumental Variables
LKYSPP	Lee Kuan Yew School of Public Policy
MNCs	Multinational Corporations
MPAC	Masterplan for ASEAN Connectivity
MS	Macroeconomic Stability
NATO	North Atlantic Treaty Organisation
NGOs	Non-governmental Organisations
NIEs	Newly Industrialised Economies
NSWs	National Single Windows
NTMs	Non-tariff Measures
NUS	National University of Singapore
OBOR	One Belt One Road
ODA	Official Development Assistance
OECD	Organisation for Economic Co-operation and Development
OLS	Ordinary Least Square
PPP	Purchasing Power Parity
QE	Quantitative Easing
QLID	Quality of Life and Infrastructure Development
R&D	Research & Development
RCEP	Regional Comprehensive Economic Partnership
REER	Real Effective Exchange Rates
RER	Real Exchange Rate
ROC	Republic of China
RSVI	"Ranked" Standardised Value of Indicator
SCO	Shanghai Cooperation Organisation
SEA	Southeast Asia
SEZs	Special Economic Zones
SMEs	Small and Medium Enterprises
SVAR	Structural Vector Autoregressive
UIP	Uncovered Interest Parity
UK	United Kingdom
UN	United Nations

UNCTAD	United Nations Conference on Trade and Development
UNDP	United Nations Development Programme
US	United States
VAP	Vientiane Action Plan
VND	Vietnam Dong
WCY	World Competitiveness Yearbook
WEF	World Economic Forum
WIR 2017	World Investment Report 2017
WTO	World Trade Organisation
YDI	ASEAN Youth Development Index

List of Figures and Tables

Chapter 1

Figure 1.1: Growth of Real GDP in Selected Economies, 2000–2016 6
Figure 1.2: Share of Trade as a Percentage of GDP in Selected Economies, 2000–2016 7
Figure 1.3: Actual and Projected Young Dependency Ratios among ASEAN-10, 2015–2030 11
Figure 1.4: Actual and Projected Old Dependency Ratios among ASEAN-10, 2015–2030 13
Figure 1.5: Five-year Average Growth Rate of Nominal Exports in Goods and Services by Region, 1991–2015 17

Table 1.1: ASEAN's Basic Social Development Indicators, 1990 and 2015 7
Table 1.2: Selected Economic Indicators of ASEAN-10, 2015 9
Table 1.3: ASEAN-10's Performance in Selected Social Development Indicators, 2015 10

Chapter 3

Figure 3.1: ACI Competitiveness Framework 44
Figure 3.2: Overall Competitiveness — 2000, 2013 and 2014 48
Figure 3.3: Macroeconomic Stability — 2000, 2013 and 2014 50
Figure 3.4: Macroeconomic Stability (Economic Vibrancy) — 2000, 2013 and 2014 50
Figure 3.5: Macroeconomic Stability (Openness to Trade and Services) — 2000, 2013 and 2014 50
Figure 3.6: Macroeconomic Stability (Attractiveness to Foreign Investors) — 2000, 2013 and 2014 51
Figure 3.7: Government and Institutional Setting — 2000, 2013 and 2014 53
Figure 3.8: Government and Institutional Setting (Government Policies and Fiscal Sustainability) — 2000, 2013 and 2014 53
Figure 3.9: Government and Institutional Setting (Institutions, Governance and Leadership) — 2000, 2013 and 2014 53
Figure 3.10: Government and Institutional Setting (Competition, Regulatory Standards and Rule of Law) — 2000, 2013 and 2014 54
Figure 3.11: Financial, Businesses and Manpower Conditions — 2000, 2013 and 2014 56
Figure 3.12: Financial, Businesses and Manpower Conditions (Financial Deepening and Business Efficiency) — 2000, 2013 and 2014 56
Figure 3.13: Financial, Businesses and Manpower Conditions (Labour Market Flexibility) — 2000, 2013 and 2014 56

Figure 3.14: Financial, Businesses and Manpower Conditions (Productivity Performance) — 2000, 2013 and 2014 57
Figure 3.15: Quality of Life and Infrastructure Development — 2000, 2013 and 2014 59
Figure 3.16: Quality of Life and Infrastructure Development (Physical Infrastructure) — 2000, 2013 and 2014 59
Figure 3.17: Quality of Life and Infrastructure Development (Technological Infrastructure) — 2000, 2013 and 2014 59
Figure 3.18: Quality of Life and Infrastructure Development (Standard of Living, Education and Social Stability) — 2000, 2013 and 2014 60
Figure 3.19: Competitiveness over Time Analysis for Overall Competitiveness, Period B (2007–2014) against Period A (2000–2006) 61
Figure 3.20: Competitiveness over Time Analysis for Economic Vibrancy, Period B (2007–2014) against Period A (2000–2006) 61
Figure 3.21: Competitiveness over Time Analysis for Openness to Trade and Services, Period B (2007–2014) against Period A (2000–2006) 62
Figure 3.22: Competitiveness over Time Analysis for Attractiveness to Foreign Investors, Period B (2007–2014) against Period A (2000–2006) 62
Figure 3.23: Competitiveness over Time Analysis for Government Policies and Fiscal Sustainability, Period B (2007–2014) against Period A (2000–2006) 64
Figure 3.24: Competitiveness over Time Analysis for Institutions, Governance and Leadership, Period B (2007–2014) against Period A (2000–2006) 64
Figure 3.25: Competitiveness over Time Analysis for Competition, Regulatory Standards and Rule of Law, Period B (2007–2014) against Period A (2000–2006) 65
Figure 3.26: Competitiveness over Time Analysis for Financial Deepening and Business Efficiency, Period B (2007–2014) against Period A (2000–2006) 65
Figure 3.27: Competitiveness over Time Analysis for Labour Market Flexibility, Period B (2007–2014) against Period A (2000–2006) 66
Figure 3.28: Competitiveness over Time Analysis for Productivity Performance, Period B (2007–2014) against Period A (2000–2006) 66
Figure 3.29: Competitiveness over Time Analysis for Physical Infrastructure, Period B (2007–2014) against Period A (2000–2006) 67
Figure 3.30: Competitiveness over Time Analysis for Technological Infrastructure, Period B (2007–2014) against Period A (2000–2006) 67
Figure 3.31: Competitiveness over Time Analysis for Standard of Living, Education and Social Stability, Period B (2007–2014) against Period A (2000–2006) 68
Figure 3.32: Median Competitiveness Web Analysis for Brunei, 2014 79
Figure 3.33: Median Competitiveness Web Analysis for Cambodia, 2014 80
Figure 3.34: Median Competitiveness Web Analysis for Indonesia, 2014 80
Figure 3.35: Median Competitiveness Web Analysis for Laos, 2014 81
Figure 3.36: Median Competitiveness Web Analysis for Malaysia, 2014 82
Figure 3.37: Median Competitiveness Web Analysis for Myanmar, 2014 82

Figure 3.38: Median Competitiveness Web Analysis for Philippines, 2014 83
Figure 3.39: Median Competitiveness Web Analysis for Singapore, 2014 84
Figure 3.40: Median Competitiveness Web Analysis for Thailand, 2014 84
Figure 3.41: Median Competitiveness Web Analysis for Vietnam, 2014 85
Figure 3.42: Maximum Competitiveness Web Analysis for Brunei, 2014 86
Figure 3.43: Maximum Competitiveness Web Analysis for Cambodia, 2014 86
Figure 3.44: Maximum Competitiveness Web Analysis for Indonesia, 2014 87
Figure 3.45: Maximum Competitiveness Web Analysis for Laos, 2014 88
Figure 3.46: Maximum Competitiveness Web Analysis for Malaysia, 2014 88
Figure 3.47: Maximum Competitiveness Web Analysis for Myanmar, 2014 89
Figure 3.48: Maximum Competitiveness Web Analysis for Philippines, 2014 90
Figure 3.49: Maximum Competitiveness Web Analysis for Singapore, 2014 90
Figure 3.50: Maximum Competitiveness Web Analysis for Thailand, 2014 91
Figure 3.51: Maximum Competitiveness Web Analysis for Vietnam, 2014 91
Figure 3.52: Weight for Each Environment by the Shapley Weightage Methodology 98

Table 3.1: Overall Competitiveness Rankings and Standardised Scores, 2000–2014 47
Table 3.2: Macroeconomic Stability Rankings and Standardised Scores, 2000–2014 49
Table 3.3: Government and Institutional Setting Rankings and Standardised Scores, 2000–2014 52
Table 3.4: Financial, Businesses and Manpower Conditions Rankings and Standardised Scores, 2000–2014 55
Table 3.5: Quality of Life and Infrastructure Development Rankings and Standardised Scores, 2000–2014 58
Table 3.6: Top 20 Percent Strongest Indicators List for Brunei, 2014 69
Table 3.7: Top 20 Percent Weakest Indicators List for Brunei, 2014 69
Table 3.8: Top 20 Percent Strongest Indicators List for Cambodia, 2014 70
Table 3.9: Top 20 Percent Weakest Indicators List for Cambodia, 2014 70
Table 3.10: Top 20 Percent Strongest Indicators List for Indonesia, 2014 71
Table 3.11: Top 20 Percent Weakest Indicators List for Indonesia, 2014 71
Table 3.12: Top 20 Percent Strongest Indicators List for Laos, 2014 72
Table 3.13: Top 20 Percent Weakest Indicators List for Laos, 2014 72
Table 3.14: Top 20 Percent Strongest Indicators List for Malaysia, 2014 73
Table 3.15: Top 20 Percent Weakest Indicators List for Malaysia, 2014 73
Table 3.16: Top 20 Percent Strongest Indicators List for Myanmar, 2014 74
Table 3.17: Top 20 Percent Weakest Indicators List for Myanmar, 2014 74
Table 3.18: Top 20 Percent Strongest Indicators List for Philippines, 2014 75
Table 3.19: Top 20 Percent Weakest Indicators List for Philippines, 2014 75
Table 3.20: Top 20 Percent Strongest Indicators List for Singapore, 2014 76
Table 3.21: Top 20 Percent Weakest Indicators List for Singapore, 2014 76
Table 3.22: Top 20 Percent Strongest Indicators List for Thailand, 2014 77
Table 3.23: Top 20 Percent Weakest Indicators List for Thailand, 2014 77

Table 3.24: Top 20 Percent Strongest Indicators List for Vietnam, 2014 78
Table 3.25: Top 20 Percent Weakest Indicators List for Vietnam, 2014 78
Table 3.26: *What-if* Competitiveness Simulation Analysis on Overall Competitiveness, 2014 92
Table 3.27: *What-if* Competitiveness Simulation Analysis on Macroeconomic Stability, 2014 93
Table 3.28: *What-if* Competitiveness Simulation Analysis on Government and Institutional Setting, 2014 93
Table 3.29: *What-if* Competitiveness Simulation Analysis on Financial, Businesses and Manpower Conditions, 2014 94
Table 3.30: *What-if* Competitiveness Simulation Analysis on Quality of Life and Infrastructure Development, 2014 94
Table 3.31: Hypothetical Example for Comparing the Shapley Weightage Methodology and the Entropy Method 97
Table 3.32: Comparison of Ranking and Index Results between Equal Weightage and Shapley Weightage Methodologies — Overall Competitiveness in 2014 99
Table 3.33: Comparison of Ranking and Index Results between Equal Weightage and Shapley Weightage Methodologies — Macroeconomic Stability in 2014 100
Table 3.34: Comparison of Ranking and Index Results between Equal Weightage and Shapley Weightage Methodologies — Government and Institutional Setting in 2014 100
Table 3.35: Comparison of Ranking and Index Results between Equal Weightage and Shapley Weightage Methodologies — Financial, Businesses and Manpower Conditions in 2014 101
Table 3.36: Comparison of Ranking and Index Results between Equal Weightage and Shapley Weightage Methodologies — Quality of Life and Infrastructure Development in 2014 101

Discussant Notes 3.2

Table 1: Industry, Manufacturing and Mining's Share of GDP in 2014 107

Chapter 4

Figure 4.1: World FDI Inflows, 1992–2015 110
Figure 4.2: FDI Inflows by Category, 1992–2015 110
Figure 4.3: Top 20 Recipients of FDI Inflows, 2014 and 2015 111
Figure 4.4: FDI Inflows into ASEAN (Billion US Dollars and Percent of World FDI, 1990–2014) 113
Figure 4.5: Percent Change in REER Levels 114
Figure 4.6: Components of Private External Financing in ASEAN, 2000–2016 115
Figure 4.7: FDI Inflows into ASEAN as Percentage of GDP and GFCF, 1990–2014 116
Figure 4.8: FDI Inflows into Individual ASEAN Economies, 1990–2014 118
Figure 4.9: FDI Inflows into ASEAN by Source Economies, 2000–2014 119
Figure 4.10: Sectoral Distribution of FDI Inflows into ASEAN, 2012–2014 121

Figure 4.11: FDI Inflows as a Share of GDP among ASEAN Member States in 1990, 2000 and 2014 123
Figure 4.12: Total FDI Inflows into ASEAN Economies from Different Data Sources, 1970–2014 145

Table 4.1: Ease of Doing Business Ranking of ASEAN Economies (out of 189 Economies), 2014 and 2015 113
Table 4.2: Contribution to FDI Inflows into ASEAN by Member State, 1990–2014 117
Table 4.3: FDI Inflows into ASEAN Member States by Source Economies in Million US Dollars, 2000–2014 120
Table 4.4: FDI Inflows into ASEAN Member States in Million US Dollars by Sector, 2012–2014 122
Table 4.5: Bivariate Correlation between FDI and GDP for ASEAN Member States, 1990–2014 124
Table 4.6: Overview of Literature 127
Table 4.7: Pairwise Correlation between Different REER Series 146
Table 4.8: Data Caveats for Data on FDI Inflows 147
Table 4.9: Data Caveats for Data on REER 148
Table 4.10: Control Variables — Sources and Definitions 149
Table 4.11: Summary Statistics 150
Table 4.12: List of Variables and Priors 152
Table 4.13: Correlation Matrix 153
Table 4.14: Empirical Findings on Determinants of FDI Inflows into ASEAN 155
Table 4.15: Using Average Monthly Change in FXR 157
Table 4.16: Using Coefficient of Variation as a Measure of Volatility 158
Table 4.17: REER as a Change in Annual Averages 159
Table 4.18: Using Bruegel's REER Monthly 41 Series 160
Table 4.19: Summary Table 161

Discussant Notes 4.3

Figure 1: FDI Inflows into ASEAN, 1990–2014 172
Figure 2: Relation between FTA and FDI Inflows — the Cases of Taiwan's Financial FDI to Viet Nam 172
Figure 3: FDI Expressed as Share of Fixed Asset Investment (FAI) 173

Chapter 6

Table 6.1: Five-year Multiplier Effects of a 1 Percent Point Positive Growth Shock on Each of the 11 Economies (Pre-2010) 223
Table 6.2: Five-year Multiplier Effects of a 1 Percent Point Positive Growth Shock on Each of the 11 Economies (Post-2010) 223
Table 6.3: Differences in Multiplier Effects for the Pre-2010 and Post-2010 Tables 224
Table 6.4: Infrastructure Investment Needs in Asia, 2010–2020: Sub-region and Sector (in 2008 Constant Prices Billion US Dollars) 225

Chapter 1

Economic Development in ASEAN: Past, Present and Future

1.1 Introduction

The Association of Southeast Asian Nations (ASEAN) is a regional organisation established in 1967 by five founding members, namely Indonesia, Malaysia, Philippines, Singapore, and Thailand. Despite its fundamental geographic contiguity, it was only after World War II that Southeast Asia was regarded as a single geopolitical region in the global context.[1] Located between the Asia-Pacific and the Indian subcontinent, Southeast Asia is a region of vibrancy with remarkable potentials for upgraded development and connectivity. Most ASEAN economies are blessed with rich natural resources including oil and gas, mineral deposits, wood, rubber and fertile land for agricultural development.

Southeast Asia has come a long way in terms of building and strengthening its regional integration. There were two predecessors to ASEAN, namely the Association of Southeast Asia and MAPHILINDO, which were founded in 1961 and 1963, respectively.[2] The first comprised the former Federation of Malaya, Philippines and Thailand, while the latter included Malaysia, Philippines and Indonesia. Both fell short of becoming a viable regional grouping due to the territorial disputes and conflicts among the member states. Subsequently, driven by a common goal of peace and stability, ASEAN was established on 8 August 1967. Since its creation, the membership of the association has expanded to include five other Southeast Asian countries namely Brunei (in 1984), Vietnam (in 1995), Laos (in 1997), Myanmar (in 1997) and Cambodia (in 1999).[3]

Following the momentous milestone in establishing the ASEAN Economic Community (AEC) in 2015, the year 2017 marks another achievement for ASEAN as it celebrates its golden jubilee anniversary. Currently made up of 10 members with nominal Gross Domestic Product (GDP) reaching 2.6 trillion US dollars,[4] ASEAN has evolved into an emerging growth centre in Asia. Given its current growth rate, which outpaces many developed nations including Japan and the United States (US), ASEAN is projected to rise as the fourth largest economy by 2030, after the US, the European Union (EU) and China.[5] Moreover, as Section 1.2 will discuss in greater detail, economic growth has translated to rapid poverty reduction, rising income and improving living standards for ASEAN residents.

---

[1] See Weatherbee (2009).

[2] *Ibid.*

[3] See the overview of establishment of ASEAN and its expansion in the official website, http://asean.org/asean/about-asean/overview/.

[4] See ASEAN Secretariat (2017a).

[5] See Heng (2015).

Over time, ASEAN has been instrumental in bolstering regional economic integration through the establishment of free trade agreements (FTAs) and multilateral initiatives. ASEAN's institutional structure has been augmented with the adoption of the ASEAN Charter in 2007. Nonetheless, stark development divides still persist within ASEAN. This is a cause for concern as inclusivity is one of the foundations for a resilient and prosperous ASEAN community as envisaged in the ASEAN Community Vision 2025.[6] Moreover, potential disruptive mega-trends including fundamental demographic transition and rapid technological advancements associated with the Fourth Industrial Revolution stand to create both challenges and opportunities for continued economic development in ASEAN.

In the tradition of the Asia Competitiveness Institute (ACI) at the Lee Kuan Yew School of Public Policy (LKYSPP), National University of Singapore (NUS), our research publications make a distinctive contribution to the literature by focusing on pertinent regional and national economic issues of ASEAN as one of our flagship projects.[7] The subsequent chapters of this book will cover the development of ASEAN institutional framework and prevailing global economic trends on top of the annual competitiveness update as well as the corresponding policy implications for the ASEAN economies. This first chapter will provide a brief summary of the progress achieved by ASEAN over the past 50 years, describe the long-term issues which will affect all ASEAN members and outline ACI's development vision for ASEAN in the years to come.

1.2 Regional Integration and Economic Development in ASEAN since 1967

The establishment and continued relevance of ASEAN 50 years since its founding is considered an unlikely success, even a "miracle", by its observers.[8] ASEAN was created during a time of great regional turmoil. It was during the height of the Cold War between the US, the Soviet Union and their respective allies which manifested in intensifying communist insurgencies and civil wars in Cambodia, Laos and Vietnam. Meanwhile, Malaysia and Philippines were engaged in territorial disputes over eastern Sabah (also known as North Borneo prior the formation of Malaysia). Indonesia, under President Sukarno, was pursuing the *Konfrontasi* policy against the newly created Malaysia throughout 1963–1966.[9] The regional geopolitics was further muddled by the separation of Malaysia and Singapore in 1965 after a series of race riots.

In addition to this tumultuous backdrop, diversity within Southeast Asia added another layer of complex challenges to regional integration. Dubbed the "Balkans of Asia", Southeast Asian

---

[6] Please see full details in the official website of ASEAN Community Vision 2025, http://www.asean.org/wp-content/uploads/images/2015/November/aec-page/ASEAN-Community-Vision-2025.pdf.

[7] See Tan *et al.* (2013, 2015, 2017a and 2017b) for previous publications on ASEAN. See Tan *et al.* (2017c, 2017d, 2017e, 2017f and 2017g) for other flagship research projects on Greater China, India and Indonesia.

[8] See Mahbubani and Sng (2017).

[9] *Konfrontasi* was a policy of hostility launched by Indonesia's President Sukarno from 1963 to 1966 in opposition to the creation of Malaysia by the amalgamation of the Federation of Malaya, North Borneo and Sarawak. While there was no declared war, numerous raids were organised by Indonesian volunteers in the border area between Indonesia and East Malaysia on the island of Borneo. The conflict ended in 1966 following the ouster of President Sukarno.

countries are very diverse in terms of cultures, languages, religions and political systems. The region is home to sizeable populations of Muslims, Christians, Buddhists, Hindus and followers of other folk religions. At the same time, political systems range from constitutional monarchies to democracies with local characteristics and single-party states. These fundamental differences have persisted until this day.

Nevertheless, the collective thirst for regional security among ASEAN's prospective member states provided the case for a cohesive regional organisation. Regime change in Indonesia in 1965 and 1966 and the resultant end of *Konfrontasi* under the new government headed by President Suharto paved the way for regional reconciliation and restoration of relations. This created the impetus for the formation of ASEAN with the Bangkok Declaration. At the time of its founding, ASEAN did not aspire towards a deeply integrated regional structure via complex institutional arrangements *à la* the EU model. Instead, the organisation set for itself, in the Bangkok Declaration, seven modest objectives which centred on the promotion and preservation of regional harmony amid a highly uncertain geopolitical landscape.[10]

Drawing lessons from episodes of bilateral and regional tensions in the not-so-distant past, the founding fathers of ASEAN agreed that regional collaboration must be based on mutual respect for national sovereignty and regional diversity. Over time, the "ASEAN Way", which emphasises consensus-based decision making, informality and consultation, as well as non-interference in domestic affairs, has emerged as the fundamental principle underpinning all ASEAN's initiatives.[11] Therefore, unlike the EU, ASEAN maintains a minimalistic formal institutional structure. Such an approach to integration has allowed member states to focus on the more urgent task of nation-building and to act jointly while maintaining their autonomy in all regional efforts.[12] The organisation has achieved success beyond expectation in terms of managing relations among its members; establishing multilateral initiatives aimed at preserving regional peace and stability such as the 1997 Southeast Asia Nuclear Weapon Free Zone Treaty and the 2002 Declaration on the Conduct of Parties in the South China Sea, to mention a few; as well as encompassing almost all Southeast Asian states.[13]

While the *raison d'être* for ASEAN in 1967 was primarily political, economic cooperation has also been fundamental throughout the bloc's history. The first ASEAN Summit in Bali in February 1976 saw the formalisation of regional economic initiatives with the signing of the ASEAN Preferential Trading Agreement (APTA), the ASEAN Industrial Projects, the ASEAN Industrial Complementation and the ASEAN Industrial Joint Ventures. The goal of APTA was to promote intra-ASEAN trade through the implementation of preferential tariffs and non-tariff measures (NTMs) on a product-by-product basis. The other three agreements were aimed at establishing inter-governmental industrial projects between members as well as facilitating

---

[10] The Bangkok Declaration is accessible from: http://asean.org/the-asean-declaration-bangkok-declaration-bangkok-8-august-1967/ (accessed on 15 March 2018).

[11] See Acharya (2001) for details on the emergence of the "ASEAN Way".

[12] See Sukma (2014).

[13] Timor-Leste, which gained independence in 2002, remains the only Southeast Asian country which is still not a member of ASEAN.

resource pooling and specialisation of complementary products. These agreements were in line with the export-led industrialisation strategy pursued by the ASEAN-5 countries.

By the late 1980s and early 1990s, multilateral trade initiatives were gaining momentum across the globe, making deeper economic integration a top priority in ASEAN's agenda. The need for closer economic cooperation was also motivated by China's emergence as a key destination for foreign direct investment (FDI) to Asia which threatens ASEAN's economic competitiveness. At the Singapore Summit in 1992, the ASEAN Free Trade Area (AFTA) was launched. The member states at the time — Brunei, Indonesia, Malaysia, Philippines, Singapore and Thailand — pledged to reduce the Common Effective Preferential Tariff (CEPT) rates on products in the Inclusion Lists to 20 percent by 1998–2000,[14] and eventually 0–5 percent by 2008. Subsequently, AFTA was extended to the new members — Cambodia, Laos, Myanmar and Vietnam (CLMV) — with special dispensations for these less developed countries in terms of deadlines for implementation of the tariff commitments.

Besides trade in goods, ASEAN was among frontrunners in the developing world in formalising commitment to promote investment and intra-regional trade in services. Member states signed the ASEAN Framework Agreement on Services (AFAS) in 1995 which aimed to liberalise trade in services in Southeast Asia beyond the scope and depth of the World Trade Organisation (WTO)'s General Agreement on Trade in Services (GATS). This was followed by the launch of the ASEAN Investment Area (AIA) in 1998, which was then elevated into the ASEAN Comprehensive Investment Agreement (ACIA) in 2009.

In 1997, the Asian Financial Crisis (AFC) erupted, denting the prospects of growth for economies in the region. The more developed ASEAN-6 were hit harder than the CLMV countries as they suffered an average 8 percent contraction in national GDP.[15] The crisis led to a collective rethink of regional economic cooperation. The ASEAN Vision 2020 was adopted in December 1997, in which ASEAN leaders reaffirmed their commitment to integration through the implementation of AFTA, AFAS and AIA. At the same time, the Vision expanded the integration agenda to include "closer consultations in macroeconomic and financial policies".[16]

Furthermore, ASEAN sought to forge closer ties with economies outside Southeast Asia. ASEAN's engagement with China, Japan and South Korea culminated in a host of ASEAN+3 initiatives, of which the two most important ones in the immediate aftermath of the AFC were the ASEAN+3 Chiang Mai Initiative (CMI)[17] and the Asian Bond Markets Initiative (ABMI).[18] Promulgated in 2000 and 2003, these two projects serve to enhance the financial safety nets in the

[14] This deadline was later moved to 2003.

[15] See Asian Development Bank Institute (2014).

[16] See ASEAN Secretariat (1997).

[17] Launched at the ASEAN+3 Finance Ministers' Meeting in Chiang Mai in 2000, the CMI was originally a currency swap arrangement between ASEAN, China, Japan and South Korea. The CMI was later multilateralised in 2009 to become a self-managed US dollar liquidity pool from which a member state can swap its local currency for US dollars in the event of a balance of payments or liquidity crisis. See Kawai *et al.* (2014).

[18] The ABMI aims to develop efficient and liquid bond markets in Asia to better utilise Asian savings for Asian investments. The initiative would also contribute to the mitigation of currency and maturity mismatches in financing. See Kurihara (2012).

region. In December 2005, ASEAN held the first East Asia Summit (EAS) with the participation of the bloc's Plus Three partners, as well as India, Australia and New Zealand. Together, they become the ASEAN+6 grouping. ASEAN went on to sign FTAs with all the Plus Six countries between 2004 and 2009. In 2011, the EAS was boosted with the inclusion of US and Russia.

Meanwhile, rising uncertainties in the global economic landscape, which were most painfully made salient by the AFC, have alerted ASEAN to the need to redefine and strengthen itself. Thus, the ASEAN Charter was adopted in 2007. The Charter bolstered the bloc's institutional framework, designating the ASEAN Summit as the highest policy-making body and expanding the role of the ASEAN Secretariat in facilitating and monitoring the implementation of regional integration initiatives. In addition, ASEAN took on additional objectives, most notably to promote an ASEAN identity as well as to play a central and active role in relations with its external partners.[19] However, notwithstanding the increasing institutionalisation of ASEAN, the ASEAN Way has remained the *modus operandi* of the bloc.

Continuous efforts in strengthening economic integration can be seen in the ratification of the ASEAN Trade in Goods Agreement (ATIGA) in 2009, and ongoing negotiation on the ASEAN Trade in Services Agreement (ATISA). These were conducted under the overarching framework of the AEC, one leg of the ASEAN Community which also includes Political-security and Socio-cultural elements. The AEC aims to transform ASEAN into a highly competitive "single market and production base" which is integrated into the world economy with equitable economic development. Its formal launch on 31 December 2015 was an important milestone, though much remains to be done to fully realise the ambitious agendas of the AEC blueprint. At the same time, ASEAN members are ardent supporters of other multilateral initiatives such as the Regional Comprehensive Economic Partnership (RCEP), the One Belt One Road (OBOR) initiative and the Comprehensive and Progressive Trans-Pacific Partnership (CPTPP).

Over the past five decades, ASEAN economies have experienced remarkable economic development. In particular, robust growth in the 1960s, 1970s and 1980s among the forerunners, including Singapore, Malaysia, Indonesia and Thailand, played a part in contributing to the East Asian Miracle.[20] Furthermore, after decades of war and civil strife, Cambodia, Laos and Vietnam have started to take off following economic reforms in these countries. Meanwhile, it is hoped that Myanmar will become the next development success story after its democratic transition. In recent years, ASEAN members have been on a positive growth trajectory. As shown in Figure 1.1, ASEAN-10 have averaged an annual real GDP growth rate of 5.2 percent between 2000 and 2016. In addition, the region has demonstrated increasing resilience where growth quickly rebounded after brief periods of economic slowdown during the early-2000s burst of the dot-com bubble and the 2008–2009 global financial crisis.

ASEAN's economic success is highly dependent on the member states' ability to attract FDI and the performance of their export sectors. As Chapter 4 discusses in more detail, FDI inflows

[19] See ASEAN Secretariat (2007).

[20] East Asia Miracle is a term coined in World Bank (1993) which identified eight Asian economies including Hong Kong, Japan, South Korea and Taiwan, Indonesia, Malaysia, Thailand and Singapore as those which had achieved spectacular economic growth with equitable income distribution and improved welfare from the 1960s to the early 1990s.

Figure 1.1: Growth of Real GDP in Selected Economies, 2000–2016

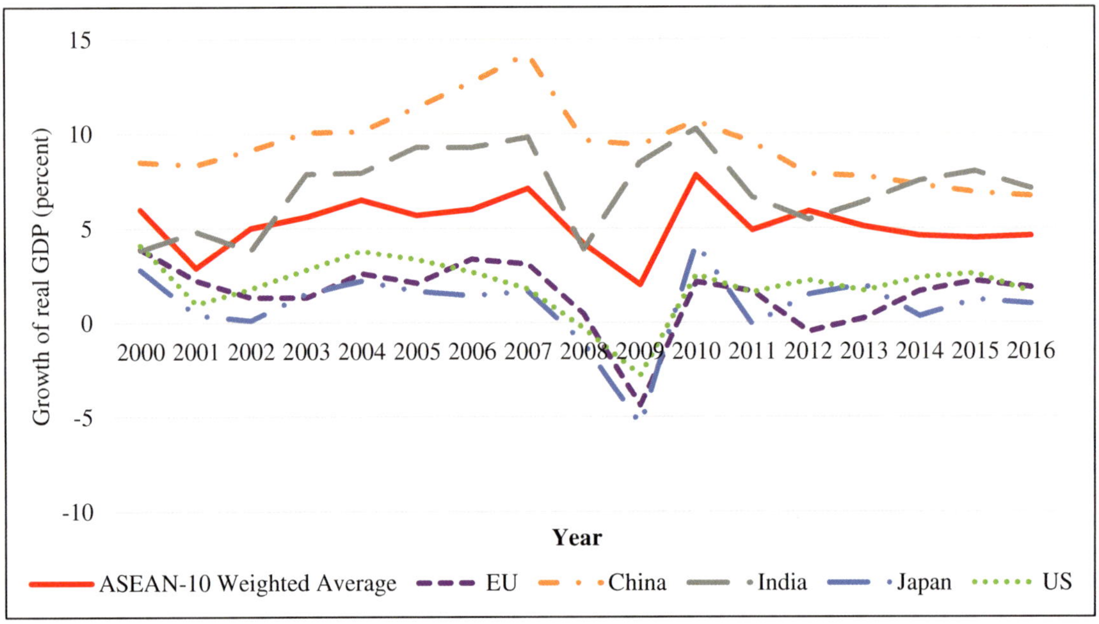

Note: The average GDP growth rate for ASEAN-10 is calculated as the weighted average of annual GDP growth rates of its members, with the weights being each member's share in the regional GDP.
Source: Authors' calculation based on data from the World Bank World Development Indicators.

into ASEAN countries rose from 12.8 billion US dollars to 132.8 billion US dollars, or 6.3 percent of total world FDI to 10.8 percent between 1990 and 2014.[21] Meanwhile, as shown in Figure 1.2, trade plays a more significant role in ASEAN as compared to other regions such as the EU, North America or the three major East Asian economies of China, Japan and South Korea. Trade in goods and services constituted more than 100 percent of GDP on average in ASEAN-10 economies over the period 2000–2016. ASEAN as an organisation has been instrumental in improving members' attractiveness to investors and connecting them to the global market. This is particularly true for the less developed CLMV countries as more than half of the total FTAs applied in CLMV ride on ASEAN's partnership with other economies. For instance, six out of eight FTAs currently enforced in Laos are associated with ASEAN.[22]

ASEAN member states have also performed admirably in terms of social development. Table 1.1 displays how ASEAN's basic social indicators have changed between 1990 and 2015. As seen from the table, robust economic growth has lifted millions out of poverty. The proportion of population living below 1.25 dollars a day, adjusted for purchasing power parity (PPP), has fallen by more than two-third from 47 percent in 1990 to 14 percent in 2015. Meanwhile, the

[21] Based on data from the United Nations Conference on Trade and Development (UNCTAD). Data includes intra-ASEAN FDI.

[22] See https://aric.adb.org/fta-country for a comprehensive listing of bilateral and plurilateral FTAs in which CLMV are engaged.

Figure 1.2: Share of Trade as a Percentage of GDP in Selected Economies, 2000–2016

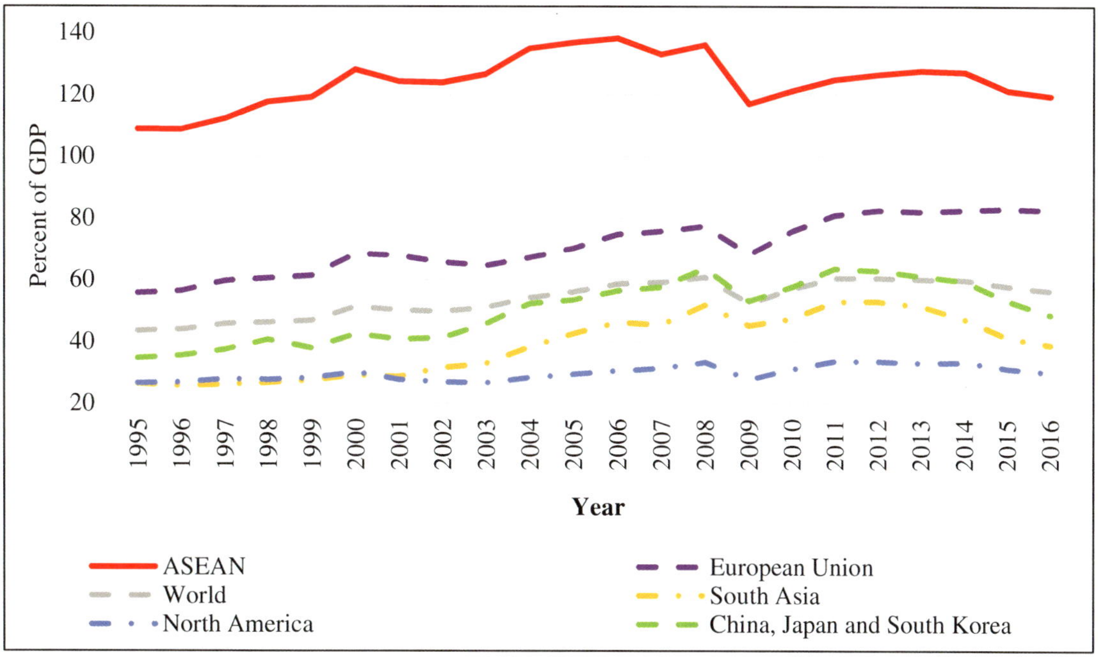

Source: World Bank World Development Indicators.

Table 1.1: ASEAN's Basic Social Development Indicators, 1990 and 2015

Indicators	1990	2015
Poverty Rate* (percentage of population living below 1.25 dollars a day, adjusted for PPP)	47.0	14.0
Adult Literacy Rate (percentage of population aged 15+)	85.0	94.5
Infant Mortality Rate (per 1,000 live births)	47.8	21.0
Life Expectancy (years)	65.4	72.5

Note: *Data on poverty rate do not include Brunei and Singapore. Data on the other indicators cover all 10 ASEAN countries.

Source: ASEAN Secretariat (2017b), World Bank World Development Indicators and Euromonitor Passport.

region has made headway in terms of basic healthcare provision. Between 1990 and 2015, average life expectancy across ASEAN-10 has risen from 65.4 years to 72.5 years, while the average infant mortality rate has dropped by more than half from 47.8 to 21 per 1,000 live births.

Thus, ASEAN countries have achieved remarkable socio-economic transformation over the past few decades. The organisation has contributed to this development success story by maintaining peace and harmony in Southeast Asia while serving as a key platform for regional economic cooperation. Today, ASEAN as a single entity is the seventh largest economy in the world, and it is projected to be the fourth largest by 2030. However, future development is not guaranteed. As the next section illustrates, the organisation and its member states are confronted with both opportunities and challenges to their future development.

1.3 Opportunities and Challenges for ASEAN's Future Development

The year 2017 marked the golden jubilee of ASEAN. There is much to be celebrated in terms of ASEAN's resilience and the member states' economic success. However, it is also a time for reflection on key factors which will determine ASEAN's future development trajectory. Common long-term issues which shall affect all 10 ASEAN countries include the persistent development divide in ASEAN, demographic transition, the Fourth Industrial Revolution, rising protectionist sentiments and gaps in ASEAN's regional integration agenda.

1.3.1 Development Divide in ASEAN

As described in Section 1.2, the ASEAN countries are diverse in terms of culture, language, religion, and customs. Furthermore, there are stark differences among the member states in terms of their natural endowment. For instance, the land area of Indonesia is about 2,555 times that of Singapore, while its population is 653 times that of Brunei.[23] While Malaysia is blessed with abundant natural resources for agricultural and industrial development, resource-poor Singapore can only rely on its strategic position in the Straits of Malacca and the ingenuity of its people for economic growth.

Apart from such fundamental differences, another aspect which calls for greater attention is the development disparity among ASEAN economies. The development gap is particularly evident between the latecomers to ASEAN, namely CLMV, and the founding members.[24] One of the reasons contributing to the divide is CLMV's late restoration of peace and stability. CLMV were plunged into years of war and conflict after decolonisation. After recovery from the turmoil, CLMV began to liberalise and open up their economies only in the late 1970s, 1980s and 1990s. As a result, they have lagged behind their neighbours in the region, particularly Indonesia, Malaysia, Singapore and Thailand which started economic reforms in the 1960s.

The development divide in ASEAN is multifaceted. Comparisons of the primary economic indicator of real average income as depicted in Table 1.2 shows an apparent income gap between CLMV and the ASEAN-6. In 2015, the real GDP per capita of CLMV were below 2,000 US dollars (constant 2010 prices), while the richest three economies, namely Brunei, Malaysia and Singapore, have reached five-digit average income levels. As the region's best performer, Singapore's real GDP per capita in 2015 was about 49 times that of Cambodia, the lowest in the region.

---

[23] According to World Bank's World Development Indicators, Indonesia owns a land area of 1,811,570 km^2, the largest in ASEAN, while Singapore's land area is 709 km^2, the smallest in ASEAN. For population size, Indonesia has the largest population of 261.1 million while Brunei has the smallest population of 0.4 million in ASEAN in 2016.

[24] See Severino (2007), Menon (2013) and Pomfret (2013).

Table 1.2: Selected Economic Indicators of ASEAN-10, 2015

Country	GDP (constant 2010 prices billion US dollars)	GDP per Capita (constant 2010 US dollars)	Trade Openness (percentage of GDP)	FDI Inflows (million US dollars/percentage of GDP)	Ease of Doing Business Ranking (out of 189 economies)
Brunei	13.6	32,661.9	84.9	173.2/1.3	101
Cambodia	15.9	1,024.9	127.9	170.1/9.4	135
Indonesia	988.1	3,827.5	41.9	16,641.5/1.9	114
Laos	10.4	1,556.7	85.8	1,118.7/7.8	148
Malaysia	330.1	1,074.5	133.6	11,121.5/3.8	18
Myanmar	70.3	1,342.3	47.4	282.4/4.7	177
Philippines	266.1	2,615.7	62.7	4,936.8/1.7	95
Singapore	289.2	52,244.6	329.9	70,579.5/23.8	1
Thailand	393.7	5,733.9	126.6	5,699.7/1.4	26
Vietnam	154.5	1,651.2	178.8	1,180.0/6.1	78

Source: World Bank World Development Indicators; World Bank Doing Business Indicators 2015 and UNCTAD.

Continuous efforts towards deeper integration and liberalisation in ASEAN including the recent establishment of the AEC have provided the impetus for reforms and transition process in CLMV.[25] In addition, CLMV have benefited from ASEAN's role as a gateway to the global economy. Nevertheless, the extent to which these transitional economies have managed to leverage on regional integration for economic development has varied greatly. On the one hand, Vietnam has successfully transformed into an investors' darling with remarkable improvement in its business environment and rising FDI inflows. In 2015, it was ranked 78th out of 189 countries in terms of ease of doing business by the World Bank and constituted 9.3 percent of total FDI inflows in ASEAN. On the other hand, Cambodia, Laos and Myanmar have not been as successful. Together, they only made up less than 4.5 percent of regional FDI while being in the bottom 30 percent of the World Bank's 2015 Ease of Doing Business Ranking. It is worth noting, however, that even Vietnam, the most developed country among CLMV, still lags far behind Singapore, Malaysia and Thailand in terms of FDI attraction and ease of doing business.

Apart from economic development, disparity in social development between CLMV and ASEAN-6 is also noticeable. As shown in Table 1.3, the average human development index for CLMV in 2015 was 0.597, far below the ASEAN-6's average at 0.782 even though Vietnam's index value was close to Philippine's and Indonesia's. Poverty remains rampant in Cambodia and Laos as more than a quarter of the population still lived below 1.25 US dollars in PPP terms as of 2015. In addition, much remain to be done in terms of improving basic healthcare in Cambodia, Laos and Myanmar as illustrated by the relatively high infant mortality rates in these countries (see Table 1.3).

[25] See Plummer and Chia (2009).

Table 1.3: ASEAN-10's Performance in Selected Social Development Indicators, 2015

Country	Human Development Index	Poverty Rate (percentage of population living below 1.25 PPP dollars a day)	Adult Literacy Rate (percentage of population aged 15+)	Infant Mortality Rate (per 1,000 live births)
Brunei	0.865	NA	96.4	8.5
Cambodia	0.563	24	77.2	27.5
Indonesia	0.689	9	95.4	22.9
Laos	0.586	29	79.9	50.4
Malaysia	0.789	NA	94.6	7
Myanmar	0.556	NA	93.1	41.4
Philippines	0.682	19	96.6	22.1
Singapore	0.925	NA	96.8	2.1
Thailand	0.740	18	94.0	10.8
Vietnam	0.683	17	94.5	17.6
CLMV Average	**0.597**	**19***	**86.2**	**34.2**
ASEAN-6 Average	**0.782**	**13***	**95.6**	**12.2**

Note: NA denotes that data are not available. Average poverty rates for CLMV and ASEAN-6 are taken from ASEAN Secretariat (2017b).
Source: ASEAN Secretariat (2017b), World Bank, World Bank World Development Indicators and Euromonitor Passport.

ASEAN leaders do acknowledge that the prevailing development gap between CLMV and the other countries may lead to the emergence of a two-tier ASEAN which will obstruct regional integration.[26] In order to tackle regional disparity, the Initiative for ASEAN Integration (IAI) was launched in 2000 with the objective of bridging the development divide. Financial and technical support dedicated to CLMV under IAI is a concrete step taken to overcome the infrastructure and financial constraints in CLMV's reforms progress, which in turn help to promote economic activities and trade flows. The Masterplan on ASEAN Connectivity 2025 (MPAC 2025) also complements the IAI in strengthening regional integration through a focus on regional connectivity improvement, which is also a critical enabling factor to facilitate cross-border economic development. Nevertheless, the onus is also on the transitional CLMV to revitalise economic reform momentum so as to achieve growth breakthroughs and catch up with the ASEAN-6.

1.3.2 Demographic Transition

Demographic transition will play a key role in the next phase of ASEAN economic development. As summarised in Bloom and Williamson (1998) as well as Bloom *et al.* (2003), views on the relationship between population dynamics and economic growth can be distinguished into three

[26] See ASEAN Secretariat (2016).

main camps of pessimists, optimists, and neutralists. The pessimists see a negative relationship between population growth and economic growth. This can be traced back to the Malthusian theory which argued that population would outgrow limited resources and eventually put a strain on economic expansion.[27] On the other hand, the optimists argue that growth in population enables economies of scale which will eventually lead to economic growth.[28] Meanwhile, the neutralists suggest that population growth has no significant effects on economic growth due to a lack of cross-country evidence. In the case of the East Asian miracle economies, Bloom and Williamson (1998) found that population dynamics accounted for one-third of their per capita income growth. This association between demographic trends with economic growth in East Asia is also supported by similar findings in Mason (2001).

ASEAN's population has witnessed an expansion from 521 million people in 2000 to 639 million people in 2016. According to a recent report by the ASEAN Secretariat, with an average growth rate of 1.3 percent annually over the period of 2000–2016, ASEAN's population constituted about 9 percent of the world's total population in 2016, of which 213 million or one-third are aged between 15 and 34.[29] Meanwhile, the average young population is projected to peak at over 220 million in 2038.

However, there are considerable heterogeneities in the demographic composition among ASEAN economies. As seen in Figure 1.3, except for Singapore and Thailand, the young

Figure 1.3: Actual and Projected Young Dependency Ratios[30] among ASEAN-10, 2015–2030

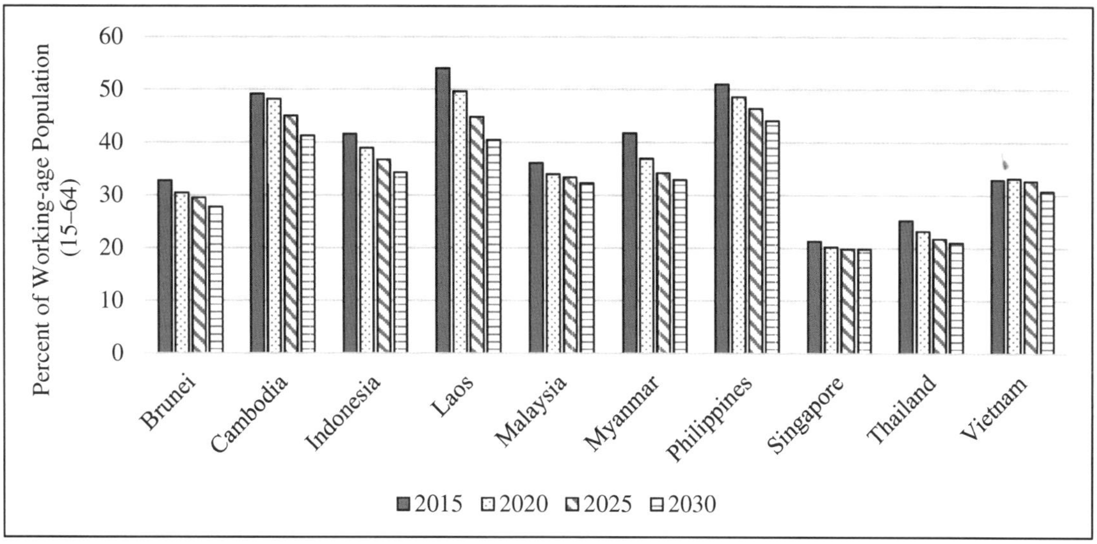

Source: United Nations, World Population Prospects 2017.

[27] See Malthus (1798).

[28] See Kuznets (1967).

[29] See ASEAN Secretariat (2017c).

[30] Calculated as percentage of population aged 0–14 to the working-age population (15–64).

dependency ratios in ASEAN countries are at least 30 percent, and such a trend is expected to continue past 2030. In particular, the young dependency ratios of Laos and Philippines were more than 50 percent in 2015 while that of Cambodia was about 49 percent. In other words, there is one child aged between 0 and 14 for every two adults aged between 15 and 64 in these economies. While this may indicate added financial burden for working people with children in Cambodia, Laos and Philippines, it also means that these countries will be experiencing a youth bulge in the near future as the young dependents grow to join the workforce.

As Lin (2012) has argued, a youth bulge can be a double-edged sword which either creates a demographic dividend or a demographic bomb. The youth bulge will yield demographic dividend if young people manage to enter workforce and reduce dependency ratio in an economy. The expansion in the productive working population relative to the dependent population will contribute to economic growth.[31] In contrast, if an economy is incapable of absorbing this growing labour force, high youth unemployment may fuel increasing youth crime, creating socio-political instability. In this case, the youth bulge is said to have turned into a demographic bomb.[32]

In recognition of the potential impacts of a youth bulge in economic development, it is imperative that ASEAN economies such as Cambodia, Laos and Philippines are prepared to harness the demographic dividend. This requires a resilient economic system which can accommodate the growing labour force. In addition, education reforms are also essential in order to produce skilled labour with relevant skillsets for future job market demands. Multiple initiatives have been launched in order to reap the demographic dividend through engagement of young people in ASEAN's development agenda. One of these is the development of the First ASEAN Youth Development Index (YDI). The YDI Report which was launched in 2017 seeks to serve as the basis for evidence-based policies in delivering effective outcomes for youth development. In line with the findings by World Bank (2011) and Lin (2012), the report has highlighted the importance of employment and opportunity for youth development in ASEAN. Meetings at ministerial level are also conducted biennially in overseeing ASEAN cooperation agenda on youth. Furthermore, the importance of youth in realising ASEAN development goal is also reflected in the World Economic Forum (WEF) on ASEAN 2017 as one of the key themes is about young people.[33]

At the same time, there are economies in ASEAN which will experience rapidly aging population. As seen in Figure 1.4, old dependency ratios in Singapore and Thailand at 16.0 and 14.8 percent, respectively, were among the highest in ASEAN in 2015. This is the result of fundamental demographic shifts in both economies. For Singapore, life expectancy at birth has risen from 65.7 years to 82.6 years while fertility rate has dropped from 5.8 to 1.2 births per woman between 1960 and 2015. Similarly, for Thailand, life expectancy has increased from 54.7 years to 75.1 years, while fertility rate has reduced from 6.1 to 1.5 births per woman over the same period.[34] Given the trends of declining birth rate and rising life expectancies, the United Nations

[31] See Reher (2011).

[32] See World Bank (2011).

[33] See Chainey (2017).

[34] Based on World Development Indicators database of the World Bank.

Figure 1.4: Actual and Projected Old Dependency Ratios[35] among ASEAN-10, 2015–2030

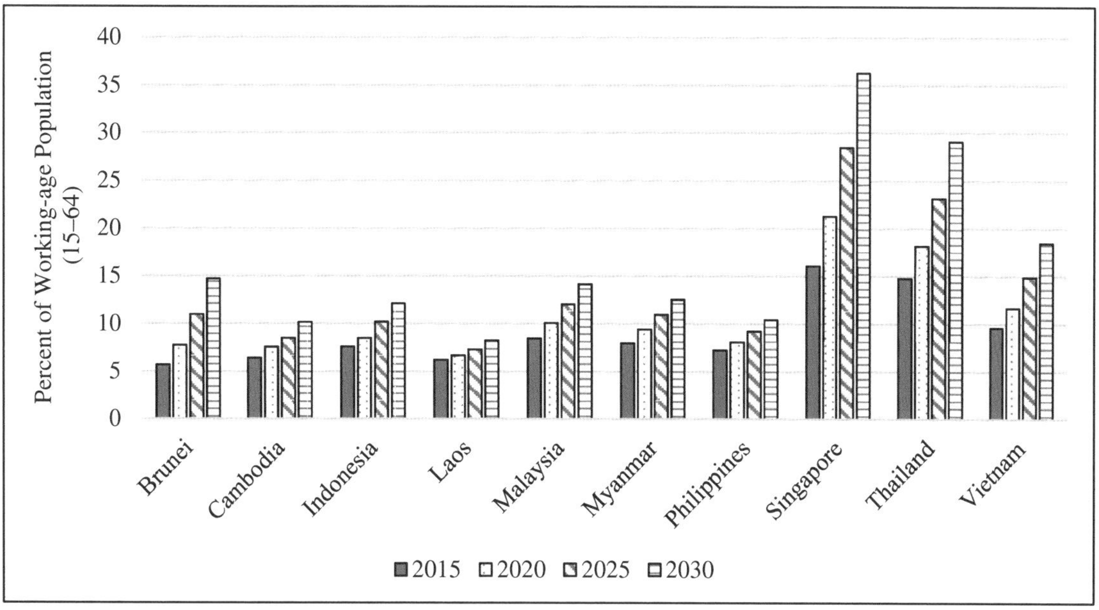

Source: United Nations, World Population Prospects 2017.

has forecasted that there will be about a twofold increase in old dependency ratio in both Singapore and Thailand by 2030 (see Figure 1.4). Besides these two countries, Vietnam will also have to contend with an aging population in the near future. While the country is still enjoying a golden population structure with twice the number of working persons as compared to the number of dependents, the risk of it "growing old before growing rich" is real. As seen from Figure 1.4, Vietnam's old dependency ratio in 2015 was high for its level of development: at 9.6 percent, it was the third highest in ASEAN, well above economies which are more developed such as Indonesia and Malaysia.[36]

A high old dependency ratio means that the labour force has to support a higher number of elderly. This creates additional strains to the government's budget under the burden of higher public spending on healthcare and pension. Furthermore, a smaller working-age population also means less domestic resources for productive investments as this group tends to save while the older population tends to dissave to meet retirement and medical needs. At the same time, an ageing population also indicates slower growth of the labour force, which may contribute to rising labour costs and erode economic competitiveness in Singapore, Thailand and Vietnam. In a recent empirical study on the growth dynamics of ASEAN countries, Greater China economies and sub-national economies in India and Indonesia by ACI, it was found that lower-middle-income economies with high old dependency ratio are more prone to experiencing growth

[35] Calculated as percentage of population aged 65+ to the working-age population (15–64).

[36] See Vu *et al.* (2018, forthcoming) for a more detailed discussion on Vietnam's aging population.

slowdown. Clearly, the ageing population will be a major issue for governments in Singapore, Thailand and Vietnam to grapple with in the next phase of their development.

1.3.3 The Fourth Industrial Revolution

Besides demographic transition, another mega-trend with tremendous potential impacts on the economic future of ASEAN is the Fourth Industrial Revolution. Past industrial revolutions have largely shaped today's world.[37] The First can be traced back to the 18th century in Britain when water and steam power led to mechanisation and kick-started the age of industrialisation. Following that, electricity emerged as a new source of energy and fuelled the Second Industrial Revolution in the 19th century. Almost a century later, information and communications technology (ICT) helped to drive the Third Industrial Revolution with breakthroughs in automation. Today, we are standing on the brink of the Fourth Industrial Revolution which involves a fusion of technological advances across digital, physical and biological fields.[38]

Past industrial revolutions have indeed brought about remarkable changes. Deane (1980) has summarised their impacts into three main dimensions of social and economic structure, productivity and living standard, and economic growth rate. One of the most evident changes is the transformation of mainly a rural and agrarian society to an industrial and urban-based society. Similar to its predecessors, the Fourth Industrial Revolution is expected to bring about more disruption in how the world operates. However, this is going to happen at an exponential rate rather than a linear pace as in previous revolutions.[39]

In fact, we have seen how innovations associated with the Fourth Industrial Revolution have penetrated our lives in a wide range of activities from taxi booking to daily transactions. The emergence of new technologies such as artificial intelligence and robotics have also disrupted a great number of industries and businesses in almost all aspects including production, distribution, sales, marketing, and research and development. For instance, instead of broadcasting through traditional media of television and radio, marketing can now be conducted through customised advertisements on online platforms like Facebook and Google.

While it is still too early to assess the full implications of the current wave of technological surge, there is no doubt that it will bring about both challenges and opportunities to individuals, businesses and governments. Being more than just a buzzword made popular after the 2016 WEF, it is expected that the Fourth Industrial Revolution will lead to significant productivity and efficiency gains.[40] This will consequently contribute to a larger scale of production, and hence economic growth. In addition, the Fourth Industrial Revolution has the potential to bring about broad-based betterment of global income level and living standards.[41] Advancements in transport and communication technologies, in particular, have made life more convenient than ever through improvement in physical connectivity as well as people-to-people connection.

---

[37] See Deane (1980) and More (2002).

[38] See Schwab (2015).

[39] *Ibid.*

[40] See Park (2017).

[41] See Schwab (2015).

At the same time, the Fourth Industrial Revolution stands to create major disruptions to the income distribution and job market structure. One of the major concerns is the "Great Decoupling" that is already happening in the US and other developed economies. According to Brynjolfsson and McAfee (2014), Western economies are experiencing a "decoupling" where income inequality is widening despite robust GDP and productivity growth. This phenomenon has been partially attributed to the labour market polarisation driven by technological innovations. On the one hand, low- and middle-skilled jobs will be displaced by computers and machines in the aftermath of industrial automation and digitalisation. On the other hand, the economy will see rising demand for high-skilled positions and jobs which are not replaceable by machines, such as those in the service sectors.[42]

The need for retooling and reskilling is great given the expected scale of labour market disruptions caused by the Fourth Industrial Revolution. According to a report which covers 15 of the world's largest economies by the WEF, there will be a net loss of 5.1 million jobs spanning the period 2015–2020, of which about two-thirds will come from the family of office and administrative jobs.[43] Furthermore, as predicted by Frey and Osborne (2017), computerisation may put about 47 percent of jobs in US at risk. Fuei (2017) estimated that a quarter of jobs is expected to be highly susceptible to automation and computerisation. Given such a trend, there has been growing call for the implementation of universal basic income, especially in developed economies. While the idea has been rejected in Switzerland in a referendum,[44] pilot studies on universal basic income are still ongoing in Finland and Netherlands.[45]

Workers in developing economies are not unsusceptible to technological disruptions either. As population size expands over time, approximately 600 million new jobs are essential to cater for the young population entering the workforce by 2030, of which the majority will have to be concentrated in Asia and Sub-Saharan Africa.[46] Thus, an unknown future of jobs with many low-skilled manufacturing and production positions at stake is a cause for concern. The new wave of technological disruptions may render a developing country's advantage in low labour cost moot, as additive manufacturing technologies such as 3D printing are able to replace unskilled, labour-intensive tasks at a much cheaper cost and faster rate. For instance, a recent report by the World Bank revealed that 3D printing has enabled the athletic footwear company Adidas to replace 1,000 low-skilled workers in Vietnam with 160 technicians in Germany and the US.[47]

The Fourth Industrial Revolution will also create new opportunities and challenges for businesses. The relationship between businesses and customers has changed as the process of buying and selling moves to online platforms. Easy access to information such as reviews of a product or a restaurant means that the customer–vendor relationship has evolved to become more interactive. More importantly, digitalisation will offer new avenues for companies to reach into the global market, enable cost-saving improvements in operations and transform the ways in which

[42] See World Economic Forum (2016a).

[43] *Ibid*.

[44] See Minder (2016).

[45] See Manjoo (2017), Coppola (2017) and *The Economist* (2017).

[46] See Raja and Ampah (2016) as well as Choi (2017).

[47] See Hallward-Driemeier and Nayyar (2017).

goods and services are delivered to consumers. Moreover, advances in Internet of Things and big data technology promise to allow companies to gain unprecedentedly detailed insights about consumers' behaviour, creating new opportunities for growth.

Thus, the Fourth Industrial Revolution will prove to be a boon for economies which can adapt to it well and a bane for those which fail to do so. In this context, constant industrial rejuvenation and upgrading, developing strong digital capacity for firms, especially small and medium enterprises (SMEs), as well as education reforms to cultivate a future-ready labour force with future-proof skills focusing on science, technology, engineering and mathematics (collectively known as the STEM fields) are vital policy priorities for ASEAN economies.

Moreover, adequate ICT infrastructure is essential as it underpins the adoption of key technological innovations of the Fourth Industrial Revolution. In this respect, ASEAN member states still lag behind other countries, as shown by their rankings in the WEF's Network Readiness Index.[48] Except for Singapore which ranked top among 139 economies surveyed in 2016 and Malaysia which topped the category of emerging and developing Asia (ranked 31st overall), other ASEAN economies have performed rather unconvincingly. For instance, Thailand was ranked 62nd out of 139, Indonesia was ranked 73rd while Vietnam was ranked 79th. Meanwhile, Cambodia, Laos and Myanmar were counted among the economies with the weakest ICT infrastructure as they were ranked 109th, 104th and 133rd. This indicates the need for a comprehensive strategy and sustained effort to prepare ASEAN economies for the Fourth Industrial Revolution.

1.3.4 The Rise of Protectionist Sentiments

Against the backdrop of potential major changes brought about by demographic forces and the Fourth Industrial Revolution, it is worrying for ASEAN economies that the global trade landscape is undergoing significant shifts. As shown in Figure 1.5, the average growth rate in world's exports of goods and services has come to its lowest level in more than two decades at 2.8 percent for the period 2011–2015. For East Asia and Pacific, the average growth rate of exports has dropped to less than 5 percent between 2011 and 2015, down from an average of 10 percent between 1991 and 2010. The trend of significant reduction in growth rates of exports in goods and services between 2011 and 2015 in all regions across the world has raised the spectre of trade deglobalisation.[49]

Indeed, key international organisations including the International Monetary Fund (IMF), the WTO, and the World Bank have sounded warnings about potential disruptions on international trade as a result of growing protectionist sentiments.[50] A recent report on the G20 economies has shown that newly introduced protectionist measures have been on the rise since 2009.[51] The rise of protectionism is driven to a large extent by fear over job loss due to globalisation and trade deficits in Western economies, as illustrated by the 2016 Brexit vote and President Trump's "America First" policy. However, protectionism will inadvertently result in more harms than

[48] See World Economic Forum (2016b).

[49] See Donnan (2018) and Swanson (2018).

[50] See Kihara and Umekawa (2017), Kutlina-Dimitrova and Lakatos (2017) as well as World Trade Orgranisation (2017).

[51] See Evenett and Fritz (2017).

Figure 1.5: Five-year Average Growth Rate of Nominal Exports in Goods and Services by Region, 1991–2015

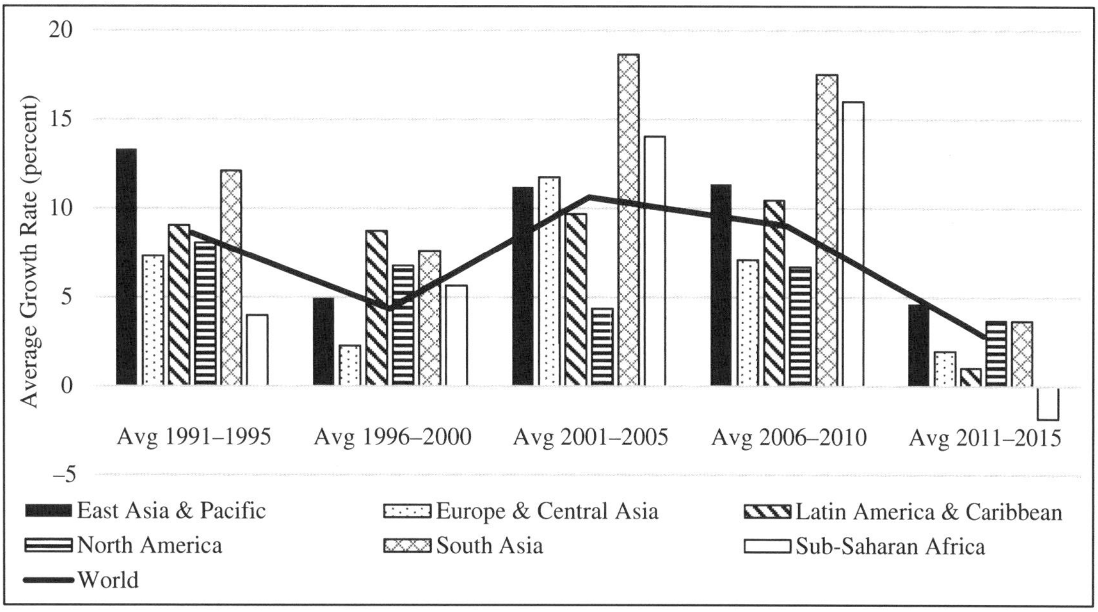

Source: World Bank World Development Indicators.

gains, culminating in a situation where everyone loses. The simulation analysis by Kutlina-Dimitrova and Lakatos (2017) has shown that in the worst-case scenario, WTO members' withdrawal from tariff commitments in all existing trade agreements would generate a real income loss of 211 billion US dollars, of which East Asia and the Pacific would experience the largest loss of 33 billion US dollars or about 16 percent of the aggregate decline.

The rise in protectionist sentiment will hurt ASEAN economies, given that they have benefited handsomely from globalisation. Exports have served as an important engine of growth, both directly and indirectly through knowledge and technology spillovers. Indeed, the success of the Singapore, Malaysia, Indonesia and Thailand in the 1970s has been attributed in large part to their export-led industrialisation strategy.[52] Drawing from the experience of their more developed counterparts, the transitional economies in Southeast Asia, namely Cambodia, Laos, Vietnam and Myanmar, have also adopted the export-led growth model. As a result, ASEAN economies are tremendously open, with trade constituting more than 100 percent of regional GDP on average (see Figure 1.2 in Section 1.2).

ASEAN has persisted in strengthening regional integration. The member states are working towards meeting the goals of the AEC blueprint while actively participating in other multilateral initiatives such as RCEP and OBOR. As the chair of ASEAN for 2018, Singapore has vowed to augment the regional economic integration effort.[53] In fact, more robust ties among ASEAN

[52] See World Bank (1993), Chow and Kellman (1993) as well as Page (1994).

[53] See Cheong (2017).

countries and regional partners in Asia are now more critical than ever given the socio-economic uncertainties and protectionist sentiments in Western economies.

1.3.5 Gaps in ASEAN's Regional Integration Agenda

In the next phase of ASEAN's development, gaps in the bloc's regional integration agenda must also be addressed. As mentioned in Sections 1.2 and 1.3.3, important elements of the AEC blueprint remain unfulfilled despite its official establishment in December 2015. One key initiative to be completed is the establishment of the ASEAN Single Window (ASW). The ASW, comprising 10 National Single Windows (NSWs), is envisaged to expedite customs clearance and reduce transaction costs, thus facilitating a more seamless intra-regional flow of goods. Despite an extended deadline set in 2015, Cambodia, Laos and Myanmar are still in the progress of developing their NSWs, causing setbacks to the launch of a fully functional ASW. Besides the ASW, there must be renewed effort to complete the bloc's agenda on reducing non-tariff barriers to trade.

In addition, it is important that ASEAN policy-makers reassess whether the current institutional arrangements of the regional grouping will continue to serve member states well in the future. While the ASEAN Way has been effective in resolving disagreements through informal dialogue and negotiation, emergence of new challenges as the bloc grows may call for a more solid institutional mechanism in ASEAN. Furthermore, as the regional grouping deepens integration under the ASEAN Community, inadequate central authority in upholding compliance among the member states might lead to ineffective collaboration.

Finally, the socio-cultural aspect of integration is equally important. To build support for deeper integration, it is imperative that ASEAN pursues inclusive development and ensures that economic development translates to tangible improvements in people's welfare. At the same time, ASEAN should seek to promote greater awareness of the ASEAN Community and facilitate more people-to-people exchanges among the member countries in order to foster a true "ASEAN identity". The fulfilment of the ASEAN Socio-Cultural Community Blueprint is a crucial first step in this effort.

1.4 Development Vision and Strategies for ASEAN-10

Recognising that community building is a dynamic process, ASEAN leaders have committed to formulating a post-2015 agenda even before the formal launch of the ASEAN Community in December 2015. Signed on 12 December 2014, the Nay Pyi Taw Declaration set out key elements of the ASEAN Community's Post-2015 Vision which included[54]: (i) promoting Southeast Asia as a region of peace, stability and prosperity; (ii) promoting ASEAN as a people-oriented community; (iii) maintaining an outward-looking ASEAN, enhancing ASEAN centrality and ASEAN's relevance in the global community, and (iv) strengthening ASEAN's institutional

[54] The Nay Pyi Taw Declaration on the ASEAN Community's Post-2015 Vision is accessible from: www.asean.org/storage/images/pdf/2014_upload/Nay%20Pyi%20Taw%20Declaration%20on%20the%20ASEAN%20Communitys%20Post%202015%20Vision%20w.annex.pdf (accessed on 15 March 2018).

capacity. Subsequently, these principles helped to motivate the ASEAN Community Vision 2025 after its launch in 2015.

In terms of economic integration, the implementation of the AEC Blueprint 2015 has achieved substantial success in facilitating the regional free trade agenda, including liberalising trade and investment flows, streamlining market regulations, facilitating skilled labour mobility, promoting equitable development, and fostering strong collaborations with external partners. Building upon these pertinent foundations, the AEC Blueprint 2025 proposes five interdependent and reinforcing characteristics, namely: (i) A Highly Integrated and Cohesive Economy; (ii) A Competitive, Innovative, and Dynamic ASEAN; (iii) Enhanced Connectivity and Sectoral Cooperation; (iv) A Resilient, Inclusive, People-Oriented, and People-Centred ASEAN; and (v) A Global ASEAN.[55] These pillars are expected to support strategies outlined in the ASEAN Community Vision 2025.

ASEAN's future development should be anchored in the pursuit of balanced, sustainable and inclusive economic development. While the institutional fabric of ASEAN needs to be strengthened to facilitate better regional cooperation,[56] the ten-member bloc should not be side-tracked from its growth trajectory by seeking to transform itself into a highly bureaucratic and complex organisation similar to the EU. As also argued elsewhere, the regional grouping should not lose its pragmatism.[57] Given the differences in development levels and fundamental socio-political diversity within the bloc, it is not the right time for ASEAN to actively work towards political integration in the same fashion as the EU. Concentration on growth and economic development to substantially narrow the prevailing development gap should be the way forward.

The ACI proposes a comprehensive policy roadmap to achieve ASEAN's aspiration to become the fourth largest economy in the world by 2030, drawing on our works on the Asia Economic Connectivity Vision 2030 (AECV), which is discussed in great detail in Chapter 1 of our *2014 Annual Competitiveness Ranking and Simulation Study for ASEAN-10 and Development Strategies to Enhance Asia Economic Connectivity*,[58] as well as the development vision outlined in Chapter 5 of the *2015 Annual Competitiveness Analysis, Agricultural Productivity and Development Vision for ASEAN-10*.[59] The roadmap can be crystallised as five integrative and mutually reinforcing elements with actionable policy recommendations. These strategies can be fine-tuned in accordance with the progress of ASEAN's existing regional initiatives, as well as the pace of domestic reforms in individual member countries.

Element 1: ASEAN as a Highly Integrated Manufacturing Hub and Single Market Connected by High-quality Infrastructure Networks

Home to more than 600 million people which provide the third largest labour force in the world behind China and India, ASEAN is well positioned to benefit from the relocation of manufacturing facilities from China due to rising labour cost in the latter. Riding this expected southward

[55] See ASEAN Secretariat (2015).

[56] See Chapter 2 for a thoughtful discussion on strengthening the ASEAN Charter by Professor Tommy Koh.

[57] See Asian Development Bank Institute (2014) and Intal *et al.* (2014).

[58] See Tan *et al.* (2015).

[59] See Tan *et al.* (2017a).

shift of FDI from China, the 10-member bloc has the potential to become a leading manufacturing base in Asia, driven largely by Malaysia, Thailand, Indonesia, Vietnam and, to a lesser extent, Cambodia, Laos and Myanmar. However, to grasp this opportunity, it is imperative that ASEAN develops a strong and competitive private sector. Concomitantly, the growth of private enterprises would facilitate the growth of the middle class in the region, thereby increasing domestic and regional demand, which will in turn further spur the development of the regional manufacturing sector. A prerequisite for the region to achieve this lofty ambition is for it to be seamlessly connected by a strong infrastructure network, complemented by robust trade facilitation mechanisms in order to reduce trade costs and improve economic competitiveness of all ASEAN members.

Thus, the first element in our development agenda envisages that ASEAN will become a highly integrated hub for trade and investment as well as a key node in the global value chain. The realisation of this element would require ASEAN member states to implement the following policy measures:

i. Deepening cooperation on the trade facilitation agenda. Consolidating the newly adopted ASEAN Seamless Trade Facilitation Indicators (ASTFI) to monitor trade liberalisation, along with the AEC 2025 Trade Facilitation Strategic Action Plan to reduce transaction costs by 10 percent by 2020 and double intra-regional trade by 2025;
ii. Fully establishing the digital NSWs in all ASEAN Member States and widening the ASW's scope to cover more documents/forms and stakeholders in these participating economies, so that cargo clearance process is expedited, and the costs and time associated are lowered;
iii. Taking concrete steps towards resolving the NTM issue, especially those involving environmental, health, safety, security, technical and cultural concerns, by streamlining procedures for standard recognition and conformance measures, increasing information exchange on laws, rules, and regulatory regimes, and reducing red-tape requirements for certificates, permits or licenses;
iv. Accelerating the negotiations and implementation of ATISA for greater integration of the service sector;
v. Building a conducive investment climate through streamlining rules and regulations and substantially reducing the costs of doing business;
vi. Completing the built-in agenda of the ACIA by speeding up the progressive liberalisation of investment restrictions on manufacturing, agriculture, and forestry and mining;
vii. Identifying opportunities for upgrading manufacturing capabilities within the global value chain and encouraging inter-industry linkages for deepening the value chains;
viii. Developing cost-effective manufacturing clusters through partnership with industrial partners in Japan, South Korea, Greater China, the US and the EU;
ix. Promoting technology and knowledge transfers from multinational corporations (MNCs) to local enterprises;
x. Particularly for CLMV, designating special industrial and economic zones with preferential tax treatment for MNCs as a springboard for regulatory, corporate and institutional development; and

xi. Promoting intra-regional information sharing and learning, especially on joint industrial projects between ASEAN members and external partners.

As mentioned, strategies for future ASEAN integration must also seek to promote intra-region connectivity. Connectivity encompasses physical, institutional and people-to-people dimensions, and the MPAC 2025 articulates ASEAN's commitment to promote all three elements in tandem. While agreeing with this principle, our development vision emphasises the need to alleviate the regional physical infrastructure bottlenecks as the most urgent task for ASEAN's development. Specifically, the following measures must be put in place:

xii. Establishing an efficient integrated transport network within ASEAN and with the neighbouring countries via road, railway, airports, ports, inland waterway and ferry links;
xiii. Developing an institutional framework for public–private partnerships in infrastructure development, consolidating existing public and private financial resources;
xiv. Establishing an ASEAN Single Maritime Market to augment maritime logistics; and
xv. Capitalising on multilaterally funded projects, especially via OBOR, to upgrade railway lines, energy generation plants and port facilities.

Element 2: ASEAN as a Productive Food Basket of Asia and the World

Home to some of the world's most prominent exporters of agricultural products including Malaysia, Thailand, and Vietnam, ASEAN has the potential to become a productive food basket of Asia and the whole world. Endowed with vast fertile land, conducive climate, abundant labour, and a mix of lowlands and uplands, in addition to diverse natural landscapes (forests, rivers, and coastlines), this region offers unlimited opportunities for agribusiness not just in crop and livestock, but also in food supply chain management and agricultural infrastructure. Furthermore, as discussed in Chapter 3 of Tan *et al.* (2017a), agriculture remains a vital economic sector in the majority of ASEAN member states. Agricultural growth is thus paramount to both regional food security and economic competitiveness.

Going forward, ASEAN member states should seek to improve agriculture productivity, leverage on regional integration mechanism for agricultural development and seek to guard against the risks of climate change through technological innovations. In addition, ASEAN's members, especially the less developed CLMV, may learn from Malaysia whose agriculture sector is the most productive in the region.[60] In particular, the following policies should be pursued:

i. Identifying agriculture niches based on endowment and core competencies of the member states, with the view of making them internationally competitive in those products;
ii. Developing agri-based industries and fostering strong linkages between primary sectors and resource-based manufacturing;
iii. Integrating smallholder producers to the agribusiness value chains as a key step to alleviate rural poverty;

---

[60] See Tan *et al.* (2017a).

iv. Upgrading agricultural infrastructure, such as drainage and irrigation system as well as transport networks, to improve farmers' access to markets;
v. Supporting farmers' access to capital and new technologies through preferential credit schemes and credit extension services;
vi. Executing the ASEAN Regional Guidelines on Food Security and Nutrition Policy endorsed at the 39th Meeting of the ASEAN Ministers for Agriculture and Forestry (AMAF) in 2017 to enhance food sustenance and nutrition cooperation, as well as the ASEAN Public–Private Partnership Regional Framework for Technology Development in the Food, Agriculture and Forestry Sectors, and the ASEAN guidelines on Prudent Use of Anti Microbials in Livestock[61];
vii. Enabling sustainable production and equitable distribution of agricultural products;
viii. Preparing to address climate change and disaster impacts on vulnerable areas of the region through intra- and inter-regional collaborations such as the ASEAN Climate Resilience Network and other regular monitoring efforts; and
ix. Promoting and facilitating intra-ASEAN cooperation on agricultural research and development as well as technological sharing to enhance regional agricultural total factor productivity.

Element 3: ASEAN as an Innovative, Resilient and Future-ready Growth Centre

The next policy priority in ACI's development agenda is for ASEAN to develop clusters and industries which are resilient to future shocks, particularly technological disruptions arising from the Fourth Industrial Revolution. Given the polarising nature of digitalisation in which nimble firms are rewarded with improved efficiency and opportunities for rapid growth while inadaptable firms will become increasingly uncompetitive, fostering digital capacity is critical. Therefore, Element 3 of our development vision revolves around the following policy initiatives:

i. Increasing investment in ICT infrastructure across the bloc and ensuring equal access to telecommunication and Internet services in both urban and rural areas;
ii. Implementing appropriate regulatory frameworks which facilitate innovation and the adoption of technology;
iii. Supporting the best practices on open data, increased productivity and efficiency, new digital services delivery, and aiding SMEs with accessing these technologies;
iv. Specifically, through partnerships with ICT vendors and consultants, providing firms, especially SMEs, with a reference list of sector-specific proven digital solutions suitable to SMEs' needs;
v. Furthermore, through partnerships with banks and other financial institutions, provide SMEs with access to loans to defray the cost of acquiring or developing new digital capabilities;
vi. Empowering SMEs through e-commerce by taking advantage of the digital connection, low cost, and low market entry barriers to amplify cross-border trade, investment flows, consumer base, and their participation in supply chains;

[61] See ASEAN Secretariat (2017d).

vii. Providing training to upgrade the workforce for the digital economy;
viii. Fostering close collaboration between businesses, industry association and higher learning institutes to ensure that tertiary education can meet industry needs; and
ix. Develop deep capabilities in cybersecurity and network management.

At the same time, it must be noted that breakthroughs in robotics and additive manufacturing technologies (e.g. 3D printing) threaten to erode ASEAN economies' competitiveness in low-cost manufacturing. Thus, as the region pushes forward to achieve its aspiration to become the next manufacturing hub as outlined in Element 1, it is also crucial for ASEAN to diversify its economic structure, seeking to develop services in tandem with manufacturing sector as a key engine of growth and source of employment creation.

Element 4: ASEAN as an Inclusive and Equitable Community

Narrowing the development gap and promoting equitable economic development is a key pillar of the AEC blueprint. While the emphasis has been on identifying and providing technical assistance and capacity building programmes for CLMV, much remains to be done for the gap to be substantially reduced so that CLMV can become the next growth frontier in ASEAN. One way to achieve this is to encourage greater expansion of regional production networks to CLMV. The spread of such networks through FDI, largely from Japan and Europe, has been the cornerstone of economic development in the East Asian newly industrialised economies (NIEs), namely Hong Kong, Singapore, South Korea and Taiwan, and subsequently China. This phenomenon could be described as the "flying geese model" as proposed by Kaname Akamatsu.

To be sure, migration of industries from developed economies does not automatically result in upgraded development in the host countries. FDI inflows must be accompanied by the growth of knowledge-intensive manufacturing activities instead of only low value-added processes. Furthermore, there must be effective technological transfers between MNCs and local enterprises. Building on the IAI framework, ASEAN policy-makers should look to implement the following strategies:

i. Fostering economic cooperation with extra-regional partners in tandem with the effort to deepen regional integration within Southeast Asia;
ii. Facilitating intraregional technology and knowledge transfers from top performers to CLMV, exploiting synergies across different member states;
iii. Encouraging investment from Singapore, Thailand and Malaysia to CLMV drawing on the Vietnam–Singapore Industrial Park model;
iv. Promoting intra-regional learning and technical assistance in terms of institutional capability-building and macroprudential management to improve CLMV's resilience to economic crises;
v. For CLMV, identifying and attracting industrial activities with potential for technological upgrading; and
vi. Providing tax incentives to promote the integration of local firms especially SMEs to the supply chains of MNCs as well as transfer of technological expertise from the latter to the former;

In addition, fostering SMEs across all ASEAN economies is crucial to achieve inclusive development in the region. As discussed in Tan *et al.* (2017h), the overwhelming majority of business establishments in ASEAN are SMEs. They are also major employers, constituting more than half of the workforce in many member states. Traditional fiscal measures such as handouts and tax breaks do play a role in alleviating the immediate constraints faced by SMEs. However, for developing economies especially CLMV, such policies place considerable strains on governments' budgets. In addition, because of the large number of SMEs in these economies, actual benefits accrued to individual firms may be too small to create any long-term impacts.

Thus, it is more effective for regional governments to focus on playing a facilitative role, specifically through the following policies:

vii. Deepening domestic reforms with particular emphasis on addressing market distortions in favour of inefficient state-owned enterprises which crowd out the private sector;
viii. Improving ease of doing business by reducing bureaucratic red tape and building a rule-based, transparent and facilitative business environment;
ix. Alleviating information asymmetries which hinder linkages and synergies between MNCs and SMEs by building business information matrices; and
x. Engaging industry captains to help SMEs address their weaknesses; and
xi. Designing suitable supportive policies for SMEs based on empirical research on SMEs' efficiency and productivity.

Element 5: ASEAN as a Major Force for Regional and Global Economic Integration

A globally connected ASEAN as a fulcrum of multilateral platforms has been the cornerstone of ASEAN's strategy to manage relations with extra-regional powers, affirm ASEAN members' relevance on the world stage and promote international economic cooperation to member states' benefits. Over the past five decades, ASEAN has been rather successful in bringing together a wide array of developed and emerging economic powers under the umbrella of the ASEAN+1 FTAs as well as the ASEAN+x forums such as the EAS.

However, there are worrying mega-trends which threaten to upend ASEAN's traditional engagement mechanisms with external partners, especially the bloc's centrality in the regional economic architecture. The upsurge in populism and anti-globalisation forces as evidenced by Brexit and election victories of nationalistic leaders or parties in US and Europe has unleashed tremendous global economic uncertainties. No less important is the meteoric rise of China, whose economic and geopolitical clout has been felt deeply in Asia and globally. The question of ASEAN unity also becomes more pertinent than ever in light of Sino-American competition for influence in the Asia-Pacific, with a real risk of the 10-member bloc "devolving into a house divided against itself".[62] The raw memory of ASEAN's unprecedented failure to issue a joint communique at the 2012 ASEAN Summit chaired by Cambodia due to disagreements over the South China Sea dispute is a vivid early warning sign about the potential loss of unity within ASEAN.

[62] See Mahbubani (2015).

Balancing power rivalry without choosing sides while driving regional cooperation efforts towards stemming the protectionist tide and promoting economic development is the way forward for ASEAN. ACI's vision for ASEAN-10 thus calls on the member states to bolster ASEAN unity so that the regional grouping can play a central role in the drive towards deeper economic integration in Southeast Asia and more broadly the Asia-Pacific. This can be achieved through the following:

i. ASEAN playing a leading role in the negotiation process of the RCEP, with the aim for it to become an encompassing trade agreement which delivers tangible benefits for ordinary residents in member states;
ii. Bridging gaps between RCEP and the CPTPP as pathways to the Free Trade Area of the Asia-Pacific (FTAAP); deepening economic relations with economies in the Asia-Pacific Economic Cooperation (APEC) forum;
iii. Promoting multilateral talks, dialogues, and forums such as the EAS to consolidate trust and stability in the region, thus avoiding taking sides with any major global powers;
iv. Uniting in articulating ASEAN's collective interests in multilateral initiatives such as the APEC forum and the OBOR;
v. Leveraging ASEAN members' status as a founding member of the Asian Infrastructure Investment Bank (AIIB) to shape the governance structure and operational guidelines of this institution so as to ensure funding from the OBOR supplement efforts to bolster MPAC and enhance intra-ASEAN connectivity;
vi. Strengthening trust among ASEAN member states; identifying fault lines which may heighten the threats of ASEAN disunity; and
vii. Pushing for the conclusion of the Code of Conduct on the South China Sea with China and emphasising peaceful means of resolving the dispute.

Singapore's tenure as the ASEAN Chairman for 2018 will give our development vision a boost as there are synergies between the city-state's aspirations for ASEAN and the abovementioned agenda. Singapore envisions to make the regional community ready for disruptive technologies, equip the citizens with future-ready skills, and enhance the smart cities' capabilities.[63] Specifically, Singapore's main priorities for consolidating the ASEAN bloc include connecting the member economies smoothly via a network of smart cities, boosting cybersecurity, enabling cross-border transactions at lower costs especially for migrant workers, and strengthening regional interdependence. The 2018 ASEAN Chairman also seeks to galvanise regional support for creating a rule-based order for cyberspace, deter cyberthreats, terrorism risks, and transnational crimes.

Regarding free trade and investment, Singapore aims to fortify ASEAN's economic and financial resilience against external shocks while deepening ties with other powers so that all the participating entities are able to enjoy a stake in the region's growing prosperity. To this end, the new chairman seeks to intensify its efforts to secure a high-quality RCEP. The longer-term goal

[63] See https://www.asean2018.sg/About/ASEAN-2018 (accessed on 15 March 2018).

is for the realisation of the FTAAP. In addition, Singapore plans to encourage regional business cooperation by pushing for the ASW as well as an ASEAN-wide self-certification regime which allows authorised exporters to self-certify their products' standards and eligibility for preferential treatment.[64]

1.5 Roadmap of the Book

The rest of the book is organised as follows. Chapter 2 contains a speech by Professor Tommy Koh, Ambassador, Singapore's Ambassador-at-Large, on the ASEAN Charter which is a key legal and constitutional mechanism of the regional grouping. ASEAN was founded on the ASEAN Way which upholds the principles of consensus decision-making and non-interference in the domestic affairs among member states. The current informal institutional arrangement might impede the region from forging ahead, although it has maintained peace and stability for the past 50 years. Professor Koh's discourse sheds light on the making of the ASEAN Charter and his vision on how the Charter can be supplemented to serve the interests of all ASEAN members in the coming decades.

Chapter 3 provides an update on ACI's competitiveness analysis of ASEAN-10. On top of the annual rankings of economic competitiveness for the 10 ASEAN countries from 2000 to 2014 derived using a comprehensive and rigorous ACI's methodological framework, we also present our breakthrough in using Shapley Weightage methodology in assigning weight to each environment objectively. Moreover, through our assessments of each economy's relative strengths and weaknesses, we provide a constructive policy roadmap for domestic reforms in each member country. In line with the ASEAN Community Vision 2025, ACI's research seeks to contribute to the realisation of the regional goals in achieving sustainable, prosperous, and inclusive development.

Acknowledging the importance of FDI as a source of capital and technology diffusion to ASEAN, Chapter 4 undertakes an empirical investigation on the determinants of FDI in ASEAN. As the notion of competitiveness at the macroeconomic level is intrinsically tied to the issue of maintaining a competitive exchange rate, we use real effective exchange rates (REER) as a proxy of competitiveness and examine how its levels and volatility affect the FDI inflows in the region. The application of alternative definitions of REER and data sources also add another layer of robustness check to our study. We then draw policy implications pertaining to the exchange rate policies in ASEAN for the region to remain as an attractive destination for global FDI inflows.

As OBOR gathers pace on the global stage, Chapter 5 provides timely insights on the initiative from two luminaries — Minister K. Shanmugam, Singapore's Minister for Home Affairs and Minister for Law, and Professor Liew Mun Leong, Chairman of Surbana Jurong and Changi Airport Group, as well as Provost Chair and Professor of National University of Singapore. As stressed in the remarks by Minister Shanmugam, it is crucial to understand OBOR in a holistic manner, taking into account geopolitical trends, history and current international situation. In addition, the Minister also thoughtfully delves on the implications of OBOR for the regional

[64] See Young (2017).

economic and security architecture as well as geopolitics. Meanwhile, Professor Liew Mun Leong provides a geo-economic perspective to OBOR, contemplating the future role of OBOR as a new growth engine for the global economy.

Chapter 6 summarises the key research findings presented in this book. We tie up the thrusts of Chapters 2 to 5, highlighting the core agenda of strengthening regional integration for ASEAN to forge ahead while bridging the development gap among the member states. Furthermore, the chapter outlines policy implications for positioning ASEAN in OBOR and stimulating FDI inflows into ASEAN economies. Finally, we discuss possible future research agendas on ASEAN.

References

Acharya, Amitav. 2001. *Constructing A Security Community in Southeast Asia: ASEAN and the Problem of Regional Order*. London: Routledge.

ASEAN Secretariat. 1997. "ASEAN Vision 2020", available at: http://www.asean.org/?static_post=asean-vision-2020 (accessed on 15 March 2018).

ASEAN Secretariat. 2007. "The ASEAN Charter", available at: http://www.asean.org/storage/images/ASEAN_RTK_2014/ASEAN_Charter.pdf (accessed on 15 March 2018).

ASEAN Secretariat. 2015. *ASEAN Economic Community Blueprint*. Jakarta: ASEAN Secretariat.

ASEAN Secretariat. 2016. *Initiative for ASEAN Integration (IAI) Work Plan III*. Jakarta: ASEAN Secretariat.

ASEAN Secretariat. 2017a. *ASEAN Statistical Leaflet — Selected Key Indicators*. Jakarta: ASEAN Secretariat.

ASEAN Secretariat. 2017b. *ASEAN Statistical Report on Millennium Development Goals 2017*. Jakarta: ASEAN Secretariat.

ASEAN Secretariat. 2017c. *First ASEAN Youth Development Index*. Jakarta: ASEAN Secretariat.

ASEAN Secretariat. 2017d. *ASEAN Economic Integration Brief*. Jakarta: ASEAN Secretariat.

Asian Development Bank Institute. 2014. *ASEAN 2030: Toward a Borderless Economic Community*. Tokyo: Asian Development Bank Institute.

Bloom, David E., David Canning, and Jaypee Sevilla. 2003. *The Demographic Dividend: A New Perspective on the Economic Consequences of Population Change*. California: RAND.

Bloom, David E., and Jeffrey G. Williamson. 1998. "Demographic Transitions and Economic Miracles in Emerging Asia". *World Bank Economic Review* 12(3): 419–455.

Brynjolfsson, E., and A. McAfee. 2014. *The Second Machine Age: Work, Progress, and Prosperity in a Time of Brilliant Technologies*. New York: W. W. Norton & Company.

Chainey, Ross. 2017. "700 Global Leaders Just Met in Cambodia. Here's What Happened". World Economic Forum, 12 May, available at: https://www.weforum.org/agenda/2017/05/700-global-leaders-just-met-in-cambodia-heres-what-happened (accessed on 15 March 2018).

Cheong, Danson. 2017. "Singapore to Push for Greater Economic Integration within ASEAN: Heng Swee Keat". *The Straits Times*, 5 December, available at: http://www.straitstimes.com/singapore/singapore-to-push-for-greater-economic-integration-within-asean-as-chair-of-regional-group (accessed on 15 March 2018).

Choi, Jieun. 2017. "The Future of Jobs and the Fourth Industrial Revolution: Business as Usual for Unusual Business". *The World Bank (blog)*, 17 July, available at: http://blogs.worldbank.org/psd/future-jobs-and-fourth-industrial-revolution-business-usual-unusual-business (accessed on 15 March 2018).

Chow, Peter C. Y., and Mitchell H. Kellman. 1993. *Trade — the Engine of Growth in East Asia*. New York: Oxford University Press.

Coppola, F. 2017. "Top Economists Endorse Universal Basic Income". *Forbes*, 31 August, available at: https://www.forbes.com/sites/francescoppola/2017/08/31/top-economists-endorse-universal-basic-income/#399ed78215ae (accessed on 15 March 2018).

Deane, P. M. 1980. *The First Industrial Revolution*. 2nd ed. Cambridge: Cambridge University Press.

Donnan, Shawn. 2018. "Seven Predictions for Trade Policy in 2018". *The Financial Times,* 15 January, available at: https://www.ft.com/content/0c65fe2a-f9dc-11e7-9b32-d7d59aace167 (accessed on 15 March 2018).

Evenett, Simon J., and Johannes Fritz. 2017. *Will Awe Trump Rules? The 21st Global Trade Alert Report*. London: CEPR Press.

Frey, Carl Benedikt, and Michael A. Osborne. 2017. "The Future of Employment: How Susceptible are Jobs to Computerisation?" *Technological Forecasting and Social Change* 114 (January): 254–280.

Fuei, Lee King. 2017. "Automation, Computerization and Future Employment in Singapore". *Journal of Southeast Asian Economies* 34(2): 388–399.

Hallward-Driemeier, Mary, and Gaurav Nayyar. 2017. *Trouble in the Making? The Future of Manufacturing-Led Development*. Washington DC: World Bank.

Heng, Swee Keat. 2015. "Singapore, a Connected and Trusted Home Base for Companies to Go Global". Opening Remarks at the 2015 Asia Competitiveness Institute Annual Conference, Singapore, 26–27 November.

Intal, Ponciano Jr., Yoshifumi Fukunaga, Fukunari Kimura, Phoumin Han, Philippa Dee, Dionisius Narjoko, and Sothea Oum. 2014. *ASEAN Rising: ASEAN and AEC Beyond 2015*. Jakarta: Economic Research Institute for ASEAN and East Asia (ERIA).

Kawai, Masahiro, Peter J. Morgan, and Pradumna B. Rana, eds. 2014. *New Global Economic Architecture: The Asian Perspective*. Cheltenham: Edward Elgar.

Kihara, Leika, and Takashi Umekawa. 2017. "IMF's Lagarde Warns Protectionism, While Now Just Words, May Come to Hurt Asia". *Reuters*, 8 November, available at: https://www.reuters.com/article/us-imf-lagarde/imfs-lagarde-warns-protectionism-while-now-just-words-may-come-to-hurt-asia-idUSKBN1D80NO (accessed on 15 March 2018).

Kurihara, Takeshi. 2012. "Achievements of Asian Bond Markets Initiative (ABMI) in the Last Decade and Future Challenges". Presentation at the OECD-ADBI 12th Roundtable on Capital Market Reform in Asia, Tokyo, 7 February.

Kutlina-Dimitrova, Zornitsa, and Csilla Lakatos. 2017. "The Global Costs of Protectionism". Policy Research Working Paper No. 8277. Washington DC: World Bank.

Kuznets, Simon. 1967. "Population and Economic Growth". *Proceedings of the American Philosophical Society* 111(3): 170–193.

Lin, Justin. 2012. "Youth Bulge: A Demographic Dividend or a Demographic Bomb in Developing Countries". World Bank. 1 May, available at: http://blogs.worldbank.org/developmenttalk/youth-bulge-a-demographic-dividend-or-a-demographic-bomb-in-developing-countries (accessed on 15 March 2018).

Mahbubani, Kishore. 2015. "ASEAN as a Living, Breathing Modern Miracle". *CIRSD Horizons (2)*: 136–148.

Mahbubani, Kishore, and Jeffery Sng. 2017. *The ASEAN Miracle: A Catalyst for Peace.* Singapore: NUS Press.

Malthus, T. R. 1798. *An Essay on the Principle of Population*. 2010 Edition.

Manjoo, F. 2017. "A Plan in Case Robots Take the Jobs: Give Everyone a Paycheck". *The New York Times*, 2 March, available at: https://www.nytimes.com/2016/03/03/technology/plan-to-fight-robot-invasion-at-work-give-everyone-a-paycheck.html?mcubz=1 (accessed on 15 March 2017).

Mason, Andrew. 2001. *Population Change and Economic Development in East Asia: Challenges Met, Opportunities Seized.* Stanford, California: Stanford University Press.

Menon, Jayant. 2013. "Narrowing the Development Divide in ASEAN: The Role of Policy". *Asian-Pacific Economic Literature* 27(2): 25–51.

Minder, Raphael. 2016. "Guaranteed Income for All? Switzerland's Voters Say No Thanks". *The New York Times*, 5 June, available at: https://www.nytimes.com/2016/06/06/world/europe/switzerland-swiss-vote-basic-income.html (accessed on 15 March 2018).

More, Charles. 2002. *Understanding the Industrial Revolution*. London: Routledge.

Page, John. 1994. "The East Asian Miracle: Four Lessons for Development Policy". In *NBER Macroeconomics Annual 1994*, edited by Stanley Fischer and Julio Rotemberg, 9: 219–282. Cambridge, MA: MIT Press.

Park, Sang-Chul. 2017. "The Fourth Industrial Revolution and Implications for Innovative Cluster Policies". AI & SOCIETY, December.

Plummer, Michael G., and Siow Yue Chia. 2009. "Benefits of the AEC". In *Realizing the ASEAN Economic Community: A Comprehensive Assessment*, edited by Michael G. Plummer and Siow Yue Chia, 164–174. Singapore: ISEAS Publications.

Pomfret, Richard. 2013. "ASEAN's New Frontiers: Integrating The Newest Members into the ASEAN Economic Community". *Asian Economic Policy Review* 8: 25–41.

Raja, Siddhartha, and Mavis Ampah. 2016. "Will the Digital Revolution Help or Hurt Employment?: Adaptation a Key to Realizing Job Gains World Bank". *Connections: 2016(2).* World Bank, Washington DC.

Reher, David S. 2011. "Economic and Social Implications of the Demographic Transition". *Population and Development Review* 37 (January): 11–33.

Schwab, Klaus. 2015. "The Fourth Industrial Revolution: What It Means, How to Respond". *Foreign Affairs*, 12 December, available at: https://www.foreignaffairs.com/articles/2015-12-12/fourth-industrial-revolution (accessed on 15 March 2018).

Severino, Rodolfo. 2007. "The ASEAN Developmental Divide and the Initiative for ASEAN Integration". *ASEAN Economic Bulletin* 24(1): 35–44.

Sukma, Rizal. 2014. "ASEAN Beyond 2015: The Imperatives for Further Institutional Changes". ERIA Discussion Paper 2014-01. Jakarta: Economic Research Institute for ASEAN and East Asia (ERIA).

Swanson, Ana. 2018. "Will 2018 be the Year of Protectionism? Trump Alone Will Decide". *The New York Times*, 3 January, available at: https://www.nytimes.com/2018/01/03/us/politics/2018-trump-protectionism-tariffs.html (accessed on 15 March 2018).

Tan, Khee Giap, Linda Low, Tan Kong Yam, and Lim Lijuan Amanda. 2013. *Annual Analysis of Competitiveness, Development Strategies and Public Policies on ASEAN-10: 2000–2010*. Singapore: Pearson Education.

Tan, Khee Giap, Sangiita Wei Cher Yoong, Sasidaran Gopalan, and Le Phuong Anh Nguyen. 2015. *2014 Annual Competitiveness Ranking and Simulation Study for ASEAN-10 and Development Strategies to Enhance Asia Economic Connectivity*. Singapore: World Scientific.

Tan, Khee Giap, Le Phuong Anh Nguyen, Sasidaran Gopalan, and Nguyen Trieu Duong Luu. 2017a. *2015 Annual Competitiveness Analysis, Agricultural Productivity and Development Vision for ASEAN-10*. Singapore: World Scientific.

Tan, Khee Giap, Le Phuong Anh Nguyen, and Nguyen Trieu Duong Luu. 2017b. *2016 Annual Competitiveness Analysis and Growth Slowdown Analysis for ASEAN-10*. Singapore: World Scientific.

Tan, Khee Giap, Peng Wang, and Teleixi Xie. 2017c. *2016 Growth Slowdown Analysis by Income Thresholds and Annual Update of Competitiveness Analysis for 34 Greater China Economies*. Singapore: World Scientific.

Tan, Khee Giap, Sasidaran Gopalan, Jigyasa Sharma, and Kong Yam Tan. 2017d. *Inaugural 2016 Ease of Doing Business Index on Attractiveness to Investors, Business Friendliness and Competitive Policies (EDB Index ABC) for 21 States and Federal Territories of India*. Singapore: World Scientific.

Tan, Khee Giap, Sasidaran Gopalan, Anuja Tandon, and Kong Yam Tan. 2017e. *2016 Annual Competitiveness and Growth Slowdown Analysis for Sub-National Economies of India*. Singapore: World Scientific.

Tan, Khee Giap, Mulya Amri, and Nursyahida Binte Ahmad. 2017f. *2016 Annual Competitiveness Analysis and Development Strategies for Indonesian Provinces*. Singapore: World Scientific.

Tan, Khee Giap, Mulya Amri, Nursyahida Binte Ahmad, and Kong Yam Tan. 2017g. *2016 Growth Slowdown Analysis, Ease of Doing Business Index, and Annual Competitiveness Studies of Indonesia's Sub-National Economies*. Singapore: World Scientific.

Tan, Khee Giap, Mulya Amri, Sasidaran Gopalan, Nursyahida Ahmad, Duy Nguyen, Zhou Shida, Jigyasa Sharma, Hui Yin Chuah, and Lim Tao Oei. 2017h. *Productivity Tracking and Efficiency Monitoring of Singapore's Small and Medium Enterprises*. Singapore: Asia Competitiveness Institute.

The Economist. 2017. "If Universal Basic Income Took Off: Giving Money to Everyone". 3 July, available at: http://worldif.economist.com/article/13518/giving-money-everyone (accessed on 15 March 2018).

Vu, Tien Loc, Khee Giap Tan, Nguyen Trieu Duong Luu, and Duy Nguyen. 2018 (forthcoming). *Balanced, Sustainable and Competitiveness Enhancement Study for Vietnam: A Critical Evaluation with Development Potentials*. Singapore: Asia Competitiveness Institute.

Weatherbee, D. E. 2009. *International Relations in Southeast Asia: The Struggle for Autonomy*. Lanham, MD: Rowman and Littlefield.

World Bank. 1993. *The East Asian Miracle: Economic Growth and Public Policy*. Washington DC: World Bank.

World Bank. 2011. *World Development Report 2011: Conflict, Security, and Development*. Washington DC: World Bank.

World Economic Forum. 2016a. *The Future of Jobs: Employment, Skills and Workforce Strategy for the Fourth Industrial Revolution*. Geneva: World Economic Forum.

World Economic Forum. 2016b. *The Global Information Technology Report 2016: Innovating in the Digital Economy*. Geneva: World Economic Forum.

World Trade Organisation. 2017. *Annual Report 2017*. Geneva: World Trade Organisation.

Young, Charissa. 2017. "Vivian Balakrishnan sets out Singapore's priorities as 2018 ASEAN chair". *The Straits Times*, 5 December, available at: http://www.straitstimes.com/singapore/vivian-balakrishnan-sets-out-singapores-priorities-as-2018-asean-chair (accessed on 15 March 2018).

Chapter 2

The ASEAN Charter at 10: Prospects and Retrospect

2.1 Introductory Notes

The year 2017 marks another milestone in the history of the Association of Southeast Asian Nations (ASEAN) with the celebration of its golden jubilee as a regional grouping. Having braved the external challenges including the 1997 Asian Financial Crisis and the 2008–2009 Global Financial Crisis, the remarkable performance of ASEAN as a whole is proven as it evolved into the world's seventh largest economy and is projected to rise to the fourth spot by 2030. Some pundits deem this success a miracle[1] as ASEAN has performed well economically, while unity and peace remain well preserved, notwithstanding the fact that the foundation of ASEAN in 1967 was motivated in large part by concerns over rising regional tensions due to territorial disputes and conflicting ideologies.

Characterised by great heterogeneity in terms of development level, resource endowment, culture, and political ideology, the regional grouping has progressed based on the "ASEAN Way", which stresses the principles of non-interference and consensus-based decision-making. Such a loose institutional setting and informal *modus operandi* in managing regional affairs has provided a certain extent of assurance in terms of domestic sovereignty to the member states as they participate in regional initiatives. Over the past five decades, ASEAN has been able to foster closer regional cooperation through the establishment of multilateral agreements in many areas, ranging from economic integration to non-proliferation of nuclear weapons and transboundary air pollution.

Nonetheless, there are shortcomings to ASEAN's informal integration model which must not be overlooked. First is the lack of legal commitment to regional initiatives as compliance to most of the agreements signed is on a voluntary basis. The lack of a central authority to uphold compliance among the member states might cause the agreements to end up delayed or even unrealised. Thus, ASEAN's informal setting may slow the progress of regional integration and hamstrung the ability of the bloc to cope with emerging challenges in an increasingly uncertain global landscape. Second, there is an absence of a credible dispute settlement mechanism in ASEAN which is usually deemed a critical feature for successful community building.[2] While past disagreements within the bloc have been resolved through dialogue and negotiation, the ASEAN Way may not always be effective in dealing with new complex disputes as the scope and depth of regional integration expands.

ASEAN leaders are keenly aware that the weak institutional framework built upon a two-page founding document — the Bangkok Declaration — will not always be sufficient to meet the needs and aspirations of member states. Therefore, community building in ASEAN has evolved over time. The Bali Concord II, which envisioned a comprehensive integration of ASEAN as a

[1] See Mahbubani (2017) and Mahbubani and Sng (2017).

[2] See Hew (2005).

single community, was signed at the ninth ASEAN Summit in 2003. This was followed by the concrete Vientiane Action Plan (VAP) in 2004 which set out, for the first time, ASEAN's formal commitment to formulate a Charter.[3] The proposal was later solidified in the 2005 Kuala Lumpur Declaration which stated that the ASEAN Charter would act as ASEAN's legal and institutional framework.[4] Furthermore, the Charter would serve as the cornerstone for a dispute settlement regime among ASEAN members.[5]

Having gone through extensive discussion and negotiation processes which involved representatives from all of the member states, the Charter was eventually adopted in 2007. The Charter set out 15 objectives for ASEAN, an extension from seven in the Bangkok Declaration. Besides, fundamental principles which reflect ASEAN's norms and values are also enshrined in the Charter. Optimists like Chalermpalanupap (2009) saw the Charter as a paradigm shift, acting as a legally binding agreement which would allow ASEAN to be recognised as a juridical entity internationally. The Charter also streamlined governance of the association: Article 7 affirmed the ASEAN Summit as the supreme policy-making body of the grouping. On the other hand, Seah (2009) suggested that the principle of non-interference, one of the core values of the ASEAN Way, has been eroded in the post-Charter period.

The ASEAN Charter is definitely not a panacea for all issues and is imperfect, as recognised by insiders who have been actively involved in the design process.[6] However, as clearly stated in Article 50, the Charter is an evolving document which may be reviewed from time to time. While the ASEAN Way is still deeply entrenched and enshrined in Article 20, the charter, to a certain extent, has strengthened the legal and institutional structure of ASEAN as a regional entity. More importantly, it reiterates the commitment among leaders of the member states in forging cohesion and deeper integration in the region. The ASEAN Charter shall contribute in setting the paths ahead, laying the foundation for a rule-based association as ASEAN celebrates 50 years of its founding and the establishment of the ASEAN Community.

At this juncture, it is timely to reflect on the nature of the Charter and envisage how ASEAN may move forward as a community in the bloc's next phase of development. The rest of this chapter will be a reprint of a lecture by Professor Tommy Koh, Singapore's Ambassador-at-Large, on the making of the ASEAN Charter and the next course of actions. Professor Koh's reflections shall yield useful inputs for ASEAN policy-makers in the journey ahead.

2.2 The ASEAN Charter at 10: Prospects and Retrospect[7]

2.2.1 Introduction

In exactly five days, ASEAN will be celebrating its 50th anniversary. This is therefore an early celebration of ASEAN's birthday. I consider my job as a member of the High-Level Task Force

[3] The idea for the ASEAN Charter was in fact not new. See Section 2.2 and Chalermpalanupap (2009).

[4] See the complete Kuala Lumpur Declaration here, http://asean.org/asean/asean-charter/kuala-lumpur-declaration/

[5] See Woon (2009).

[6] See Koh *et al.* (2009).

[7] This section is a reprint with permission of the ASEAN Lecture delivered by Professor Tommy Koh, Ambassador-At-Large at the Ministry of Foreign Affairs of Singapore, at the ISEAS–Yusof Ishak Institute on 3 August 2017.

(HLTF) and as its second chairman, one of the most important in my life and career. Drafting the ASEAN Charter is historically as important as drafting the constitution of a country or the Charter of an international organisation with one difference. You usually draft a constitution of a country or the Charter of an international organisation at the time of their founding. In the case of ASEAN, we were drafting its Charter when it was 40 years old. I would like to dedicate this lecture to the members of the HLTF and their assistants. I would also like to recognise some members of the Singapore delegation who are here this morning and to thank them for a memorable year of good work and comradeship.

In my lecture, I will focus on three points. First, I will give a brief account of the history of the making of the Charter. Second, I will explain why I consider the Charter to be a revolutionary document. Third, I will review some of the suggestions for amending the Charter.

2.2.2 The Making of the ASEAN Charter

According to my good friend, Professor Walter Woon, the author of the Commentary on the ASEAN Charter, the first person to propose a Charter for ASEAN was the legendary Foreign Minister of the Philippines, General Carlos P. Romulo. He did this at the seventh ASEAN Foreign Ministers Meeting, in Jakarta, in 1974. Romulo was ahead of his time and the idea languished with the senior officials for 30 years.

Thirty years after Romulo's proposal, the 10th ASEAN Summit, held in Vientiane, in 2004, adopted the VAP. In the Annex to the VAP, there was a commitment to work towards the development of an ASEAN Charter. In that same year, the ASEAN Secretariat, then led by Secretary-General, Ong Keng Yong, put up a paper containing a review of the institutional framework of ASEAN and the need for ASEAN to have legal personality. The senior officials produced a draft Charter for the consideration of their Ministers.

In 2005, the ASEAN Foreign Ministers agreed to work towards the promulgation of an ASEAN Charter. At the 11th ASEAN Summit, held in Kuala Lumpur, in 2005, the leaders adopted the Declaration on the Establishment of the ASEAN Charter. The summit also established an Eminent Persons Group (EPG). Its mandate was to put forward bold and visionary recommendations. The members of the EPG were appointed in their individual capacities and were not constrained by instructions from their respective governments. The group was chaired by a former Deputy Prime Minister of Malaysia, Musa Hitam, and included other elder statesmen of ASEAN, such as, the former President of the Philippines, Fidel Ramos, the former Foreign Minister of Indonesia, Ali Alatas and the former Deputy Prime Minister of Singapore, Professor S Jayakumar.

The EPG did not disappoint. It produced a very bold report which was accepted by the 12th ASEAN Summit, in Cebu, the Philippines, in January 2007. The Summit also appointed the HLTF to draft the ASEAN Charter. Unlike the EPG, the HLTF worked under the supervision of the ASEAN Foreign Ministers. Several of the bold and visionary proposals made by the EPG did not survive the reality test administered by the foreign ministers. For example, we were told to

---

The transcript of the lecture is also available at https://www.iseas.edu.sg/images/centres/asc/pdf/Prof-Tommy-Koh-ALS-ASEAN-Charter.pdf (accessed 10 August 2017).

ignore the EPG's proposal that ASEAN would eventually become a "union". We were also told not to include any language on "suspension, expulsion and withdrawal". We were also instructed that consensus would remain the principal mode of decision-making.

The HLTF had two chairmen, Ambassador Rosario Manalo of the Philippines and myself. Rosario chaired the first eight meetings and I chaired the last five. The two of us and Walter Woon have edited a book on the making of the ASEAN Charter. I hope that you have read our book. I would be happy to answer any question you may have on the work of the HLTF and the drafting process.

2.2.3 ASEAN Charter: A Revolutionary Document

I would now like to turn to my second point. I wish to explain why I regard the ASEAN Charter as a revolutionary document.

First, the Charter is a revolutionary document because it seeks to make a paradigm change to the nature of ASEAN. Pre-Charter, ASEAN was strong on networks but weak on institutions. ASEAN was prolific in making decisions and agreements but weak on compliance. ASEAN was famous for its informality and its culture of mutual accommodation and consensus-making. Post-Charter, the ASEAN Way has not been abandoned. It has, however, been strengthened by a greater reliance on institutions and the rule of law.

Second, I consider the Charter as a revolutionary document when you consider the political reality of the 10 member states. One is an absolute monarchy, two are ruled by communist parties, one has a government formed by the military after it had overthrown an elected government, one has a power-sharing arrangement between the army and the elected government, and the remaining five are democracies with local characteristics. A friend, Michael Vatikiotis, has recently published a book entitled *Blood and Silk: Power and Conflict in Modern Southeast Asia*. The book is a reminder of the political realities of our region. It is quite remarkable that the Charter, in its Preamble, Purposes and Principles, emphasises ASEAN's commitment to: "democracy, the rule of law and good governance". In Article 2 (2)(h), the Charter also commits ASEAN to adhere to "constitutional government". This is a polite way of saying that the Charter is against the unconstitutional changes of governments. It is also remarkable that the Charter, in its Preamble, Purposes and Principles, commits ASEAN to "promote and protect human rights and fundamental freedoms".

Third, it is a miracle that ASEAN has not one but two, human rights bodies, namely, the ASEAN Intergovernmental Commission on Human Rights (AICHR) and the Commission on the Rights of Woman and Child. Why do I call it a miracle? I do so because of the 10 ASEAN member states, only four, namely, Indonesia, Malaysia, Philippines and Thailand, had national commissions of human rights. You would normally expect the minority to follow the majority and not the other way around. In this case, the majority agreed to follow the minority. This remarkable decision was made by the foreign ministers, at their meeting, held on 30 July 2007 in Manila. The Ministers met by themselves, without their staffers. Only the chairman of HLTF and the ASEAN Secretary-General were present. When the meeting was over, the Secretary-General provided the HLTF with a summary of the Ministers' decisions. The decision of the Ministers to establish an ASEAN human rights body was greeted by some of my colleagues with disbelief. I remember that my colleague from Vietnam demanded to see his minister. Ong Keng Yong had the unpleasant duty of informing us that our ministers did not want to see any of us! Post-Charter, Myanmar has established a national commission of human rights.

Fourth, I consider the Charter to be a revolutionary document because of its strong commitment to sustainable development and to the protection of the environment. The Preamble contains the following paragraph: "Resolved to ensure sustainable development for the benefit of present and future generations ..." Article 1(9) declares that one of the purposes of ASEAN is: "9. To promote sustainable development so as to ensure the protection of the region's environment, the sustainability of its natural resources, the preservation of its cultural heritage and the high quality of life of its peoples." A critic may say that these are aspirational statements and cannot be enforced. My response is to point out that aspirational statements are not without moral and political force. If an ASEAN government were to act in an irresponsible manner towards its environment, it can be held to account by its citizens and by its neighbours.

Fifth, I consider the Charter to be a revolutionary document because of its commitment to the rule of law, to international law and to the peaceful settlement of disputes. The rule of law is mentioned in the Preamble, Purposes and Principles. Article 2(2)(j) states that one of ASEAN's principles is to uphold the UN Charter and international law, including international humanitarian law. In Article 2, on Principles, we have Article 2(2)(c) on the "renunciation of aggression and of the threat or use of force or other actions in any manner inconsistent with international law." In Article 2(2)(d), we find the principle of "reliance on peaceful settlement of disputes." Taken together, I am impressed that, through the Charter, ASEAN and its member states have made such a strong commitment to the rule of law, to upholding international law and to the peaceful settlement of disputes.

Sixth, the Charter is seeking to make a paradigm change in an area in which ASEAN had been weak, namely, dispute settlement. Culturally, ASEAN's preference was for disputes between member states to be settled by consultations and negotiations. In other words, the preference was for diplomacy over the law. However, in the field of trade and economic agreements, the ASEAN member states realized that it was necessary to have a more formal, binding dispute settlement procedure. ASEAN had to keep up with the World Trade Organisation (WTO)'s dispute settlement system. The EPG recommended the establishment of dispute settlement mechanisms in all fields of ASEAN cooperation. The HLTF tried to implement the EPG's recommendation. Some members of HLTF proposed the establishment of an ASEAN Court, like the European Court of Justice. There was, however, no consensus on the proposal.

A whole Chapter of the Charter, Chapter VIII, is devoted to the settlement of disputes. Article 22 states that member states shall endeavour to resolve their disputes through dialogue, consultation and negotiations. Article 23 states that member states to a dispute may agree to settle the dispute by resorting to good offices, conciliation and medication. The Charter states that the ASEAN Chair and the Secretary-General may provide good offices, conciliation or mediation. Article 24(3) provides that disputes concerning ASEAN economic agreements shall be settled in accordance with the Vientiane Protocol on the Enhanced Dispute Settlement Mechanism. Article 25 prescribes that appropriate dispute settlement mechanisms, including arbitration, should be established for disputes concerning the Charter or other ASEAN instruments.

Seventh, the Charter has tried to rationalise and streamline ASEAN's institutional structure and to empower the Secretary-General and the Secretariat. The Charter gives the Secretary-General four deputies, two of whom would be recruited in an open exercise. Article 23(2) of the Charter states that the parties to a dispute may request the Secretary-General to exercise his good offices, mediation and conciliation. Most importantly, Article 27 of the Charter gives the Secretary-General the duty to monitor compliance and to report on non-compliance to the Summit.

Eighth, the Charter emphasises that ASEAN should be a people-oriented and people-centred organisation and all sectors of our society should benefit from ASEAN integration and community building. The Charter begins with the following words: "We, the peoples of the Member States of ASEAN". I would also point out that, 11 of the 15 Purposes of ASEAN directly affect the people's life, livelihood and well-being. We do not want ASEAN to become an elitist organisation which is out of touch with the ground. The inclusion of Chapter V of the Charter and the requirement to engage with the civil society are meant to reinforce the goal to be a people-oriented and people-centred organisation. Article 16 and Annex 2 are very significant. Annex 2 contains an extensive list of entities associated with ASEAN.

2.2.4 Reviewing and Amending the Charter

The Charter was signed on the 20th of November 2007 and came into force on the 15th of December 2008. It has been in force for nine years. The Charter is not perfect, but it appears to have worked satisfactorily. Article 48 of the Charter states that any member state may propose amendments to the Charter. Article 50 states that it may be reviewed five years after its entry into force, which was in 2013. No review of the Charter was held that year. I understand that an update of the Charter is on the current chairman's list of deliverables, and member states are presently discussing the proposed updating of certain sections of the Charter.

On track two, however, some ASEAN think-tanks, non-governmental organisations (NGOs) and individuals have expressed dissatisfaction with some provisions of the Charter. For example, they would like to do away with the principle of "non-interference in the internal affairs of ASEAN member states". They would also like the method of decision-making to be by majority vote instead of consensus. They would like the Charter to contain sanctions for non-compliance to include "suspension and expulsion".

I would respectfully point out to my friends who have made such proposals that they are impractical and may be counter-productive. ASEAN unity is of paramount importance. In the interest of unity, we are sometimes unable to take action in situations which call for urgent action such as the complex situation in the Rakhine state of Myanmar. In such situations, my heart is with the critics. However, my head tells me that there is wisdom in strategic patience. ASEAN is evolving in the right direction. If we become impatient and insist that the majority should prevail, and we should not allow the minority to block consensus, we may feel triumphant, but we may be doing harm to ASEAN. The out-voted minority may withdraw from ASEAN, leading to the break up of ASEAN. That would be a tragedy.

I take very seriously the aspiration, expressed in the Charter, for ASEAN to be a people-oriented and a people-centred organisation. One of the lessons I have learnt from Brexit is that we must not allow ASEAN to become as an elitist organisation, which is out of touch with our citizens. ASEAN must bring benefits to the citizens of ASEAN. ASEAN integration must bring benefits to small and medium-sized business as well as to big business. The ASEAN Secretariat should make a special effort to cultivate our students, young people, young parliamentarians, small and medium-sized enterprises, our sports community as well as our media and arts communities. We want the people of ASEAN to feel ownership of the organisation. I support former Foreign Minister, George Yeo's suggestion that ASEAN should make a bid to host the FIFA World Cup. Also, inspired by the success of Eurovision, I have suggested that ASEAN should hold an annual singing competition.

We can also improve the communication between our civil society and the leaders of ASEAN. The status quo is not satisfactory. The representatives of civil society complain that their meetings with ASEAN's leaders are perfunctory and scripted. On the other hand, some of ASEAN's leaders complain that the leaders of civil society are often hostile and disrespectful. I think the solution is for the ASEAN Secretariat to play the role of the liaison between ASEAN and the civil society. Ambassador Ong Keng Yong, when he was the Secretary-General, had acted as a bridge between the two sides.

Finally, I think we should try to find an issue in the field of human rights in which there would be a consensus to take action. My suggestion would be to focus on human trafficking. I hope that AICHR would consider this suggestion sympathetically.

2.2.5 Conclusion

I shall conclude. I believe in ASEAN and salute it on the occasion of its 50th birthday. I salute ASEAN for having kept the peace in Southeast Asia for 50 years. I salute ASEAN for enabling the ASEAN economies to grow and integrate. I salute ASEAN for the indispensable role it plays as the convener and neutral chairman of our region's institutions and networks. I believe that the ASEAN Charter has helped to strengthen ASEAN by augmenting its institutions and the rule of law. I believe that ASEAN has a bright future provided that we remember the advice given by Singapore's founding Foreign Minister, Mr S Rajaratnam, on the 8th of August 1967, in Bangkok. He urged the ASEAN member states to embrace the ASEAN spirit and to act in accordance with it. He defined the ASEAN spirit as the willingness of the ASEAN member states to consider making adjustments to their national policies for the sake of the greater good of ASEAN.

References

Chalermpalanupap, Termsak. 2009. "In Defence of the ASEAN Charter". In *The Making of the ASEAN Charter*, edited by Tommy Koh, Rosario G Manalo and Walter Woon. Singapore: World Scientific.

Hew, Dennis. 2005. "Towards an ASEAN Charter: Regional Economic Integration". In *Framing the ASEAN Charter: An ISEAS Perspective*, edited by Rodolfo C. Severino. Singapore: ISEAS — Yusof Ishak Institute.

Koh, Tommy. 2017. "The ASEAN Charter at 10: Prospects and Retrospect". Lecture at the ISEAS-Yusof Ishak Institute, Singapore, 3 August.

Koh, Tommy, Rosario G. Manalo, and Walter C. M. Woon. 2009. *The Making of the ASEAN Charter*. Singapore: World Scientific.

Mahbubani, Kishore. 2017. "How Fear, Luck and Golf Brought Asean Together". *The Straits Times*, 18 March, available at: http://www.straitstimes.com/opinion/how-fear-luck-and-golf-brought-asean-together (accessed on 15 March 2018).

Mahbubani, Kishore, and Jeffery Sng. 2017. *The ASEAN Miracle: A Catalyst for Peace.* Singapore: NUS Press.

Seah, Daniel. 2009. "The ASEAN Charter". *The International and Comparative Law Quarterly* 58 (1):197–212.

Woon, Walter. 2009. "The ASEAN Charter Dispute Settlement Mechanisms". In *The Making of the ASEAN Charter*, edited by Tommy Koh, Rosario G Manalo and Walter Woon. Singapore: World Scientific.

Chapter 3
2017 Update on Annual Competitiveness Analysis for ASEAN-10

3.1 Introduction

As discussed in Chapter 1, the Association of Southeast Asian Nations (ASEAN) has developed from a regional grouping founded by five member states five decades ago to today's dynamic bloc which possesses remarkable potentials to grow as the world's fourth largest economy by 2030. Leveraging on its deepened economic integration as well as geographical advantages between the Asia-Pacific and the Indian sub-continents, ASEAN as a whole has emerged as an increasingly significant economic player in the global economy. On the social front, ASEAN has also achieved high human development with an average Human Development Index (HDI) of 0.71 in 2015.[1]

Nonetheless, as analysed in great detail in Chapter 4 of the *2016 Annual Competitiveness Analysis and Growth Slowdown Analysis for ASEAN-10*,[2] the fourth instalment of our publication series on ASEAN, while increased integration and reforms in Cambodia, Laos, Myanmar and Vietnam (CLMV) have generated some positive outcomes, it is questionable if their robust growth momentum will be sustainable. Structural weaknesses in industrial productivity and enterprises' capacity as well as the gaps in infrastructure and human capital has to be overcome in order to fuel future development. On the other hand, the forerunners in ASEAN are confronted with a different set of challenges. Among these is the issue of population ageing. Singapore, for instance, is projected to have old-age dependency ratio of 61 dependents per 100 working-age persons in 2050 according to the United Nations, which is the highest in ASEAN.

In light of this, ACI has crafted a comprehensive and rigorous methodological framework not only to produce annual rankings of competitiveness for ASEAN but also to provide an ingenious policy roadmap for individual member states to identify challenges that need to be addressed to achieve greater competitiveness on their respective pathways to sustainable and inclusive economic development. In contrast to other existing global competitiveness rankings, ACI's framework adopts a customised approach through the lens of each ASEAN economy with its own distinct characteristics, challenges and opportunities. Instead of a one-size-fits-all solution, our methodology represents a tailored approach in evaluating and improving national competitiveness for a region as diverse as ASEAN.

While ASEAN has celebrated its golden anniversary in 2017, the consensus is that more development effort is still required especially in terms of bridging the gap between the

[1]According to the Technical notes in Human Development Report 2016 by United Nations Development Programme (UNDP), a country with HDI that ranges from 0.7 to 0.799 is categorised in high human development grouping. See UNDP (2016).

[2]See Tan *et al.* (2017).

transitional CLMV economies and the more economically mature countries. With this latest competitiveness ranking and simulation study covering data from 2000 to 2014, ACI seeks to contribute to the future pathway of ASEAN beyond its 50 years and turn ASEAN into a competitive and sustainable region. Moreover, in this edition, we will introduce the Shapley weightage approach, a breakthrough which enables objective weightage of the different competitiveness dimensions in a comprehensive index.

Following the introduction, Section 3.2 details the methodology and data used to derive the rankings as well as our trademark *What-if* simulation analysis. This policy simulation makes ACI's contribution more instructive than other competitiveness indices which merely report the rankings. Section 3.3 discusses the ranking results, sheds light on the top 20 percent strongest and weakest indicators for individual ASEAN member countries and reports the results of the *What-if* simulation. Section 3.4 explains the Shapley weightage methodology as a robustness check to our vanilla competitiveness framework and presents the corresponding results. Finally, Section 3.5 concludes with policy implications.

3.2 ACI Competitiveness Framework and Methodology

3.2.1 Literature Review on Competitiveness

The notion of regional or *in situ* competitiveness has been explored in various ways. Initially, in the 1980s, "competitiveness" was considered as part of the private sector domain, especially in relation to firm performance.[3] Over time, the discourse expanded onto the domain of macroeconomics, as shown by the establishment of "Council on Competitiveness" or similar institutions in various advanced industrialised countries. Some scholars have argued that it was primarily firms that compete, not nations, regions, or places.[4] However, the performance of those firms depends on various factors that are embedded in the firm's location. These include quality of labour and infrastructure, governance, costs of doing business, as well as the performance of competing and complementary firms around the area.[5]

Two of the most highly cited cross-country competitiveness studies at the moment are the World Competitiveness Yearbook (WCY) by the IMD World Competitiveness Centre and the World Economic Forum's Global Competitiveness Report (GCR). The WCY defines competitiveness as composed of four factors: (i) economic performance, (ii) government efficiency, (iii) business efficiency, and (iv) infrastructure. Each factor is further made up of five criteria, so that there are 20 criteria in total. The WCY uses equal weights such that each criterion contributes 5 percent weight, and each factor contributes 25 percent weight to the overall competitiveness index.[6] Most of the data used are statistical indicators sourced from international, regional and national organisations. However, substantial perception data sourced from executive surveys supplement the statistical data.

---

[3] See Porter (1980).

[4] See Krugman (1994).

[5] See Camagni (2002), Kitson *et al.* (2004) and Bristow (2010).

[6] See IMD World Competitiveness Center (2014).

The GCR breaks down its Global Competitiveness Index into three sub-indices: (i) basic requirements, (ii) efficiency enhancers, and (iii) innovation and sophistication factors.[7] Each of the three sub-indices has a different number of pillars. The basic requirements sub-index has four pillars: institutions, infrastructure, macroeconomic environment, and health and primary education. The efficiency enhancers sub-index is composed of six pillars: higher education and training, goods market efficiency, labour market efficiency, financial market development, technological readiness, and market size. Lastly, the sub-index on innovation and sophistication factors consists of two pillars: business sophistication and innovation. Most of the data that make up these pillars and sub-indices come from executive opinion surveys.

3.2.2 ACI Competitiveness Framework

While the notion of competitiveness has been defined in various ways, ACI's approach to competitiveness is eclectic and comprehensive as it takes into account different factors that collectively shape the ability of a nation or region to achieve substantial and inclusive economic development over a sustained period of time.

In line with this overarching thrust, ACI defines competitiveness through four environments: (i) Macroeconomic Stability (MS), (ii) Government and Institutional Setting, (iii) Financial, Businesses and Manpower Conditions, and (iv) Quality of Life and Infrastructure Development. These four environments carry equal weightage (25 percent) in the computation of the Overall Competitiveness score. Following a nested approach, each environment comprises three sub-environments of the same weightage (33.3 percent) (see Figure 3.1). While giving different weights to different environments and sub-environments based on their importance seems more appropriate, the method is nonetheless arbitrary and contentious. Thus, equal distribution of weight reflects a balanced view towards the different factors that make up an overall notion of competitiveness.

ACI's framework provides a holistic, integrated and systematic way of examining national competitiveness. Two environments are specifically related to economic performance, namely Macroeconomic Stability (MS) and Financial, Businesses and Manpower Conditions (FBMC). MS encompasses aggregated macroeconomic conditions which include: (i) Economic Vibrancy, (ii) Openness to Trade and Services, and (iii) Attractiveness to Foreign Investors. FBMC, on the other hand, represents the micro-economy, particularly firms and factors that impact their performances. FBMC thus comprises: (i) Financial Deepening and Business Efficiency, (ii) Labour Market Flexibility, and (iii) Productivity Performance). The remaining two environments are institutional and social in character. Government and Institutional Setting (GIS) covers efficacy of government institutions and rule of law. This environment consists of: (i) Government Policies and Fiscal Sustainability, (ii) Institutions, Governance and Leadership, and (iii) Competition, Regulatory Standards and Rule of Law. Lastly, Quality of Life and Infrastructure Development (QLID) combines infrastructure, health and education services, environmental standards and social security. The three sub-environments are: (i) Physical Infrastructure, (ii) Technological Infrastructure, and (iii) Standard of Living, Education and Social Stability.

---

[7] See World Economic Forum (2014).

Figure 3.1: ACI Competitiveness Framework

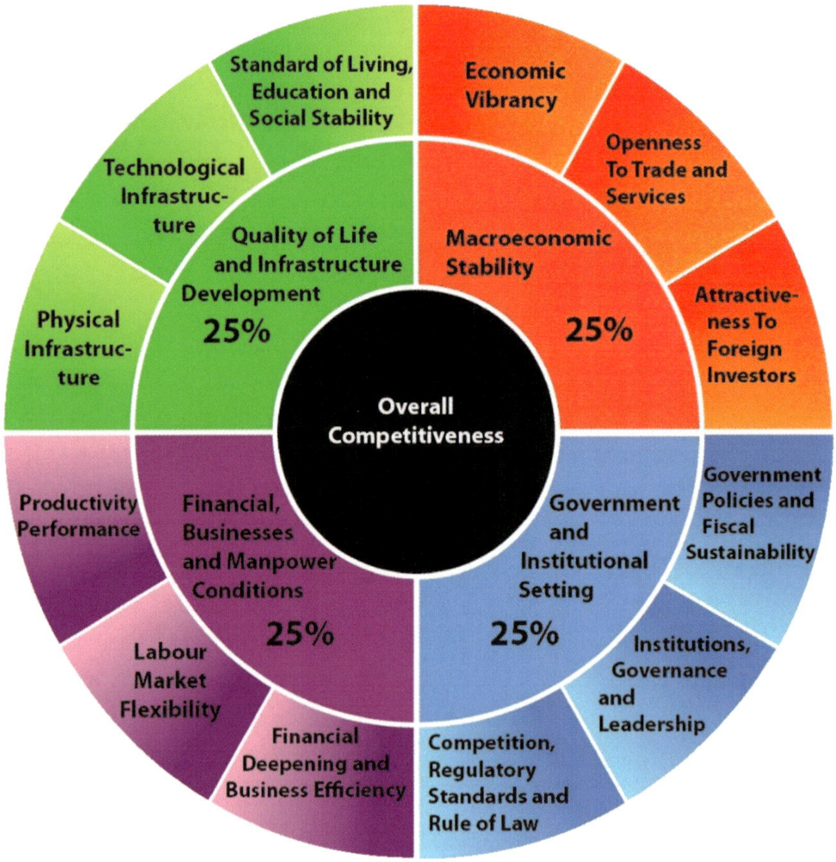

Source: Asia Competitiveness Institute.

There are in total 121 indicators in ACI's competitiveness rankings and simulations for ASEAN-10 economies in the period 2000–2012 (see Appendix 1). The extensive number of indicators ensures robust interpretation of each environment and sub-environment in the Overall Competitiveness score. Depending on data availability, some environments and sub-environments may have more indicators than others. Nonetheless, this is not an issue as they simply average out. This also allows a certain amount of flexibility in adding or removing indicators when updating the rankings in the future, so long as the overall structure of the four environments and 12 sub-environments remains unchanged.

3.2.3 Data Sources

The data for the 121 indicators used in this study are collected from various sources, of which the bulk come from official data sources such as the World Bank World Development Indicators, Asian Development Bank (ADB) and World Economic Forum GCI. Other sources include Economist Intelligence Unit (EIU), Global Market Information Database (GMID), UNESCO Institute for Statistics, International Monetary Fund (IMF) World Economic Outlook Database, United Nations Conference on Trade and Development (UNCTAD), IMD WCY, International

Telecommunication Union Information and Communication Technology (ICT) Indicators Database, United Nations Development Programme (UNDP), Reporters Without Border, Freedom House, and The Pew Research Centre.

3.2.4 Computation of Standardised Scores Using Equal Weights

The next important question in terms of methodology is how to aggregate the different types of data into one coherent index. Given 121 different indicators in this research, all in different value or quantity terms, such as GDP in millions of US dollars, or population in number, how do we resolve these different units of measurement?

The ACI uses the statistical methodology of "standardised score". The standardised score is a relative comparison to see how well the performance of a certain economy is in comparison to the average economy. Therefore, the unit of measurement is no longer relevant. The standardised score has no unit of measurement because it simply measures relative performance among economies.

In statistical terms, it measures how many standard deviations away each economy is from the average economy (see Appendix 2 for technical explanation). If an economy has a standardised score of zero, it is an average performer in terms of that particular indicator. Having a negative score means the economy performs below average. Having a positive score, on the other hand, means above-average performance.

The farther away the score is from zero, the farther away is the performance of the said economy from the ASEAN average. If an economy has a high positive score, it means it is much above the average score. The standardised scores for each indicator are then aggregated at the sub-environment level and then reaggregated at the environment level, and finally aggregated again at the overall level. This allows the comparison of the performance of 10 ASEAN economies at different levels from the Overall Competitiveness to specific indicators in four environments.

3.2.5 *What-if* Competitiveness Simulation Analysis

A competitiveness ranking in itself is like a beauty contest; it merely identifies who are doing well and who are facing challenges but stops short of giving more constructive advice on improving the rankings. The ACI index goes one step further by tackling the "so what?" question. What is the policy implication of a competitiveness ranking result for a particular economy? The data used in the ACI index allow us to do an in-depth analysis of the performance of each economy according to the different indicators, sub-environments, and environments. By analysing the data, we are able to identify not just the Overall Competitiveness ranking but also specific indicators for which the economy is doing well or struggling. This allows us to come up with policy recommendations for each economy.

The ACI has come up with the *What-if* competitiveness simulation that is based on an improvement of each economy's top 20 percent weakest indicators,[8] and a recalculation of the standardised score based on such improvement. To do this, we first look at each economy and sort the different indicators for each economy from the highest to the lowest score. This allows us to identify the 24 weakest indicators, or the bottom 20 percent of the indicators, that each economy has.

[8] In a list of 121 indicators, the weakest are listed at the bottom and the top 20 percent strongest are listed at the top.

Then, we raise the values of these 24 weakest indicators to the average level. This means their average score is raised to zero if it has been negative in the original ranking. For other economies which are already competitive, we leave their scores alone. Their scores are not discounted if they are already competitive. Once these scores are raised, we recalculate the ranking, assuming that other economies stay constant. We do this simulation one by one for each economy. Each economy would then have a new, improved standardised score. This allows us to answer the question: If a particular economy improves on its set of weakest indicators, and assuming other economies remain constant, how would that economy's competitiveness ranking improve?

3.3 Competitiveness Analysis of ASEAN-10 Economies, 2000–2014

In this section, we present the Overall Competitiveness rankings as well as the rankings for the four environments as derived from the standardised scores for each economy over the period 2000–2014. The scores for individual sub-environments are visualised in the median and maximum web analysis. Findings on the *What-if* competitiveness simulation are also discussed.

3.3.1 Overall Competitiveness

Table 3.1 shows the Overall Competitiveness rankings along with the standardised scores of individual ASEAN member states over the period of 2000–2014. In the year 2014, Singapore demonstrated a consistent performance and remained at the top in the region for the 14th consecutive year. Nonetheless, there is slight dip in its score from 2.0924 in 2013 to 2.0152 in 2014, thus narrowing its competitiveness gap with Malaysia which ranked second in 2014 with a score of 1.0568.

One point worth highlighting here is that Brunei has overtaken Thailand and ranked third for the first time throughout the study period. This is due to the significant improvement in Brunei's score to 0.5322 from 0.4169 in 2013 while Thailand experienced a drop in its scores from 0.5301 in 2013 to 0.4477 in 2014. Meanwhile, the largest country in ASEAN, Indonesia has graduated into the rank of economies with positive, or above-average, scores (0.0412) in the region and maintained its ranking at the fifth since 2002. Philippines is ranked sixth in 2014 with a slight improvement in its competitiveness standardised score as compared to that in 2013.

The less developed members of ASEAN remained at the bottom of the ranking in 2014. Vietnam, while maintaining its seventh place, seems to catch up with the Philippines as illustrated in the narrower score gap *vis-à-vis* Philippines. Cambodia appears to have firmly overtaken Laos and Myanmar at the eighth position. Laos, at the ninth place, has fared worse in 2014 with a score of –0.9241 relative to 2013, while Myanmar has seen a notable increase in its score from −1.6044 in 2013 to −1.5501 in 2014.

Figure 3.2 depicts the 10 ASEAN economies' performances in 2000, 2013 and 2014. Uneven improvement in competitiveness within ASEAN can be observed as countries such as Philippines and Vietnam converge towards the regional average while Cambodia, Laos, and Thailand deteriorate in 2014 as compared to 2013. Brunei, Indonesia and Malaysia have demonstrated an optimistic outlook with consistent inch up in terms of the overall competitiveness scores. Singapore, while remaining as the top performer in the region, has witnessed a continuous downturn since 2000.

Table 3.1: Overall Competitiveness Rankings and Standardised Scores, 2000–2014

Overall Competitiveness										
	1		2		3		4		5	
Rank	**Economy**	**Score**	**Economy**	**Score**	**Economy**	**Score**	**Economy**	**Score**	**Economy**	**Score**
2000	Singapore	2.1621	Malaysia	0.9531	Thailand	0.5312	Brunei	0.3726	Indonesia	−0.1154
2001	Singapore	2.1217	Malaysia	0.9244	Thailand	0.6068	Brunei	0.4012	Philippines	−0.1615
2002	Singapore	1.9824	Malaysia	1.0491	Thailand	0.7477	Brunei	0.3706	Indonesia	−0.1851
2003	Singapore	1.9862	Malaysia	1.0605	Thailand	0.7429	Brunei	0.3786	Indonesia	−0.1185
2004	Singapore	1.9573	Malaysia	1.0743	Thailand	0.7228	Brunei	0.4158	Indonesia	−0.0784
2005	Singapore	1.9964	Malaysia	1.0657	Thailand	0.7177	Brunei	0.3724	Indonesia	−0.1784
2006	Singapore	1.9752	Malaysia	1.0799	Thailand	0.6692	Brunei	0.3891	Indonesia	−0.0500
2007	Singapore	2.0327	Malaysia	1.0678	Thailand	0.5723	Brunei	0.3339	Indonesia	0.0134
2008	Singapore	2.1041	Malaysia	0.9589	Thailand	0.5329	Brunei	0.3576	Indonesia	0.0719
2009	Singapore	2.1526	Malaysia	0.8578	Thailand	0.5334	Brunei	0.3588	Indonesia	0.0957
2010	Singapore	2.0811	Malaysia	0.9320	Thailand	0.5284	Brunei	0.4283	Indonesia	0.1185
2011	Singapore	2.0865	Malaysia	1.0434	Thailand	0.5002	Brunei	0.3939	Indonesia	0.0521
2012	Singapore	2.0839	Malaysia	1.0235	Thailand	0.4857	Brunei	0.4101	Indonesia	−0.0059
2013	Singapore	2.0924	Malaysia	0.9763	Thailand	0.5301	Brunei	0.4169	Indonesia	−0.0180
2014	Singapore	2.0152	Malaysia	1.0568	Brunei	0.5322	Thailand	0.4477	Indonesia	0.0412

Overall Competitiveness										
	6		7		8		9		10	
Rank	**Economy**	**Score**	**Economy**	**Score**	**Economy**	**Score**	**Economy**	**Score**	**Economy**	**Score**
2000	Philippines	−0.1844	Vietnam	−0.3895	Cambodia	−0.8558	Laos	−1.1893	Myanmar	−1.2845
2001	Indonesia	−0.1706	Vietnam	−0.3566	Cambodia	−0.8453	Laos	−1.1146	Myanmar	−1.4055
2002	Philippines	−0.2204	Vietnam	−0.3054	Cambodia	−0.8706	Laos	−1.1411	Myanmar	−1.4272
2003	Vietnam	−0.2882	Philippines	−0.3128	Cambodia	−0.9569	Laos	−1.1474	Myanmar	−1.3446
2004	Philippines	−0.2918	Vietnam	−0.3587	Cambodia	−0.9058	Laos	−1.0884	Myanmar	−1.4472
2005	Philippines	−0.2423	Vietnam	−0.3335	Cambodia	−0.9063	Laos	−1.0248	Myanmar	−1.4668
2006	Philippines	−0.2734	Vietnam	−0.3563	Cambodia	−0.9029	Laos	−1.0292	Myanmar	−1.5016
2007	Philippines	−0.2761	Vietnam	−0.3169	Cambodia	−0.9196	Laos	−1.0062	Myanmar	−1.5013
2008	Vietnam	−0.3073	Philippines	−0.3146	Cambodia	−0.9218	Laos	−1.0024	Myanmar	−1.4792
2009	Vietnam	−0.2047	Philippines	−0.4541	Laos	−0.8709	Cambodia	−0.9565	Myanmar	−1.5122
2010	Vietnam	−0.2180	Philippines	−0.4661	Cambodia	−0.9396	Laos	−0.9687	Myanmar	−1.4958
2011	Philippines	−0.3959	Vietnam	−0.4262	Cambodia	−0.8434	Laos	−0.8933	Myanmar	−1.5173
2012	Philippines	−0.3163	Vietnam	−0.4318	Cambodia	−0.6984	Laos	−0.9770	Myanmar	−1.5738
2013	Philippines	−0.3214	Vietnam	−0.4365	Cambodia	−0.7529	Laos	−0.8825	Myanmar	−1.6044
2014	Philippines	−0.3133	Vietnam	−0.3987	Cambodia	−0.9071	Laos	−0.9241	Myanmar	−1.5501

Source: Asia Competitiveness Institute.

Figure 3.2: Overall Competitiveness — 2000, 2013 and 2014

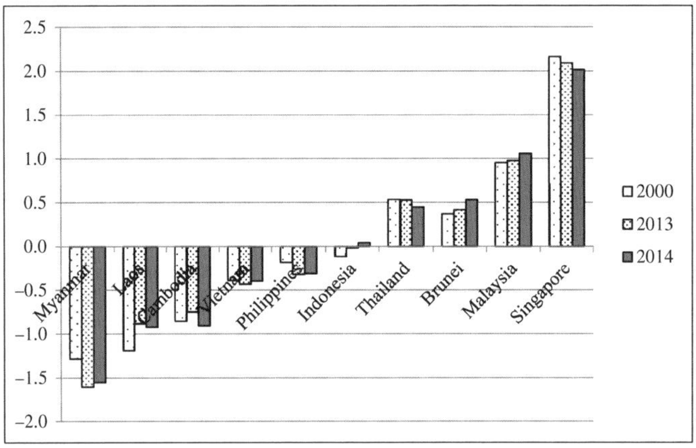

Source: Asia Competitiveness Institute.

3.3.2 Macroeconomic Stability

Table 3.2 presents the rankings and standardised scores for the first environment, Macroeconomic Stability, over the period of 2000–2014. Singapore has once again remained at the top throughout the study period, while the gap between Thailand and Malaysia has widened since Malaysia was overtaken by Thailand in 2013. Indonesia remained to be ranked at the fourth despite a dip in its score (0.3968) as compared to the previous year (0.4328). Vietnam seems to have decidedly overtaken Philippines for two consecutive years at the sixth place despite slight improvement in Philippines' score to −0.5150 in 2014 relative to −0.5647 in 2013. Although Cambodia's score plunged to its lowest (−0.8807) over the study period, it remained at eighth in 2014 while Laos and Myanmar took the ninth and 10th place, respectively.

The relative performances of the 10 ASEAN member states as well as the evolution of competitiveness in Macroeconomic Stability are illustrated in Figure 3.3. Laos appears to make the most remarkable leap in its score in 2014 relative to 2000. Brunei, Laos and Thailand registered moderate improvement in 2014 as compared to 2000, while the rest fared worse over the same period. The Philippines, in particular, has experienced continuous drop in its score for this environment.

Among the three sub-environments constituting Macroeconomic Stability, Brunei's score improved to positive level for Economic Vibrancy in 2014 (Figure 3.4) while Vietnam continued to catch up with the forerunners in terms of Openness to Trade and Services (Figure 3.5). Likewise, Malaysia's score in terms of Attractiveness to Foreign Investors experienced the largest leap among its peers in 2014 (Figure 3.6).

On the flip side, Cambodia's score for Economic Vibrancy deteriorated further in two consecutive years of 2013 and 2014. Its performance in Attractiveness to Foreign Investors also plunged to negative level relative to the positive score in 2000. Besides, competitiveness of

Table 3.2: Macroeconomic Stability Rankings and Standardised Scores, 2000–2014

	Macroeconomic Stability									
	1		2		3		4		5	
Rank	Economy	Score	Economy	Score	Economy	Score	Economy	Score	Economy	Score
2000	Singapore	2.1846	Malaysia	0.8498	Thailand	0.6423	Indonesia	0.3645	Brunei	–0.1940
2001	Singapore	2.0775	Malaysia	0.8187	Thailand	0.6765	Indonesia	0.3119	Brunei	0.0289
2002	Singapore	1.9981	Malaysia	0.8583	Thailand	0.7194	Indonesia	0.4046	Brunei	–0.0088
2003	Singapore	2.1469	Malaysia	0.8096	Thailand	0.6324	Indonesia	0.5578	Brunei	–0.1227
2004	Singapore	2.1565	Malaysia	0.8119	Thailand	0.7392	Indonesia	0.4439	Brunei	–0.1678
2005	Singapore	2.1525	Malaysia	0.8500	Thailand	0.7088	Indonesia	0.3852	Brunei	–0.1144
2006	Singapore	2.1087	Malaysia	0.8244	Thailand	0.7035	Indonesia	0.5099	Brunei	–0.1137
2007	Singapore	2.1002	Malaysia	0.8765	Thailand	0.6963	Indonesia	0.5527	Philippines	–0.2618
2008	Singapore	2.0978	Malaysia	0.7631	Indonesia	0.7401	Thailand	0.6948	Brunei	–0.1861
2009	Singapore	2.1904	Indonesia	0.7242	Thailand	0.7021	Malaysia	0.6173	Brunei	–0.1518
2010	Singapore	2.2118	Malaysia	0.6677	Indonesia	0.6528	Thailand	0.5624	Brunei	0.0404
2011	Singapore	2.2279	Malaysia	0.7262	Indonesia	0.6879	Thailand	0.4381	Brunei	0.0618
2012	Singapore	2.1837	Malaysia	0.6854	Thailand	0.6128	Indonesia	0.5869	Brunei	0.0683
2013	Singapore	2.2628	Thailand	0.6861	Malaysia	0.6019	Indonesia	0.4328	Brunei	0.0164
2014	Singapore	2.1709	Thailand	0.7317	Malaysia	0.6255	Indonesia	0.3968	Brunei	0.2478

	Macroeconomic Stability									
	6		7		8		9		10	
Rank	Economy	Score	Economy	Score	Economy	Score	Economy	Score	Economy	Score
2000	Philippines	–0.3168	Vietnam	–0.4087	Cambodia	–0.5220	Myanmar	–1.2605	Laos	–1.3393
2001	Vietnam	–0.2531	Philippines	–0.3782	Cambodia	–0.5041	Laos	–1.1269	Myanmar	–1.6513
2002	Vietnam	–0.2814	Philippines	–0.2855	Cambodia	–0.6154	Laos	–1.1121	Myanmar	–1.6773
2003	Vietnam	–0.3652	Philippines	–0.4320	Cambodia	–0.6946	Laos	–1.2426	Myanmar	–1.2896
2004	Philippines	–0.3913	Vietnam	–0.5231	Cambodia	–0.5870	Laos	–1.0586	Myanmar	–1.4236
2005	Philippines	–0.4555	Vietnam	–0.4861	Cambodia	–0.5934	Laos	–0.9150	Myanmar	–1.5321
2006	Philippines	–0.3636	Vietnam	–0.5327	Cambodia	–0.6962	Laos	–0.8826	Myanmar	–1.5577
2007	Brunei	–0.2887	Vietnam	–0.5234	Cambodia	–0.7982	Laos	–0.8623	Myanmar	–1.4913
2008	Philippines	–0.4392	Vietnam	–0.5435	Cambodia	–0.7938	Laos	–0.9309	Myanmar	–1.4024
2009	Vietnam	–0.4429	Philippines	–0.6829	Laos	–0.7673	Cambodia	–0.8363	Myanmar	–1.3528
2010	Vietnam	–0.4667	Philippines	–0.5249	Cambodia	–0.8153	Laos	–1.0066	Myanmar	–1.3217
2011	Philippines	–0.4943	Vietnam	–0.6635	Cambodia	–0.7458	Laos	–0.9025	Myanmar	–1.3359
2012	Philippines	–0.3842	Vietnam	–0.5851	Cambodia	–0.7721	Laos	–0.9963	Myanmar	–1.3994
2013	Vietnam	–0.4568	Philippines	–0.5647	Cambodia	–0.6464	Laos	–0.8541	Myanmar	–1.4780
2014	Vietnam	–0.4130	Philippines	–0.5150	Cambodia	–0.8807	Laos	–0.9205	Myanmar	–1.4433

Source: Asia Competitiveness Institute.

Figure 3.3: Macroeconomic Stability — 2000, 2013 and 2014

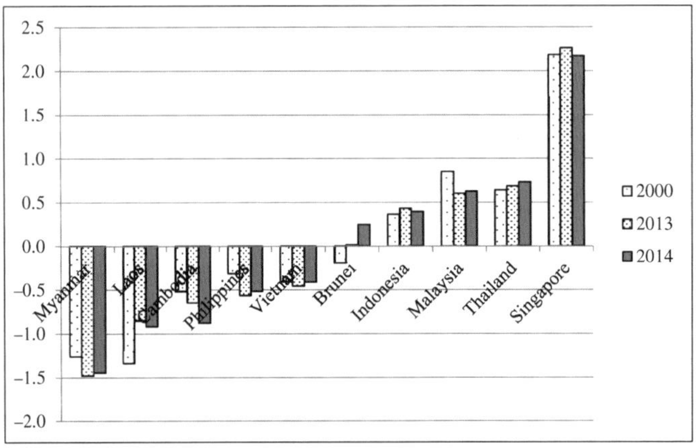

Source: Asia Competitiveness Institute.

Figure 3.4: Macroeconomic Stability (Economic Vibrancy) — 2000, 2013 and 2014

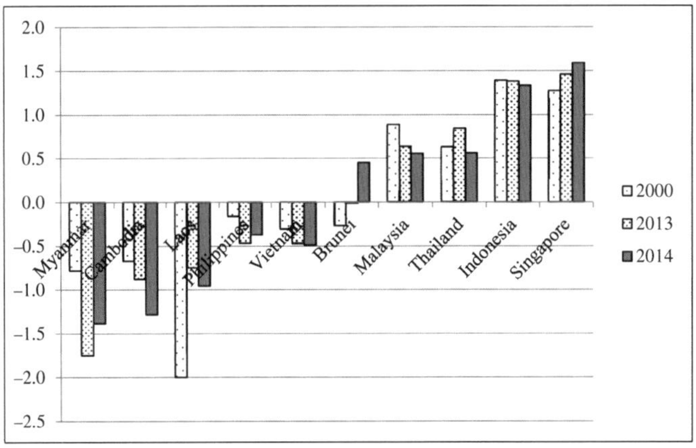

Source: Asia Competitiveness Institute.

Figure 3.5: Macroeconomic Stability (Openness to Trade and Services) — 2000, 2013 and 2014

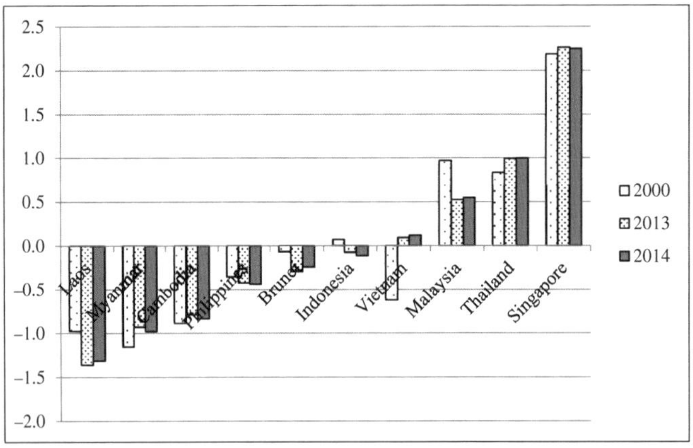

Source: Asia Competitiveness Institute.

Figure 3.6: Macroeconomic Stability (Attractiveness to Foreign Investors) — 2000, 2013 and 2014

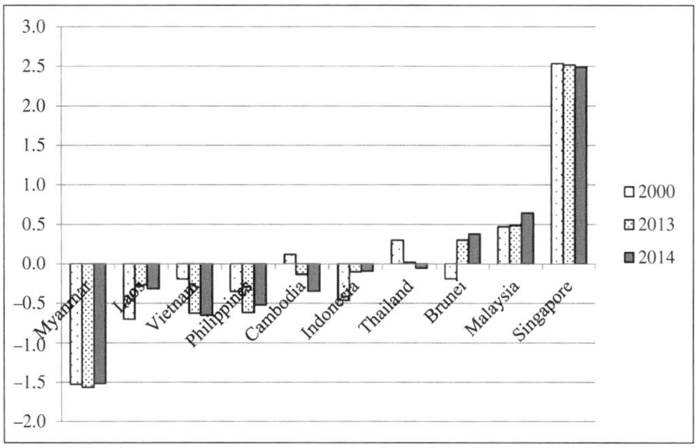

Source: Asia Competitiveness Institute.

Myanmar and Laos also seems to have eroded in 2014 as compared to 2000 in terms of Economic Vibrancy and Openness to Trade and Services, respectively.

3.3.3 Government and Institutional Setting

The same duo, Singapore and Malaysia, dominated the first and second places in the rankings for Government and Institutional Setting throughout the study period (see Table 3.3). Singapore continues to be ahead of Malaysia and other neighbours despite a narrowed gap between the two in 2014 as compared to 2013. Thailand's performance in this environment experienced a notable dip in 2014 and enabled Brunei to firmly overtake its ranking at the third since 2010. The scores of Philippines, Indonesia and Vietnam which were ranked fifth, sixth and seventh, respectively, have witnessed some improvement between 2013 and 2014 although they remained negative or below regional average. Laos, Cambodia and Myanmar remained lagging behind their peers and were ranked at the eighth, ninth and 10th places, respectively.

As seen in Figure 3.7, among four above-average performers, only Malaysia made steadfast improvement in Government and Institutional Setting in 2014 relative to 2000. On the other hand, Cambodia, Myanmar, Philippines, and Vietnam fared worse over time and dropped further from the average score.

In terms of sub-environment, Philippines' score for Government Policies and Fiscal Sustainability remained above average in 2014 despite a slight dip relative to 2013, while Brunei dropped further below average as compared to the score in 2000 (Figure 3.8). Apart from Laos which improved in all three sub-environments over the study period (Figures 3.8–3.10), the remaining ASEAN members showed inconsistent performance over three environments, of which most fared better in one or two sub-environments while deteriorating in others. This reflects some rooms for improvement in terms of good governance and institution for the ASEAN member states.

Table 3.3: Government and Institutional Setting Rankings and Standardised Scores, 2000–2014

	Government and Institutional Setting									
	1		2		3		4		5	
Rank	Economy	Score	Economy	Score	Economy	Score	Economy	Score	Economy	Score
2000	Singapore	2.2937	Malaysia	0.7786	Thailand	0.5409	Brunei	0.4489	Philippines	–0.0852
2001	Singapore	2.2819	Malaysia	0.7781	Thailand	0.5476	Brunei	0.3870	Philippines	–0.0453
2002	Singapore	2.1754	Malaysia	0.9528	Thailand	0.6567	Brunei	0.2602	Philippines	–0.1370
2003	Singapore	2.1470	Malaysia	0.9180	Thailand	0.8302	Brunei	0.2487	Vietnam	–0.1745
2004	Singapore	2.0646	Malaysia	1.0267	Thailand	0.7027	Brunei	0.4226	Philippines	–0.2498
2005	Singapore	2.0475	Malaysia	1.0893	Thailand	0.6890	Brunei	0.4037	Philippines	–0.1794
2006	Singapore	2.1149	Malaysia	0.9818	Thailand	0.6208	Brunei	0.4364	Philippines	–0.2331
2007	Singapore	2.1935	Malaysia	0.9685	Thailand	0.5390	Brunei	0.4345	Philippines	–0.2245
2008	Singapore	2.3680	Malaysia	0.7715	Thailand	0.4567	Brunei	0.4400	Vietnam	–0.2976
2009	Singapore	2.4651	Malaysia	0.5640	Thailand	0.4444	Brunei	0.4057	Indonesia	–0.2248
2010	Singapore	2.3205	Malaysia	0.7618	Brunei	0.5035	Thailand	0.4125	Indonesia	–0.1437
2011	Singapore	2.2518	Malaysia	0.9586	Brunei	0.5349	Thailand	0.3902	Indonesia	–0.3295
2012	Singapore	2.2843	Malaysia	0.9430	Brunei	0.4711	Thailand	0.2583	Philippines	–0.1923
2013	Singapore	2.2463	Malaysia	0.9417	Brunei	0.5178	Thailand	0.3499	Philippines	–0.1692
2014	Singapore	2.2851	Malaysia	1.0322	Brunei	0.4421	Thailand	0.1916	Philippines	–0.1345

	Government and Institutional Setting									
	6		7		8		9		10	
Rank	Economy	Score	Economy	Score	Economy	Score	Economy	Score	Economy	Score
2000	Vietnam	–0.3486	Indonesia	–0.5787	Cambodia	–0.7935	Laos	–1.1262	Myanmar	–1.1300
2001	Vietnam	–0.2904	Indonesia	–0.5197	Cambodia	–0.8326	Laos	–1.0360	Myanmar	–1.2707
2002	Vietnam	–0.2176	Indonesia	–0.4675	Cambodia	–0.8424	Laos	–1.0618	Myanmar	–1.3188
2003	Philippines	–0.3251	Indonesia	–0.4147	Laos	–0.9875	Myanmar	–1.1182	Cambodia	–1.1238
2004	Vietnam	–0.2644	Indonesia	–0.4217	Laos	–0.9308	Cambodia	–0.9839	Myanmar	–1.3661
2005	Vietnam	–0.2849	Indonesia	–0.5316	Cambodia	–0.9385	Laos	–0.9565	Myanmar	–1.3386
2006	Indonesia	–0.2519	Vietnam	–0.3892	Laos	–0.9224	Cambodia	–0.9674	Myanmar	–1.3899
2007	Indonesia	–0.3602	Vietnam	–0.3925	Laos	–0.8848	Cambodia	–0.9496	Myanmar	–1.3239
2008	Philippines	–0.3246	Indonesia	–0.4261	Laos	–0.8640	Cambodia	–0.9674	Myanmar	–1.1564
2009	Vietnam	–0.2798	Philippines	–0.4877	Laos	–0.7624	Cambodia	–0.9228	Myanmar	–1.2016
2010	Vietnam	–0.3166	Philippines	–0.4025	Laos	–0.9295	Cambodia	–0.9779	Myanmar	–1.2282
2011	Philippines	–0.3429	Vietnam	–0.4744	Cambodia	–0.8101	Laos	–0.8756	Myanmar	–1.3031
2012	Vietnam	–0.3756	Indonesia	–0.4119	Cambodia	–0.7466	Laos	–0.7899	Myanmar	–1.4405
2013	Indonesia	–0.4125	Vietnam	–0.4429	Laos	–0.7919	Cambodia	–0.8484	Myanmar	–1.3909
2014	Indonesia	–0.3317	Vietnam	–0.4344	Laos	–0.8673	Cambodia	–0.9715	Myanmar	–1.2116

Source: Asia Competitiveness Institute.

Figure 3.7: Government and Institutional Setting — 2000, 2013 and 2014

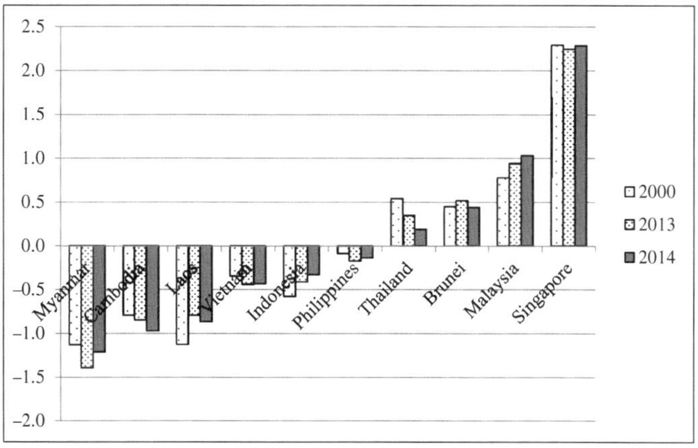

Source: Asia Competitiveness Institute.

Figure 3.8: Government and Institutional Setting (Government Policies and Fiscal Sustainability) — 2000, 2013 and 2014

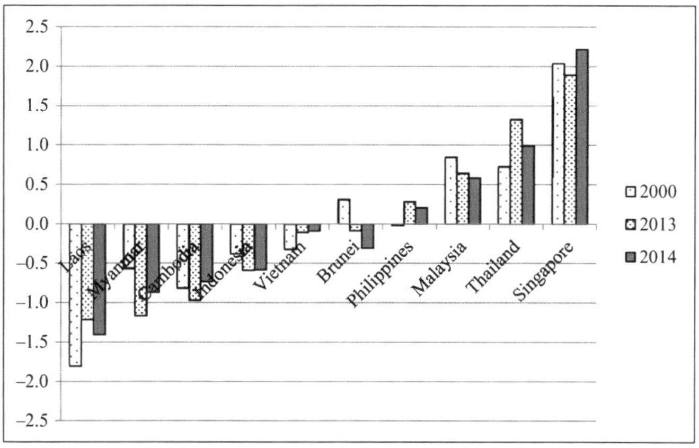

Source: Asia Competitiveness Institute.

Figure 3.9: Government and Institutional Setting (Institutions, Governance and Leadership) — 2000, 2013 and 2014

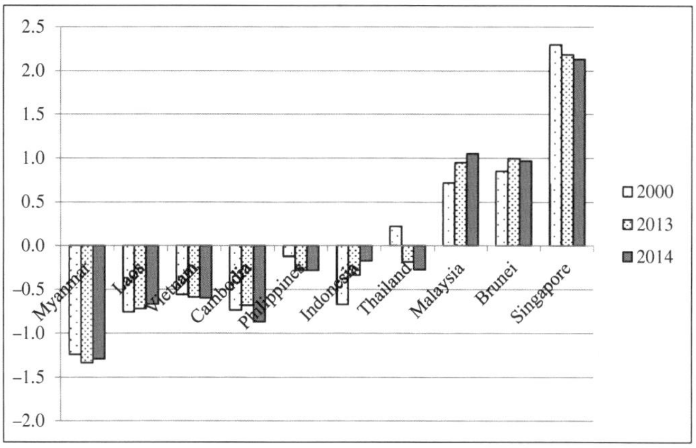

Source: Asia Competitiveness Institute.

Figure 3.10: Government and Institutional Setting (Competition, Regulatory Standards and Rule of Law) — 2000, 2013 and 2014

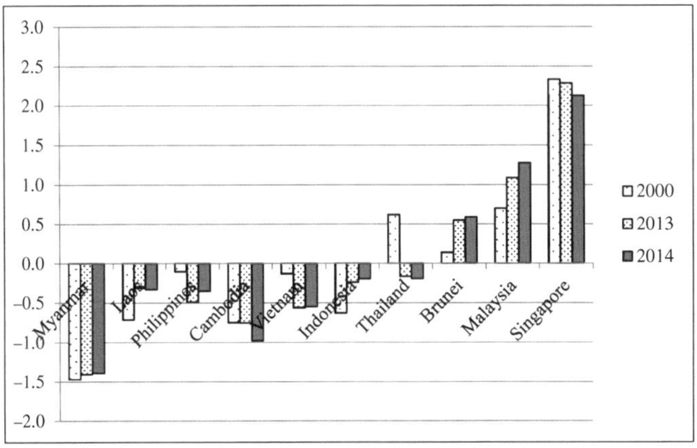

Source: Asia Competitiveness Institute.

3.3.4 Financial, Businesses and Manpower Conditions

Table 3.4 and Figure 3.11 show the rankings and standardised scores for Financial, Businesses and Manpower Conditions from 2000 to 2014. After being a champion in this environment for 14 consecutive years, Singapore was overtaken for the first time by Malaysia which has substantially improved its score from 1.4985 in 2013 to 1.6273 in 2014, while Singapore's score dropped from 1.5693 to 1.3232 over the same period. The ranking for other member states remained the same in the past three years. A closer scrutiny, however, highlighted the narrower gap between Thailand and Brunei in 2014 which are ranked third and fourth, respectively. Similarly, for Philippines and Vietnam, which are at the sixth and seventh positions, a plunge in the score of the former as well as a significant leap in the score of the latter had shrunk the gap between the two economies. Indonesia continues to witness improvement in its score despite the same ranking at the fifth. In the bottom three, Laos improved markedly while Cambodia and Myanmar fared worse.

The standardised scores of individual ASEAN member states for the three sub-environments are illustrated in Figures 3.12–3.14. Interestingly, each sub-environment is championed by different economies. Singapore topped the Financial Deepening and Business Efficiency sub-environment, while Malaysia and Brunei took the top spot for Labour Market Flexibility and Productivity Performance, respectively. One point worth highlighting here is that for each sub-environment, there are only three economies which made it to above average while the rest have negative scores in 2014. In particular, Philippines, Vietnam and Singapore had plunged from positive score in 2000 to negative level in 2014 in terms of Labour Market Flexibility, signifying a growing restrictiveness in labour flow in these economies. In terms of Productivity Performance, Brunei has surpassed all ASEAN member states at large margin and topped the region.

Table 3.4: Financial, Businesses and Manpower Conditions Rankings and Standardised Scores, 2000–2014

	Financial, Businesses and Manpower Conditions									
	1		2		3		4		5	
Rank	Economy	Score	Economy	Score	Economy	Score	Economy	Score	Economy	Score
2000	Singapore	1.8846	Malaysia	1.2700	Thailand	0.5267	Brunei	0.2646	Indonesia	–0.0210
2001	Singapore	1.9099	Malaysia	1.1592	Thailand	0.6945	Brunei	0.2699	Philippines	–0.0701
2002	Singapore	1.5633	Malaysia	1.4114	Thailand	0.9515	Brunei	0.3136	Vietnam	–0.1486
2003	Singapore	1.4880	Malaysia	1.4645	Thailand	0.8605	Brunei	0.4510	Vietnam	–0.0372
2004	Singapore	1.4765	Malaysia	1.4563	Thailand	0.8159	Brunei	0.4308	Indonesia	–0.0538
2005	Singapore	1.6562	Malaysia	1.2916	Thailand	0.8575	Brunei	0.2729	Vietnam	–0.0121
2006	Singapore	1.6281	Malaysia	1.4368	Thailand	0.7533	Brunei	0.3487	Vietnam	–0.1020
2007	Singapore	1.6275	Malaysia	1.4856	Thailand	0.5231	Brunei	0.3527	Indonesia	0.0364
2008	Singapore	1.7300	Malaysia	1.3656	Thailand	0.5240	Brunei	0.2364	Indonesia	0.1160
2009	Singapore	1.6908	Malaysia	1.3606	Thailand	0.5571	Brunei	0.2543	Vietnam	0.0946
2010	Singapore	1.5765	Malaysia	1.4394	Thailand	0.6897	Brunei	0.2934	Vietnam	0.0670
2011	Singapore	1.6336	Malaysia	1.5208	Thailand	0.7637	Brunei	0.1008	Indonesia	0.0579
2012	Singapore	1.6487	Malaysia	1.5194	Thailand	0.7009	Brunei	0.2392	Indonesia	0.0153
2013	Singapore	1.5693	Malaysia	1.4985	Thailand	0.7453	Brunei	0.2932	Indonesia	0.1363
2014	Malaysia	1.6723	Singapore	1.3232	Thailand	0.5671	Brunei	0.5261	Indonesia	0.2875

	Financial, Businesses and Manpower Conditions									
	6		7		8		9		10	
Rank	Economy	Score	Economy	Score	Economy	Score	Economy	Score	Economy	Score
2000	Vietnam	–0.1256	Philippines	–0.1602	Laos	–1.0766	Cambodia	–1.2395	Myanmar	–1.3232
2001	Indonesia	–0.1332	Vietnam	–0.2082	Laos	–1.1108	Cambodia	–1.2396	Myanmar	–1.2716
2002	Philippines	–0.2044	Indonesia	–0.2393	Laos	–1.1822	Cambodia	–1.1956	Myanmar	–1.2698
2003	Indonesia	–0.2712	Philippines	–0.2946	Cambodia	–1.1097	Laos	–1.1184	Myanmar	–1.4329
2004	Vietnam	–0.0710	Philippines	–0.3023	Cambodia	–1.1210	Laos	–1.1943	Myanmar	–1.4371
2005	Philippines	–0.0593	Indonesia	–0.2808	Laos	–1.1101	Cambodia	–1.1611	Myanmar	–1.4548
2006	Indonesia	–0.2168	Philippines	–0.2258	Cambodia	–0.9822	Laos	–1.1822	Myanmar	–1.4578
2007	Vietnam	–0.0207	Philippines	–0.3451	Cambodia	–0.9695	Laos	–1.1612	Myanmar	–1.5287
2008	Vietnam	–0.0560	Philippines	–0.2601	Cambodia	–0.9273	Laos	–1.0946	Myanmar	–1.6339
2009	Indonesia	0.0647	Philippines	–0.3845	Laos	–0.9285	Cambodia	–1.0215	Myanmar	–1.6877
2010	Indonesia	0.0625	Philippines	–0.5980	Laos	–0.9006	Cambodia	–0.9646	Myanmar	–1.6654
2011	Vietnam	–0.2562	Philippines	–0.3687	Cambodia	–0.9359	Laos	–0.9584	Myanmar	–1.5575
2012	Philippines	–0.4246	Vietnam	–0.4260	Cambodia	–0.6165	Laos	–1.0506	Myanmar	–1.6059
2013	Philippines	–0.3491	Vietnam	–0.5127	Cambodia	–0.7198	Laos	–1.0235	Myanmar	–1.6376
2014	Philippines	–0.4753	Vietnam	–0.4763	Cambodia	–0.8090	Laos	–0.9586	Myanmar	–1.6569

Source: Asia Competitiveness Institute.

Figure 3.11: Financial, Businesses and Manpower Conditions — 2000, 2013 and 2014

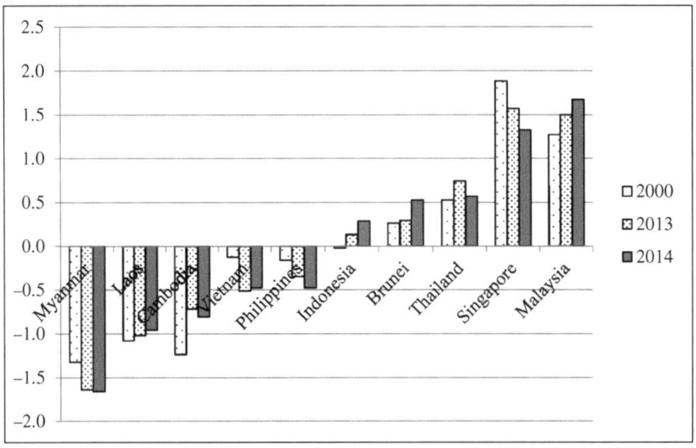

Source: Asia Competitiveness Institute.

Figure 3.12: Financial, Businesses and Manpower Conditions (Financial Deepening and Business Efficiency) — 2000, 2013 and 2014

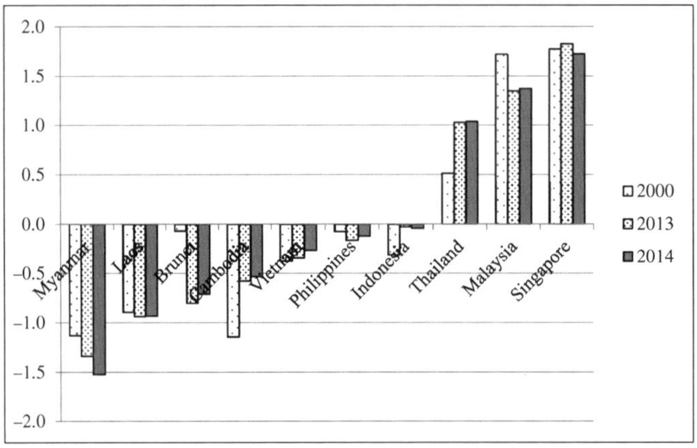

Source: Asia Competitiveness Institute.

Figure 3.13: Financial, Businesses and Manpower Conditions (Labour Market Flexibility) — 2000, 2013 and 2014

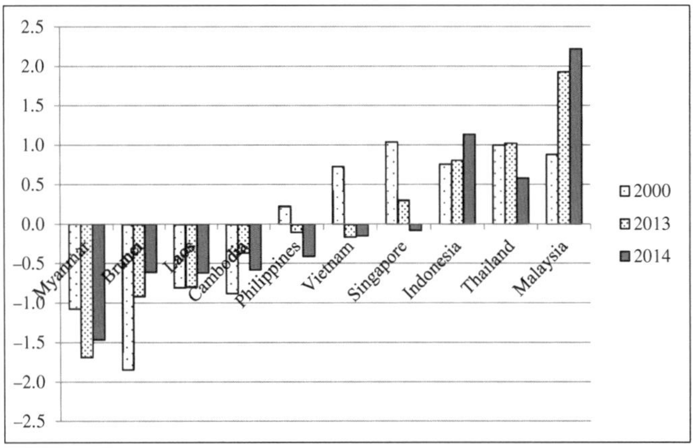

Source: Asia Competitiveness Institute.

Figure 3.14: Financial, Businesses and Manpower Conditions (Productivity Performance) — 2000, 2013 and 2014

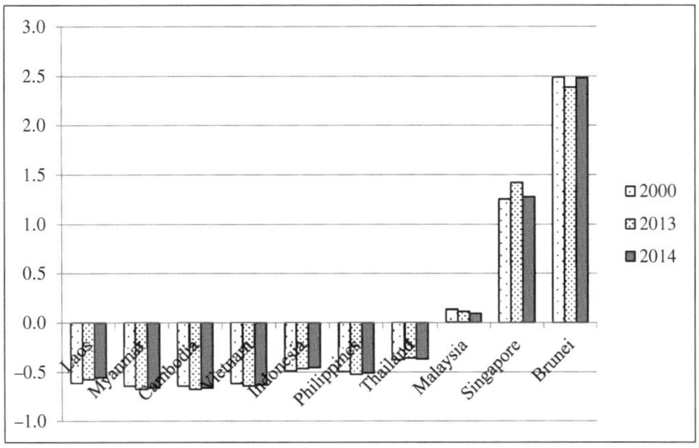

Source: Asia Competitiveness Institute.

3.3.5 Quality of Life and Infrastructure Development

In the ranking for Quality of Life and Infrastructure Development (Table 3.5), Singapore topped the ranking throughout the study period (2000–2014) followed by Brunei. Malaysia remained at the third after being overtaken by Brunei since 2013. Thailand maintained its ranking at the fourth despite a slight drop in the score. The remaining six ASEAN members performed below average in this environment since 2000. Philippines retained its fifth position after surpassing Indonesia in 2013, followed by Vietnam at the seventh. As the performance of Cambodia further deteriorated, Laos has managed to overtake Cambodia and emerged as the eighth. Despite a notable improvement in the score between 2013 and 2014, Myanmar stayed at the 10th place with a significant lag behind Cambodia.

As seen in Figure 3.15, besides Indonesia, Laos, Philippines, and Vietnam, all economies, especially Myanmar, have fared worse since 2000 for this environment. Among the four economies which improved over time, Laos and Vietnam have witnessed the most significant improvement in the scores. More alarmingly, extra effort is required in improving performance of Myanmar, which is the only economy in the region that scored below −1.5 in this environment. While the fall in scores between 2013 and 2014 seem insignificant for Singapore and Thailand, the eroding competitiveness in this environment also calls for more attention from the stakeholders.

As reflected in its ranking at environment level, Singapore topped the rankings for all three sub-environments (see Figures 3.16–3.18). This is followed by Malaysia which ranked second, except for the Standard of Living, Education and Social Stability, where it was overtaken by Brunei (see Figure 3.18). Although much effort is still required to improve the competitiveness in the other two sub-environments, Thailand and Vietnam appear to have improved significantly in terms of Technological Infrastructure as their scores turned from negative in 2000 to positive in 2014. On the flip side, the scores of Malaysia and Thailand for Standard of Living, Education and Social Stability have shown a marked drop in 2014 relative to 2000. More alarmingly, Myanmar had witnessed a drop in scores for all three sub-environments over the study period.

Table 3.5: Quality of Life and Infrastructure Development Rankings and Standardised Scores, 2000–2014

	Quality of Life and Infrastructure Development									
	1		2		3		4		5	
Rank	Economy	Score	Economy	Score	Economy	Score	Economy	Score	Economy	Score
2000	Singapore	2.0777	Brunei	0.9353	Malaysia	0.8222	Thailand	0.3637	Philippines	−0.1579
2001	Singapore	2.0516	Brunei	0.8877	Malaysia	0.8693	Thailand	0.4612	Philippines	−0.1399
2002	Singapore	2.0129	Brunei	0.8840	Malaysia	0.8788	Thailand	0.5955	Philippines	−0.2349
2003	Singapore	1.9430	Malaysia	0.9324	Brunei	0.8956	Thailand	0.5664	Philippines	−0.1647
2004	Singapore	1.9374	Brunei	0.9364	Malaysia	0.8955	Thailand	0.5618	Philippines	−0.1949
2005	Singapore	1.9547	Malaysia	0.9385	Brunei	0.8949	Thailand	0.5528	Philippines	−0.2539
2006	Singapore	1.8983	Malaysia	0.9941	Brunei	0.8552	Thailand	0.5481	Indonesia	−0.2375
2007	Singapore	2.0227	Malaysia	0.8425	Brunei	0.8062	Thailand	0.4781	Indonesia	−0.1765
2008	Singapore	1.9860	Brunei	0.9001	Malaysia	0.8286	Thailand	0.3966	Indonesia	−0.1505
2009	Singapore	2.0038	Brunei	0.8836	Malaysia	0.7853	Thailand	0.3654	Vietnam	−0.1658
2010	Singapore	2.0169	Brunei	0.8351	Malaysia	0.7702	Thailand	0.3984	Indonesia	−0.1090
2011	Singapore	2.0175	Malaysia	0.8602	Brunei	0.8374	Thailand	0.3571	Indonesia	−0.2133
2012	Singapore	2.0236	Malaysia	0.8503	Brunei	0.8231	Thailand	0.3252	Indonesia	−0.2135
2013	Singapore	2.0835	Brunei	0.7987	Malaysia	0.7662	Thailand	0.2863	Philippines	−0.1707
2014	Singapore	2.0429	Brunei	0.8499	Malaysia	0.7720	Thailand	0.2476	Philippines	−0.0913

	Quality of Life and Infrastructure Development									
	6		7		8		9		10	
Rank	Economy	Score	Economy	Score	Economy	Score	Economy	Score	Economy	Score
2000	Indonesia	−0.2155	Vietnam	−0.6377	Cambodia	−0.7859	Laos	−1.1010	Myanmar	−1.3010
2001	Indonesia	−0.3280	Vietnam	−0.6469	Cambodia	−0.7388	Laos	−1.0975	Myanmar	−1.3186
2002	Indonesia	−0.4215	Vietnam	−0.5463	Cambodia	−0.7501	Laos	−1.1048	Myanmar	−1.3135
2003	Indonesia	−0.3325	Vietnam	−0.5440	Cambodia	−0.7934	Laos	−1.1140	Myanmar	−1.3887
2004	Indonesia	−0.2742	Vietnam	−0.5407	Cambodia	−0.8411	Laos	−1.0619	Myanmar	−1.4183
2005	Indonesia	−0.2709	Vietnam	−0.5219	Cambodia	−0.8530	Laos	−1.0278	Myanmar	−1.4134
2006	Philippines	−0.2503	Vietnam	−0.3743	Cambodia	−0.8966	Laos	−1.0508	Myanmar	−1.4862
2007	Philippines	−0.2474	Vietnam	−0.3018	Cambodia	−0.8766	Laos	−1.0240	Myanmar	−1.5231
2008	Philippines	−0.1994	Vietnam	−0.2979	Cambodia	−0.8959	Laos	−1.0083	Myanmar	−1.5592
2009	Indonesia	−0.1929	Philippines	−0.2063	Laos	−0.9199	Cambodia	−0.9297	Myanmar	−1.6236
2010	Vietnam	−0.1350	Philippines	−0.2947	Cambodia	−0.9109	Laos	−0.9458	Myanmar	−1.6252
2011	Vietnam	−0.2667	Philippines	−0.3367	Laos	−0.7445	Cambodia	−0.7948	Myanmar	−1.7161
2012	Philippines	−0.2343	Vietnam	−0.3000	Cambodia	−0.5929	Laos	−0.9796	Myanmar	−1.7020
2013	Indonesia	−0.2269	Vietnam	−0.2902	Cambodia	−0.7224	Laos	−0.7729	Myanmar	−1.7516
2014	Indonesia	−0.1925	Vietnam	−0.2237	Laos	−0.8404	Cambodia	−0.8597	Myanmar	−1.7047

Source: Asia Competitiveness Institute.

Figure 3.15: Quality of Life and Infrastructure Development — 2000, 2013 and 2014

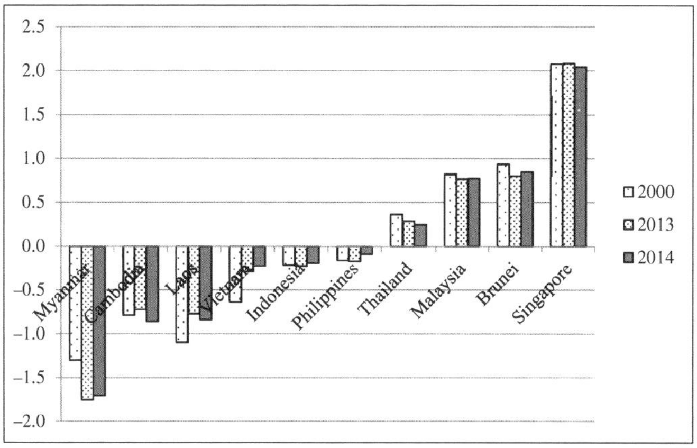

Source: Asia Competitiveness Institute.

Figure 3.16: Quality of Life and Infrastructure Development (Physical Infrastructure) — 2000, 2013 and 2014

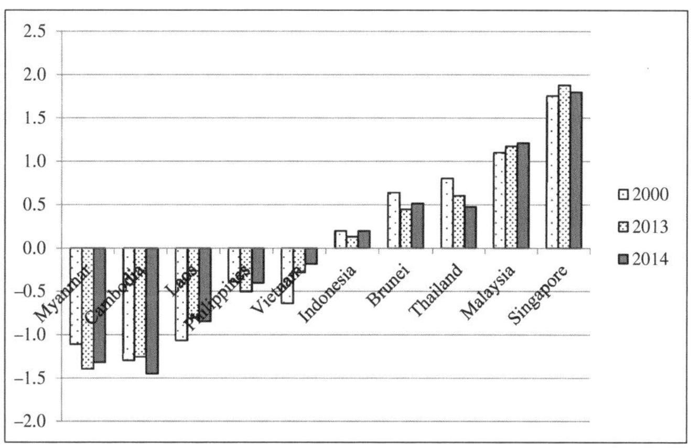

Source: Asia Competitiveness Institute.

Figure 3.17: Quality of Life and Infrastructure Development (Technological Infrastructure) — 2000, 2013 and 2014

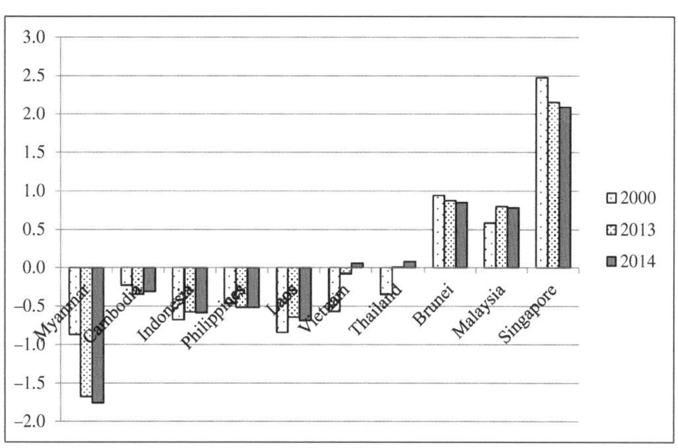

Source: Asia Competitiveness Institute.

Figure 3.18: Quality of Life and Infrastructure Development (Standard of Living, Education and Social Stability) — 2000, 2013 and 2014

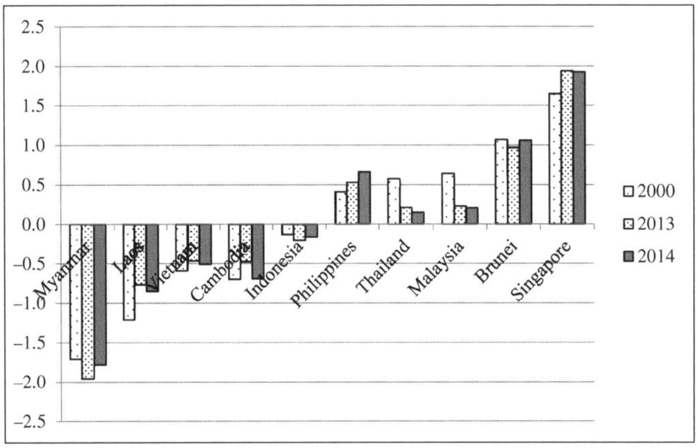

Source: Asia Competitiveness Institute.

3.3.6 Competitiveness over Time Analysis

For a better comparison of the competitive performances over time, we split the study period into two sub-periods, 2000–2006 (Period A) and 2007–2014 (Period B). Our Competitiveness over Time (COT) analysis is conducted for Overall Competitiveness as well as each of the 12 sub-environments, which is instructive for policy-making as it reveals where individual economies are losing competitiveness. For all COT Figures (3.19–3.31), countries above the 45-degree line improved their competitiveness in Period B relative to Period A; below the line means the performance has worsened in Period B as compared to Period A; and on the line means no change over both sub-periods.

As shown in Figure 3.19 for Overall Competitiveness, Singapore, located at the top of the 45-degree line, is consistent with its top-notch performance detailed in Section 3.3.1. Brunei, Cambodia and Vietnam are on the 45-degree line, indicating constant competitiveness in both periods. Indonesia and Laos have performed better in Period B than in Period A as shown by their positions above the line. In contrast, the competitiveness of Malaysia, Myanmar, Philippines and Thailand have deteriorated in Period B relative to Period A as demonstrated by their positions below the line.

In Figure 3.20 for Economic Vibrancy, a sub-environment under Macroeconomic Stability, Indonesia not only stands at the top among all member states but also performs better in Period B than in Period A. This is followed by Singapore which takes the second place and also shows improvement in Period B relative to Period A. Among the bottom four economies, Laos and Myanmar show marked improvement over time, while Vietnam and Cambodia are losing in competitiveness in this sub-environment. The competitiveness of Brunei, Malaysia, Philippines and Thailand in Economic Vibrancy seems to stay stagnant over the period as reflected by their positions close to the line.

In the remaining two sub-environments under Macroeconomic Stability, most ASEAN economies are clustered along the 45-degree line, which indicates little to no improvement in competitiveness, with the exception of Singapore, Thailand and Vietnam lying above the line for Openness to Trade and Services (see Figure 3.21), and Brunei, Indonesia and Laos which fared better over time in terms of Attractiveness to Foreign Investors (see Figure 3.22).

Figure 3.19: Competitiveness over Time Analysis for Overall Competitiveness, Period B (2007–2014) against Period A (2000–2006)

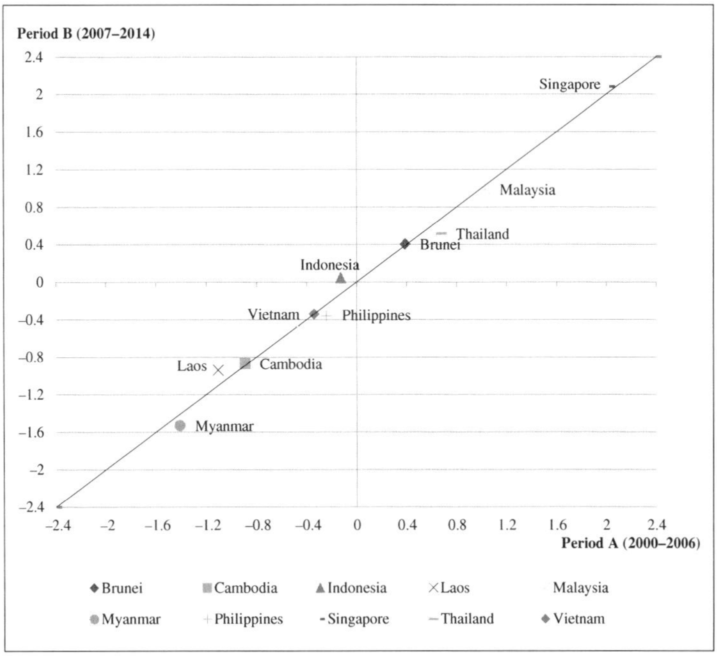

Source: Asia Competitiveness Institute.

Figure 3.20: Competitiveness over Time Analysis for Economic Vibrancy, Period B (2007–2014) against Period A (2000–2006)

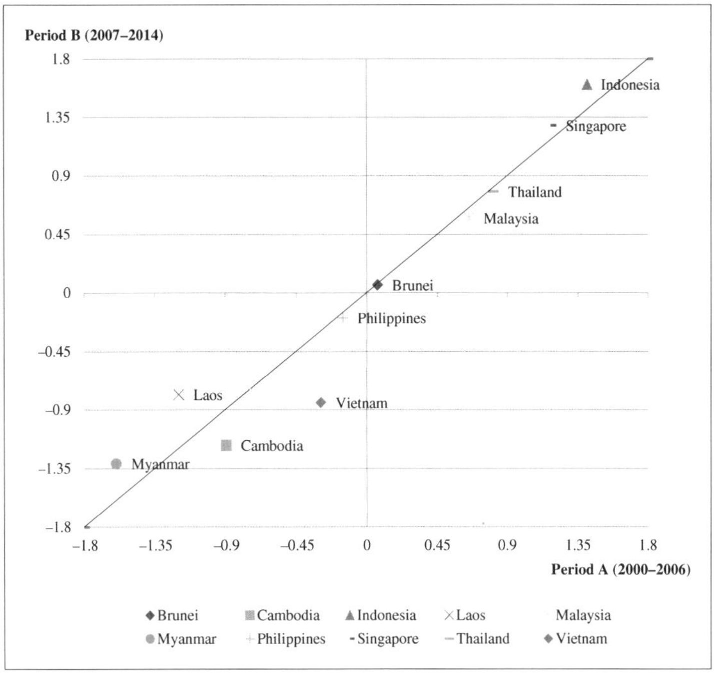

Source: Asia Competitiveness Institute.

Figure 3.21: Competitiveness over Time Analysis for Openness to Trade and Services, Period B (2007–2014) against Period A (2000–2006)

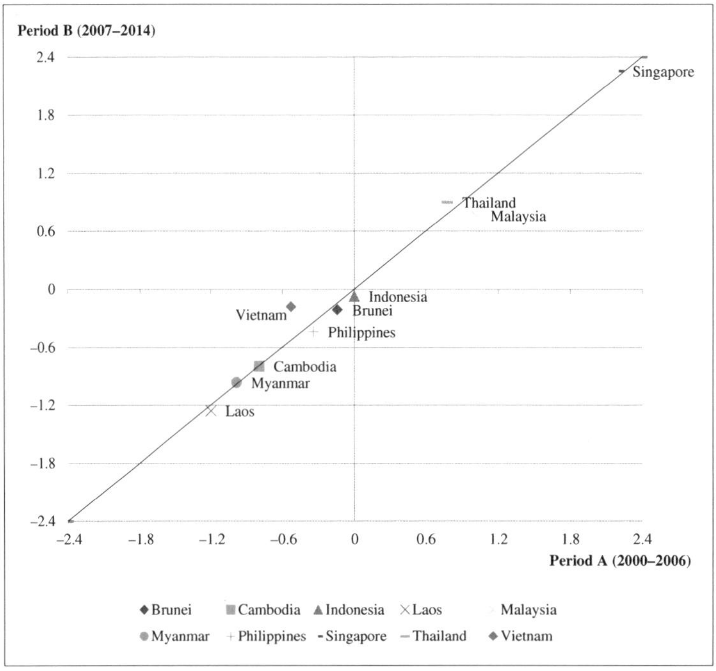

Source: Asia Competitiveness Institute.

Figure 3.22: Competitiveness over Time Analysis for Attractiveness to Foreign Investors, Period B (2007–2014) against Period A (2000–2006)

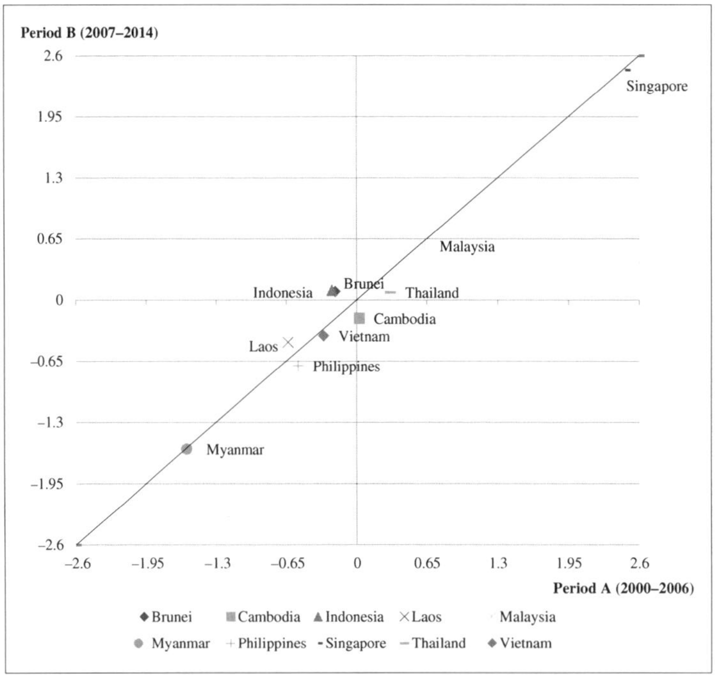

Source: Asia Competitiveness Institute.

As seen in Figures 3.23–3.25, Singapore remains at the top and far ahead of its peers for all three sub-environments under Government and Institutional Setting with improvement in Period B as compared to Period A. The performance of ASEAN economies is encouraging by as shown by the improvement of Laos, Myanmar, Philippines and Thailand in terms of Government Policies and Fiscal Sustainability, while Brunei, Indonesia and Laos fared better in Competition, Regulatory Standards and Rule of Law in Period B as compared to Period A. Nonetheless, among the bottom three, only Laos shows significant improvement in all sub-environments in Period B relative to Period A, while Cambodia and Myanmar have only shown little or no improvement as they cluster around the 45-degree line. This signifies that more effort is required to catch up with the other economies in the region.

Among the three sub-environments under Financial, Businesses and Manpower Conditions, Singapore maintained its top spot for Financial Deepening and Business Efficiency (Figure 3.26) while Malaysia and Brunei have been the most competitive in terms of Labour Market Flexibility (Figure 3.27) and Productivity Performance (Figure 3.28), respectively. However, while Singapore and Malaysia have become more competitive over time in terms of Financial Deepening and Business Efficiency, and Labour Market Flexibility, respectively, Brunei's competitiveness in Productivity Performance appears to be eroding as it fared worse in Period B relative to Period A. It is alarming to note that in the sub-environment of Productivity Performance, all ASEAN members except Singapore are clustered on the 45-degree line, signifying their stagnant productivity over the two sub-periods.

In Figures 3.29–3.31 for the three sub-environments under Quality of Life and Infrastructure Development, Singapore's performance indicated a worrying sign in terms of Technological Infrastructure as shown by its significant deterioration in Period B relative to Period A (Figure 3.30). On the bright side, Indonesia and Laos have made positive progress in Standard of Living, Education and Social Stability. Nonetheless, Malaysia and Thailand have fared significantly worse in the same sub-environment. Indonesia and Thailand have demonstrated improved competitiveness in Technological Infrastructure albeit deterioration in Physical Infrastructure, which indicates challenges in balancing development in both sub-environments. It is also alarming to note a distinct gap between Myanmar and its peers in terms of Technological Infrastructure, and Standard of Living, Education and Social Stability. Moreover, Myanmar's competitiveness has deteriorated markedly in Period B relative to Period A.

Our COT analysis shows that the performance of ASEAN member states vary in different sub-environments over the study period. In line with the overall competitiveness performance in 2014, Singapore has topped most sub-environments by a large margin. Brunei and Malaysia are catching up with Singapore and even overtook the city-state in some sub-environments. However, the intensification of globalisation which leads to an increasingly competitive economy coupled with internal challenges has posed new threats to some of the ASEAN economies, particularly Philippines and Thailand. For the transitional economies in ASEAN, Vietnam in particular has stood out with significant strides and emerged as a new investor darling among multinational corporations (MNCs) and other foreign investors. While Cambodia, Laos and Myanmar have shown optimistic sign of entering their take-off development stage, there remains a wide gap with other forerunners in the region in all sub-environments.

Figure 3.23: Competitiveness over Time Analysis for Government Policies and Fiscal Sustainability, Period B (2007–2014) against Period A (2000–2006)

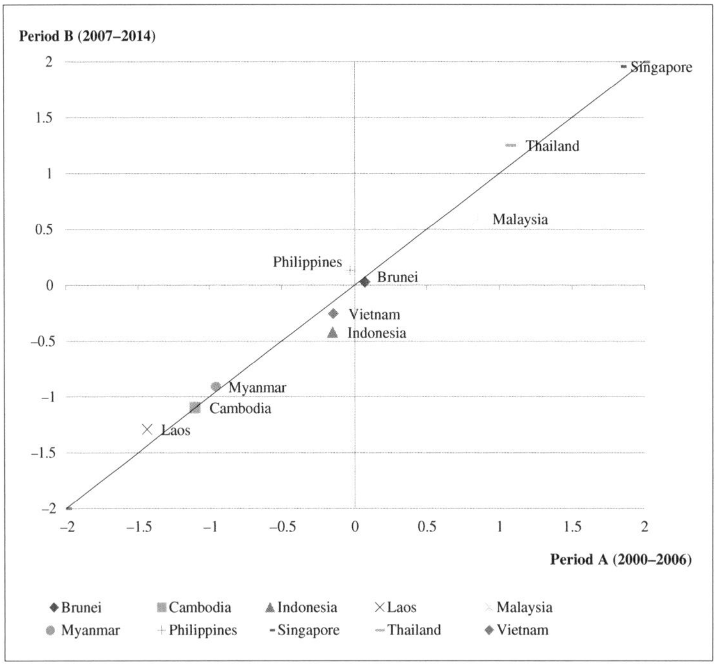

Source: Asia Competitiveness Institute.

Figure 3.24: Competitiveness over Time Analysis for Institutions, Governance and Leadership, Period B (2007–2014) against Period A (2000–2006)

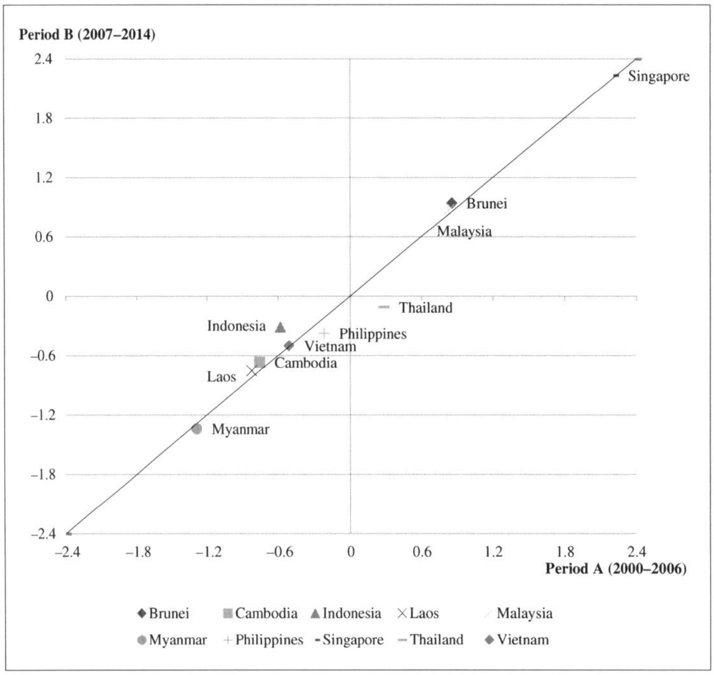

Source: Asia Competitiveness Institute.

Figure 3.25: Competitiveness over Time Analysis for Competition, Regulatory Standards and Rule of Law, Period B (2007–2014) against Period A (2000–2006)

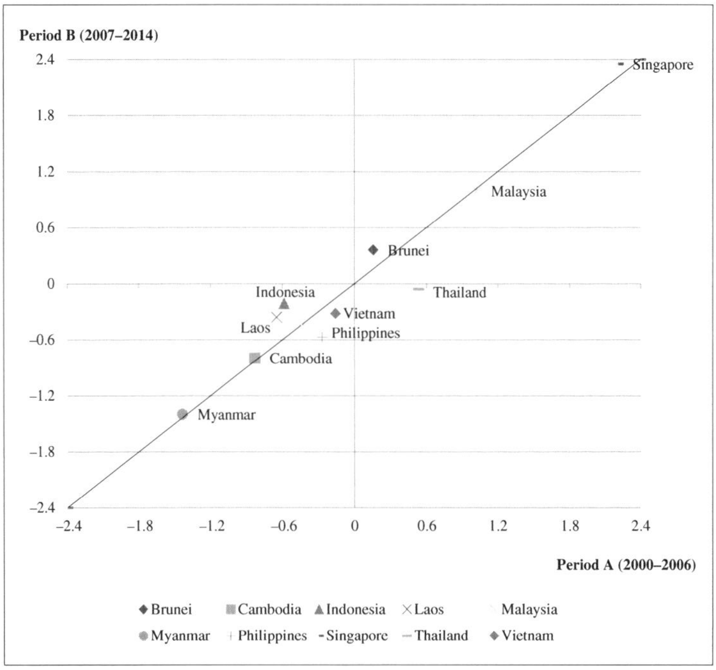

Source: Asia Competitiveness Institute.

Figure 3.26: Competitiveness over Time Analysis for Financial Deepening and Business Efficiency, Period B (2007–2014) against Period A (2000–2006)

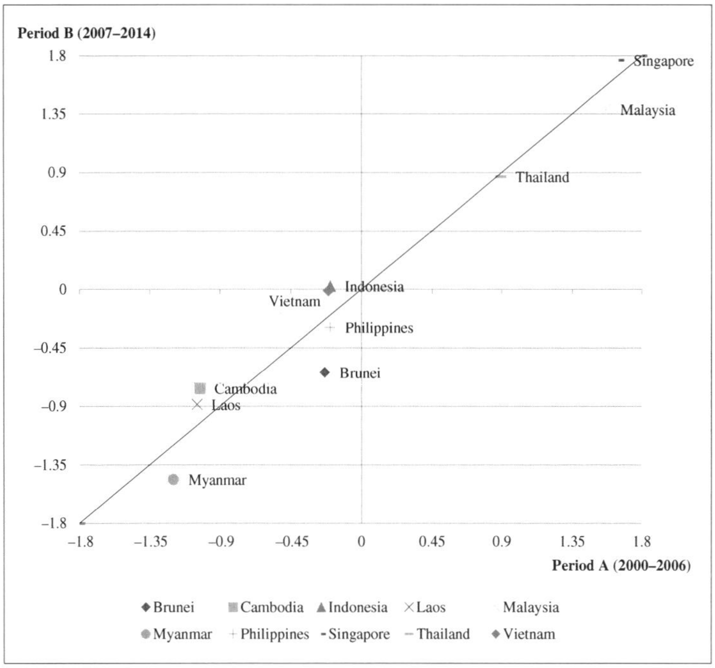

Source: Asia Competitiveness Institute.

Figure 3.27: Competitiveness over Time Analysis for Labour Market Flexibility, Period B (2007–2014) against Period A (2000–2006)

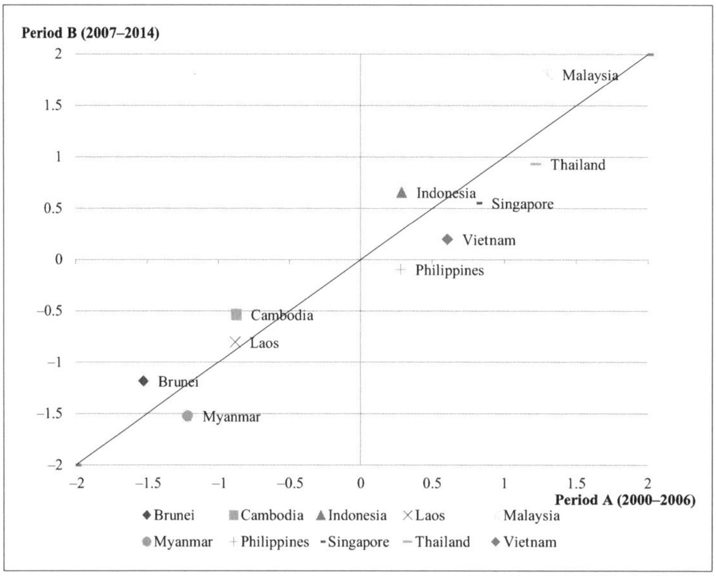

Source: Asia Competitiveness Institute.

Figure 3.28: Competitiveness over Time Analysis for Productivity Performance, Period B (2007–2014) against Period A (2000–2006)

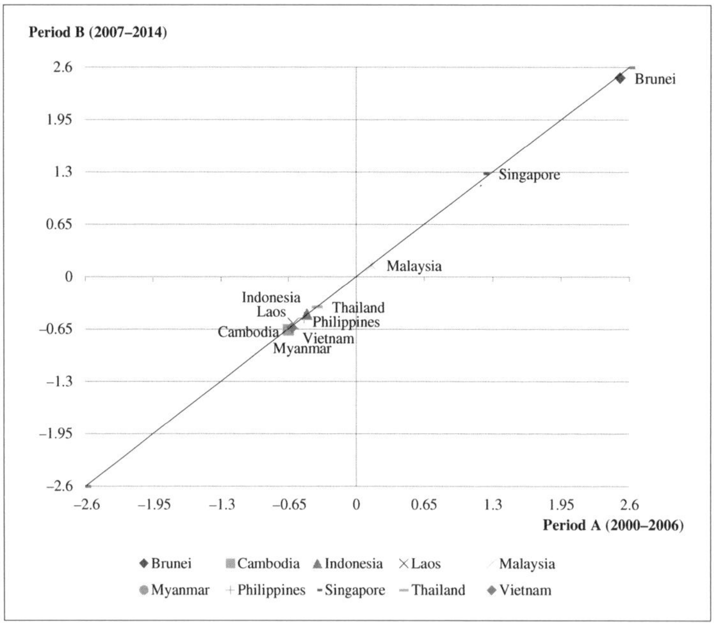

Source: Asia Competitiveness Institute.

Figure 3.29: Competitiveness over Time Analysis for Physical Infrastructure, Period B (2007–2014) against Period A (2000–2006)

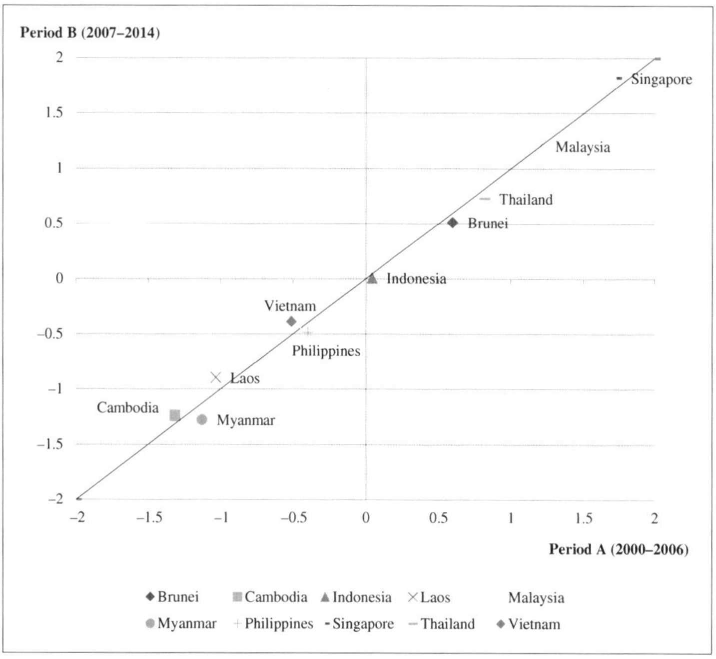

Source: Asia Competitiveness Institute.

Figure 3.30: Competitiveness over Time Analysis for Technological Infrastructure, Period B (2007–2014) against Period A (2000–2006)

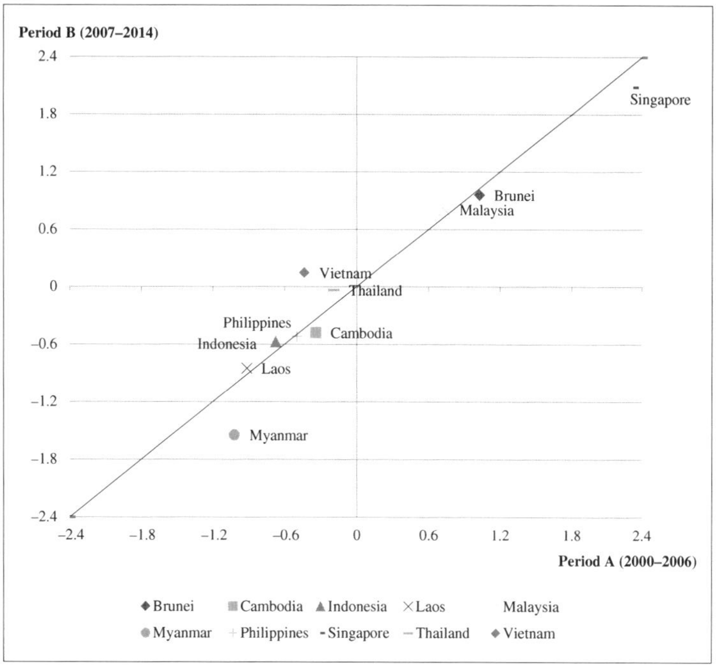

Source: Asia Competitiveness Institute.

Figure 3.31: Competitiveness over Time Analysis for Standard of Living, Education and Social Stability, Period B (2007–2014) against Period A (2000–2006)

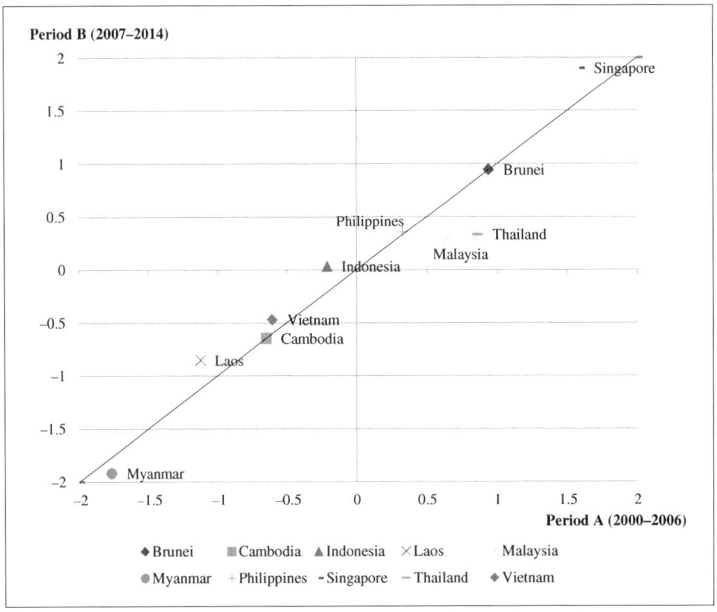

Source: Asia Competitiveness Institute.

3.3.7 Maximising Strengths and Minimising Weaknesses

In this section, the top 20 percent strongest indicators and top 20 percent weakest indicators for individual ASEAN economies will be first discussed. This is followed by the analysis of spider web charts depicting each economy's competitiveness in each sub-environment *vis-à-vis* the ASEAN median and maximum (set by the regional top performer).

3.3.7.1 *Top 20 Percent Strongest and Weakest Indicators*

Brunei's top 20 percent strongest and top 20 percent weakest indicators are listed in Tables 3.6 and 3.7, respectively. Being highly dependent on oil in its economy, Brunei is vulnerable to the unpredictable oil market. This makes venturing into new source of growth a policy priority. Strong value added per worker in agriculture and industry (#1 and #2 in Table 3.6) are catalysts for the economic restructuring process. This can also be complemented by gross domestic savings of the people (#4) which is one of the most notable strengths in the economy. While economic growth matters, the government does not overlook the importance of environment as reflected in its third strongest indicator, government environmental protection policies.

On the other hand, high labour cost in terms of both management and production dimensions (#120 and #121 in Table 3.7) may hamper the economic development and restructuring in Brunei. Potential investors might also be turned away due to its poor claims on private sector (#117), tax burden (#118) and lack of ease of starting business (#119). Weak financial sector as

Table 3.6: Top 20 Percent Strongest Indicators List for Brunei, 2014

Rank	20 Percent Strongest Indicator	Score	Environment
1	Agriculture, Value Added Per Worker	2.9465	FBMC
2	Industry, Value Added Per Worker	2.7915	FBMC
3	Government Environmental Protection Policies	2.1918	GIS
4	Gross Domestic Savings	2.1023	MS
5	Current Account Balance	2.0586	MS
6	Access to Print Media	1.9747	QLID
7	Government Consumption Expenditure	1.9597	GIS
8	Personal Computers	1.9177	QLID
9	Inflation	1.8901	MS
10	Religious Unrest	1.7549	QLID
11	High Quality Management Staff	1.7525	FBMC
12	Sovereign Debt Risk	1.7266	FBMC
13	Political Change	1.6369	GIS
14	Air Quality	1.6229	QLID
15	Information and Communication Technology (ICT) Expenditure	1.5761	QLID
16	Integrity of Legal System	1.5275	GIS
17	Corporate Income Tax	1.5128	MS
18	Public Security and Safety	1.4479	QLID
19	Human Development Index	1.3452	QLID
20	Secondary Schooling	1.3122	QLID
21	Government Responsiveness	1.2651	GIS
22	Internet Subscribers	1.2448	QLID
23	Quality of Judiciary	1.2420	GIS
24	Government Stability	1.2240	GIS

Source: Asia Competitiveness Institute.

Table 3.7: Top 20 Percent Weakest Indicators List for Brunei, 2014

Rank	20 Percent Weakest Indicator	Score	Environment
98	Population	−0.8536	QLID
99	Exports of Goods and Services	−0.8574	MS
100	Net Foreign Assets	−0.8683	GIS
101	Labour Force	−0.8936	FBMC
102	International Tourism Receipts	−0.9032	MS
103	International Reserves	−0.9158	GIS
104	Tax Revenue/Government Revenue	−0.9173	GIS
105	Market Capitalisation	−0.9314	FBMC
106	Health Expenditure	−0.9378	QLID
107	Imports of Goods and Services	−0.9399	MS
108	Output Services (Value Added)	−0.9421	MS
109	Government Revenue (Including Grants)	−0.9450	GIS
110	Regional Competitiveness	−0.9928	GIS
111	Tax Revenue	−0.9971	GIS
112	Gross Domestic Product	−1.0171	MS
113	Listed Domestic Companies	−1.0270	FBMC
114	Real GDP Growth	−1.0303	MS
115	Domestic Credit Provided by the Financial Sector	−1.0335	FBMC
116	Deposit Interest Rate	−1.0472	GIS
117	Claims on Private Sector	−1.3977	FBMC
118	Tax Burden	−1.4216	GIS
119	Ease of Starting Business	−1.7668	GIS
120	Cost of Management Staff	−1.8198	FBMC
121	Cost of Production Labour	−1.9665	FBMC

Source: Asia Competitiveness Institute.

reflected in domestic credit provided by the financial sector and deposit interest rate (#115 and #116) is also a potential hindrance to development in Brunei.

For Cambodia, labour cost emerges as one of its top strengths at #12 and #16 in Table 3.8. Notable efforts have been made in strengthening the private sector, as shown in claims on private sector (#1) and corporate income tax (#10). While there are optimistic prospects in economic performance, development progress seems to be imbalanced as social indicators such as lack of public services provision, especially in education (#111, #112 and #120 in Table 3.9) and infrastructure (#115, #118 and #119) are among the weakest indicators for Cambodia. Hence, more efforts are needed to channel the economic benefits towards improving social conditions for a comprehensive development in Cambodia.

Table 3.8: Top 20 Percent Strongest Indicators List for Cambodia, 2014

Rank	20 Percent Strongest Indicator	Score	Environment
1	Claims on Private Sector	2.6061	FBMC
2	Telecommunications System	2.3892	QLID
3	Freedom of Religion	2.2361	QLID
4	Freedom of Speech	1.5275	QLID
5	Unemployment Rate	1.2734	FBMC
6	Real GDP Growth	1.2210	MS
7	Government Environmental Protection Policies	1.1503	GIS
8	Daily Organic Water Pollutant Emissions	1.1496	QLID
9	Exchange Rate Appreciation	0.9360	GIS
10	Corporate Income Tax	0.9348	MS
11	Health Expenditure	0.8117	QLID
12	Cost of Management Staff	0.7806	FBMC
13	International Monetary Fund Credit	0.7723	GIS
14	External Debt	0.7679	GIS
15	Freedom of Press	0.6667	QLID
16	Tax Revenue/Government Revenue	0.6387	GIS
17	Cost of Production Labour	0.6240	FBMC
18	Traffic Congestion	0.5785	QLID
19	Cellular Mobile Telephone Subscribers	0.4230	QLID
20	Tax Burden	0.2514	GIS
21	Foreign Owned Companies	0.1233	MS
22	Urban Population Growth	0.0852	QLID
23	Openness to Trade	0.0636	MS
24	Political Change	−0.0254	GIS

Source: Asia Competitiveness Institute.

Table 3.9: Top 20 Percent Weakest Indicators List for Cambodia, 2014

Rank	20 Percent Weakest Indicator	Score	Environment
98	Government Revenue (Including Grants)	−1.0142	GIS
99	Lack of Corruption	−1.0181	GIS
100	Gross Domestic Product	−1.0207	MS
101	Listed Domestic Companies	−1.0270	FBMC
102	Tax Revenue	−1.0279	GIS
103	Intellectual Property Rights Protection	−1.0332	GIS
104	Lack of Cronyism	−1.0369	GIS
105	Government Consumption Expenditure	−1.0393	GIS
106	Information and Communication Technology (ICT) Expenditure	−1.0445	QLID
107	Internet Subscribers	−1.0552	QLID
108	Effectiveness of Legal System	−1.0897	GIS
109	Gross Domestic Savings	−1.1277	MS
110	Quality of Police	−1.1288	GIS
111	Availability of Scientists and Engineers	−1.1662	FBMC
112	Human Development Index	−1.1808	QLID
113	Interest Rate Spread	−1.2020	GIS
114	Urban Population	−1.3671	QLID
115	Electric Power	−1.4391	QLID
116	Quality of Judiciary	−1.6063	GIS
117	Money Supply Growth (M2)	−1.6519	MS
118	Access to Water	−1.6998	QLID
119	Access to Sanitation	−2.1104	QLID
120	Literacy Rate	−2.1347	QLID
121	Air Quality	−2.2943	QLID

Source: Asia Competitiveness Institute.

Being the largest economy in ASEAN, Indonesia's population size has contributed to abundant and low-cost labour force (#3, #4, #13 and #22 in Table 3.10). The top two indicators, valued added in agriculture and industry (#1 and #2), have shown that Indonesia is dependent on dualistic economic structure. In addition, Indonesia has also performed well in services sector (#5), which indicates a balanced development across three main sectors.

Nonetheless, less conducive business environment may hinder economic activities in Indonesia. Improvement is needed in removing trade barriers (#111 in Table 3.11) in order to increase openness to trade (#108). Macroeconomic factors including quality of central bank, money supply, inflation, external debt and exchange rate appreciation (#109, #114,

Table 3.10: Top 20 Percent Strongest Indicators List for Indonesia, 2014

Rank	20 Percent Strongest Indicator	Score	Environment
1	Output Agriculture (Value Added)	2.7812	MS
2	Output Industry (Value Added)	2.7234	MS
3	Population	2.6490	QLID
4	Labour Force	2.5769	FBMC
5	Output Services (Value Added)	2.3189	MS
6	Deposit Interest Rate	1.8276	GIS
7	Freedom of Speech	1.5275	QLID
8	Gross Fixed Capital Formation	1.4589	MS
9	Tax Burden	1.4101	GIS
10	Gross Domestic Product	1.2035	MS
11	Political System Risk	1.1359	GIS
12	Availability of Scientists and Engineers	0.8342	FBMC
13	Cost of Management Staff	0.7806	FBMC
14	Market Capitalisation	0.7259	FBMC
15	Government Revenue (Including Grants)	0.7052	GIS
16	Tax Revenue	0.6937	GIS
17	Regional Competitiveness	0.6922	GIS
18	Freedom of Press	0.6834	QLID
19	Listed Domestic Companies	0.6696	FBMC
20	Legislature/Parliament (Functioning of Government System)	0.6233	GIS
21	Rail Facilities	0.5576	QLID
22	Cost of Production Labour	0.5236	FBMC
23	Interest Rate Spread	0.5215	GIS
24	Secondary Schooling	0.5125	QLID

Source: Asia Competitiveness Institute.

Table 3.11: Top 20 Percent Weakest Indicators List for Indonesia, 2014

Rank	20 Percent Weakest Indicator	Score	Environment
98	Labour Market Rating	−0.6727	FBMC
99	Domestic Credit Provided by the Financial Sector	−0.6812	FBMC
100	Institutional Sophistication	−0.6816	GIS
101	Lending Rate	−0.7184	GIS
102	Freedom of Religion	−0.7454	QLID
103	Domestic Credit to Private Sector	−0.7883	FBMC
104	Health Expenditure	−0.8230	QLID
105	Policy Towards Private Enterprise Rating	−0.8281	GIS
106	Government Stability	−0.8474	GIS
107	Lack of Discrimination Against Investors	−0.8646	MS
108	Openness to Trade	−0.8653	MS
109	Quality of Central Bank/Monetary Authority	−0.8879	GIS
110	Internet Subscribers	−0.9233	QLID
111	Barriers to Trade	−0.9339	GIS
112	Access to Sanitation	−1.0141	QLID
113	Information and Communication Technology (ICT) Expenditure	−1.0445	QLID
114	Money Supply (M2)	−1.1430	GIS
115	Primary Schooling	−1.1936	QLID
116	Unemployment Rate	−1.5242	FBMC
117	Inflation	−1.5846	MS
118	Real GDP Growth	−1.9069	MS
119	International Monetary Fund Credit	−2.1695	GIS
120	External Debt	−2.1848	GIS
121	Exchange Rate Appreciation	−2.6786	GIS

Source: Asia Competitiveness Institute.

#117, #120 and #121) remain the top weaknesses in Indonesia. While labour supply is a strength for Indonesia as discussed earlier, it is also crucial to not overlook the quality of the labour market (#98).

As commonly seen in most rapidly growing economies, Laos is also experiencing high urban population growth (#1 in Table 3.12). Among its top 20 percent strengths are manpower cost (#7 and #12), political stability (#13) and a relatively conducive business environment (#17, #18 and #20).

However, the quality of human capital remains a key challenge for Laos to keep up with the market demand for skilled labour (#108, #109, #111, and #119 in Table 3.13). Connectivity advancement should remain top on the priority (#103, #112, and #116) as this will not only encourage economic activity but also facilitate the distribution of growth outcomes.

Table 3.12: Top 20 Percent Strongest Indicators List for Laos, 2014

Rank	20 Percent Strongest Indicator	Score	Environment
1	Urban Population Growth	2.2645	QLID
2	Telecommunications System	1.3990	QLID
3	Daily Organic Water Pollutant Emissions	1.1496	QLID
4	Gross Fixed Capital Formation	1.0208	MS
5	International Monetary Fund Credit	0.8239	GIS
6	Unemployment Rate	0.7910	FBMC
7	Cost of Management Staff	0.7806	FBMC
8	Real GDP Growth	0.7612	MS
9	External Debt	0.7276	GIS
10	Government Environmental Protection Policies	0.6967	GIS
11	Traffic Congestion	0.6302	QLID
12	Cost of Production Labour	0.6240	FBMC
13	Political Change	0.5996	GIS
14	Government Consumption Expenditure	0.5297	GIS
15	Corporate Governance	0.4600	GIS
16	Labour Unrest	0.4585	QLID
17	Corporate Income Tax	0.4013	MS
18	Levelness of Playing Field	0.3691	MS
19	Religious Unrest	0.3687	QLID
20	Claims on Private Sector	0.3407	FBMC
21	Electric Power	0.3341	QLID
22	Telephone Main Lines	0.3070	QLID
23	Exchange Rate Appreciation	0.2789	GIS
24	Monopolies and Cartel	0.2729	GIS

Source: Asia Competitiveness Institute.

Table 3.13: Top 20 Percent Weakest Indicators List for Laos, 2014

Rank	20 Percent Weakest Indicator	Score	Environment
98	Lack of Market Distortion due to State-Ownership	–0.9571	GIS
99	Net Foreign Assets	–0.9984	GIS
100	Human Development Index	−1.0129	QLID
101	Political System Risk	−1.0131	GIS
102	Listed Domestic Companies	−1.0270	FBMC
103	Internet Subscribers	−1.0442	QLID
104	Information and Communication Technology (ICT) Expenditure	−1.0445	QLID
105	Government Revenue (Including Grants)	−1.0456	GIS
106	Gross Domestic Product	−1.0691	MS
107	Tax Revenue	−1.0720	GIS
108	Secondary Schooling	−1.0978	QLID
109	University and Post-Graduate Education	−1.1263	QLID
110	Money Supply Growth (M2)	−1.1648	MS
111	Availability of Scientists and Engineers	−1.2380	FBMC
112	Port Facilities	−1.2933	QLID
113	Health Expenditure	−1.3900	QLID
114	Freedom of Press	−1.4451	QLID
115	Access to Water	−1.4834	QLID
116	Cellular Mobile Telephone Subscribers	−1.5634	QLID
117	Current Account Balance	−1.7634	MS
118	Regional Competitiveness	−1.7658	GIS
119	Literacy Rate	−1.7933	QLID
120	Lending Rate	−2.1781	GIS
121	Interest Rate Spread	−2.4800	GIS

Source: Asia Competitiveness Institute.

Despite being the second most competitive economy in ASEAN, Malaysia still lags far behind the top performing economy, Singapore. As Malaysia surpassed Singapore for the first time throughout the study period in the environment of Financial, Businesses and Manpower Conditions, it is imperative to tap on its rich talent pool (#3, #4 and #24 in Table 3.14) in order to expedite the catching-up process. Furthermore, its sound institutional capacity (#2, #6, #9, #15, and #18) and well-functioning financial system (#10, #16, and #22) also make it an attractive investment destination for local and foreign investors.

However, several indicators (#115, #120, and #121 in Table 3.15) have exposed high fiscal vulnerability in Malaysia which poses credible threat to macroeconomic environment of the country. Expanding urban population (#101) has also led to problems such as traffic congestion (#110) and pollution (#119) which the policy-makers need to be heedful of.

Table 3.14: Top 20 Percent Strongest Indicators List for Malaysia, 2014

Rank	20 Percent Strongest Indicator	Score	Environment
1	Listed Domestic Companies	1.9739	FBMC
2	Legislature/Parliament (Functioning of Government System)	1.9335	GIS
3	High Quality Management Staff	1.7525	FBMC
4	Availability of Scientists and Engineers	1.6508	FBMC
5	Rail Facilities	1.5566	QLID
6	Integrity of Legal System	1.5275	GIS
7	Ease of Starting Business	1.5035	GIS
8	Monopolies and Cartel	1.5020	GIS
9	Bureaucracy/Red Tape	1.4609	GIS
10	Quality of Banking and Financial System	1.4459	FBMC
11	Extent of Staff Training	1.3955	FBMC
12	Money Supply (M2)	1.3630	GIS
13	Barriers to Trade	1.3581	GIS
14	Local Road System	1.3068	QLID
15	Government Responsiveness	1.2651	GIS
16	Domestic Credit to Private Sector	1.2580	FBMC
17	Transparency of Processes for Investors	1.2546	MS
18	Transparency of Government	1.2546	GIS
19	Corporate Governance	1.2517	GIS
20	Levelness of Playing Field	1.2423	MS
21	Intellectual Property Rights Protection	1.2284	GIS
22	Domestic Credit Provided by the Financial Sector	1.2254	FBMC
23	Government Stability	1.2240	GIS
24	Labour Market Rating	1.1959	FBMC

Source: Asia Competitiveness Institute.

Table 3.15: Top 20 Percent Weakest Indicators List for Malaysia, 2014

Rank	20 Percent Weakest Indicator	Score	Environment
98	Access to Print Media	−0.0256	QLID
99	Exchange Rate Appreciation	−0.0389	GIS
100	Health Expenditure	−0.0589	QLID
101	Urban Population Growth	−0.0693	QLID
102	Deposit Interest Rate	−0.0848	GIS
103	Industry, Value Added Per Worker	−0.0914	FBMC
104	GDP Per Capita	−0.1017	MS
105	University and Post-Graduate Education	−0.1369	QLID
106	Tax Burden	−0.1672	GIS
107	Telecommunications System	−0.1752	QLID
108	Government Environmental Protection Policies	−0.2932	GIS
109	Claims on Private Sector	−0.3157	FBMC
110	Traffic Congestion	−0.3271	QLID
111	Population	−0.4471	QLID
112	Labour Force	−0.5267	FBMC
113	Foreign Direct Investment Inflows	−0.5452	MS
114	Primary Schooling	−0.5627	QLID
115	Budget Balance	−0.6113	GIS
116	Freedom of Speech	−0.6547	QLID
117	Freedom of Religion	−0.7454	QLID
118	Corporate Income Tax	−1.0993	MS
119	Daily Organic Water Pollutant Emissions	−1.1495	QLID
120	International Monetary Fund Credit	−1.1856	GIS
121	External Debt	−1.3340	GIS

Source: Asia Competitiveness Institute.

Myanmar possesses immense potential in becoming the next investment hub in ASEAN (#16 in Table 3.16) albeit being a latecomer in the region. It should leverage on its large pool of low cost labour (#5, #7, and #18) as well as high literacy rate (#11) in attracting new investment. Stable financial status (#6, #9, #13, and #17) is also another strong feature in Myanmar which plays a crucial role in fuelling sustainable growth.

The list of weakest indicators in Table 3.17 reveals weak institutional capacity (#98, #99, #100, #105 and #112) and socio-political instability (#107 and #118) in Myanmar. With newly elected government in place, it is imperative to curb this weaknesses which may derail Myanmar from its development trajectory.

Table 3.16: Top 20 Percent Strongest Indicators List for Myanmar, 2014

Rank	20 Percent Strongest Indicator	Score	Environment
1	Tax Burden	1.7638	GIS
2	Deposit Interest Rate	1.5715	GIS
3	Daily Organic Water Pollutant Emissions	1.3627	QLID
4	Real GDP Growth	0.9100	MS
5	Cost of Management Staff	0.7806	FBMC
6	External Debt	0.7727	GIS
7	Cost of Production Labour	0.6240	FBMC
8	Traffic Congestion	0.5463	QLID
9	International Monetary Fund Credit	0.5395	GIS
10	Interest Rate Spread	0.2402	GIS
11	Literacy Rate	0.1977	QLID
12	Exchange Rate Appreciation	0.1521	GIS
13	Budget Balance	0.1173	GIS
14	Access to Sanitation	0.0281	QLID
15	Urban Population Growth	−0.0363	QLID
16	Foreign Direct Investment Inflows	−0.0374	MS
17	Gross Domestic Savings	−0.0519	MS
18	Labour Force	−0.0527	FBMC
19	Population	−0.1226	QLID
20	Unemployment Rate	−0.1254	FBMC
21	Claims on Private Sector	−0.2903	FBMC
22	Primary Schooling	−0.3141	QLID
23	Corporate Income Tax	−0.3324	MS
24	Output Agriculture (Value Added)	−0.3330	MS

Source: Asia Competitiveness Institute.

Table 3.17: Top 20 Percent Weakest Indicators List for Myanmar, 2014

Rank	20 Percent Weakest Indicator	Score	Environment
98	Quality of Government Policies	−1.4519	GIS
99	Legislature/Parliament (Functioning of Government System)	−1.4566	GIS
100	Quality of Regulatory Environment	−1.5031	GIS
101	Freedom of Press	−1.5414	QLID
102	Government Consumption Expenditure	−1.5421	GIS
103	Public Security and Safety	−1.5438	QLID
104	Local Road System	−1.6026	QLID
105	Government Effectiveness	−1.6107	GIS
106	Electric Power	−1.6187	QLID
107	Labour Unrest	−1.6389	QLID
108	Airport Facilities	−1.6972	QLID
109	Networked Readiness Index	−1.7570	QLID
110	Strength of Auditing and Reporting Standards	−1.7982	GIS
111	Levelness of Playing Field	−1.8209	MS
112	Quality of Stock Market Regulatory Authority	−1.8230	FBMC
113	Business Impact of Rules on FDI	−1.9068	MS
114	Quality of Banking and Financial System	−1.9208	FBMC
115	Cellular Mobile Telephone Subscribers	−2.0175	QLID
116	Monopolies and Cartel	−2.0540	GIS
117	Foreign Owned Companies	−2.0564	MS
118	Religious Unrest	−2.1454	QLID
119	Tax Revenue/Government Revenue	−2.1822	GIS
120	Extent of Staff Training	−2.2154	FBMC
121	Gross Fixed Capital Formation	−2.3528	MS

Source: Asia Competitiveness Institute.

High quality of human capital resulting from good training and education (#8, #20, #21, and #24 in Table 3.18) would have boosted the competitiveness of Philippines if there are sufficient job opportunities to be filled (#121 in Table 3.19). While foreign-owned companies find heavy presence in Philippines (#18), foreign direct investment (FDI) inflows and trade openness are rather low (#98 and #111). This is most likely due to unfavourable business environment plagued with bureaucratic inefficiency (#100, #108 and #113). Poor connectivity (#99, #101, #114, and #115) is another major hindrance to Philippines' development which should be overcome for the country to move forward.

Evolving from a port city to one of the most important global hubs, Singapore stands out with its open economic policies. This is reflected among its strongest indicators such as openness to trade (#5 in Table 3.20), and export and import (#11 and #12). High integrity and efficiency of

Table 3.18: Top 20 Percent Strongest Indicators List for Philippines, 2014

Rank	20 Percent Strongest Indicator	Score	Environment
1	Labour Activism	1.8229	QLID
2	Freedom of Speech	1.5275	QLID
3	Tax Revenue/Government Revenue	1.2996	GIS
4	Daily Organic Water Pollutant Emissions	0.9449	QLID
5	Primary Schooling	0.8748	QLID
6	Lending Rate	0.8484	GIS
7	Freedom of Religion	0.7454	QLID
8	Literacy Rate	0.6528	QLID
9	Freedom of Press	0.6527	QLID
10	Lack of Market Distortion due to State-Ownership	0.5866	GIS
11	Cost of Production Labour	0.5454	FBMC
12	Strength of Auditing and Reporting Standards	0.5223	GIS
13	Population	0.5075	QLID
14	Traffic Congestion	0.4868	QLID
15	Corporate Governance	0.4856	GIS
16	Interest Rate Spread	0.4125	GIS
17	Quality of Stock Market Regulatory Authority	0.4108	FBMC
18	Foreign Owned Companies	0.4053	MS
19	Money Supply Growth (M2)	0.3559	MS
20	High Quality Management Staff	0.3535	FBMC
21	University and Post-Graduate Education	0.3460	QLID
22	Labour Force	0.3281	FBMC
23	Tax Burden	0.3260	GIS
24	Extent of Staff Training	0.3176	FBMC

Source: Asia Competitiveness Institute.

Table 3.19: Top 20 Percent Weakest Indicators List for Philippines, 2014

Rank	20 Percent Weakest Indicator	Score	Environment
98	Foreign Direct Investment Inflows	−0.5340	MS
99	Local Road System	−0.5598	QLID
100	Bureaucracy/Red Tape	−0.5598	GIS
101	Port Facilities	−0.5647	QLID
102	Monopolies and Cartel	−0.5996	GIS
103	Levelness of Playing Field	−0.6187	MS
104	Domestic Credit to Private Sector	−0.6432	FBMC
105	Gross Fixed Capital Formation	−0.6433	MS
106	Integrity of Legal System	−0.6547	GIS
107	Money Supply (M2)	−0.6676	GIS
108	Government Responsiveness	−0.6742	GIS
109	Access to Print Media	−0.6930	QLID
110	Personal Computers	−0.6945	QLID
111	Openness to Trade	−0.7138	MS
112	Deposit Interest Rate	−0.7313	GIS
113	Institutional Sophistication	−0.7340	GIS
114	Telephone Main Lines	−0.7908	QLID
115	Airport Facilities	−0.8091	QLID
116	Political Change	−0.9237	GIS
117	Government Environmental Protection Policies	−0.9362	GIS
118	Gross Domestic Savings	−1.1587	MS
119	Urban Population Growth	−1.3815	QLID
120	Corporate Income Tax	−1.4550	MS
121	Unemployment Rate	−1.9583	FBMC

Source: Asia Competitiveness Institute.

governing institutions (#6, #7, #17, #18, #20, and #23) have contributed to a transparent and conducive business environment which in turn reinforces the competitiveness of the city state. Its top-notch ICT infrastructure (#4, #19) further strengthens its position as a host to many MNC headquarters in Southeast Asia.

Despite dominating the top spot in the rankings of Overall Competitiveness as well as the majority of sub-environments for over a decade, Singapore is not without its weaknesses (Table 3.21). Its small population (#114 and #115) and rising manpower costs (#119, #120) threaten to erode its attractiveness to MNCs as newcomers with large, young and increasingly educated workforce emerge.

Thailand manages to brave the political turmoil (#107, #117, and #118 in Table 3.22) and continues to receive high FDI inflows (#1) and international tourists (#2). Notwithstanding the

Table 3.20: Top 20 Percent Strongest Indicators List for Singapore, 2014

Rank	20 Percent Strongest Indicator	Score	Environment
1	Services, Value Added Per Worker	2.8395	FBMC
2	Budget Balance	2.7404	GIS
3	GDP Per Capita	2.6567	MS
4	Telephone Main Lines	2.6524	QLID
5	Openness to Trade	2.6279	MS
6	Quality of Central Bank/Monetary Authority	2.5650	GIS
7	Quality of Political Leadership	2.5601	GIS
8	Social Unrest	2.5261	QLID
9	Lack of Corruption	2.4635	GIS
10	Lack of Discrimination Against Investors	2.4453	MS
11	Exports of Goods and Services	2.4274	MS
12	Imports of Goods and Services	2.3574	MS
13	Institutional Sophistication	2.3069	GIS
14	Policy Towards Private Enterprise Rating	2.3034	GIS
15	International Reserves	2.2616	GIS
16	Barriers to Trade	2.2403	GIS
17	Transparency of Processes for Investors	2.2250	MS
18	Transparency of Government	2.2250	GIS
19	Networked Readiness Index	2.2212	QLID
20	Quality of Government Policies	2.2080	GIS
21	Net Foreign Assets	2.1892	GIS
22	Business Impact of Rules on FDI	2.1890	MS
23	Quality of Regulatory Environment	2.1600	GIS
24	Lack of Market Distortion due to State-Ownership	2.1304	GIS

Source: Asia Competitiveness Institute.

Table 3.21: Top 20 Percent Weakest Indicators List for Singapore, 2014

Rank	20 Percent Weakest Indicator	Score	Environment
98	Freedom of Press	0.3261	QLID
99	Tax Burden	0.1919	GIS
100	Interest Rate Spread	0.1897	GIS
101	Real GDP Growth	0.1732	MS
102	High Quality Management Staff	0.1250	FBMC
103	Unemployment Rate	0.0193	FBMC
104	Output Industry (Value Added)	−0.1637	MS
105	Government Consumption Expenditure	−0.2122	GIS
106	Foreign Direct Investment Inflows	−0.2407	MS
107	Agriculture, Value Added Per Worker	−0.3695	FBMC
108	Claims on Private Sector	−0.4377	FBMC
109	Tax Revenue/Government Revenue	−0.6210	GIS
110	Telecommunications System	−0.6353	QLID
111	Freedom of Speech	−0.6547	QLID
112	Output Agriculture (Value Added)	−0.7535	MS
113	Daily Organic Water Pollutant Emissions	−0.7600	QLID
114	Population	−0.7840	QLID
115	Labour Force	−0.8122	FBMC
116	Government Environmental Protection Policies	−0.8271	GIS
117	Deposit Interest Rate	−1.1003	GIS
118	Urban Population Growth	−1.3477	QLID
119	Cost of Management Staff	−1.8198	FBMC
120	Cost of Production Labour	−1.9665	FBMC
121	Traffic Congestion	−2.8633	QLID

Source: Asia Competitiveness Institute.

political uncertainties, attention on public services including health and education (#5, #7, and #13) are not compromised. Easily available financial access (#4 and #12) coupled with ease of starting business (#22) may catalyse the development of entrepreneurship in Thailand.

However, the political instability which is exacerbated by religious and social unrest (#111 and #112 in Table 3.23) may pose challenges to the economic recovery. Besides, it is imperative to tackle the deteriorated fiscal health (#102, #103, and #105).

Vietnam, being the leader among four transition economies (Cambodia, Laos, Myanmar and Vietnam) in ASEAN, has demonstrated its strengths in provision of public services and

Table 3.22: Top 20 Percent Strongest Indicators List for Thailand, 2014

Rank	20 Percent Strongest Indicator	Score	Environment
1	Foreign Direct Investment Inflows	2.8433	MS
2	International Tourism Receipts	2.4379	MS
3	Total Value of Stocks Traded	1.9926	FBMC
4	Domestic Credit Provided by the Financial Sector	1.7808	FBMC
5	University and Post-Graduate Education	1.6820	QLID
6	Tax Revenue	1.5515	GIS
7	Health Expenditure	1.3051	QLID
8	Gross Domestic Product	1.2439	MS
9	Government Revenue (Including Grants)	1.1988	GIS
10	Government Consumption Expenditure	1.1373	GIS
11	Net Foreign Assets	1.1372	GIS
12	Domestic Credit to Private Sector	1.1343	FBMC
13	Secondary Schooling	1.0901	QLID
14	Money Supply (M2)	1.0725	GIS
15	Unemployment Rate	1.0322	FBMC
16	Listed Domestic Companies	1.0283	FBMC
17	Regional Competitiveness	1.0054	GIS
18	Tax Revenue/Government Revenue	0.9894	GIS
19	International Reserves	0.9753	GIS
20	Money Supply Growth (M2)	0.9617	MS
21	Access to Water	0.7983	QLID
22	Ease of Starting Business	0.7937	GIS
23	Inflation	0.7907	MS
24	Access to Sanitation	0.7754	QLID

Source: Asia Competitiveness Institute.

Table 3.23: Top 20 Percent Weakest Indicators List for Thailand, 2014

Rank	20 Percent Weakest Indicator	Score	Environment
98	Levelness of Playing Field	−0.4585	MS
99	Deposit Interest Rate	−0.4833	GIS
100	Tax Burden	−0.5205	GIS
101	Exchange Rate Appreciation	−0.5345	GIS
102	External Debt	−0.5611	GIS
103	International Monetary Fund Credit	−0.6025	GIS
104	Integrity of Legal System	−0.6547	GIS
105	Government Consumption Expenditure	−0.2122	GIS
106	Freedom of Speech	−0.6547	QLID
107	Government Stability	−0.7532	GIS
108	Bureaucracy/Red Tape	−0.7538	GIS
109	Intellectual Property Rights Protection	−0.7858	GIS
110	Government Responsiveness	−0.8051	GIS
111	Religious Unrest	−0.8269	QLID
112	Social Unrest	−0.8271	QLID
113	Lack of Cronyism	−0.8285	GIS
114	Claims on Private Sector	−0.8381	FBMC
115	High Quality Management Staff	−0.8530	FBMC
116	Quality of Police	−0.8878	GIS
117	Political System Risk	−1.0131	GIS
118	Political Change	−1.1710	GIS
119	Daily Organic Water Pollutant Emissions	−1.2375	QLID
120	Real GDP Growth	−1.2613	MS
121	Primary Schooling	−1.4562	QLID

Source: Asia Competitiveness Institute.

infrastructure such as health care (#1 in Table 3.24), education (#6), access to water (#14), and ICT (#24). Moreover, the availability of large pool of low-cost workforce (#10, #15, and #16) is another key factor in attracting investors.

Despite market reforms through the *Doi Moi* (renovation) policy since 1986, the inertia resulted from a centrally planned economy, especially the dominance of an inefficient state sector continues to prevail (#101 and #113 in Table 3.25). Furthermore, although the focus on infrastructure investment has brought about upgraded development, infrastructure quality in Vietnam still lags behind that in its ASEAN peer (#108). Another point to note is that economic development in Vietnam seems to rule at the expense of the environment (#111) and have led to environmental issues in Vietnam (#98 and #103).

Table 3.24: Top 20 Percent Strongest Indicators List for Vietnam, 2014

Rank	20 Percent Strongest Indicator	Score	Environment
1	Health Expenditure	1.6156	QLID
2	Primary Schooling	1.5993	QLID
3	Money Supply (M2)	1.1607	GIS
4	Cellular Mobile Telephone Subscribers	0.9361	QLID
5	Real GDP Growth	0.8601	MS
6	Tax Revenue/Government Revenue	0.8177	GIS
7	Deposit Interest Rate	0.8090	GIS
8	Exchange Rate Appreciation	0.7879	GIS
9	Domestic Credit to Private Sector	0.7857	FBMC
10	Cost of Management Staff	0.7806	FBMC
11	Interest Rate Spread	0.7531	GIS
12	Domestic Credit Provided by the Financial Sector	0.7004	FBMC
13	Regional Competitiveness	0.6824	GIS
14	Access to Water	0.6506	QLID
15	Cost of Production Labour	0.6240	FBMC
16	Labour Force	0.6195	FBMC
17	Traffic Congestion	0.5773	QLID
18	Urban Population Growth	0.5764	QLID
19	Openness to Trade	0.5282	MS
20	Social Unrest	0.5142	QLID
21	International Monetary Fund Credit	0.4142	GIS
22	Population	0.3916	QLID
23	Internet Subscribers	0.3856	QLID
24	Information and Communication Technology (ICT) Expenditure	0.3795	QLID

Source: Asia Competitiveness Institute.

Table 3.25: Top 20 Percent Weakest Indicators List for Vietnam, 2014

Rank	20 Percent Weakest Indicator	Score	Environment
98	Daily Organic Water Pollutant Emissions	−0.7709	QLID
99	Quality of Stock Market Regulatory Authority	−0.7866	FBMC
100	Intellectual Property Rights Protection	−0.7922	GIS
101	Levelness of Playing Field	−0.7961	MS
102	Government Responsiveness	−0.8051	GIS
103	Air Quality	−0.8216	QLID
104	Urban Population	−0.8307	QLID
105	Labour Activism	−0.8466	QLID
106	High Quality Management Staff	−0.8530	FBMC
107	Government Consumption Expenditure	−0.8893	GIS
108	Local Road System	−0.8978	QLID
109	Labour Market Rating	−0.9218	FBMC
110	Budget Balance	−0.9233	GIS
111	Government Environmental Protection Policies	−0.9248	GIS
112	Sovereign Debt Risk	−0.9390	FBMC
113	Lack of Market Distortion due to State-Ownership	−0.9571	GIS
114	Labour Unrest	−0.9984	QLID
115	Strength of Auditing and Reporting Standards	−1.0177	GIS
116	Bureaucracy/Red Tape	−1.0452	GIS
117	Corporate Income Tax	−1.2661	MS
118	Secondary Schooling	−1.2691	QLID
119	Tax Burden	−1.5056	GIS
120	Freedom of Press	−1.5414	QLID
121	Corporate Governance	−1.5996	GIS

Source: Asia Competitiveness Institute.

3.3.7.2 *Median Competitiveness Web Analysis*

As another instructive roadmap for policy-makers, the spider web charts are employed to show how competitive individual ASEAN economies are in each of the 12 sub-environments relative to ASEAN-10 median and ASEAN-10 maximum.

As shown in Figure 3.32, Brunei's Institutions, Governance and Leadership, Standard of Living, Education and Social Stability, and in particular, Productivity Performance exceed the ASEAN-10 median by a large margin, indicating the paramount role of productivity level in spurring competitiveness level of Brunei. Nonetheless, Brunei lags behind the regional median

Figure 3.32: Median Competitiveness Web Analysis for Brunei, 2014

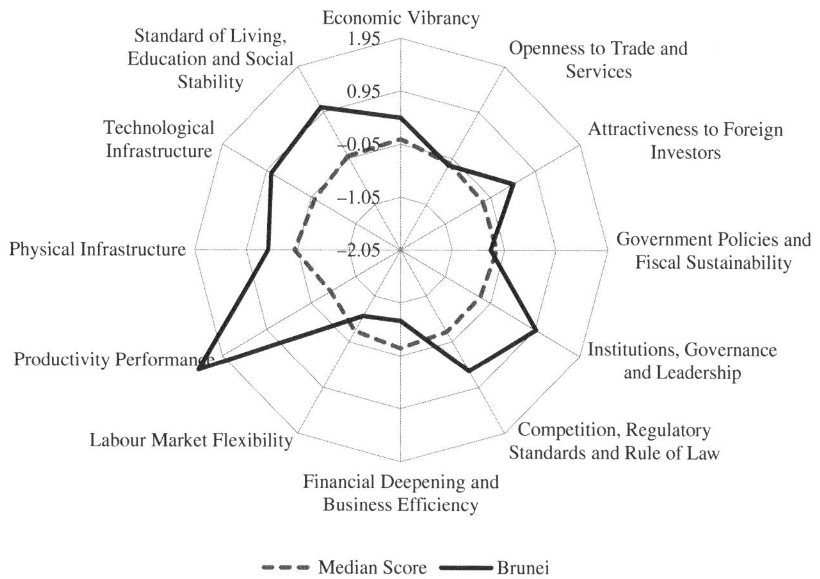

Source: Asia Competitiveness Institute.

in other areas such as Labour Market Flexibility, and Financial Deepening and Business Efficiency, hence implying more improvement in these two aspects. In addition, the prominent oil supplier's proximate position to the median level for Openness to Trade and Services, and Government Polices and Fiscal Sustainability calls for more attention in order to prevent Brunei from falling below the median.

Cambodia's performance in all 12 sub-environments are below the regional median (Figure 3.33). Physical Infrastructure and Economic Vibrancy particularly are of great concern since they are farthest away from the median scores. Fortunately, the lack in Physical Infrastructure seems to be complemented by moderate Technological Infrastructure which is close to the median level. The relatively poor institutional capacity as illustrated in the web analysis below, however, does not seem to deter foreign investors from investing in Cambodia given the proximity of Attractiveness to Foreign Investors to the median score.

Being the country with the largest population in ASEAN, Indonesia has performed remarkably well for Economic Vibrancy and Labour Market Flexibility as reflected in the well-above median scores in Figure 3.34. For most of the remaining sub-environments, Indonesia performs at a satisfactory level as the scores lie close to the ASEAN-10 median. In order to make a significant leap in the region, more efforts are needed, especially in terms of Technological Infrastructure, and Government Policies and Fiscal Sustainability, which are below the regional median.

Laos, albeit remaining far below other ASEAN members in majority of the sub-environments, has shown some heartening performance in terms of Attractiveness to Foreign Investors,

Figure 3.33: Median Competitiveness Web Analysis for Cambodia, 2014

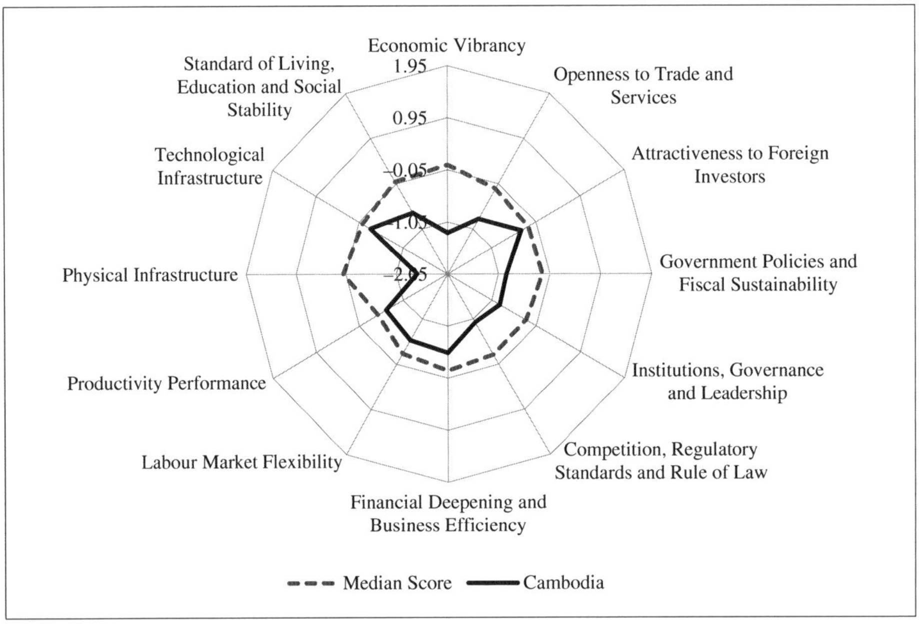

Source: Asia Competitiveness Institute.

Figure 3.34: Median Competitiveness Web Analysis for Indonesia, 2014

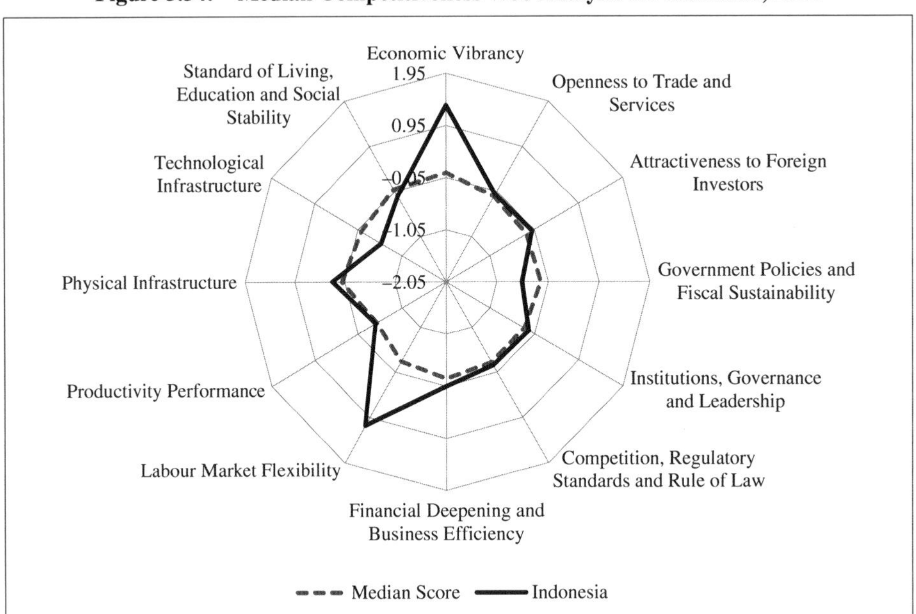

Source: Asia Competitiveness Institute.

Figure 3.35: Median Competitiveness Web Analysis for Laos, 2014

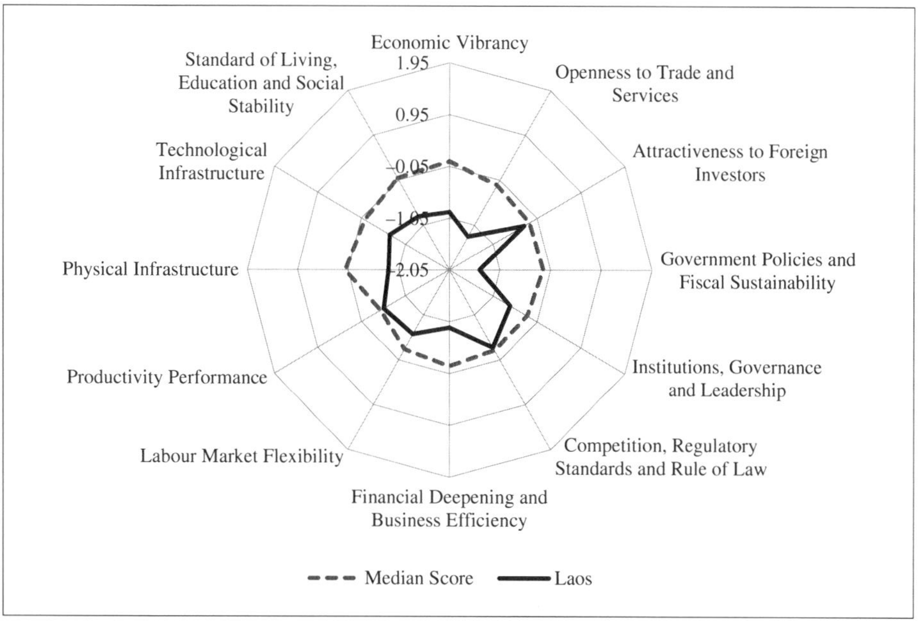

Source: Asia Competitiveness Institute.

Competition, Regulatory Standards and Rule of Law, and Productivity Performance, of which the scores for these three aspects lie closely to the regional median scores. Meanwhile, the sub-environments of Openness to Trade and Services, and Government Policies and Fiscal Sustainability which have the lowest scores among all sub-environments highlight the need to intensify trade liberalisation and improve fiscal capacity so as to bring Laos on par with the regional median (Figure 3.35).

Standing as the second most competitive country in ASEAN, Malaysia has exceeded ASEAN-10 median for all sub-environments as depicted in Figure 3.36. Labour Market Flexibility stands out among all as it exceeds the median score by the largest margin. This is aligned with its top ranking in that particular sub-environment. While the existing strengths in Competition, Regulatory Standards and Rule of Law, and Financial Deepening and Business Efficiency have placed Malaysia far ahead of the regional medians, areas such as Productivity Performance, and Standard of Living, Education and Social Stability should not be overlooked to further boost Malaysia's competitiveness level.

As expected, Myanmar, the lowest ranked country in overall competitiveness, scores below median level for all sub-environments as illustrated in Figure 3.37. Among all, Productivity Performance shows some extent of potential in catching up with the regional median, while Standard of Living, Education and Social Stability lies below the median score by the largest margin. Concerted efforts in improving multiple aspects is essential to increase the competitiveness of Myanmar and hence narrow the score gap between each sub-environment and the regional median.

Figure 3.36: Median Competitiveness Web Analysis for Malaysia, 2014

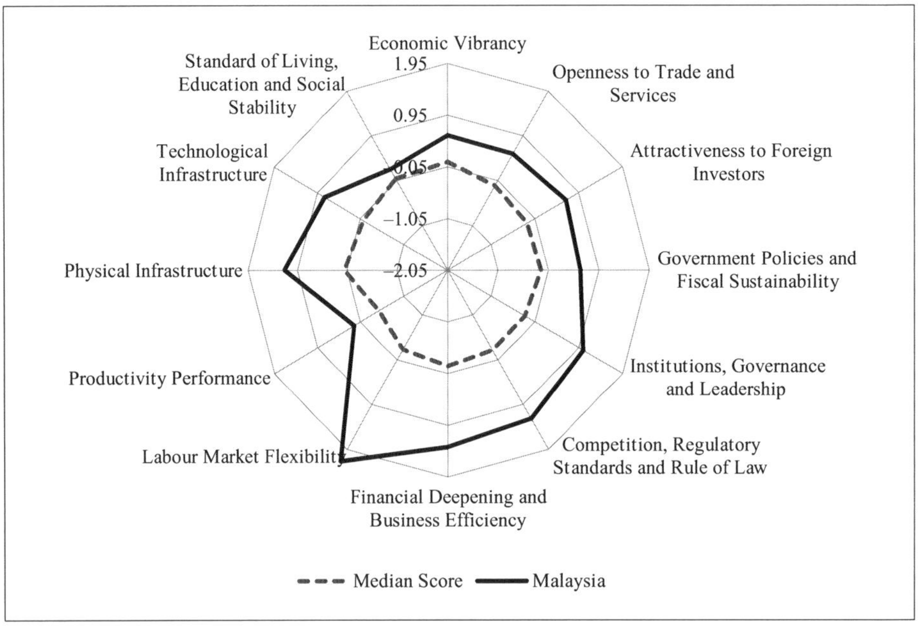

Source: Asia Competitiveness Institute.

Figure 3.37: Median Competitiveness Web Analysis for Myanmar, 2014

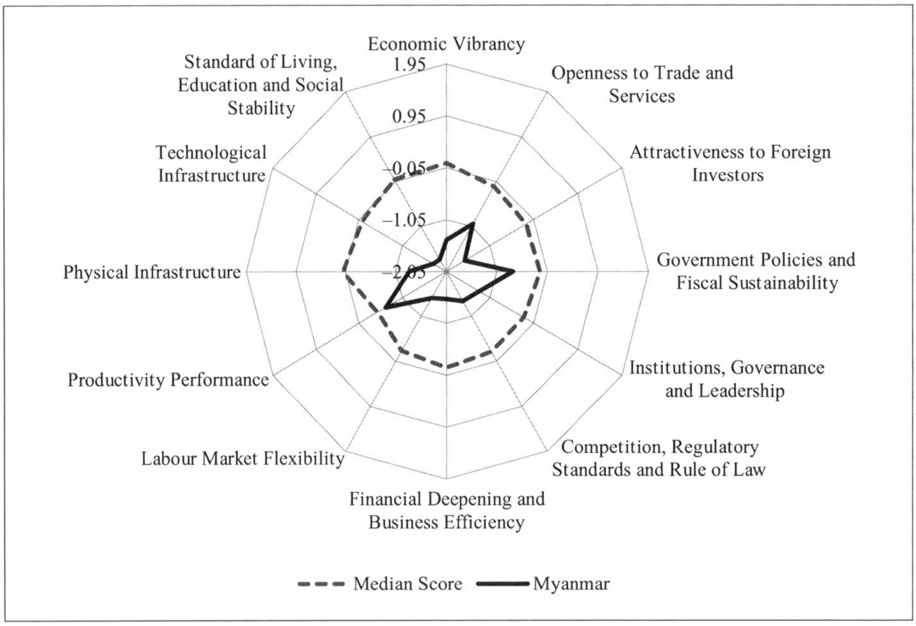

Source: Asia Competitiveness Institute.

Figure 3.38: Median Competitiveness Web Analysis for Philippines, 2014

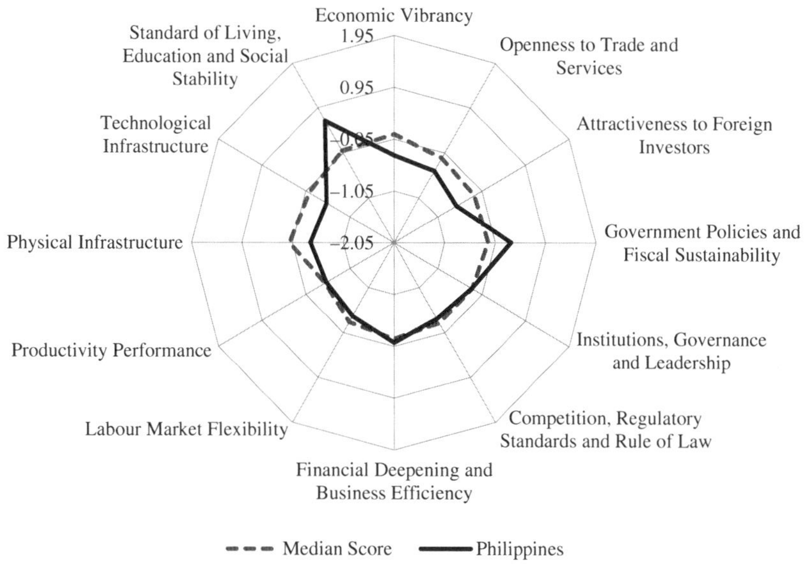

Source: Asia Competitiveness Institute.

Figure 3.38 shows that the Philippines performed strongly in terms of Government Policies and Fiscal Sustainability, and Standard of Living, Education and Social Stability at which the scores exceed the regional median by the largest margin. Despite this, it lags behind its regional peers in most sub-environments, particularly Openness to Trade and Services, and Physical Infrastructure which have the lowest scores. The Philippines should leverage on its strengths in fiscal capacity as well as social development in making significant strides in other dimensions, including infrastructural development, Economic Vibrancy, and Attractiveness to Foreign Investors.

In line with its outstanding ranking in Overall Competitiveness throughout the study period of 2000–2014, Figure 3.39 depicts significant gaps between Singapore's scores and ASEAN-10 medians in all sub-environments except for Labour Market Flexibility. While maintaining the current outstanding performance in each sub-environment, the weakest performance attained in the labour market should serve as a nudge to the policy-makers and calls for more heed in that particular area so as to retain its role as a regional champion particularly against the backdrop of rising global uncertainties.

Standing at the third after Singapore and Malaysia, Thailand lies well above ASEAN-10 median in all sub-environments except two sub-environments, namely Institutions, Governance and Leadership, and Competition, Regulatory Standards and Rule of Law (Figure 3.40) which coincides with the median scores. This indicates some room for improvement in these areas and should be prioritised by the policy-makers in order to lift the overall competitiveness level of Thailand. In addition, Productivity Performance which has the lowest score among other sub-environments deserves more attention as well.

Figure 3.39: Median Competitiveness Web Analysis for Singapore, 2014

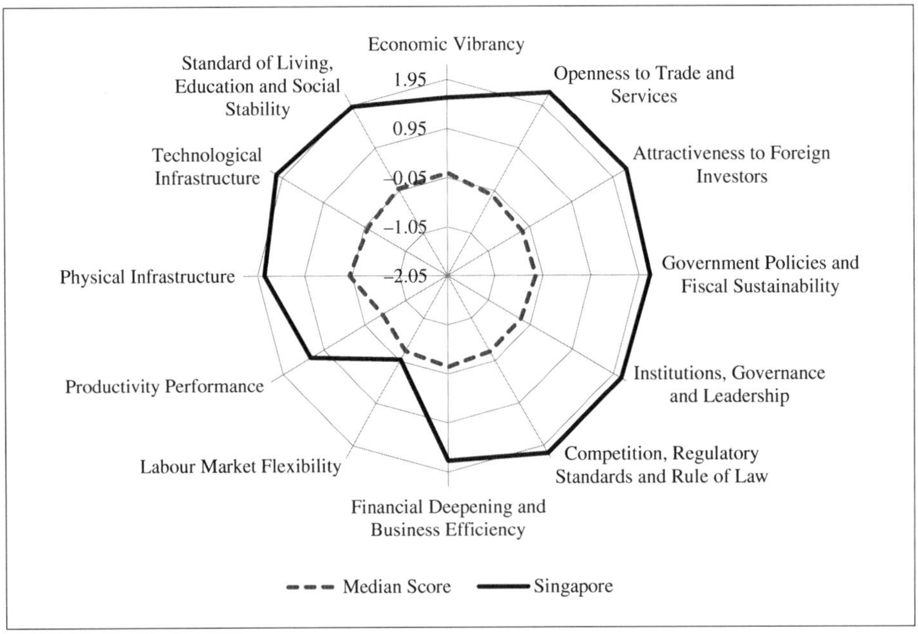

Source: Asia Competitiveness Institute.

Figure 3.40: Median Competitiveness Web Analysis for Thailand, 2014

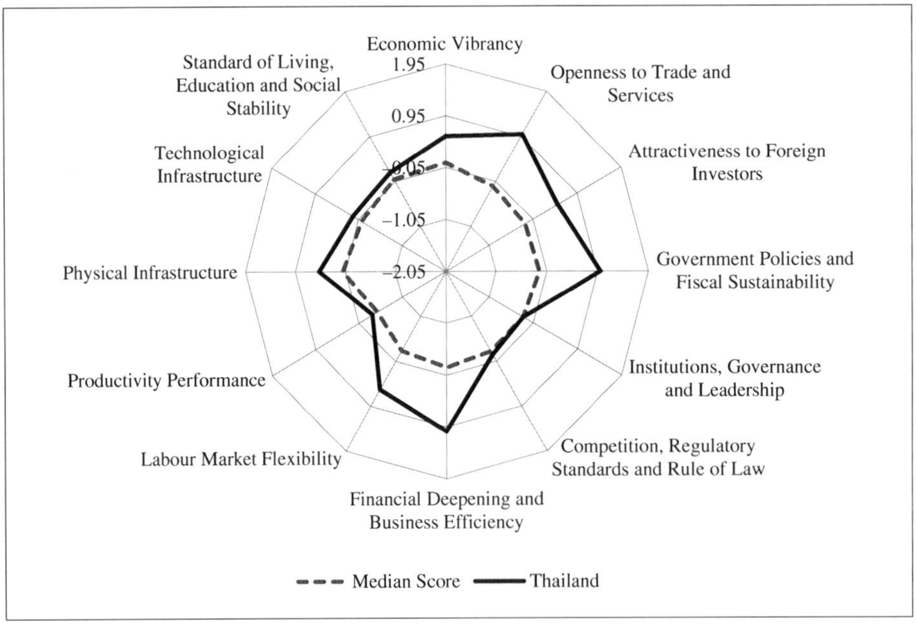

Source: Asia Competitiveness Institute.

Figure 3.41: Median Competitiveness Web Analysis for Vietnam, 2014

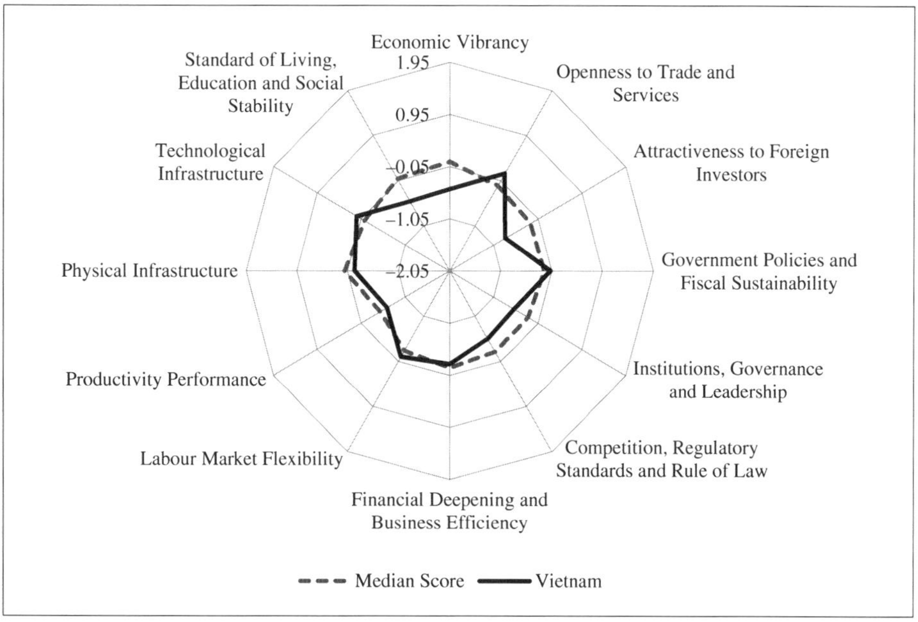

Source: Asia Competitiveness Institute.

The performance of Vietnam relative to ASEAN-10 median is rather mixed (Figure 3.41). On the one hand, the scores of the transitional economy exceeds the regional median, albeit by a small margin in terms of Openness to Trade and Services, Government Policies and Fiscal Sustainability, Labour Market Flexibility, and Technological Infrastructure. On the other hand, Vietnam lies below the median level for the remaining sub-environments except Financial Deepening and Business Efficiency which coincides with the median score. More improvement in these areas is paramount to fuel further reform in Vietnam.

3.3.7.3 *Maximum Competitiveness Web Analysis*

Maximum competitiveness web analysis presented in this sector reveals how far individual ASEAN economies are from the highest scores for each of the 12 sub-environments in the region.

As shown in Figure 3.42, Brunei has set a high standard in the region in terms of Productivity Performance. Nonetheless, more need to be done for the oil-dependent nation in multiple aspects of competitiveness, particularly Openness to Trade and Services, Government Policies and Fiscal Sustainability, and Labour Market Flexibility, which fall far below the regional maximum.

Figure 3.43 illustrates the significant gaps between Cambodia and ASEAN maximum in all sub-environments. In view of resource and capacity constraints, the policy-makers may prioritise improvement in terms of Economic Vibrancy and Physical Infrastructure which scored the lowest among all. This, in turn, may generate spillover effects in stimulating foreign investments and upgrading standard of living in Cambodia.

Figure 3.42: Maximum Competitiveness Web Analysis for Brunei, 2014

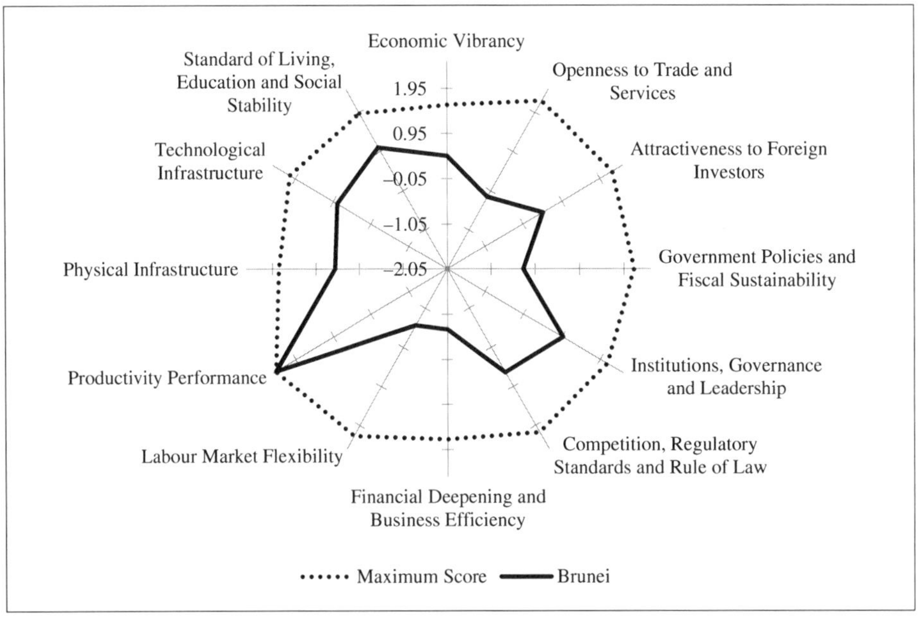

Source: Asia Competitiveness Institute.

Figure 3.43: Maximum Competitiveness Web Analysis for Cambodia, 2014

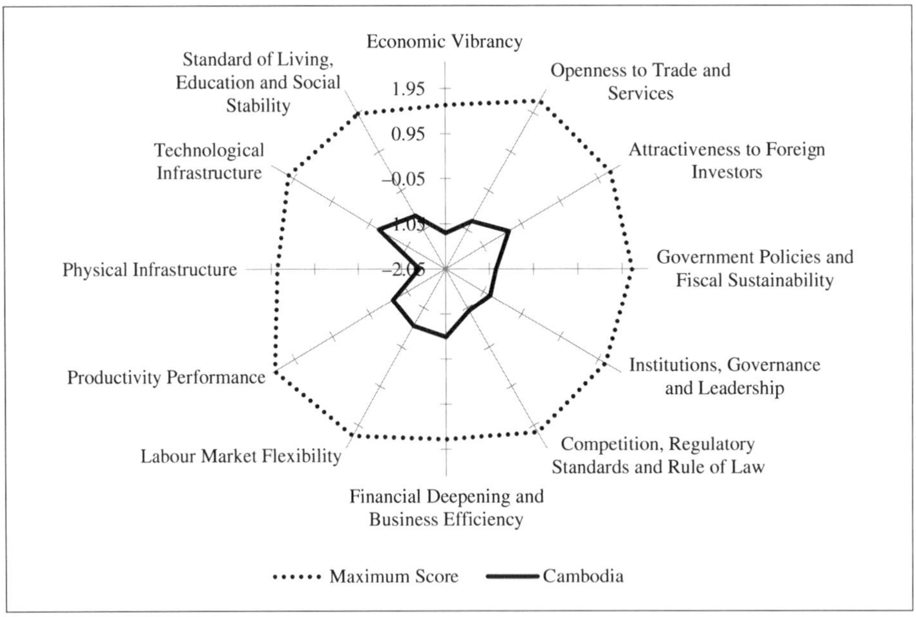

Source: Asia Competitiveness Institute.

Figure 3.44: Maximum Competitiveness Web Analysis for Indonesia, 2014

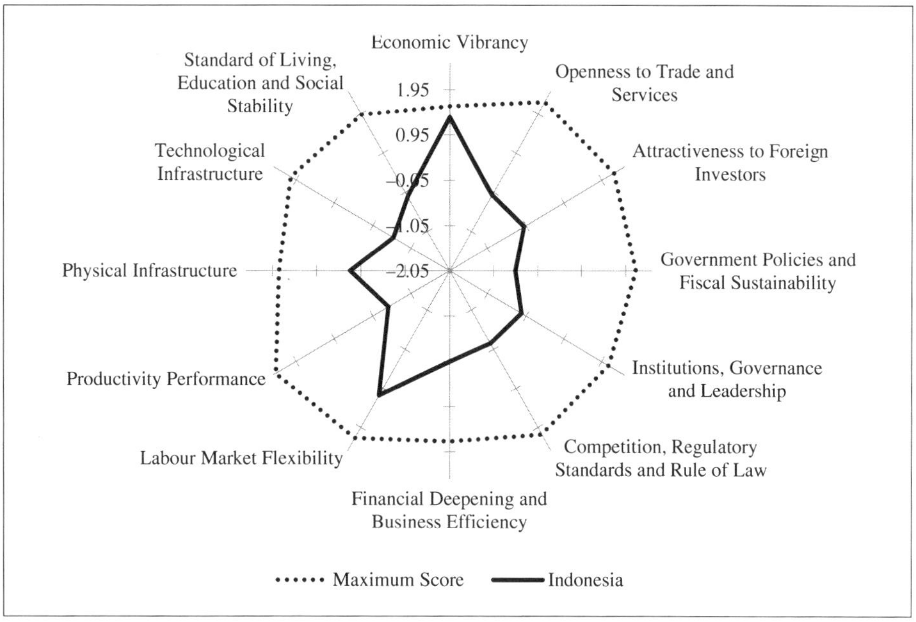

Source: Asia Competitiveness Institute.

Indonesia has demonstrated its potential to catch up with the regional top performer in the sub-environment of Economic Vibrancy (Figure 3.44). Besides that, Labour Market Flexibility and Physical Infrastructure also register positive outlook with smaller gap from the ASEAN maximum. However, more needs to be done in catching up with the regional champions in the rest of the sub-environments.

As shown in Figure 3.45, Laos unsurprisingly remains below the ASEAN maximum in all sub-environments given its weak ranking in the overall competitiveness throughout the study period. However, smaller gaps between the regional maximum and Attractiveness to Foreign Investors, and Competition, Regulatory Standards and Rule of Law provide grounds for hope for Laos to catch up with its peers in the region.

Malaysia (Figure 3.46), the second most competitive economy in ASEAN has set the regional maximum for Labour Market Flexibility. Nevertheless, it remains below regional maximum for the majority of the remaining sub-environments. The largest gap between the score and median can be found in the sub-environment of Productivity Performance. Hence, improving productivity on the back of sound macroeconomic stability can be a good starting point for the country to catch up with Singapore.

Myanmar (Figure 3.47) lags far behind the ASEAN maximum for all sub-environments. Opening up the economy as well as promoting good governance should come in tandem in order to improve the country's Attractive to Foreign Investors and Competition, Regulatory Standards and Rule of Law. Financial Deepening and Business Efficiency, Labour Market Flexibility, and Technological Infrastructure are also important elements in fostering a favourable business environment.

Figure 3.45: Maximum Competitiveness Web Analysis for Laos, 2014

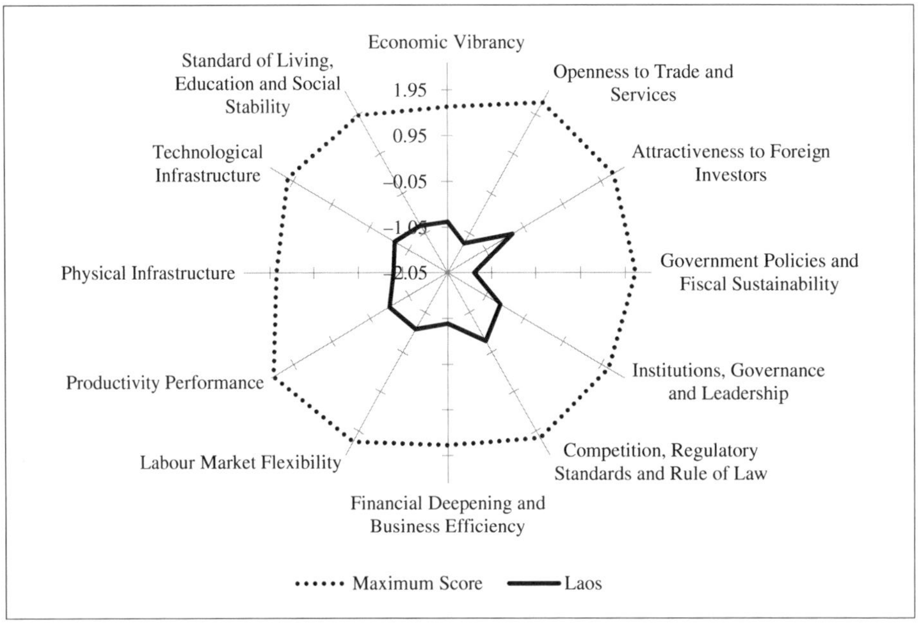

Source: Asia Competitiveness Institute.

Figure 3.46: Maximum Competitiveness Web Analysis for Malaysia, 2014

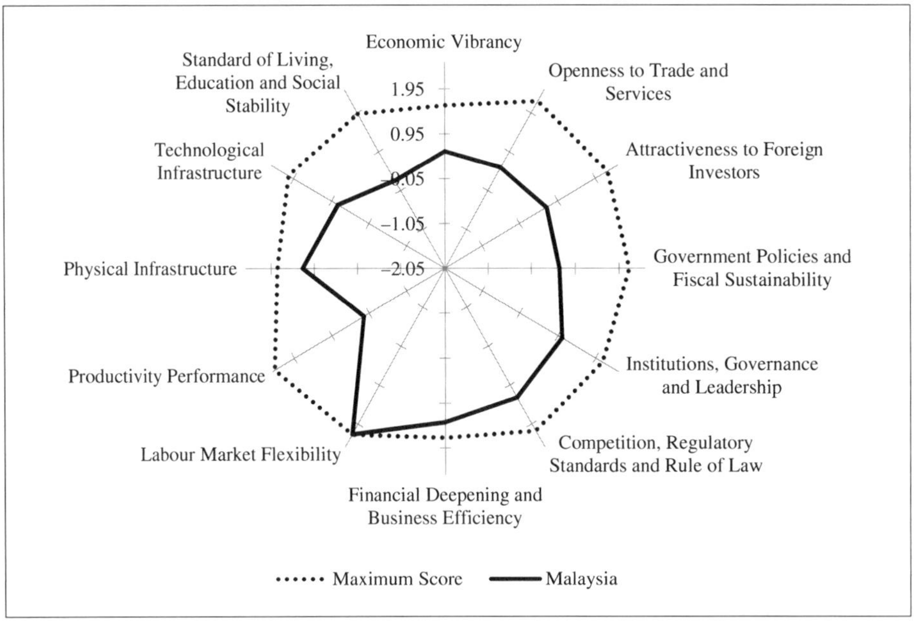

Source: Asia Competitiveness Institute.

Figure 3.47: Maximum Competitiveness Web Analysis for Myanmar, 2014

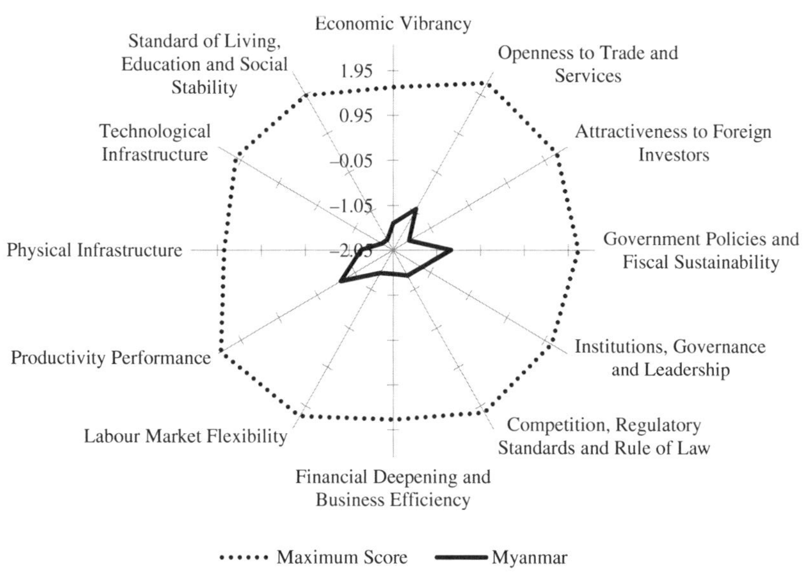

Source: Asia Competitiveness Institute.

Philippines (Figure 3.48) falls far behind the regional maximum for all sub-environments. Sub-environments of Openness to Trade and Services, Attractiveness to Foreign Investors, and Productivity Performance, in particular, have the largest gaps with the maximum scores. Reforms in these sub-environments are essential against the backdrop of increasingly integrated market. Infrastructural development should also be included in the policy agenda to support the reforms.

Being the top performer in the region, Singapore has set high benchmarks in the majority of sub-environments as illustrated in Figure 3.49. Nonetheless, it has lost domination in Labour Market Flexibility and Productivity Performance. With growing competition, especially from Malaysia and Brunei in these two sub-environments, Singapore needs to expedite its reform in the labour market as well as transformation to knowledge economy in order to retain its top position in the region.

In spite of lying below the ASEAN-10 maximum for all sub-environments (Figure 3.50), the performance of Thailand shows some encouraging signs in terms of Government Policies and Fiscal Sustainability as well as Financial Deepening and Business Efficiency. Nevertheless, evident gaps with the regional maximum in Institutions, Governance and Leadership, and Competition, Regulatory Standards and Rule of Law call for more heed in order to restore the confidence level in Thailand's institutional capacity.

Figure 3.51 shows that Vietnam lies below the regional maximum in all 12 sub-environments with the smallest gaps in terms of Openness to Trade and Services, Government Policies and Fiscal Sustainability, and Technological Infrastructure. As the rapid emergence of other transition economies including Cambodia, Laos and Myanmar pose new challenges and competition

Figure 3.48: Maximum Competitiveness Web Analysis for Philippines, 2014

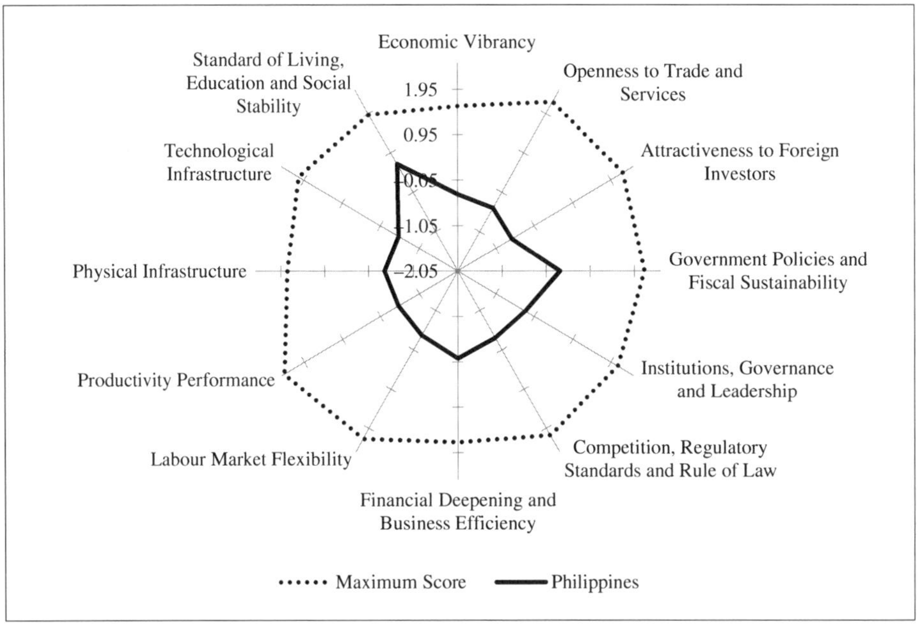

Source: Asia Competitiveness Institute.

Figure 3.49: Maximum Competitiveness Web Analysis for Singapore, 2014

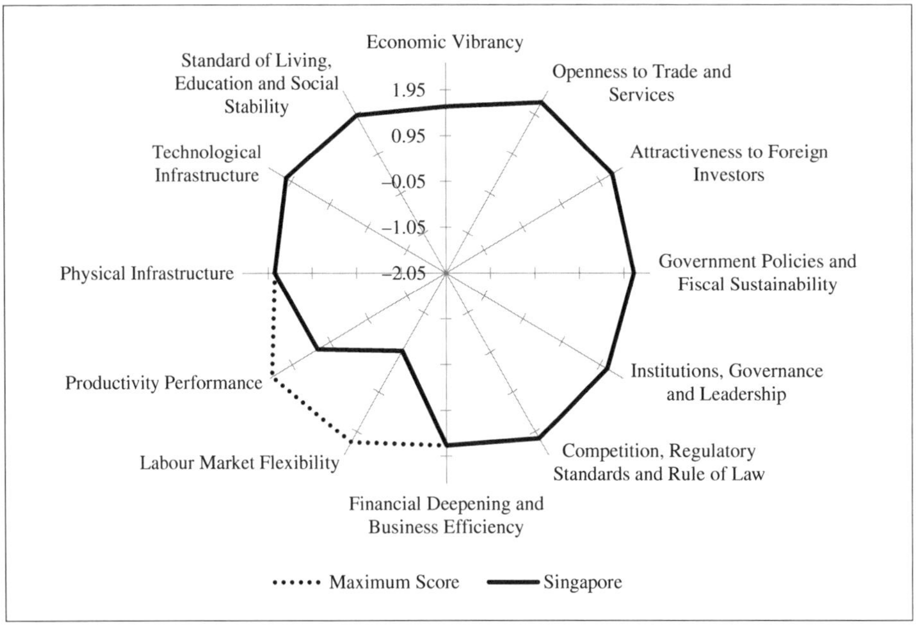

Source: Asia Competitiveness Institute.

Figure 3.50: Maximum Competitiveness Web Analysis for Thailand, 2014

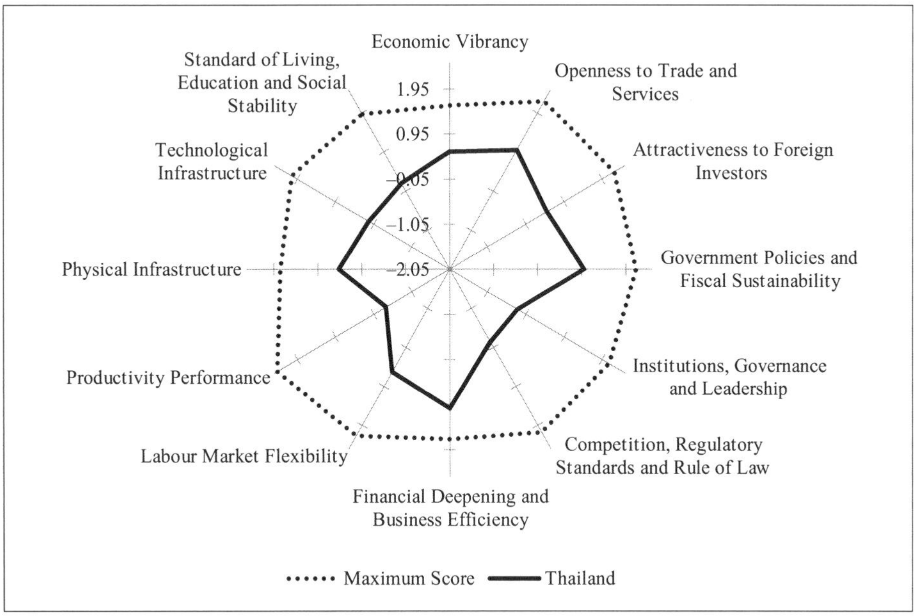

Source: Asia Competitiveness Institute.

Figure 3.51: Maximum Competitiveness Web Analysis for Vietnam, 2014

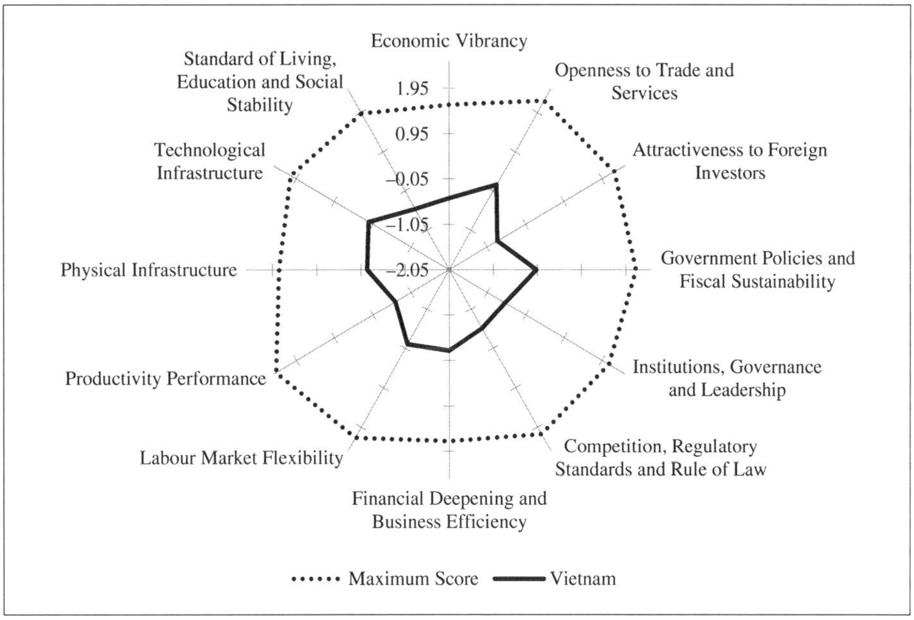

Source: Asia Competitiveness Institute.

to the country, it is important to expedite its catching-up process, particularly for Attractiveness to Foreign Investors and Productivity Performance.

3.3.8 Upgrading Competitiveness through *What-if* Simulation Analysis

This section lays out the *What-if* simulation analysis as detailed in the methodology discussion in Section 3.2.5. The simulation analysis is conducted for Overall Competitiveness as well as each environment. The comparison of standardised scores and rankings of individual ASEAN-10 economies before and after simulation is shown in Tables 3.26–3.30.

Table 3.26 illustrates the simulation analysis for Overall Competitiveness in ASEAN. Most of the ASEAN member states have shown improvement in the rankings after simulation, while the rankings of Singapore (first), Malaysia (second), Philippines (sixth) and Cambodia (eighth) remain constant but with improved scores. For instance, while Cambodia's ranking place stays constant at the eighth place, its score leaps to –0.5236 as compared to the score of –0.9071 prior to the simulation. Myanmar demonstrates the largest improvement with a leap from the last to the eighth position, while the rest of the economies rise for one rank after having the top 20 percent weakest indicators raised to the regional average level.

In Table 3.27, the effect of simulation for Macroeconomic Stability is evenly distributed. Brunei, Indonesia and Myanmar see the most significant improvement of two spots in the ranking, while the rankings of Cambodia, Singapore, Thailand and Vietnam remain constant albeit improvement in their scores after the simulation. The rest of ASEAN member states' rankings move up one place after the policy simulation.

For Government and Institutional Setting (Table 3.28), Indonesia and the transitioning economies, namely Laos, Myanmar and Vietnam climb two places after the simulation. Singapore,

Table 3.26: *What-if* Competitiveness Simulation Analysis on Overall Competitiveness, 2014

	Rank		Score	
Economy	Before	After	Before	After
Brunei	3	2	0.5322	0.9710
Cambodia	8	8	–0.9071	–0.5236
Indonesia	5	4	0.0412	0.4102
Laos	9	8	–0.9241	–0.5018
Malaysia	2	2	1.0568	1.1760
Myanmar	10	8	–1.5501	–1.0245
Philippines	6	6	–0.3133	–0.0266
Singapore	1	1	2.0152	2.1945
Thailand	4	3	0.4477	0.6443
Vietnam	7	6	–0.3987	–0.1059

Source: Asia Competitiveness Institute.

Table 3.27: *What-if* Competitiveness Simulation Analysis on Macroeconomic Stability, 2014

	Rank		Score	
Economy	**Before**	**After**	**Before**	**After**
Brunei	5	3	0.2478	0.6252
Cambodia	8	8	−0.8807	−0.6453
Indonesia	4	2	0.3968	0.6796
Laos	9	8	−0.9205	−0.6514
Malaysia	3	2	0.6255	0.7247
Myanmar	10	8	−1.4433	−0.9751
Philippines	7	6	−0.5150	−0.1821
Singapore	1	1	2.1709	2.2067
Thailand	2	2	0.7317	0.8345
Vietnam	6	6	−0.4130	−0.2847

Source: Asia Competitiveness Institute.

Table 3.28: *What-if* Competitiveness Simulation Analysis on Government and Institutional Setting, 2014

	Rank		Score	
Economy	**Before**	**After**	**Before**	**After**
Brunei	3	3	0.4421	0.8539
Cambodia	9	8	−0.9715	−0.5740
Indonesia	6	4	−0.3317	0.2226
Laos	8	6	−0.8673	−0.3756
Malaysia	2	2	1.0322	1.1911
Myanmar	10	8	−1.2116	−0.7957
Philippines	5	5	−0.1345	0.0683
Singapore	1	1	2.2851	2.3308
Thailand	4	3	0.1916	0.5067
Vietnam	7	5	−0.4344	−0.0806

Source: Asia Competitiveness Institute.

Malaysia and Brunei retain their top three rankings with better scores, while the Philippines remains at the fifth. Cambodia and Thailand progress a rank higher to the eighth and third respectively, after the simulation.

As seen in Table 3.29, half of the ASEAN member states, namely Cambodia (eighth), Malaysia (first), Myanmar (10th), Philippines (sixth) and Thailand (third) attain higher scores but

Table 3.29: *What-if* Competitiveness Simulation Analysis on Financial, Businesses and Manpower Conditions, 2014

	Rank		Score	
Economy	**Before**	**After**	**Before**	**After**
Brunei	4	2	0.5261	1.3603
Cambodia	8	8	–0.8090	–0.5811
Indonesia	5	3	0.2875	0.6113
Laos	9	8	–0.9586	–0.7245
Malaysia	1	1	1.6723	1.7282
Myanmar	10	10	–1.6569	–1.1507
Philippines	6	6	–0.4753	–0.1623
Singapore	2	1	1.3232	1.8721
Thailand	3	3	0.5671	0.7234
Vietnam	7	6	–0.4763	–0.1189

Source: Asia Competitiveness Institute.

Table 3.30: *What-if* Competitiveness Simulation Analysis on Quality of Life and Infrastructure Development, 2014

	Rank		Score	
Economy	**Before**	**After**	**Before**	**After**
Brunei	2	2	0.8499	0.9193
Cambodia	9	6	–0.8597	–0.2263
Indonesia	6	5	–0.1925	0.0823
Laos	8	6	–0.8404	–0.1887
Malaysia	3	2	0.7720	0.9274
Myanmar	10	8	–1.7047	–1.0447
Philippines	5	5	–0.0913	0.1730
Singapore	1	1	2.0429	2.1963
Thailand	4	4	0.2476	0.4425
Vietnam	7	5	–0.2237	0.0732

Source: Asia Competitiveness Institute.

remain at the same rankings post simulation for Financial, Businesses and Manpower Conditions. Only Brunei and Indonesia show remarkable jump of two spots in ranking, while the rest move up one rank after the simulation.

Table 3.30 shows how each economy fares after the simulation for Quality of Life and Infrastructure Development. The youngest ASEAN member states witness the most notable leap after the simulation at which Cambodia climb up three spots while Laos, Myanmar and Vietnam jump two places in the ranking. On the other hand, more mature economies including Brunei, Philippines, Singapore, and Thailand see no improvement in rankings albeit higher scores after the simulation.

3.4 Shapley Weightage Methodology as Robustness Check

3.4.1 Shapley Value

The Shapley value is the most commonly used solution concept in cooperative game theory. Formally, a coalition game (N, v) in cooperative game theory is defined by a set of players N and a characteristic function $v(S)$: $2^N \rightarrow R$, where it maps coalition S (or subset of players) to a real number. The function describes the expected payoffs the S players can obtain by cooperation. The Shapley value of the coalition game is an n-vector, denoted by $\Phi(v)$, satisfying a set of axioms, i.e. Individual Rationality, Efficiency, Symmetry, Additivity and Null Player.

The i-th component of $\Phi(v)$ can be determined by

$$\Phi(v) = \sum_{S \subseteq N \setminus \{i\}} \frac{|S|!(N - |S| - 1)!}{N!}(v(S \cup i) - v(S)).$$

In our context, the players will be the indicators used for the construction of the index. The coalition will be the sub-environments and environments which the indicators belong to. The desirable properties, i.e. the axioms, are meaningful for general index ranking. Individual Rationality ensures that each indicator has a positive contribution to the index score. An indicator must satisfy the Null Player axiom, so that it is economically meaningful for that indicator to be considered relevant to the index. Symmetry guarantees that if two indicators carry the same value, they are equally important in the index scoring. Efficiency and Additivity are also important mathematical properties for the construction of index.

The application of Shapley value has been well studied in various strands of literature. The concept has been used to solve the taxation and redistribution problem, as described by Aumann and Kurz (1977). It is also used in voting for public goods problems. Aumann and Myerson (1988), for instance, have studied the link or coalition formation among players using the Shapley value. Moulin (1992) studies the application of the Shapley value in fair division of unproduced goods under monetary transfer and quasi-linear utilities. Petrosjan and Zaccour (2003) study the Shapley value cost allocation in a pollution reduction setting. More recently, Hougaard *et al.* (2017) have applied the Shapley value concept to licensing under FRAND terms.[9] However, the Shapley value has not to our knowledge been applied to index ranking analysis before.

As a robustness check to the Equal Weightage approach, we would like to propose an objective weighting method based on Shapley value — the "Bottom-Up" approach.

[9] FRAND is a short notation for Fair Reasonable and Non-Discriminatory.

3.4.2 Shapley Weightage — The "Bottom-up" Approach

We first compute the Shapley value of each indicator based on the standardised value of the indicator for every city. By our definition, it measures the aggregate dispersion of the indicator, thus reflecting the inequality among the cities. More weights are assigned to those indicators with a higher Shapley value. The weights of sub-environments are computed based on both the absolute performance (standardised score) and the relative performance (weights) of indicators under that particular sub-environment. The weights of environments are computed in a similar way by considering the relevant absolute performance and the relative performance of sub-environments. The detailed description of the methodology can be found in Appendix 3.

3.4.3 Comparison between the Shapley Method and the Entropy Method

Yet another objective weight assignment method, commonly applied in the area of decision science, is entropy (Zeleny, 1982). The entropy for the indicator i is defined as

$$Entropy_i = -\frac{1}{\ln(E)}\sum_{e=1}^{E} p_{ei}\ln(p_{ei}),$$

where E is the number of economies, $p_{ei} = \frac{v_{ei}}{\sum_{e=1}^{E} v_{ei}}$ and v_{ei} is the characteristic of the raw data x_{ei}. The weightage of indicator i is, then, defined by

$$w_i = 1 - Entropy_i.$$

The interpretation of the entropy of an indicator concerns the information that the particular indicator transmits. The higher the entropy, the less the information carried, implying a lower weight assigned to that indicator.

While this method appears to be an improvement over a subjective weighting scheme, one of the important reasons why we cannot apply the entropy method for our analysis is its inability to handle negative values due to the use of logarithm operator. Thus, the alternative standardisation method, other than *z-score*, is required.

In the report *Assessing Provincial Development under the Five Development Concepts*, Institute of Applied Economics Shanghai Academy of Social Sciences has applied the entropy method to assign weights to indicators. To avoid negative values, they deploy the *max-min standardisation* method, where

$$v_{ei} = \frac{x_{ei} - \min(x_i)}{\max(x_i) - \min(x_i)}.$$

There is an important drawback to the max–min standardisation. If an economy performs the worst under an indicator, i.e. $x_{ei} = \min(x_i)$, then $v_{ei} = 0$, which cannot be computed by

Table 3.31: Hypothetical Example for Comparing the Shapley Weightage Methodology and the Entropy Method

Economy	Indicator 1	Indicator 2	Indicator 3
A	10	2	1
B	1	3	2
C	1	2	3
D	1	2	4
E	1	2	5
F	1	2	6
G	1	2	7
H	1	1	8
I	1	2	9
J	1	2	10
K	1	2	11

Source: Asia Competitiveness Institute.

natural log either. Additional assumptions must be made in the computation, i.e. ln(0) must be assigned to 0.

Another reason that the entropy method is less appropriate than the Shapley method is that, when applied to the field of index construction, the former method is very sensitive to indicators containing outliers.

Consider the following example. There are 11 economies and three indicators with different measurement units (see Table 3.31). Indicator 1 contains an outlier. All the economies perform equally in Indicator 2. There is a clear divergence of performance among all the economies in Indicator 3. We will use *z-score* standardisation for the Shapley method, and *max-min* standardisation for the entropy method.

Under the entropy method, the weights of indicators are

$$w_1^{Entropy} = 0.866, \quad w_2^{Entropy} = 0.045, \quad w_3^{Entropy} = 0.089.$$

Due to the presence of an outlier under Indicator 1, i.e. Economy A, the entropy method predicts that Indicator 1 carries the most information, thus assigning it a much higher weight relative to the rest.

Under the Shapley method, the weights of indicators are

$$w_1^{Shapley} = 0.308, \quad w_2^{Shapley} = 0.229, \quad w_3^{Shapley} = 0.463.$$

As we can observe, similar to the entropy method, the Shapley weights assign a relatively higher weight to Indicator 1 than Indicator 2 because of the presence of the outlier. However, the highest weight is assigned to Indicator 3 because of the dispersion observed, overcoming the bias that the entropy method generates due to its inability to handle outliers.

To summarise the foregoing discussion, the derivation of the final index score must be done with the help of aggregation of all relevant information, implying that all the indicators are the determinants. We should reflect on the importance of indicators which show that the economies are unequally developed (e.g. Indicator 3). However, as noted earlier, the entropy method fails to capture this feature due to the fact that such indicators convey less information than those with an outlier (e.g. Indicator 1). The Shapley method, on the other hand, offers a better alternative as it captures both the fact that economies are most unequally developed under Indicator 3 as well as the existence of the outlier in Indicator 1.

3.4.4 Findings Based on the Shapley Weightage Methodology

Figure 3.52 shows the weight of each environment in the Overall Competitiveness Index under the Shapley methodology based on data in 2014. As shown in the figure, Macroeconomic

Figure 3.52: Weight for Each Environment by the Shapley Weightage Methodology

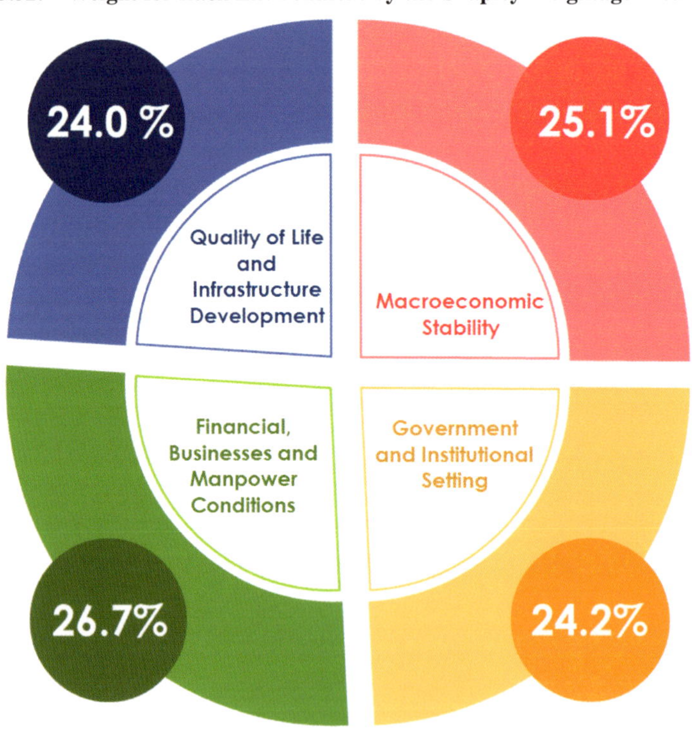

Source: Asia Competitiveness Institute.

Stability constitutes 25.1 percent of the overall index, Government and Institutional Setting 24.2 percent; Financial Businesses and Manpower Conditions 26.7 percent and finally, Quality of Life and Infrastructure Development 24 percent.

The Shapley Weightage of an environment measures the degree of unequal development among the economies in that particular environment: the more divergent the performances of the economies, the higher the Shapley weight. In this sense, Financial, Businesses and Manpower Conditions was where ASEAN countries differed from each other the most in 2014, as the Shapley weight for this environment was the highest. At a more nuanced level, an economy receives a higher score under the Shapley weightage methodology if it performs well in an environment in which there is higher inequality across all assessed economies. This adds another layer of sophistication as compared to the equal weightage methodology.

However, the newly calculated Shapley weights are not significantly different from 25 percent — the weight of each environment under the equal weightage scheme. Mathematically, there are two possible reasons that could account for this phenomenon. The first is that every surveyed economy has become equally developed in all aspects and across all indicators, sub-environments, and hence environments. This is clearly not the case in reality, where regional inequality still exists within ASEAN. Thus, we come to the second explanation, which is that the aggregate dispersion, i.e. the Shapley value, of each indicator, sub-environment, and hence environment for all the economies is rather similar across all indicators. In other words, the frontrunner economies excel, while the less developed lack behind for the majority of the indicators. Notwithstanding these nuances in the underlying explanations for the observed results, it is clear that the original results based on equal weightage are robust. Tables 3.32–3.36 show

Table 3.32: Comparison of Ranking and Index Results between Equal Weightage and Shapley Weightage Methodologies — Overall Competitiveness in 2014

Economy	Equal Weightage-based Ranking	Shapley Weightage-based Ranking	Equal Weightage-based Score	Shapley Weightage-based Score
Singapore	1	1	2.0152	2.0176
Malaysia	2	2	1.0568	1.0773
Brunei	3	3	0.5322	0.5214
Thailand	4	4	0.4477	0.4288
Indonesia	5	5	0.0412	0.0397
Philippines	6	6	–0.3133	–0.3073
Vietnam	7	7	–0.3987	–0.3943
Cambodia	8	8	–0.9071	–0.9100
Laos	9	9	–0.9241	–0.9403
Myanmar	10	10	–1.5501	–1.5328

Source: Asia Competitiveness Institute.

Table 3.33: Comparison of Ranking and Index Results between Equal Weightage and Shapley Weightage Methodologies — Macroeconomic Stability in 2014

Economy	Equal Weightage-based Ranking	Shapley Weightage-based Ranking	Equal Weightage-based Score	Shapley Weightage-based Score
Singapore	1	1	2.1709	2.2352
Thailand	**2**	**3**	**0.7317**	**0.5840**
Malaysia	**3**	**2**	**0.6255**	**0.6393**
Indonesia	4	4	0.3968	0.4221
Brunei	5	5	0.2478	0.2224
Vietnam	6	6	−0.4130	−0.3879
Philippines	7	7	−0.5150	−0.4606
Cambodia	8	8	−0.8807	−0.9261
Laos	9	9	−0.9205	−0.9453
Myanmar	10	10	−1.4433	−1.3830

Note: Bold text shows instances where a country's rank based on equal weightage methodology is different from that based on Shapley weightage methodology.
Source: Asia Competitiveness Institute.

Table 3.34: Comparison of Ranking and Index Results between Equal Weightage and Shapley Weightage Methodologies — Government and Institutional Setting in 2014

Economy	Equal Weightage-based Ranking	Shapley Weightage-based Ranking	Equal Weightage-based Score	Shapley Weightage-based Score
Singapore	1	1	2.2851	2.2630
Malaysia	2	2	1.0322	1.0613
Brunei	3	3	0.4421	0.4358
Thailand	4	4	0.1916	0.2056
Philippines	5	5	−0.1345	−0.1683
Indonesia	6	6	−0.3317	−0.3115
Vietnam	7	7	−0.4344	−0.4284
Laos	8	8	−0.8673	−0.8581
Cambodia	9	9	−0.9715	−0.9318
Myanmar	10	10	−1.2116	−1.2676

Source: Asia Competitiveness Institute.

that the ranking and index results derived from the equal weightage and Shapley weightage methodologies are largely similar to each other except for minor differences in the Macroeconomic Stability and Quality of Life and Infrastructure Development environments.

Table 3.35: Comparison of Ranking and Index Results between Equal Weightage and Shapley Weightage Methodologies — Financial, Businesses and Manpower Conditions in 2014

Economy	Equal Weightage-based Ranking	Shapley Weightage-based Ranking	Equal Weightage-based Score	Shapley Weightage-based Score
Malaysia	1	1	1.6723	1.6615
Singapore	2	2	1.3232	1.3634
Thailand	3	3	0.5671	0.5949
Brunei	4	4	0.5261	0.5314
Indonesia	5	5	0.2875	0.2202
Philippines	6	6	–0.4753	–0.4708
Vietnam	7	7	–0.4763	–0.4775
Cambodia	8	8	–0.8090	–0.8446
Laos	9	9	–0.9586	–0.9662
Myanmar	10	10	–1.6569	–1.6122

Source: Asia Competitiveness Institute.

Table 3.36: Comparison of Ranking and Index Results between Equal Weightage and Shapley Weightage Methodologies — Quality of Life and Infrastructure Development in 2014

Economy	Equal Weightage-based Ranking	Shapley Weightage-based Ranking	Equal Weightage-based Score	Shapley Weightage-based Score
Singapore	1	1	2.0429	2.0394
Brunei	2	2	0.8499	0.8495
Malaysia	3	3	0.7720	0.7769
Thailand	4	4	0.2476	0.2576
Philippines	5	5	–0.0913	–0.0699
Indonesia	6	6	–0.1925	–0.2110
Vietnam	7	7	–0.2237	–0.2285
Laos	**8**	**9**	**–0.8404**	**–0.8814**
Cambodia	**9**	**8**	**–0.8597**	**–0.8395**
Myanmar	10	10	–1.7047	–1.6930

Note: Bold text shows instances where a country's rank based on equal weightage methodology is different from that based on Shapley weightage methodology.
Source: Asia Competitiveness Institute.

3.5 Concluding Notes

In general, the Overall Competitiveness rankings do not see considerable changes, with the only exception of Brunei overtaking Thailand as the third-ranked economy for the first time over the study period of 2000–2014. The significant divide in terms of economic development level as well as progress of catching up in the ASEAN-10 is well reflected in our annual rankings where Singapore, Malaysia, Brunei and Thailand remained in the top four for 15 consecutive years, while Vietnam, Cambodia, Laos and Myanmar stayed as the bottom four. Indonesia has decidedly surpassed the Philippines at fifth position despite having a similar standardised score level to the latter in 2000. With the exception of the top five economies, the standardised scores of the remaining five economies were negative in 2014, indicating their below-average performances.

Zooming in to the environment and sub-environment levels, our analysis shows that the competitiveness results are rather diverse. Malaysia has been surging ahead, particularly in the sub-environment of Labour Market Flexibility, and broken the monopoly of Singapore in all four environments by emerging at the top for Financial, Businesses and Manpower Conditions. Laos seems to have improved consistently with marked increases in scores of all four environments. However, Myanmar witnessed a downward trend in the overall competitiveness score over the study period, while the below-median scores in all sub-environments also signify deep rooted structural weaknesses which requires attention amid the optimism of its democratic transition. The Philippines risks being outperformed by the newer members as its standardised scores in all environments except Quality of Life and Infrastructure Development plunged more negatively over time. For Vietnam, economic reforms have resulted in a leap in Openness to Trade and Services, but it still lags in other sub-environments such as Economic Vibrancy and Attractiveness to Foreign Investors; Vietnam's scores for these dimensions in 2014 were below the regional median.

As discussed in Section 3.2.5, competitiveness ranking alone does not offer insights on how to improve economic competitiveness. The top 20 percent strongest and weakest indicators discussed present a constructive approach for the ASEAN member states to consolidate their strengths and address their weaknesses in order to foster a more competitive and prosperous economy. Furthermore, our policy simulation analysis shows the potential of improvement for each country in both standardised scores and rankings if the values of the top 20 percent weaknesses were to be raised to the average.

The establishment of the ASEAN Community which envisages the creation of a resilient and cohesive regional grouping has illustrated the determination of ASEAN in forging ahead. Nonetheless, enormous work awaits the 10 member states to realise the common dream of forming a prosperous and inclusive community which will last another 50 years. The full realisation of a single market and production base as laid out in the ASEAN Economic Community (AEC) blueprint is hampered by the development divide in the region. The ongoing catching-up progress demonstrated is evident in the flexibilities granted to CLMV in implementing regional integration initiatives. Furthermore, the development divide has impeded the resolution of thorny agendas such as non-tariff barriers and trade in services.

Thus, bridging the development divide remains a priority for the bloc. This will require far-reaching domestic reforms among the transitional CLMV, to be augmented with the assistance and support from the other ASEAN forerunners. In this regard, ACI's competitiveness ranking and simulation study provides a timely and instructive roadmap for policy-makers in individual ASEAN member states as well as the region as a whole in identifying challenges and opportunities in their respective paths to growth and development. Moving forward, competition in parallel with cooperation among the ASEAN member states is the key factor in braving future challenges and propelling ASEAN forward.

References

Aumann, Robert J., and Mordecai Kurz. 1977. "Power and Taxes". *Econometrica: Journal of the Econometric Society*: 1137–1161.

Aumann, Robert J., and Roger Myerson. 1988. "Endogenous Formation of Links Between Players and Coalitions: An Application of the Shapley Value". *The Shapley Value*: 175–191.

Bristow, Gillian. 2010. *Critical Reflections on Regional Competitiveness: Theory, Policy, Practice (Routledge Studies in Human Geography).* Oxon: Routledge.

Camagni, Roberto. 2002. "On the Concept of Territorial Competitiveness: Sound or Misleading"? *Urban Studies* 39 (13): 2395–2411.

Hougaard, Jens Leth, Chiu Yu Ko, and Xuyao Zhang. "A Welfare Economic Interpretation of FRAND". (2017).

IMD World Competitiveness Center. 2014. *IMD World Competitiveness Yearbook*. Lausanne: International Institute for Management Development.

Institute of Applied Economics Shanghai Academy of Social Sciences. 2016. "五大发展理念指标体系及省级区域评估报告 Assessing Provincial Development under the Five Development Concepts (in Chinese)". Shanghai Academy of Social Sciences.

Kitson, Michael, Ronald Martin, and Peter Tyler. 2004. "Regional Competitiveness: An Elusive yet Key Concept"? *Regional Studies* 38 (9): 991–999.

Krugman, Paul. 1994. "Competitiveness: A Dangerous Obsession". *Foreign Affairs* 73 (2): 28–44.

Moulin, Hervé. 1992. "An application of the Shapley Value to Fair Division with Money". *Econometrica: Journal of the Econometric Society*: 1331–1349.

Petrosjan, Leon, and Georges Zaccour. 2003. "Time-Consistent Shapley Value Allocation of Pollution Cost Reduction". *Journal of Economic Dynamics and Control* 27 (3): 381–398.

Porter, Michael E. 1980. *Competitive Strategy: Techniques for Analyzing Industries and Competitors*. New York: Free Press.

Tan, Khee Giap, Le Phuong Anh Nguyen, and Nguyen Trieu Duong Luu. 2017. *2016 Annual Competitiveness Analysis and Growth Slowdown Analysis for ASEAN-10*. Singapore: World Scientific.

UNDP. 2016. *Human Development Report 2016*. New York: United Nations Development Program (UNDP).

World Economic Forum. 2014. *Global Competitiveness Report 2013–2014*. Geneva: World Economic Forum.

Zeleny, Milan. 1982. *Multiple Criteria Decision Making*. New York: McGraw-Hill.

Discussant Notes 3.1

Dr Lee Jae Young

Group Head and Lead Economist
ASEAN+3 Macroeconomic Research Office (AMRO)

The presented studies are timely and relevant, in particular, when globalization has been facing strong headwinds in several advanced economies recently. For decades, trade and investment have been the engines of global growth, but we should admit that our understanding about how trade and investment were shaping our economies not only in growth but also in other parts of our lives remain limited. Surge of protectionism in major advanced economies might simply reflect our lack of understanding about globalization and limited policy actions thereafter. While globalisation and, in particular, the development of global value chain was analysed and studied by many researchers, we did not clearly understand how the medium-term consequences could be. A few comments are provided.

First, while it is broadly agreed among economists that trade and investment are the key pillars of globalization, the relationship between trade and investment remains an issue. Inward FDI has been broadly seen positive for growth and employment in a host economy, but outward FDIs has been often viewed as stolen jobs and lost growth by some policymakers. How to understand FDI and trade in this globalized world remains crucial.

In the study of "impact of real effective exchange rates on trade in goods and services", FDI stock was used as proxy for production capacity. There are different types of FDIs that would have different implications on exports and other outcomes. Relationship between trade and FDI stock may need to be further elaborated which may affect the efficiency of the model. For instance, market-seeking type of FDI does involve reduced imports and may not have big impacts on export of the host country. In contrast, efficiency-seeking type of FDI which may integrate a host country into the global value chain would require importing intermediary goods or exporting final products.

Many Japanese companies expanded their investments in several ASEAN countries in response to rising cost of production in Japan due to appreciation of its currency and in search for markets as well. In many cases, these companies imported intermediary goods from Japan which in turn put into assembly with varying degrees. Recent survey by JETRO shows that Japanese overseas subsidiaries have rapidly increased their local sales in Asia but exports to other countries have been limited. In particular, as for transportation equipment, local sales accounted for about over 80 percent. Meanwhile, local contents in those FDI companies' products continued to increase, reaching around 50 to 60 percent in many sectors. Data also shows that imports and exports of these FDI companies fluctuated over years depending on degree of local content and situation of the target markets. These types of dynamics of FDI companies' activities may cause biases in model estimation.

Second, a few emerging markets and developing economies have large energy or commodity sectors in their exports and thus energy or commodity prices, which largely depend on global growth, have had significant impacts on such economies. Exchange rates of these energy or commodity exporting countries were heavily influenced by global growth that affects global demand on commodities and energy and commodity prices. By the same token, exchange rates of energy or commodity importing countries would be also affected by global energy or commodity prices in the opposite direction. Given that growth and exchange rate would be closely related, the model estimation could be inefficient. For example, in commodity-exporting countries like Indonesia and Malaysia, policymakers were concerned about losses in competitiveness in manufacturing sector due to real exchange rate appreciation during commodity boom period. Incorporating the energy or commodity price into the model could be challenging.

Third, one of the policy implications from the study, which is "competitive devaluation may not yield the desired export-boosting effect in a world of global value chains" may need to be qualified a bit, if we consider medium-term consequences. Set aside the feasibility of maintaining a medium-term competitive devaluation, if a country has succeeded in maintaining a prolonged period of cheap currency, the country might continue to have larger inflows of efficiency-seeing type of FDI which in turn might increase exports. Consequent current account surplus might result in currency appreciation of the country which may self-correct the imbalances. However, this may not apply to a prolonged period of appreciation due to surge in oil or other commodity exports that happened in many oil or other commodity-exporting countries in the past. Should the country lose competitiveness in manufacturing exports, due to commodity-boom-driven currency appreciation, the country might lose ground in manufacturing sector. In such a case, even a significant competitive devaluation might not help the country regain its prowess in manufacturing sector. This is the so-called, "Dutch Disease".

Lastly, it is true that the establishment of the AEC in 2015 shows that ASEAN is on the right track in their efforts to strengthen regional integration. However, ironically, the fact that there seems like not much resistance to economic integration which is seen in the U.S. and in Europe also implies that there is a long way to go for ASEAN integration. While it is true that ASEAN is getting more intensively integrated into the global value chain, but at the same time intra-regional integration among ASEAN members themselves remain pretty limited as often compared to the case of Europe. How to enhance economic complementarity and mutual benefits among ASEAN economies themselves remains the key task.

Discussant Notes 3.2

Dr Tham Siew Yean

Adjunct Professor, Institute of Malaysian and International Studies (IKMAS) and Senior Fellow, ISEAS-Yusof Ishak Institute, National University of Singapore

The first presentation focuses on the use of new weights, namely the Shapley weights to compute the competitiveness index for comparing the competitiveness of the ASEAN-10 member countries. The presentation compares the results using equal and Shapley weights. Although the change in weights changed some of the scores, nonetheless the competitiveness ranking of the 10 economies did not change for 2014. Using the same methodology over time shows that there is a competitiveness divide between the top four competitive economies, namely Singapore, Malaysia, Thailand and Brunei and the rest of the ASEAN-10 economies, with CLMV countries occupying the bottom four (slide 41). This is not surprising since the competitiveness divide reflects the development divide between the ASEAN economies.

I note that the simulation results show that competitiveness can improve in terms of scores and also ranking with the right solutions. Are policy recommendations based on the list of weakest indicators? How do we choose which ones to prioritise? Is it according to the scores?

Assuming that improving competitiveness is to facilitate the development needs of countries, perhaps the use of additional country specific information can help to prioritise policy choices for improving competitiveness. To illustrate, although the sectoral distribution in GDP is usually divided between agriculture, industry and services, within the context of ASEAN, it may be useful to consider the importance of extractive mining, including crude petroleum and natural gas in the economies of Southeast Asia, especially for Brunei, Indonesia, Laos, and Vietnam (Table 1).

In the case of Brunei, since country specific information indicates that it is petroleum dependent (see Table 1) and the dominance of state-owned enterprises, it is important to prioritise improvements in competitor indicators, that will enable it to diversify its economy in terms of output and enhance the role of the private sector. For example, prioritising the ease of doing business (for drawing in both domestic private and foreign players) and improving the output of services (for sectoral diversification) will help Brunei to overcome its dependence on oil.

Second, given the influence of big countries on the development of ASEAN-10 through trade and investment, what is the impact of China on the competitiveness of each of the ASEAN-10 economies?

In the second presentation on the impact of REER on Trade in Goods and Services, it uses TiVa data to examine the trade impact of exchange rates in the ASEAN-8. Several issues for further discussion are: the impact of REER and its volatility on FVA of gross exports; using

Table 1: Industry, Manufacturing and Mining's Share of GDP in 2014

Country	Share of Industry in GDP (ISIC 10-45)	Share of Manufacturing in GDP (ISIC 15-47)	Share of Mining and Quarrying in GDP (ISIC 11-14)
Brunei	68	16	52
Cambodia	27	16	11
Indonesia	42	21	21
Laos	32	9	22
Malaysia	37	23	14
Myanmar	35	20	15
Philippines	31	21	10
Singapore	26	19	7
Thailand	37	28	9
Vietnam	37	15	22

Source: World Bank World Development Indicators.

domestic value added in exports for robustness test; and the choice of traded goods. Since the REER can also potentially affect the FVA of gross exports through its impact on imported inputs, will there be any multi-collinearity problems (See for example Cheng *et al.*, 2016)? Can domestic value added (DVA) of exports be used instead of FVA for robustness checking since an increase in DVA is equivalent to a decrease in FVA? Also whether the study should focus on products that are commonly traded though GVCs such as electronics and automobiles and services rather than all commodities since natural resources have lower GVC participation? Or to investigate further sub-sectoral differences since the OECD data bank also has data by subsectors and there are sub-sectoral variations in the importance of GVC participation.

Finally, if openness in the competitiveness indicators is replaced by TiVa data for years with available data, will it affect the scores and ranking for those years?

Reference

Cheng, K.C., G. H. Hong, D. Seneviratne, and R. van Elkan. 2016. "Rethinking the Exchange Rate Impact on Trade in a World with Global Value Chains." *International Economic Journal* 30(2): 204–216.

Chapter 4

Impact of Real Effective Exchange Rates on Foreign Direct Investment Inflows to ASEAN Economies

4.1 Introduction and Motivation

Foreign Direct Investment (FDI) inflows to developing economies play a significant role in supplementing domestic capital, technology and skills, which fundamentally accelerate economic growth.[1] A growing strand of economic literature provides evidence on the impact of FDI inflows, pertaining to enhanced participation of economies in the global and regional value chains, which not only enhances export competitiveness but also favours trade facilitation by exercising comparative advantage in specific domains.[2] Indeed, as the production process becomes increasingly fragmented and diversified, access to more technology-intensive, high-income yielding activities requires participation in global and regional production networks. This also implies that competencies and institutions to attract FDI have a critical role in facilitating that process.[3]

Global FDI inflows have increased exponentially since the 1990s. As shown in Figure 4.1, notwithstanding the dips at the onset of the 21st century and during the global financial crisis (GFC), world FDI reached a peak of over 1.3 trillion US dollars in 2000 and hit a new high of over 1.9 trillion US dollars before the GFC in 2007. Though the global FDI inflows have recovered after the GFC, it has yet not been able to reach pre-GFC levels.

Figure 4.2 plots FDI inflows to developed, developing and transition economies as a share of world's FDI inflows. Even though the developed economies dominated the world FDI inflows for the most part of 1990s and 2000s, the importance of developing economies have increased over time. A closer look at the trends reveal that developed economies received about 68 percent of global FDI inflows on average from 1992 to 2000 and since then it has gradually dipped to a low of over 40 percent in 2014 before rebounding to around 55 percent in 2015.

Taken together, the share of FDI inflows to developing and transition economies have more than tripled from about 18 percent in 2000 to over 58 percent in 2014. The share of developing economies to world FDI inflows gained prominence and was larger than that of the developed economies in 2014, subsequently falling below the latter in 2015. In 2014, developing economies accounted for the largest share of about 55 percent of the world FDI inflows; however, their

[1] Among the early works, see Barro (1997), Borensztein *et al.* (1998), Mencinger (2003), Alfaro *et al.* (2004), Razin (2004), Carkovic and Levine (2005), Bosworth *et al.* (1999), and Mody and Murshid (2005). For more recent assessments, see Herzer (2012) and Iamsiraroj (2016).

[2] See for instance, Athukorala and Hill (1998), Hobday (2001), and Ng and Yeats (2003) for some of the early literature on this phenomenon of FDI and production fragmentation. Also see Van Assche and Gangnes (2010) for a relatively recent discussion.

[3] See Kaplinsky (2000) for a discussion on the proliferation of global production networks.

Figure 4.1: World FDI Inflows, 1992–2015

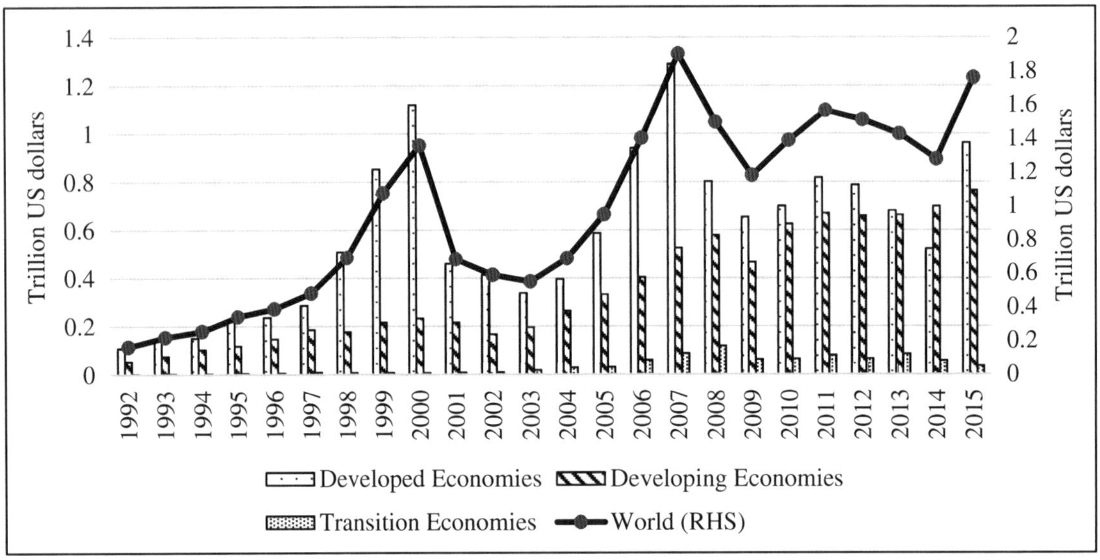

Source: Asia Competitiveness Institute based on data from United Nations Conference on Trade and Development (UNCTAD), World Investment Report 2017 (WIR 2017).

Figure 4.2: FDI Inflows by Category, 1992–2015

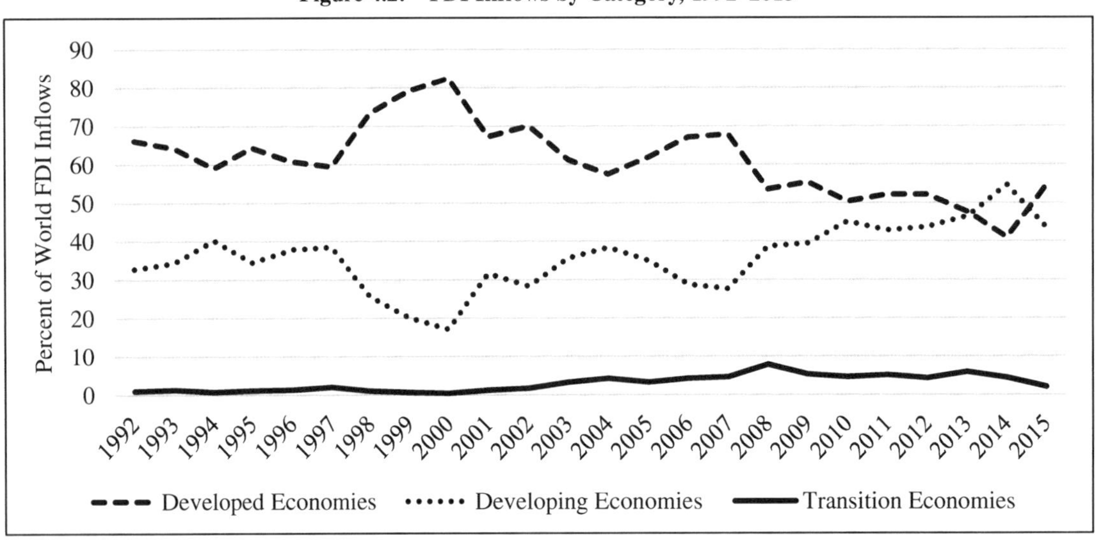

Source: Asia Competitiveness Institute based on data from UNCTAD, WIR 2017.

share slumped to over 43 percent in 2015. The share of transition economies have remained somewhat stable and low and stood at about 2 percent of world FDI inflows in 2015.

We further delve into the FDI inflows by category and focus on the top 20 recipients of FDI inflows in 2014 and 2015 (see Figure 4.3). Clearly, more than half of the 20 economies have

Figure 4.3: Top 20 Recipients of FDI Inflows, 2014 and 2015

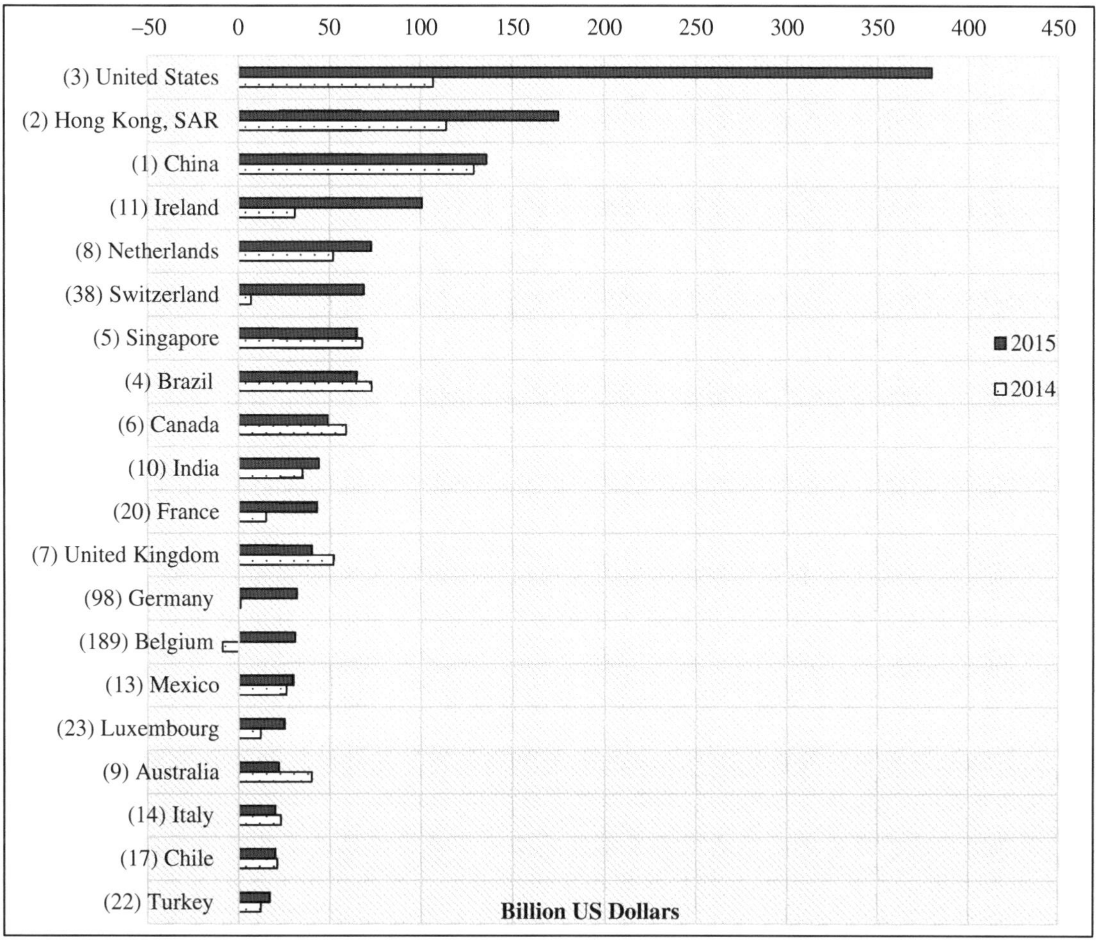

Note: Number in parenthesis denotes the rank of the economy in 2014.
Source: Asia Competitiveness Institute based on data from UNCTAD, WIR 2017.

witnessed an increase in their FDI inflows in 2015 *vis-à-vis* 2014. Concurrently, FDI inflows to most of the developed economies have increased in 2015. It is notable that about half of the largest recipients of FDI inflows are developing and transition economies.

The United States (US) was the largest recipient of FDI inflows with its value increasing by nearly four times from 107 billion US dollars in 2014 to around 380 billion US dollars in 2015, thus accounting for the highest increase (in absolute terms) in FDI inflows among the top 20 recipients. Second to the US are Hong Kong and China, which together accounted for over US$ 300 billion and ranked second and third respectively, in 2015. Apart from China and Hong Kong, Singapore and India are the only two Asian economies to appear in the list ranking sixth and 10th, respectively, in the corresponding year.

Located at the centre of the dynamic Asia-Pacific region, the 10-member Association of Southeast Asian Nations (ASEAN) has evolved as a significant recipient of global FDI inflows.

In fact, the two most developed economies in the region, namely Singapore and Malaysia, were early adopters of export-led growth strategies based on foreign investment.[4] In particular, the hallmark of Singapore's growth strategy is a combination of export-led industrialisation, with a focussed attention on specific global multinational corporations (MNCs) to attract FDI, which has translated into rapid expansion of its industrial sector. For Malaysia, FDI inflows have contributed significantly to its transition from a low-income to a middle-income economy with a robust export-oriented industrial base. Among the older, more mature ASEAN-6 economies, Thailand, Indonesia, and Philippines are also active hosts of FDI while the transition economies of ASEAN, namely Cambodia, Laos, Myanmar and Vietnam (CLMV), have increasingly been recognised as the new FDI frontiers given their abundant resources, low-cost educated workforce, and proactive FDI policies.

As a 2014 report by the Organisation for Economic Cooperation and Development has pointed out, the degrees of openness to FDI correspondingly vary across different ASEAN member states which are widely noted for the distinct heterogeneity in their development stages.[5] Almost all governments in ASEAN impose at least one sectorial restriction, while members such as Vietnam and Laos have horizontal equity restrictions for listed companies at 49 percent and 20 percent, respectively. Sectors which are commonly subject to foreign ownership restrictions in ASEAN include banking, retail, telecommunications, and transport. Restrictions of land ownership among foreign investor remain widespread with the majority of the ASEAN member states only allowing for long leases of land. Furthermore, as shown in Table 4.1, notable variations can be observed in ease of doing business across the regional grouping.

Notwithstanding the prevailing restrictions of foreign investment, sustained inflows of FDI continue to be emphasised as a key driver of growth in ASEAN, as the regional bloc took economic integration to a new height with the formal establishment of the ASEAN Economic Community (AEC) on 31 December, 2015. As stipulated in the AEC blueprint, ASEAN recognises that "a free and open investment regime is key to enhancing ASEAN's competitiveness in attracting FDI," which in turn will "promote and ensure dynamic development of ASEAN economies."[6] Principal measures for enhancing FDI inflows as identified in the AEC blueprint include the following: (i) progressive liberalisation of ASEAN member states' investment regime to achieve free and open investment, (ii) creating a more transparent, consistent and predictable investment environment, (iii) providing enhanced protection to all investors and their investments, and (iv) promoting ASEAN as an integrated investment and production network.

As seen in Figure 4.4, FDI inflows into ASEAN have been rising remarkably since the early 1990s, with two notable exceptions owing to external shocks, namely the 1997–1998 Asian Financial Crisis (AFC) and the 2008–2009 GFC. In absolute terms, FDI inflows into ASEAN steadily increased from around 13 billion US dollars in 1990 to about 36 billion US dollars in 1997 when the AFC erupted, and hit the historic high in 2014 at about 133 billion US dollars in 2014, notwithstanding the dips in 2008 and 2009 during the GFC. Likewise, FDI inflows into

[4] See Tan *et al.* (2015) for details on Singapore and Malaysia's development strategies.

[5] See OECD (2014).

[6] See ASEAN Secretariat (2008).

Table 4.1: Ease of Doing Business Ranking of ASEAN Economies (out of 189 Economies), 2014 and 2015

Country	2014	2015
Brunei	98	101
Cambodia	134	135
Indonesia	117	114
Laos	155	148
Malaysia	20	18
Myanmar	178	177
Philippines	86	95
Singapore	1	1
Thailand	28	26
Vietnam	72	78

Source: World Bank.

Figure 4.4: FDI Inflows into ASEAN (Billion US Dollars and Percent of World FDI, 1990–2014)

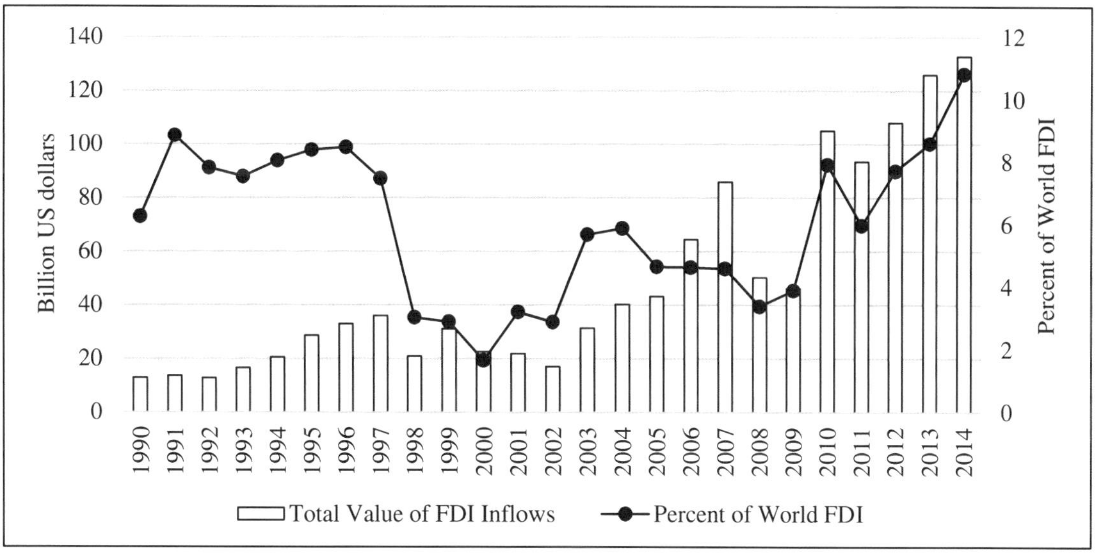

Source: Asia Competitiveness Institute based on data from UNCTAD.

ASEAN as a share of world's total FDI inflows rose significantly from over 6 percent in 1990 to around 11 percent in 2014.

Among the various determinants of FDI inflows well documented in the literature, one of the important factors that ASEAN economies have to pay attention to in order to sustain the interest of global investors is cost competitiveness, broadly represented by Real Effective Exchange

Figure 4.5: Percent Change in REER Levels

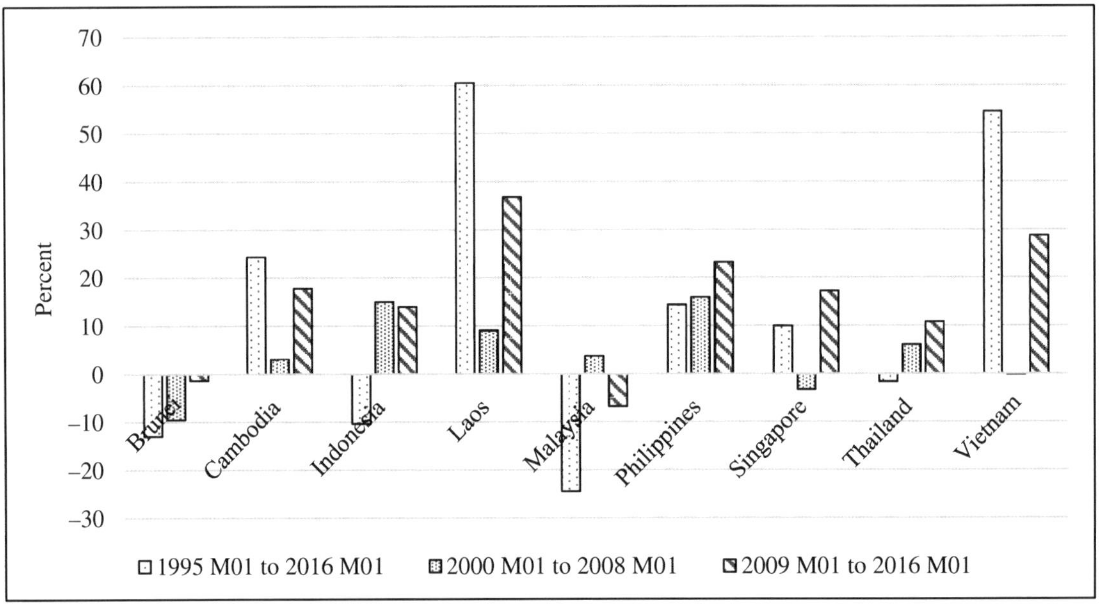

Source: Asia Competitiveness Institute based on data from Bruegel.

Rates (REER). Figure 4.5 plots the percent change in REER levels for nine ASEAN economies for three periods. For the entire period under consideration (1995 M01 to 2016 M01), we observe that the currencies of five out of nine ASEAN economies have appreciated in the last two decades. While the Lao kip appreciated the most (over 60 percent), the Singapore dollar and Philippine peso appreciated by only around 10 and 14 percent, respectively. The Malaysian ringgit depreciated the most (24 percent) over the last two decades followed by the Brunei dollar (12 percent) and Indonesian rupiah (10 percent).

With the exception of the Singapore dollar, Vietnamese dong and Brunei dollar, almost all the other ASEAN currencies appreciated during the pre-GFC period (2000 M01 to 2008 M01). Subsequently, even in the post-GFC period (2009 M01 to 2016 M01) most of the ASEAN currencies appreciated, raising concerns about an appreciating REER which will have a significant bearing on ASEAN's external competitiveness. A persistent appreciation of REER could lead to a loss of export competitiveness of the ASEAN region, which in turn could affect the economic growth of the ASEAN economies, moving forward, which makes it important for the policy-makers to understand the impact of movements in exchange rates and their volatility.

To what degree do movements in REER, both in terms of levels and volatility, determine FDI inflows into ASEAN economies? While there have been some works that already exist in this area, most of the literature is either cross-sectional in nature or covers only a subset of ASEAN, particularly the relatively more developed economies of ASEAN-5. Considering the diversity of ASEAN both in terms of the FDI inflows as well as the existence of multiple exchange rate regimes, we undertake an empirical assessment to understand how REER movements in levels and volatility impact FDI inflows into the region.

The remainder of this chapter is structured as follows. In Section 4.2, we will discuss the importance of FDI as a source of external financing for ASEAN. The section further elaborates on the trends and patterns of FDI inflows to ASEAN as a whole and to its member economies. In Section 4.3, we discuss the theory of interest drawing on the general literature on impact of exchange rates on FDI, besides providing a literature on the determinants of FDI specific to the region. Section 4.4 provides a detailed description of the data used in our empirics, and Section 4.5 focuses on broad analytical framework and methodology highlighting the empirical model to be tested. Finally, Sections 4.6 and 4.7 deal with empirical results and robustness checks, respectively, and Section 4.8 concludes the chapter and outlines some policy implications.

4.2 Importance of Foreign Direct Investment (FDI) Inflows as a Source of External Financing: Trends and Patterns

Non-trade external financing sources have assumed greater importance in ASEAN over the last two decades. Net resource flows include direct investments, portfolio investments, financial derivatives (other than reserves) and employee stock options as well as other investments. Figure 4.6 illustrates that direct investment emerges as the most significant component of external financing for ASEAN over 2000–2016. While the magnitude of ASEAN's average annual direct inflows

Figure 4.6: Components of Private External Financing in ASEAN, 2000–2016

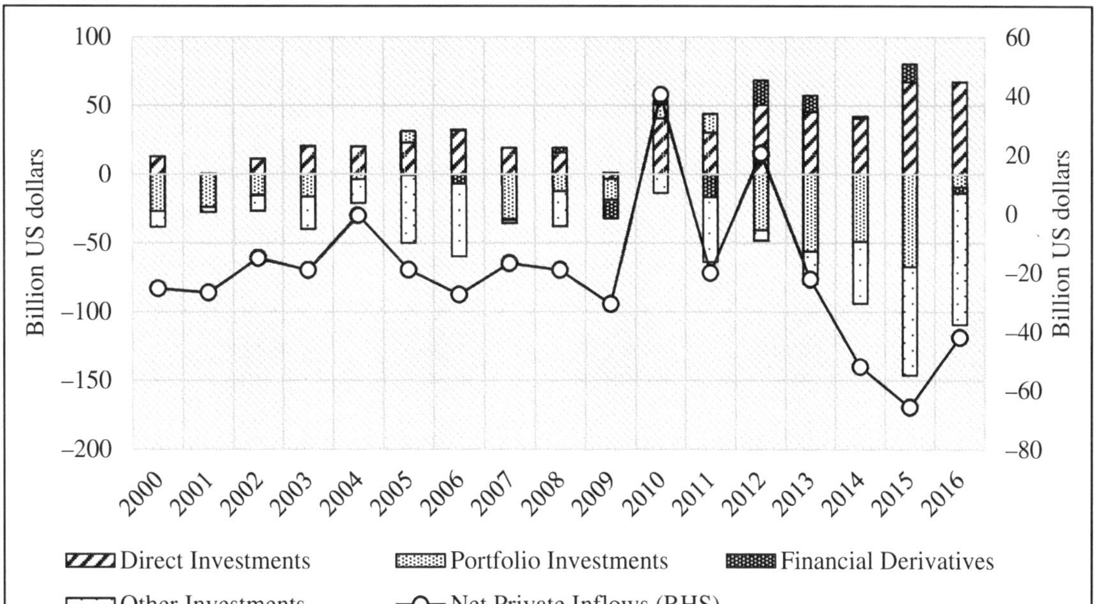

Source: Asia Competitiveness Institute based on data from the International Monetary Fund (IMF).

of FDI was just about 29 billion US dollars over the period of 2000–2016, its value increased from over 12 billion US dollars in 2000 to over 67 billion US dollars in 2016.

Despite an increasing share of FDI inflows, ASEAN accounted for a total private outflow largely because of outflow of portfolio investment and other investments. Financial derivatives (other than reserves) and employee stock options continue to contribute a very small share of ASEAN's total private inflows. Nonetheless, direct investment continues to contribute a significant share of total private inflows to ASEAN. The remainder of the section will discuss the trends and patterns in ASEAN's FDI inflows at the national level.

FDI inflows to ASEAN as a share of ASEAN's Gross Domestic Product (GDP) increased from over 3 percent in 1990 to about 5.4 percent in 2014 (see Figure 4.7). ASEAN's FDI inflows as a percent of GDP have been relatively stable from 1990 to 2014 when compared to ASEAN's FDI inflows as a percent of Gross Fixed Capital Formation (GFCF). FDI inflows as a percent of GFCF increased from under 10 percent in 1992 to over 20 percent in 1999. Two significant dips are noticed after 1999 and 2008 following the AFC and GFC, respectively.

Nonetheless at the national level, FDI inflows into individual ASEAN member states have been uneven throughout the period from 1990 to 2014 (see Table 4.2). Singapore consistently led the 10-member bloc as an FDI host, accounting for more than half of total FDI inflows to ASEAN since 2000. However, between 2010 and 2014 Singapore's share of FDI inflows declined slightly from over 52 percent to around 51 percent. Malaysia's and Thailand's contribution to FDI inflows

Figure 4.7: FDI Inflows into ASEAN as Percentage of GDP and GFCF,[7] 1990–2014

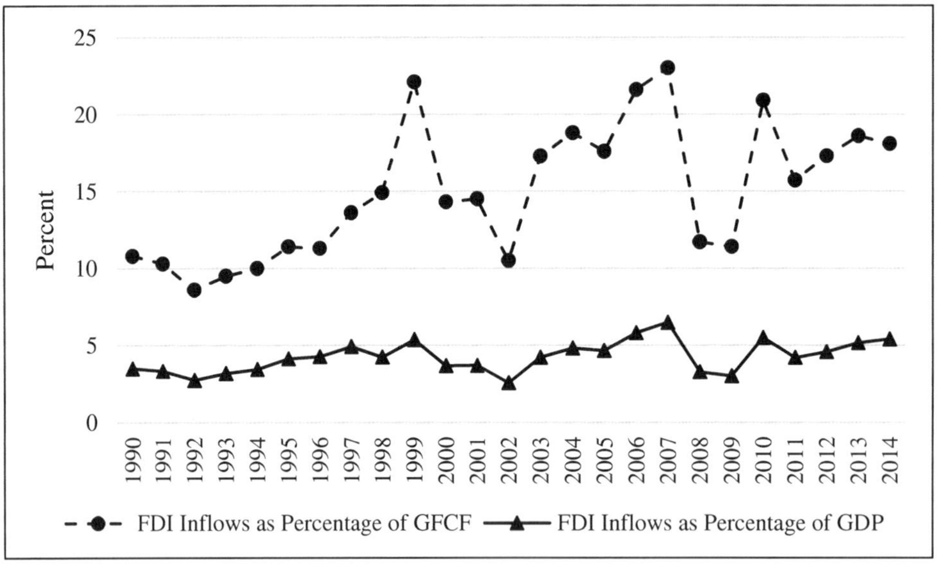

Source: Asia Competitiveness Institute based on data from UNCTAD.

[7] FDI inflows as a percent of GFCF used from Southeast Asia region data. With the exception of Myanmar, all ASEAN countries were accounted for in the South East region with Timor-Leste being the only non-ASEAN economy included in the region.

Table 4.2: Contribution to FDI Inflows into ASEAN by Member State, 1990–2014

	Share of Regional FDI Inflows (percent)						
Economy	**1990–1999**	**2000–2009**	**2010**	**2011**	**2012**	**2013**	**2014**
Brunei	1.5	1.7	0.5	0.7	0.8	0.6	0.4
Cambodia	0.6	1	1.3	1.5	1.7	1.5	1.3
Indonesia	9.7	6.7	13.1	20.9	17.7	14.9	17
Laos	0.2	0.3	0.3	0.3	0.3	0.3	0.5
Malaysia	21.3	9.9	8.6	13.1	8.6	9.6	8.1
Myanmar	1.6	1	6.3	1.2	0.5	0.5	0.7
Philippines	5.3	3.9	1.2	2	1.9	3	4.7
Singapore	39.8	51.8	52.4	51.4	52.4	51.4	50.8
Thailand	14.1	15.4	8.7	1.3	8.5	11.1	9.5
Vietnam	5.9	8.4	7.6	8	7.7	7.1	6.9

Source: Asia Competitiveness Institute based on data from UNCTAD.

into ASEAN went down significantly from about 21 percent and 14 percent between 1990 and 1999 to over 8 percent and 9 percent, respectively, in 2014. In contrast, Indonesia has seen an impressive surge in its share of FDI inflows from around 10 percent between 1990 and 1999 to about 17 percent in 2014. Among the transitional economies, Vietnam and, to a lesser extent, Cambodia and Laos have registered an increasing share of total regional FDI inflows from 1990 to 2014, while Myanmar's share slipped from about 2 percent between 1990 and 1999 to less than 1 percent in 2014.

In absolute terms, as shown in Figure 4.8, FDI inflows to Singapore rose more than 10 times from over 5 billion US dollars in 1990 to around 68 billion US dollars in 2014. Despite experiencing outflows of FDI from 1999 to 2001, Indonesia rebounded strongly and came second to Singapore between 2010 and 2014, with FDI inflows totalled at around 23 billion US dollars in 2014. Thailand stood at the third place although it registered a decline from about 14 billion US dollars in 2013 to over 12 billion US dollars in 2014. Malaysia and Vietnam came at the fourth and fifth place in 2014 with FDI inflows of about 11 billion US dollars and 9 billion US dollars, respectively, followed by Philippines, Cambodia, Myanmar, Laos and Brunei. Overall, all 10 ASEAN member states have seen significant increase in FDI inflows between 1990 and 2014.

In addition, we also measure the coefficient of correlation between FDI inflows into individual ASEAN member states with that of ASEAN as a whole between 1990 and 2014. We find that Singapore has the highest correlation with the aggregate inflows of FDI into ASEAN (0.98), followed by Cambodia (0.96), Laos (0.92) and Vietnam (0.87). The oil-rich Brunei and the relatively closed Myanmar have the lowest correlation of 0.09 and 0.40, respectively. Interestingly, the correlation of FDI inflows into Indonesia (0.91) is higher than that of Malaysia (0.84), Thailand (0.76) and Philippines (0.73). It is evident from the correlation analysis that the evolution of FDI inflows into ASEAN economies has been largely consistent with the regional trends, with the exception of Brunei and Myanmar.

Figure 4.8: FDI Inflows into Individual ASEAN Economies, 1990–2014

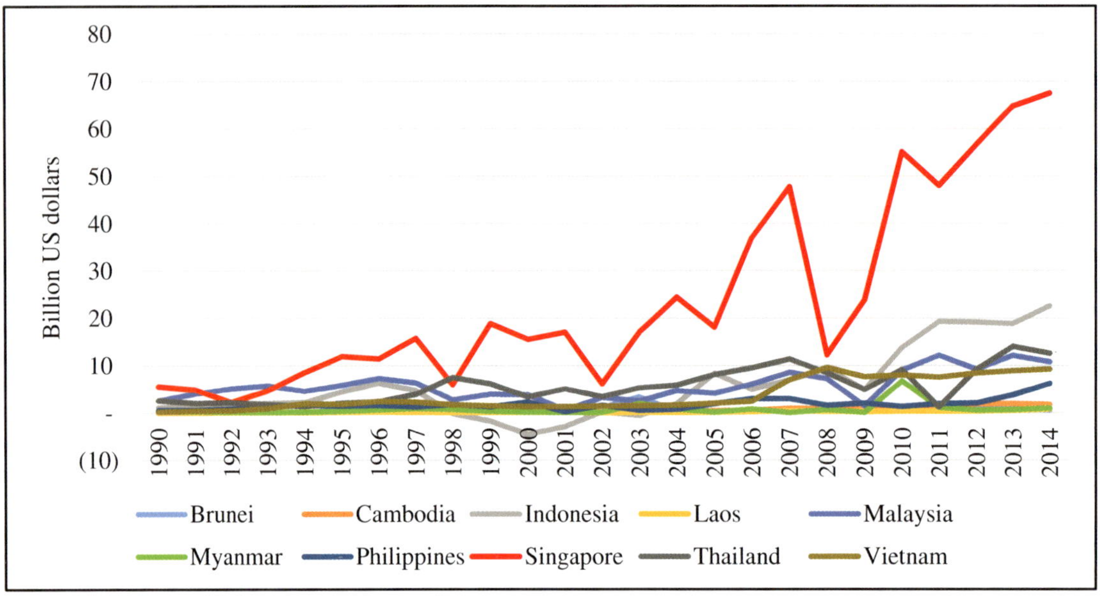

Source: Asia Competitiveness Institute based on data from UNCTAD.

Figure 4.9 illustrates FDI inflows to ASEAN by source country. On average, Japan has been the largest contributor of FDI inflows to ASEAN, contributing to about 13 percent of total FDI inflows between 2000 and 2014, followed by the US which accounted for an FDI inflows of about 11 percent and Netherlands at around 8 percent. Together, these three economies constituted to more than 30 percent of FDI inflows into ASEAN during 2000–2014, indicating ASEAN's reliance on extra-regional major powers as a source of investment.

Meanwhile, the United Kingdom (UK) accounted for about 6 percent of FDI inflows into ASEAN over the same period. Indonesia and Singapore are the only two intra-ASEAN investors in the top-10, contributing to around 5 and 4 percent of FDI inflows, respectively. China registers for about 4 percent of total inflows, while Australia and South Korea round out the top-10 with a share of about 3 percent each between 2000 and 2014. In terms of regions, the European Union (EU) remains the most important source of FDI inflows to ASEAN, followed by ASEAN itself, with Indonesia and Singapore being the most important sources of intra-regional FDI (see Figure 4.9).

Table 4.3 shows the distribution of FDI inflows into individual ASEAN member economies by source countries for the period from 2000 to 2014. The EU was the top investor in three out of 10 ASEAN economies, namely Brunei, Malaysia and Singapore. Meanwhile, ASEAN is the most significant source of FDI for Cambodia, Indonesia and Vietnam, which signifies the enormous potential of intra-regional investment flows as a driver of growth, particularly for the newer, less developed members. China's importance as a source of FDI seems to be rising as it constitutes the highest amount of FDI inflows to Laos and Myanmar. Japan invests the most in Thailand, Indonesia and Vietnam.

Figure 4.9: FDI Inflows into ASEAN by Source Economies, 2000–2014

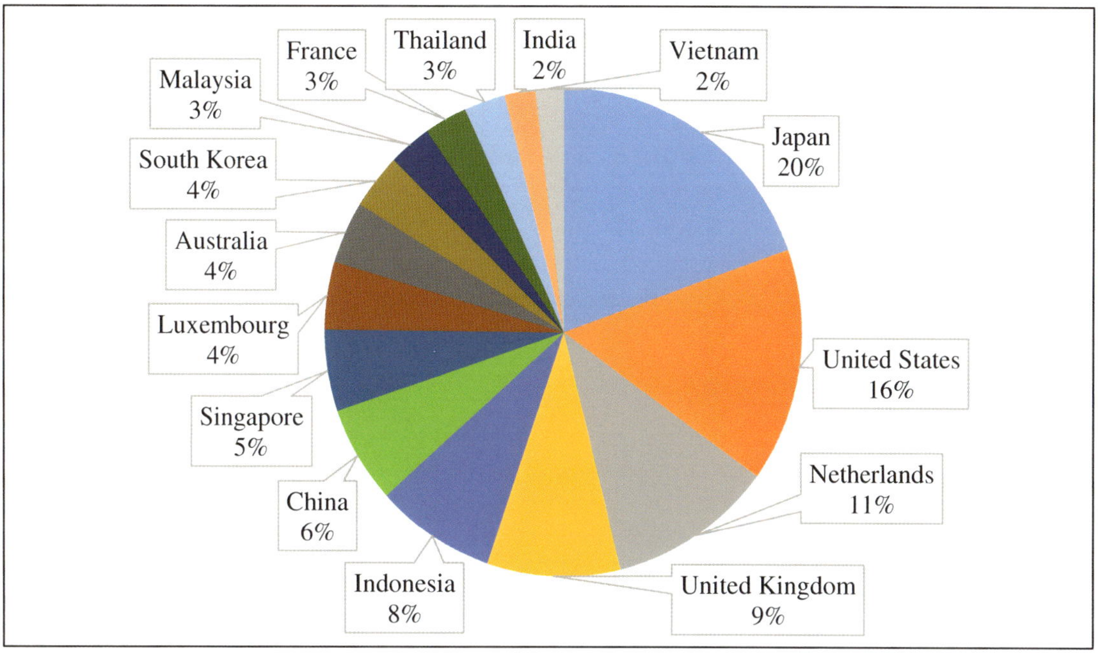

Source: Asia Competitiveness Institute based on data from ASEAN Secretariat.

We now turn to a sector-wise analysis of FDI inflows to ASEAN. The service sector attracts the most FDI into ASEAN with financial and insurance, wholesale and retail trade and other services accounting for more than half of the cumulative FDI inflows between 2012 and 2014 (see Figure 4.10). Manufacturing is the second most important sector, which attracted about 20 percent of total FDI inflows during the same period. Real estate ranks fifth, accounting for over 8 percent of FDI inflows into ASEAN, followed by mining and quarrying and agriculture, forestry and fishing with equal shares of about 2 percent each of the cumulative inflows during 2012–2014.

A breakdown of FDI inflows into the 10 ASEAN member economies between 2012 and 2014 by sector reveals that the bulk of FDI inflows into the service sector went to Singapore (see Table 4.4). In particular, Singapore, one of the world's major service hubs, topped the ASEAN region in terms of FDI inflows into financial and insurance, wholesale and retail trade, real estate and transportation and storage sector. Meanwhile, Indonesia attracted the most FDI inflows into manufacturing over the period 2012–2014, followed by Vietnam. Indonesia also led the regional bloc in terms of FDI inflows into agriculture, forestry and fishing as well as information and communication, reflecting the country's efforts to boost foreign investment in recent years. Malaysia was the top FDI destination among the 10 ASEAN members for mining and quarrying.

As seen in Table 4.4, competition among the ASEAN member economies for FDI seems to be intensifying, particularly in the manufacturing sector, highlighting the importance of

Table 4.3: FDI Inflows into ASEAN Member States by Source Economies in Million US Dollars, 2000–2014

Source Economy	Brunei	Cambodia	Indonesia	Laos	Malaysia	Myanmar	Philippines	Singapore	Thailand	Vietnam
Intra-ASEAN	454.8	2,680.0	52,206.7	769.1	18,618.2	2,634.9	407.8	34,536.5	13,885.6	12,523.6
Australia	8.9	221.4	2,743.4	57.6	1,116.0	24.3	314.1	20,776.2	886.6	458.8
Canada	113.8	45.0	646.0	0.9	447.0	55.5	7.3	4,305.3	2,073.6	607.7
China	20.6	2,068.2	4,158.1	1,047.6	417.2	4,720.9	38.0	22,172.0	3,264.9	2,446.9
European Union	8,730.4	672.2	8,457.4	138.1	21,170.0	2,439.5	–462.5	141,912.0	9,655.0	8,954.3
India	9.6	59.0	–352.5	4.6	3.6	70.5	–2.1	13,712.3	118.5	161.3
Japan	886.2	247.3	30,526.1	70.3	13,509.1	139.8	3,556.8	19,585.6	38,064.2	11,802.0
New Zealand	129.9	1.6	18.9	0.3	449.9	0.0	–4.0	489.6	42.9	26.8
Pakistan	0.3	0.0	0.1	0.0	5.3	0.0	–0.1	95.0	4.9	0.5
South Korea	38.1	1,171.2	4,302.7	89.0	1,097.1	300.7	100.5	2,866.1	1,810.3	10,992.3
Russia	0.0	64.0	–0.2	25.2	20.0	28.3	0.0	0.0	211.2	729.5
United States	74.1	212.2	3,389.1	4.5	9,354.0	275.2	6,341.8	62,425.8	9,717.6	6,262.6
Others	391.9	2,051.8	10,148.8	1,244.0	23,258.4	2,562.1	19,106.0	148,889.8	24,088.8	19,703.1

Source: Asia Competitiveness Institute based on data from ASEAN Secretariat.

Figure 4.10: Sectoral Distribution of FDI Inflows into ASEAN, 2012–2014

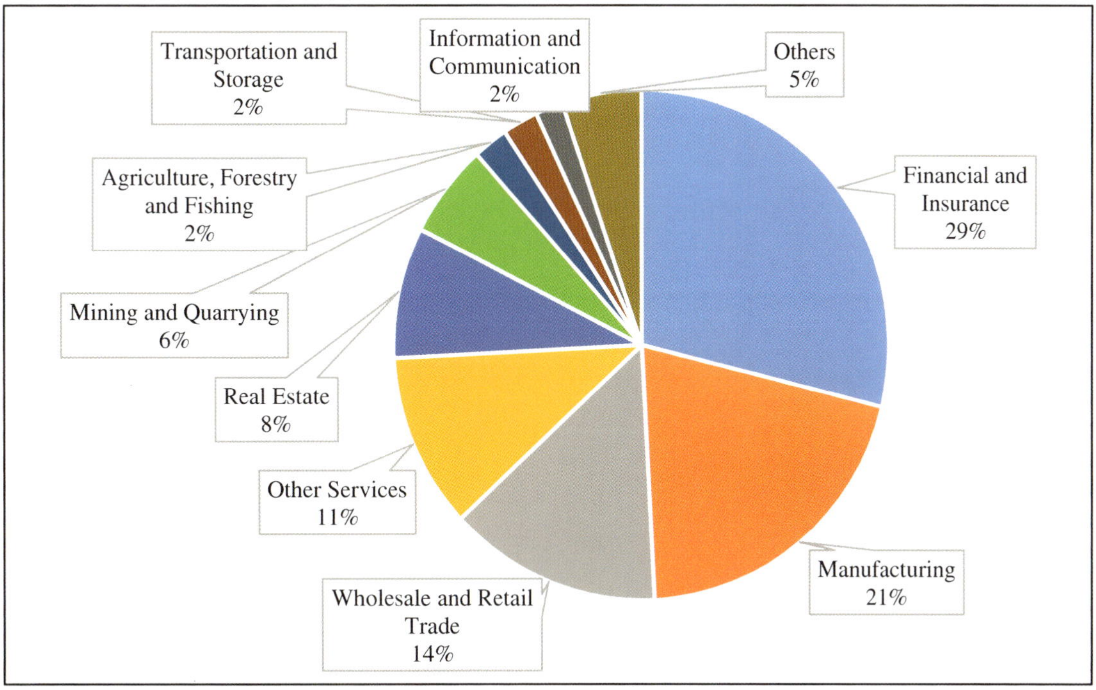

Source: Asia Competitiveness Institute based on data from ASEAN Secretariat.

cost competitiveness in attracting FDI. A case in point is Malaysia, which has not managed to overtake Singapore as a regional service centre but seems to be losing FDI in manufacturing to economies with low-cost, abundant labour such as Indonesia and Vietnam. Likewise, although Thailand was the second most attractive host for FDI in financial and insurance and real estate, it still came at a distant second to Singapore. Meanwhile, FDI inflows into manufacturing in Thailand were only the third largest in the region, after Indonesia and Vietnam.

Figure 4.11 shows the magnitude of FDI inflows to the 10 ASEAN economies as a proportion of their GDP relative to ASEAN average in 1990, 2000 and 2014. With the exceptions of Brunei, Malaysia and Myanmar, FDI inflows as a share of GDP generally went up over the period 1990–2014. Notable increases can be observed for Cambodia and Laos, whose shares of FDI inflows as a percent of GDP more than doubled from over 4 and 2 percent to about 11 and 6 percent, respectively, between 2000 and 2014. Correspondingly, Cambodia's and Laos' FDI inflows as a share of GDP exceeded the regional average in 2014. The contribution of FDI inflows to GDP has also increased for Indonesia, Vietnam and, to a lesser extent, Philippines during 1990–2014. Singapore, the region's most open economy, also saw a remarkable increase in FDI inflows as a proportion of GDP from about 14 percent in 1990 to over 16 percent in 2000 and to about 22 percent in 2014.

Table 4.4: FDI Inflows into ASEAN Member States in Million US Dollars by Sector, 2012–2014

Sector	Brunei	Cambodia	Indonesia	Laos	Malaysia	Myanmar	Philippines	Singapore	Thailand	Vietnam
Financial and Insurance	174.0	959.0	3,051.4	52.7	5,664.7	0.0	982.0	87,620.7	8,294.7	4.6
Manufacturing	164.9	1,535.2	25,222.8	39.7	9,542.7	672.5	1,458.2	3,257.4	13,525.3	19,372.5
Wholesale and Retail Trade	137.5	0.0	4,292.1	24.0	2,103.3	0.0	214.7	44,666.4	–1,072.9	790.5
Other Services	0.0	0.0	0.0	0.0	47.2	0.0	171.9	0.0	12.4	57.2
Real Estate	0.0	18.8	3,037.1	8.8	2,041.3	73.8	387.8	18,705.5	3,935.2	2,598.9
Mining and Quarrying	1,587.7	17.4	6,849.0	116.1	10,468.5	2,720.0	237.0	0.0	–225.6	163.8
Agriculture, Forestry and Fishing	0.0	895.7	6,834.2	3.8	571.0	87.3	22.3	0.0	24.8	144.1
Transportation and Storage	10.1	0.0	2,362.3	0.5	292.1	818.9	101.9	4,580.7	179.2	209.2
Information and Communication	–3.1	0.0	5,020.3	0.3	739.7	0.0	38.0	0.0	729.1	270.3

Source: Asia Competitiveness Institute based on data from ASEAN Secretariat.

Figure 4.11: FDI Inflows as a Share of GDP among ASEAN Member States in 1990, 2000 and 2014

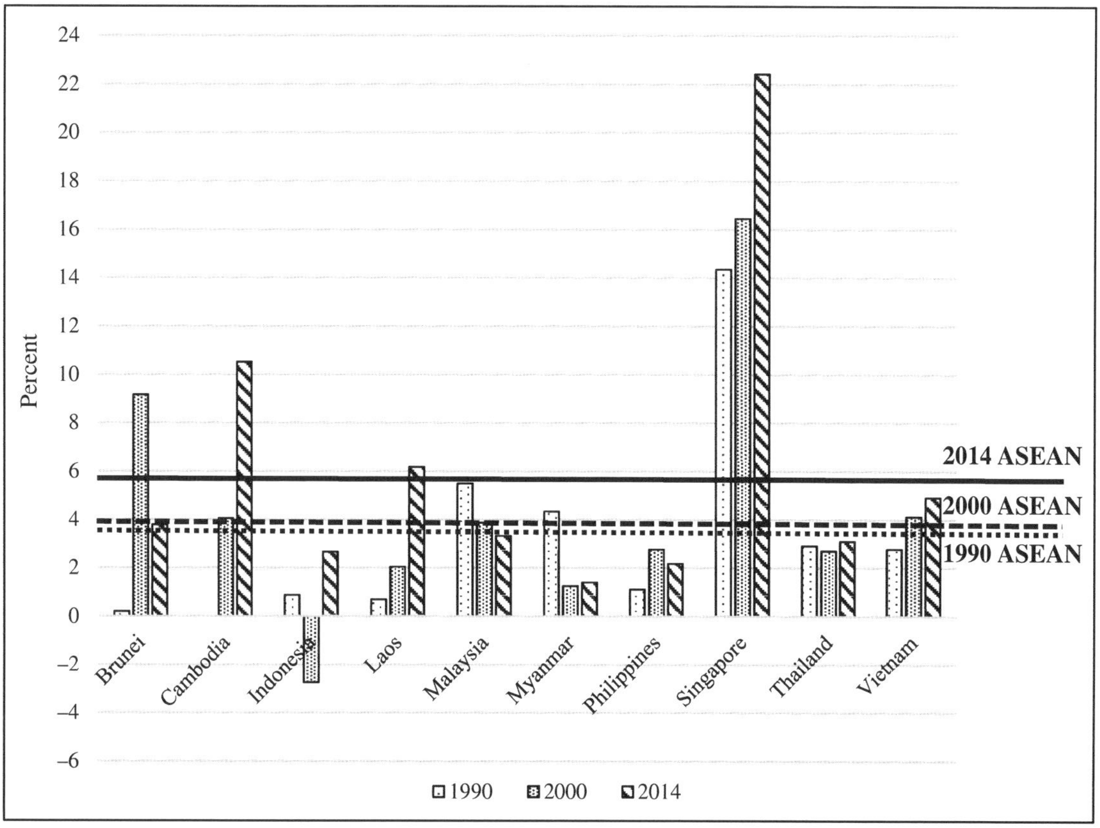

Source: ACI based on data from UNCTAD.

As a final exercise, we check if larger national output is associated with greater FDI inflows by comparing FDI inflows into individual ASEAN member states with their respective GDP during the four periods 1990–2014, 1990 to the AFC (1998), the AFC to the GFC (1999–2008) and after the GFC (2009–2014). The results are presented in Table 4.5. We find a strong positive correlation between GDP and FDI for the majority of ASEAN economies, except for Brunei and Myanmar, with Cambodia demonstrating the highest correlation throughout the period of 1990–2014 (0.98), followed by Indonesia (0.94) and Singapore (0.92). However, following the GFC Brunei seems to step up its efforts in attracting FDI as evident in the high correlation between its output and FDI inflows (0.94) during 2009–2014. In contrast, Myanmar, Thailand and, to a lesser extent, Vietnam show a weaker correlation between FDI inflows and GDP in the aftermath of the GFC.

Our analysis shows that there exists significant unevenness for FDI inflows across different economies in ASEAN. This asymmetry can be attributed to the existing disparities in a host of developmental, structural and institutional factors across ASEAN economies. Before we proceed

Table 4.5: Bivariate Correlation between FDI and GDP for ASEAN Member States, 1990–2014

Period	Brunei	Cambodia	Indonesia	Laos	Malaysia	Myanmar	Philippines	Singapore	Thailand	Vietnam
1990–2014	0.09	0.98	0.94	0.91	0.78	0.30	0.72	0.92	0.66	0.91
1990–1998	0.81	0.89	0.96	0.92	0.76	0.58	0.73	0.82	−0.20	0.91
1999–2008	−0.36	0.93	0.89	0.86	0.83	0.05	0.51	0.51	0.84	0.92
2009–2014	0.94	0.88	0.96	0.86	0.86	−0.34	0.77	0.90	0.62	0.89

Source: Asia Competitiveness Institute based on data from UNCTAD.

to outlining our empirical model, we offer an overview of the existing theoretical and empirical literature in Section 4.3.

4.3 Literature Review

In this section, the discussion proceeds in two parts. The first part will summarise the existing theories and the general literature on the nexus between REER and FDI inflows. The second part will discuss the literature specific to ASEAN economies and focus on the determinants of FDI and its association with exchange rates.

4.3.1 General Empirical Literature

How do movements in REER (levels and volatility) affect FDI inflows? Both the theoretical and empirical literature are ambiguous. However, the literature points to some directions as to what to expect from the nexus between exchange rate movements both in their levels and volatility and FDI inflows.

The literature posits that the exchange rate effects operate broadly through the valuation channel which can affect FDI inflows through three specific ways. At the outset, it must be clarified that we expect to see a positive relationship between the depreciation of the host country's currency and its FDI inflows.[8] This can come about in three specific ways operating through the valuation channel, as discussed below.

The first is through wealth effects. When there is depreciation of the host country's currency, it makes its assets cheap and can in turn encourage FDI inflows.[9]

Second is what can be termed as demand effects. When there is depreciation of the host country's currency, it makes it less attractive to repatriate profits to the home country, which in turn leads to higher reinvestment of retained earnings in the host country. Hence a positive effect of depreciation is observed as it triggers more inflows of FDI.[10]

The third effect relates to cost competitiveness. There is a subtle difference observed in the literature with respect to the cost competitiveness effects of exchange rate movements on FDI

[8] See Froot and Stein (1991), Goldberg and Klein (1998) as well as Blonigen (1997).

[9] See Chakrabarti and Scholnick (2002).

[10] See Goldberg and Klein (1998).

inflows, which to a large extent depend on the nature of FDI inflows. In other words, if FDI inflows are export-promoting in nature, then a REER depreciation induces FDI as firms using the host country as an export platform experience lowering of export costs; conversely, if FDI is domestic-market oriented/commodity seeking, REER depreciation induces FDI because of wealth effects. However, the caveat is that if the country is part of a supply chain and has low value-add, changes in REER levels might not have a significant effect although REER volatility might.

While the above effects hold in general, there are some important caveats regarding exchange rate expectations which can actually confound the positive impacts of a host country depreciation. If there are strong expectations of sustained and further depreciation in the host country's currency, it can hold back further FDI to that country. Further, expectations of depreciation of the host country's currency can also reduce repatriation of retained earnings. Finally, if further depreciation in the host country's currency is expected in future, then based on Uncovered Interest Parity (UIP), the interest rates in that country will go up, and therefore cost of credit will go up, leading to a reduction in FDI into that country.

Besides the influence of REER levels on FDI, volatility of REER matters too for FDI, and there is a large strand of both theoretical and empirical literature that examines this relationship. At the risk of simplifying a complex strand of literature, there are two possible conflicting effects that the literature points to when examining the impact of exchange rate volatility on FDI inflows. Higher REER volatility can induce FDI inflows into a country if FDI is export substituting in nature. This implies that an increase in REER volatility between the firms' home country and the host country could motivate the firm to serve the host country through a local production facility rather than exports, which to a reasonable degree will insulate it against the risk of uncertainties imposed by exchange rate volatility. Empirically, some notable papers such as Cushman (1988), Stokman and Vlar (1996), De MÈnil *et al.* (1999), Pain and Van Welsum (2003) find a significantly positive relationship between REER volatility and FDI inflows in the host country.

On the other hand, another body of literature also suggests that higher exchange rate volatility can deter firms from moving to the host country because of risk aversion reasons. To be sure, a firm planning to undertake an investment in a country that is prone to greater exchange rate fluctuations might imply a riskier stream of profits. This, coupled with the sunk costs involved in the investment activity would encourage the firm to place on hold its investment rather than undertake it.[11] In other words, as summarised by Goldberg (2009), considering that exchange rate volatility introduces additional risks to the return on a firm's investment, the expected values of its investment projects are reduced, which deters FDI accordingly. This hypothesis is also supported empirically by studies such as Darby *et al.* (1999), Byrne and Philip (2003), Bénassy-Quéré *et al.* (2001).

Similar to the case of movements of REER (in levels), one of the key points to be noted from the related literature is that the relationship between REER volatility and FDI inflows depends on the nature of FDI inflows. If FDI is horizontal or domestic-market oriented in nature, an increase in REER volatility could induce FDI because costs of exporting become high, which

---

[11] See, for instance, the discussion in Goldberg (2009) and Foad (2005).

leads firms to serve the domestic market by establishing a base in the host country. The intuition, as alluded to earlier, is that the firm attempts to establish an early base in the country in order to avoid dealing with exchange rate risks since they already know that they are going to serve the specific host country market. However, if the nature of FDI is vertical or export-oriented, we expect to see a negative relationship between REER volatility and FDI, *viz.* an increase in REER volatility is likely to deter FDI, for the risk aversion reasons elaborated earlier.

Overall, the current state of knowledge is that REER both in terms of levels and volatility may have an ambiguous impact on FDI. The lack of consensus might be partly due to the heterogeneity of the studies, reflecting the complex nature of FDI itself.

4.3.2 Empirical Literature on ASEAN Economies

As noted earlier briefly, most empirical literature on FDI and exchange rates relating to ASEAN economies cover only a subset of them, clustered often around ASEAN-5 (Indonesia, Singapore, Malaysia, Philippines, and Thailand) or include them as part of a larger panel of East Asian or developing economies. For instance, Bayoumi and Lipworth (1997), Sazanami *et al.* (2003) and Goldberg and Klein (1998) are some papers that examine the relationship between bilateral real exchange rate (RER) and Japanese FDI inflows. While the first two include all ASEAN-5 economies in their analysis, Goldberg and Klein (1998) exclude Singapore. Kiyota and Urata (2004) for example include all ASEAN economies (except Laos) and investigate the relationship between RER and Japanese FDI. The general consensus from these papers appear to be that a RER appreciation is significantly and negatively associated with FDI inflows into these economies. In addition, there are also a few country papers like Pham and Nguyen (2013) who focus on Vietnam specifically and find that a 1 percent depreciation of the Vietnamese Dong (VND) leads to an increase of about 0.2 percent in FDI inflows.

There are fewer studies which explicitly focus on the impact of exchange rate volatility on FDI inflows in the context of ASEAN, and even those handful of studies offer conflicting results. Kiyota and Urata (2004) and Udomkerdmongkol *et al.* (2009) for instance argue that increased exchange rate volatility deters FDI. Gottschalk and Hall (2008) on the other hand found that an increase in volatility in bilateral dollar exchange rates is positively associated with US FDI, but negatively associated with Japanese FDI into ASEAN-4 (Indonesia, Malaysia, Philippines, and Thailand). Dhakal *et al.* (2010) established that increased exchange rate volatility is favourable to FDI inflows into ASEAN-4.

To sum up, we can say that while there is some consensus in literature on the relationship between REER and FDI inflows to ASEAN, the impact of REER volatility remains ambiguous. If we consider the broader literature on determinants of FDI inflows into ASEAN, only two studies, namely Hsieh and Hong (2005) as well as Nwosu *et al.* (2013), include exchange rates as a possible determinant in their empirical model, although the results are insignificant. This discussion clearly points to a gap in the existing literature about understanding the importance of exchange rates on FDI inflows in a panel context. In this light, this chapter attempts to make a modest contribution to the existing literature by estimating a fixed-effects model to examine the impact of both REER levels and volatility on FDI inflows to ASEAN. A summary of the literature review is provided in Table 4.6.

Table 4.6: Overview of Literature

Citation	Topic	Countries Covered	Period of Study	Methodology	Dependent Variable(s)	Independent Variable(s)	Findings
Bayoumi, T. and G. Lipworth. 1997. "Japanese Foreign Direct Investment and Regional Trade." IMF Working Paper WP/97/103, International Monetary Fund, Washington DC.	Relationship between real bilateral exchange rates and Japanese FDI	21 countries (US, Canada, Australia, France, Germany, Italy, Netherlands, Belgium, New Zealand, Spain, UK, Hong Kong, Taiwan, Korea, India, Mexico, Malaysia, Philippines, Singapore, Thailand, Indonesia)	1982–1995	Fixed-effects model (logarithmic form)	Real FDI outflows from Japan to 20 of her major trading partners	1. Real bilateral exchange rates; 2. Real investment in Japan; 3. Real investment in the recipient country; 4. One-year lagged real investment in Japan; 5. One-year lagged real investment in the recipient country; 6. One-year lagged FDI stock	1. The main driving forces for Japanese FDI are domestic conditions and exchange rate, but the distribution of FDI has reflected the investment climate of recipient countries. After one year, a depreciation of the local currency by 6 percent would generate around a 10-percent increase in FDI.
Goldberg, L.S. and M.W. Klein. 1997. "Foreign Direct Investment, Trade and Real Exchange Rate Linkages in Southeast Asia and Latin America."	Relationship between real bilateral exchange rates and Japanese and US FDI	7 developing countries in Southeast Asia (Indonesia, Malaysia, Philippines, Thailand) and Latin America (Argentina, Brazil, Chile)	1978–1993 or 1994 (depending upon the country)	Fixed-effects model (logarithmic form)	Real direct investment from either the United States or Japan	1. Real bilateral exchange rates between the host country's currency and US dollar; 2. Real bilateral exchange rates between the host country's currency and Japanese yen; 3. GDP of the source country;	1. When the developing countries' currencies depreciate with respect to the yen, there is a corresponding increase in direct investment from Japan; 2. A 1-percent depreciation with respect to the yen causes an increase in direct investment from Japan to the Southeast Asian countries of 3 percent.

(Continued)

Table 4.6: (*Continued*)

Citation	Topic	Countries Covered	Period of Study	Methodology	Dependent Variable(s)	Independent Variable(s)	Findings
NBER Working Paper 6344, National Bureau of Economic Research, Cambridge.						4. One-year lagged GDP of the source country; 5. One-year lagged GDP of the host country; 6. One-year lagged bilateral real exchange rates with respect to both yen and US dollar	However, the effect is highly statistically significant only when one also controls for the exchange rate movements of the developing country currency relative to the US dollar; 3. In general, real exchange rates have the most significant effect on FDI for Southeast Asia. A real depreciation of the currencies of the Southeast Asian countries with respect to the yen both increases FDI from Japan and decreases FDI from the US.
Baek, I. and T. Okawa. 2001. "Foreign exchange rates and Japanese foreign direct investment in Asia." *Journal of Economics and Business* 53: 69–84.	Relationship between nominal exchange rates and Japanese FDI	6 countries (South Korea, Hong Kong, Singapore, Malaysia, Indonesia, Thailand)	1983–1992	Pooled OLS	Japanese FDI in each country for each sector (8 sectors) in dollars	1. Log of nominal exchange rate of the yen per dollar; 2. Log of nominal exchange rate of host country's currency per dollar; 3. Labour input in host country; 4. Labour input in Japan; 5. Wage rate in Japan; 6. Wage rate in host country; 7. Import tariff	1. An appreciation of the yen against the dollar or against the Asian currencies significantly increases FDI (at 1 percent level). The results for the aggregate manufacturing sector are generally consistent with those for individual sectors; 2. Nominal exchange rates of the Asian currencies per dollar do not significantly affect FDI,

							suggesting that a depreciation of those countries' currencies against the dollar does not induce Japanese FDI in manufacturing unless it results in a depreciation of the currencies against the yen. However, they have a significant impact in chemical and electrical machinery sectors.
Sazanami, Y., S. Yoshimura and K. Kiyota. 2003. "Japanese Foreign Direct Investment to East Asia and Exchange Rate Policies: Some Longer Term Policy Implications after the Crisis." *Keio Economic Studies* 40 (1): 1–26.	Relationship between real bilateral exchange rates and Japanese FDI	8 countries (Hong Kong, Korea, Taiwan, Indonesia, Malaysia, Philippines, Singapore, Thailand)	1978–2000	Feasible generalised least square estimation method	Log of ratio of real FDI outflows from Japan to respective East Asian countries to host country's real GDP	1. Log of real exchange rate of East Asian currencies against the yen; 2. Log of relative labour cost between Japan and East Asian countries; 3. Agglomeration effect in East Asia (One-year lagged cumulative Japan's FDI to host country scaled by host country's GDP, log form); 4. Dummy capturing the effect of the Asian	1. Coefficients of RER are negative and statistically significant at 1 percent level, implying that the decline in the RER attracts Japanese FDI to East Asia; 2. The ASEAN-4 plus Singapore dummy gave better results than the ASEAN-4 dummy. The ASEAN-4 plus Singapore dummy is positive and statistically significant at 1–5 percent level in total FDI and in chemical, precision and electrical machinery industries. ASEAN-4 dummy is statistically significant in textile industry at a

(Continued)

Table 4.6: (Continued)

Citation	Topic	Countries Covered	Period of Study	Methodology	Dependent Variable(s)	Independent Variable(s)	Findings
						Financial Crisis (1 after 1997, 0 otherwise); 5. ASEAN-4 dummy; 6. ASEAN-4 plus Singapore dummy	5 percent level, but is statistically significant only at a 10 percent level in wood and pulp, precision machinery, transportation machinery; 3. Asian Financial Crisis dummy is not statistically significant for total FDI and most industries.
Kiyota, K. and S. Urata. 2004. "Exchange Rate, Exchange Rate Volatility and Foreign Direct Investment." *World Economy* 27 (10): 1501–1536.	Relationship between real exchange rate and exchange rate volatility and Japanese FDI	127 countries (including 9 ASEAN countries — Brunei, Cambodia, Indonesia, Malaysia, Myanmar, Philippines, Singapore, Thailand, Vietnam)	1990–2000	Feasible generalised least square estimation method	Log of ratio of FDI from Japan to country I as a proportion of country i's GDP	1. Log of real exchange rate; 2. Unexplained part of real exchange rate volatility (defined as the deviation of the actual value from the value explained by the failure of the law of one price). Real exchange rate volatility is the variance of the changes in the real exchange rate. Explained parts of real exchange rate volatility are fitted values obtained from a gravity equation; 3. Time trend	A depreciation of the host country currency attracts FDI. Large volatility in exchange rates discourages FDI. Overvaluation of the currency discourages FDI. A flexible but stable exchange rate system is needed to successfully attract FDI.

Xing, Y. and G. Wan. 2006. "Exchange Rates and Competition for FDI in Asia." *World Economy* 29 (4): 419–434.	Relationship between real exchange rate and relative Japanese FDI to ASEAN-4 versus to China	China and ASEAN-4 (Indonesia, Malaysia, Philippines, Thailand)	1981–2002	Fixed-effects model (logarithmic form)	Relative Japanese FDI into one of ASEAN-4 compared to that into China (ratio of FDI flow into an ASEAN-4 country versus the FDI flow into China)	1. Relative yen exchange rates of the Chinese yuan and ASEAN-4's currencies; 2. Relative market size (GDP of ASEAN-4/GDP of China); 3. Difference in GDP growth rates; 4. Relative trade openness between ASEAN-4 country and China	1. RER is found to be negative and statistically significant, implying that appreciation of currency would discourage FDI.
Gottschalk, S. and S. Hall. 2008. "Foreign Direct Investment and Exchange Rate Uncertainty in South-east Asia." *International Journal of Finance and Economics* 13: 349–359.	Relationship between exchange rate volatility and Japanese and US FDI	4 countries (Indonesia, Malaysia, Philippines, Thailand)	1982–2001	Arrellano–Bond method for dynamic panel	Difference of log of real US or Japanese FDI stock in country *i*	1. Real rate of return reported by affiliates in location *i* ; 2. GARCH estimate of the variance of exchange rate in location *i* ; 3. GARCH estimate of the correlation between the exchange rate in location *i* and the	1. An increase in the local rate of return has a positive impact on FDI from the US and Japan. In addition, the positive coefficient of the yen/dollar volatility indicates that a rise in the volatility of the yen results in an increase in both outward US and outward Japanese FDI; 2. There is significant evidence that an increase in the volatility of

(Continued)

Table 4.6: (*Continued*)

Citation	Topic	Countries Covered	Period of Study	Methodology	Dependent Variable(s)	Independent Variable(s)	Findings
						exchange rate in location *j*; 4. Variance of the Japanese exchange rate; 5. Correlation of the dollar exchange rate of location *i* with the yen/dollar	bilateral dollar exchange rates would probably make the ASEAN-4 more attractive for outward US investment but not for Japanese outward investment. The coefficient of this variable is positive in the estimation of US FDI and negative in the estimation of Japanese FDI. This may suggest that US FDI has a longer maturity than Japanese FDI; 3. Only the correlation of the ASEAN-4 exchange rates with the Indonesian ringgit and with the Japanese yen matters for US FDI. The more correlated these are in absolute terms, the more the US investors are attracted by the region.
Udomk-erdmongkol, M., O. Morrisey and H. Gorg. 2009. "Exchange Rates and Outward Foreign Direct Investment:	Relationship between real exchange rate and US FDI	16 emerging market economies (Bolivia, Chile, Colombia, Costa Rica, Dominican Republic, Paraguay, Uruguay, Venezuela,	1990–2002	Fixed-effects model	Real US FDI inflows to country *i*	1. Change in log of real effective exchange rate index; 2. Log of real bilateral exchange rates; 3. Log of the temporary component of bilateral	1. A current devaluation (appreciate on) increases (decreases) FDI inflows in that year; 2. Foreign investors will postpone FDI if they expect local currency depreciation but may bring forward FDI if they expect an appreciation; 3. Exchange rate

US FDI in Emerging Economies." *Review of Development Economics* 13 (4): 754–764.		Morocco, South Africa, Tunisia, China, Pakistan, Malaysia, Philippines, Thailand)				exchange rates; 4. Manufacturing as a share of GDP; 5. Inflation; 6. Exports as a share of GDP; 7. GDP per capita; 8. Portfolio investment adjusted by GDP; 9. Number of telephone mainlines; 10. Real GDP growth; 11. Asia dummy	volatility discourages FDI inflows; 4. An expected devaluation has a much greater deterrent effect on FDI for Asia than for Latin America as expected devaluation in Asia implies abandoning the peg to the US dollar.
Dhakal, D., R. Nag, G. Pradhan, K.P. Upadhyaya. 2010. "Exchange Rate Volatility and Foreign Direct Investment: Evidence from East Asian Countries." *International Business & Economics Research* 9 (7): 121–128.	Relationship between real exchange rate and exchange rate volatility and FDI inflows	6 countries (China, Indonesia, Malaysia, Philippines, South Korea, Thailand)	China (1982–2005), Indonesia (1981–2005), Malaysia (1974–2005), Philippines (1977–2005), South Korea (1976–2005), Thailand (1975–2005).	Error Correction Model (ECM)	FDI inflow to country *i*	1. Current account balance in country *i*; 2. Openness in country *i* (sum of export and import divided by GDP); 3. Real exchange rate with US dollar of country *i*	Exchange rate volatility has a favourable effect on FDI. These countries have continued to attract considerable FDI inflows while also experiencing a great deal of volatility in exchange rates.

(Continued)

Table 4.6: (*Continued*)

Citation	Topic	Countries Covered	Period of Study	Methodology	Dependent Variable(s)	Independent Variable(s)	Findings
Pham, T.H.H. and T.D. Nguyen. 2013. "Foreign Direct Investment, Exports and Real Exchange Rate Linkages in Vietnam: Evidence from a Co-Integration Approach." *Journal of Southeast Asian Economies* 30 (3): 250–262.	Relationship between real exchange rate and FDI inflows	Vietnam	1994–2010	Panel cointegration and Instrumental Variables (IV) analysis	Real FDI flows into Vietnam from country *i*	1. Real bilateral exchange rate between the VND and the foreign currency; 2. Real exports from Vietnam to FDI source countries	A 1-percent real depreciation of the VND leads to an increase of 0.172 percent in inward FDI flows.
Lily, Jaratin, Mori Kogid, Dullah Mulok, and Rozilee Asid. 2014. "Exchange Rate Movement and Foreign Direct Investment in ASEAN Economies." *Economics Research International* 2014: 1–10.	Relationship between real exchange rate and FDI inflows	4 countries (Singapore, Malaysia, Philippines, Thailand)	1971–2011	Error Correction Model (ECM)-based Auto-regressive Distributed Lag (ARDL) model	Real FDI inflows	Real exchange rate between the local currency and US dollar	1. There are long-run cointegration relationships between FDI and the exchange rate for Malaysia, Philippines and Singapore, but none in Thailand; 2. Singapore and Philippines show long-run bidirectional causality between exchange rate and FDI. Long-run unidirectional causality running from exchange rate to FDI exists in Malaysia.

							Short-term unidirectional running from exchange rate to FDI exists in Singapore; 3. Since this study refers to the foreign exchange rate as the number of home currency units per foreign currency, the negative relationship implies that the appreciation (a fall in the exchange rate) of the local currency has a positive impact on FDI inflows.
Koojaroenprasit, S. 2015. "Determinants of Foreign Direct Investment in AEC Countries." *International Journal of Economic Research* 12 (1): 113–120.	Determinants of FDI inflows	Indonesia, Malaysia, Philippines, Singapore, Thailand, Vietnam	1997–2012	Random-effects model	FDI inflows	1. GDP per capita in host country (market size); 2. Real wage; 3. Trade openness; 4. Inflation rate; 5. Exchange rate of host country's currency against US Dollar; 6. Corporate tax rate;	The coefficient of market size and corporate tax rate are positive and significant at 1 percent. R&D is positive and significant at 5 percent. Real wage is negative and significant at 5 percent. Trade openness is negative and significant at 10 percent. Inflation (negative), exchange rate (positive), infrastructure (positive)

(*Continued*)

Table 4.6: (*Continued*)

Citation	Topic	Countries Covered	Period of Study	Methodology	Dependent Variable(s)	Independent Variable(s)	Findings
						7. Telephone lines user per 100 people; 8. High-technology exports R&D; 9. Dummy variables for Asian Financial Crisis 1997–1998 and global financial crisis 2007–2008	and financial crises (positive) are not significant.
Hoang, H.H. and D.H. Bui. 2015. "Determinants of Foreign Direct Investment in ASEAN: A Panel Approach." *Management Science Letters* 5: 213–222.	Determinants of FDI inflows	Indonesia, Malaysia, Philippines, Singapore, Thailand, Vietnam	1991–2009	Random-effects model	FDI inflows	1. Market size of host country (GDP); 2. Exchange rate of host country's currency against US dollar; 3. Real interest rate; 4. General index of political risk; 5. Skilled labour to number of employees; 6. Monthly average wage in the manufacturing sector; 7. Productivity (GDP per employee); 8. Control of corruption	Market size (+), trade openness (+), the quality of the infrastructure (+) are macroeconomic factors that have a positive impact on FDI inflows. Exchange rate (+) and real interest rate (–) have a significant impact on FDI inflows. However, inflation rate (–) and financial development (+) have no statistically significant impact on FDI inflows. Finally, political risk (+) and institutional quality (+) strongly influence FDI inflows in the region. Nominal labour cost, human capital, labour productivity are positive and statistically significant.

						index; 9. Trade openness; 10. Inflation rate; 11. Telephone and mobile phone users per 100 people; 12. Domestic credit provided by banking sector (percent of GDP)	
Xaypanya, P., P. Rangkakulnuwat and S.W. Paweenawat. 2015. "The Determinants of Foreign Direct Investment in ASEAN: The First Differencing Panel Data Analysis." *International Journal of Social Economics* 42 (3): 239–250.	Determinants of FDI inflows	ASEAN-5 (Indonesia, Malaysia, Philippines, Singapore, Thailand) and ASEAN-3 (Cambodia, Laos, Vietnam)	2000–2011	First differencing pooled OLS	FDI inflows	1. Real exchange rate (RER); 2. Inflation rate; 3. GDP of host country; 4. Number of telephone lines; 5. Trade openness; 6. Official development assistance (ODA) (for ASEAN-3)	For ASEAN-3: RER is negative and insignificant, inflation rate is negative and significant at 5 percent, GDP is positive but insignificant, telephone lines are positive and significant at 1 percent, trade openness is positive and significant at 1 percent, ODA is negative and insignificant. For ASEAN-5: RER is positive and insignificant, inflation rate is positive and significant at 5 percent, GDP is positive and significant at

(Continued)

Table 4.6: (*Continued*)

Citation	Topic	Countries Covered	Period of Study	Methodology	Dependent Variable(s)	Independent Variable(s)	Findings
							1 percent, telephone lines are positive and significant at 10 percent, trade openness is negative and significant at 1 percent.
Nwosu, E.O., A. Orji, N. Urama, J.I. Amuka. 2013. "Regional Integration and Foreign Investment: The Case of ASEAN Countries." *Asian Economic and Financial Review* 3 (12): 1670–1680.	Determinants of FDI inflows	ASEAN-10	Not stated	Fixed- and random-effects model	1. Intra-ASEAN FDI inflows; 2. Inter-ASEAN FDI inflows	1. Market size (GDP); 2. Exchange rate; 3. Inflation rate; 4. Lagged log of FDI from rest of world (when independent variable is intra-ASEAN FDI); 5. Lagged log of intra-ASEAN FDI (when independent variable is inter-ASEAN FDI)	Random Effects: Market size is statistically significant for both intra- and extra-ASEAN FDI, implying that both intra- and extra-ASEAN FDI are market-seeking. Exchange rate behaviour in ASEAN has a statistically significant and negative effect on extra-ASEAN FDI, while its effect on intra-ASEAN FDI is negative but not significant. Inflation is negative but statistically insignificant for extra-ASEAN FDI. Inflation is positive and statistically significant for intra-ASEAN FDI. Fixed Effects: Exchange rate is negative and significant for intra-ASEAN FDI, but negative and insignificant for extra-ASEAN FDI. Market size is positive and

							significant for extra-ASEAN FDI, but positive and insignificant for intra-ASEAN FDI. Inflation is positive and significant for intra-ASEAN FDI, and negative and insignificant for extra-ASEAN FDI.
Hattari, R., R.S. Rajan and S. Thangavelu. 2008. "Understanding Intra-ASEAN FDI Inflows: Trends, Determinants and The Role of China and India." Unpublished paper.	Determinants of FDI inflows	China, India, Malaysia, Philippines, Singapore, Thailand	1990–2005	Gravity model	Bilateral FDI flows (Ln (1+FDI))	1. Nominal GDP of host country and source country; 2. Common language; 3. Distance between host and source country's capitals; 4. Difference in GDP per capita of the host and source countries; 5. Lagged exports from source country to host country; 6. Volatility of exchange rate of source country with respect to host country;	We considered 3 specifications: without the control variables (regression 1), with the control variables (regression 2), regression 2 without lagged export (regression 3). In 3 specifications, market sizes remain statistically and economically significant. Common language and distance only stay statistically significant with correct sign in regression (1). They, however, turned statistically insignificant when we included the control variables but remain with correct signs. Intra-ASEAN dummy is positive and statistically

(Continued)

Table 4.6: (*Continued*)

Citation	Topic	Countries Covered	Period of Study	Methodology	Dependent Variable(s)	Independent Variable(s)	Findings
						7. Host country's political risk index; 8. Average corporate tax rates in host country; 9. ASEAN dummy (1 if the bilateral FDI flows are between ASEAN countries); 10. Free trade agreement dummy	significant in all 3 specifications. It indicates that when we control distance, common language, and control variables on average an ASEAN country would directly invest 1.2 million dollars more to another ASEAN country. The difference in GDP per capita between host and source countries is negative, implying that the lower the degree of income divergence between the countries, the more likely there is to be bilateral FDI flows between the countries. The coefficients of exchange rate values and volatility are both positive but are not statistically significant. Similar to any other investors, ASEAN countries takes into the account the political

							risk of their neighbours when they are directly investing as indicated in political risk results of positive sign and statistically significant. FTA dummy is positive in regression 2 but is statistically insignificant. Corporate tax rate has a negative sign and is statistically significant though weakly economically significant. Lagged exports from source to host economy show up with a positive sign but are not statistically significant.
Ismail, N.W. 2009. "The Determinant of Foreign Direct Investment in ASEAN: A Semi-Gravity Approach." *Transition Studies Review* 16 (3): 710–722.	Determinants of FDI inflows	ASEAN-9 (Cambodia excluded)	1995–2003	Semi-gravity model	Bilateral FDI flows (Ln(1+FDI))	1. GDP of source country and host country; 2. Distance as a proxy for transportation cost; 3. Common border; 4. Common language; 5. Regional market size;	Both source and host country's GDP are positive and statistically significant. Distance and border are both negatively significant. Language dummy is positive and statistically significant. The coefficient of extended market for host country which includes

(Continued)

Table 4.6: (*Continued*)

Citation	Topic	Countries Covered	Period of Study	Methodology	Dependent Variable(s)	Independent Variable(s)	Findings
						6. Extended market for host country (economies belonging to the same free trade area); 7. Capital labour ratio; 8. Absolute difference of GDP per capita; 9. Real exchange rate, 10. Real interest rate; 11. Inflation rate; 12. Openness; 13. Government budget balance; 14. Infrastructure; 15. Skilled labour availability	economies belonging to the same free trade area is positive but insignificant. The estimation includes a time effect dummy which is highly significant. The measure of regional market for the host country, weighted with relative inverse distance, is positive and significant which implies that the regional market in ASEAN is still important factor for attracting foreign investors. Regarding two variables that are related to factor endowment, absolute difference in income per capita and the ratio of capital and labour are both positive and highly statistically significant. The coefficient of the real exchange rate is positive and significant at the 90 percent significance level. This result suggests that a depreciation/devaluation of the host currency stimulates more investment to the country since it

							induces a reduction in local production costs in term of foreign currency. The coefficient of inflation is negative and statistically significant. The coefficient of the real interest rate is negative but insignificant. The coefficient of the government budget balance is positive and statistically significant.
Hsieh, W.J. and M.C. Hong. 2005. "The Determinants of Foreign Direct Investment in Southeast Asian Transition Economies." In *Proceedings of the Eighth Conference on Cross-Strait Chinese Culture and Management*, Sichuan University, China.	Determinants of FDI inflows	Cambodia, Vietnam, Laos, Myanmar	1990–2001	Fixed-effects model	FDI inflows	1. One-period lagged FDI inflows; 2. One-period lagged GDP per capita; 3. One-period lagged real GDP growth rate; 4. One-period lagged trade openness; 5. One-period lagged government expenditure on education; 6. Exchange rate of host country's current against 1 US dollar;	The most important determinants are the one-period lagged FDI inflows, GDP per capita, and the degree of openness. The Asian Financial Crisis is shown to have deterred FDI inflows in these countries. Two out of three broad categories — the cost-related factors (real wage rate and exchange rate) and investment environment improving factors (government education expenditure and government budget balance as a share of GDP) — are statistically insignificant.

(*Continued*)

Table 4.6: (*Continued*)

Citation	Topic	Countries Covered	Period of Study	Methodology	Dependent Variable(s)	Independent Variable(s)	Findings
						7. Real wage rate; 8. Ratio of government budget balance to GDP; 9. Asian Financial Crisis dummy (1 for 1997–2001)	The only category found to be significant in attracting FDI is the fundamental macroeconomic factors.
Mehrens, D., B. Maniam and J. Bexley. 2002. "A Survey of Determinants of US Foreign Direct Investment in ASEAN-5 Countries." *Journal of Economics and Economic Education Research* 3 (1): 87.	Determinants of US FDI inflows	Indonesia, Malaysia, Philippines, Singapore, Thailand	1985–1999	Pooled OLS	Ratio of US FDI to host country's GDP	1. GNP per capita; 2. Host country's total exports; 3. US exports to the host country; 4. Inflation rate; 5. Exchange rate fluctuations; 6. Composite risk index (including political risk, economic risk, and financial risk); 7. Perception of corruption in the host country	Determinants included the size of the host country's economy, the host country's total exports, US exports to the host country, inflation rate, exchange rate fluctuations, composite risk index (including political risk, economic risk, and financial risk), and the perception of corruption in the host country. This model was tested using ordinary least square (OLS) regression. Overall, the model was shown to be a good predictor of US FDI in Thailand, Singapore, Malaysia, and Indonesia. However, the model was not a good indicator of US FDI in the Philippines.

Source: Compiled by the Asia Competitiveness Institute.

4.4 Data Description, Statistical Computation and Sources

For our study, we compile a panel dataset of nine ASEAN economies,[12] covering the time period from 1995 to 2014. Data on annual FDI inflows into ASEAN at the national level is reported by ASEANstats, Euromonitor, UNCTAD and the World Bank. The sources use similar definitions of FDI inflows, but they differ in terms of coverage. Figure 4.12 demonstrates that FDI data series available from different sources almost overlap each other. For the empirics, we use data from UNCTAD to calculate the annual growth rates of FDI inflows. This is because UNCTAD provides the longest and most comprehensive FDI series for all 10 ASEAN countries.

With regard to our key independent variable, REER, it is important to note that REER is available from various sources such as UNCTAD, the Bruegel Institute, Bank for International Settlements (BIS) and the International Monetary Fund (IMF). Among these sources, the IMF provides data only for Malaysia, Philippines and Singapore, while BIS data is available only for the ASEAN-5. While UNCTAD covers all 10 ASEAN economies, it only reports annual data which is not ideal as we prefer monthly data to calculate our measure of REER volatility. As

Figure 4.12: Total FDI Inflows into ASEAN Economies from Different Data Sources, 1970–2014

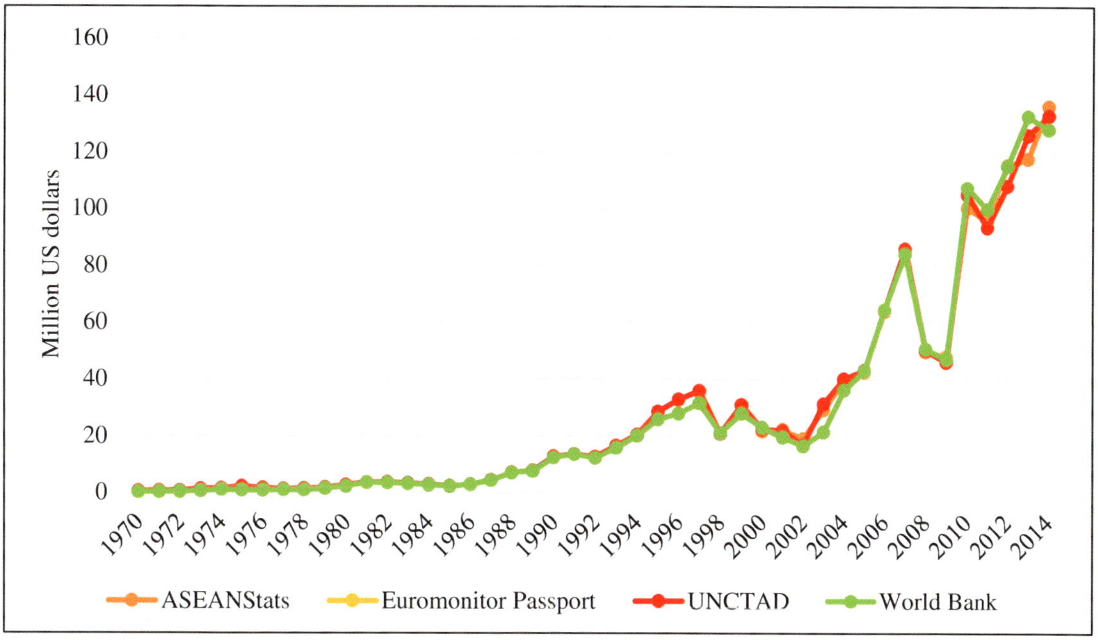

Source: ASEANstats, Euromonitor Passport, UNCTAD and World Bank World Development Indicators.

[12] There are officially 10 countries in ASEAN region, including Myanmar. However, complete data for Myanmar are not available.

Table 4.7: Pairwise Correlation between Different REER Series

Economy	UNCTAD and Bruegel Monthly 138	UNCTAD and Bruegel Monthly 41	Bruegel Monthly 138 and Bruegel Monthly 41
Brunei	0.653	0.539	0.943
Cambodia	0.960	0.965	0.998
Indonesia	0.987	0.951	0.992
Laos	0.997	0.981	0.990
Malaysia	0.835	0.782	0.979
Myanmar	N.A.	N.A.	N.A.
Philippines	0.971	0.964	0.999
Singapore	0.995	0.864	0.998
Thailand	0.990	0.990	0.789
Vietnam	0.973	0.976	0.999

Notes: We calculate annual average REER at base year 2007 using the two monthly REER series from Bruegel. We rebase UNCTAD's series to 2007 to match with Bruegel's data. We drop Myanmar from the sample because Bruegel only reports REER data for Myanmar from April 2012 onwards.
Source: Asia Competitiveness Institute based on data from UNCTAD and Bruegel.

Bruegel provides monthly data, it is most suitable for our purpose, and the series provided is a Consumer Price Index (CPI)-based REER.

As Myanmar's data is only available from April 2012 onwards, the country is dropped from the sample. In addition, Bruegel also provides an alternative REER Monthly 41 series for the period 1990–2014. We use this series for robustness check later in Section 4.7. Table 4.7 displays the pairwise correlation between the annual average REER calculated from the Bruegel's REER Monthly 138 series, the Bruegel's REER Monthly 41 series and UNCTAD's annual REER data. Clearly, the three series are highly correlated with one another; therefore, it is unlikely that the empirical results will be sensitive to the choice of REER series. Tables 4.8 and 4.9 provide a snapshot of the data caveats for FDI inflows and REER, respectively.

Table 4.10 summarises the definitions and data sources for all independent variables used in our empirics. Our priors (discussed in detail in Section 4.5) for the directions of association between these variables and the annual growth rate of FDI inflows are indicated in the first column of the table.

Table 4.11 presents a summary statistics of the variables that will be used in our empirics. It shows that average REER index is estimated to be around 104 with a variation of about 5 when measured by between standard deviation. However, the within standard deviation of REER index is found to be 11.77. Having discussed in detail the nature and availability of data, we now introduce the empirical methodology in Section 4.5.

Table 4.8: Data Caveats for Data on FDI Inflows

Indicator	Source	Definition	Level of Aggregation	Coverage	Time Period & Data Frequency
FDI Inflows	ASEANStats	Net FDI = Equity + Net Inter-company Loans + Reinvested Earnings	National	All ASEAN economies.	2000–2014 (Annual)
	Euromonitor Passport	"Foreign Direct Investment (FDI) is investment made to acquire a lasting interest in or effective control over an enterprise operating outside of the economy of the investor. FDI inflows are the net value of inward direct investment made by non-resident investors in the reporting economy, including reinvested earnings and intra-company loans, net of repatriation of capital and repayment of loans."	National	ASEAN economies, except for Cambodia (1977–1991); Laos (1977–1987); Myanmar (1978–1979, 1981–1982).	1977–2014 (Annual)
	UNCTAD	"Foreign Direct Investment inflows and outflows comprise capital provided (either directly or through other related enterprises) by a foreign direct investor to a FDI enterprise, or capital received by a foreign direct investor from a FDI enterprise. FDI includes the following three components: equity capital, reinvested earnings and intra-company loans. Data on FDI flows are presented on net bases (capital transactions' credits less debits between direct investors and their foreign affiliates). Net decreases in assets or net increases in liabilities are recorded as credits (with a positive sign), while net increases in assets or net decreases in liabilities are recorded as debits (with a positive sign). Hence, FDI flows with a negative sign indicate that at least one of the three components of FDI is negative and not offset by positive amounts of the remaining components. These are called reverse investment or disinvestment."	National	All ASEAN economies.	1970–2014 (Annual)
	World Bank (World Development Indicators)	"Foreign direct investment refers to direct investment equity flows in the reporting economy. It is the sum of equity capital, reinvestment of earnings, and other capital. Direct investment is a category of cross-border investment associated with a resident in one economy having control or a significant degree of influence on the management of an enterprise that is resident in another economy. Ownership of 10 percent or more of the ordinary shares of voting stock is the criterion for determining the existence of a direct investment relationship. Data are in current U.S. dollars."	National	ASEAN economies, except for Brunei (1970–2000); Laos (1970–1991); Indonesia (1970–1980); Myanmar (1970, 1976, 1978–1979, 1981–1982, 1986, 1988).	1970–2014 (Annual)

Source: Compiled by Asia Competitiveness Institute.

Table 4.9: Data Caveats for Data on REER

Indicator	Index	Source	Definition	Coverage	Time Period	Data Frequency
REER	GDP deflator (2005 = 100)	UNCTAD	Each of the country's exchange rates against other major currencies (i.e. nominal exchange rates) is deflated by the price indices of the country and the corresponding partner countries to calculate the real exchange rate. The weighted average (geometric mean) of the real exchange rates is then calculated using the annual value of country's trade with the respective countries as its weights. It is then converted into an index and aggregated into various trade and economic country groups.	ASEAN-10	1998–2014 (except Indonesia 2003–2014)	Annual
	CPI (2007 = 100)	Bruegel Institute	The REER is calculated from nominal effective exchange rate and a measure of the relative price or cost between the country under study and its trading partners. See working paper: http://bruegel.org/wp-content/uploads/imported/publications/120315_ZD_REER_WP_01.pdf.	ASEAN-9 (Myanmar excluded) for annual series, ASEAN-10 for monthly series	1960–2015 (Annual) 1992–2015 (Annual) 1995–2016 (Monthly)	Annual, Monthly
	CPI (2010 = 100)	BIS	REER are geometric weighted averages of bilateral exchange rates adjusted by relative consumer prices. The weighting pattern is time-varying.	Indonesia, Malaysia, Philippines, Singapore, Thailand	1994–2016	Monthly
	CPI (2010 = 100)	IMF	REER is the nominal effective exchange rate (a measure of the value of a currency against a weighted average of several foreign currencies) divided by a price deflator or index of costs.	Malaysia, Philippines, Singapore	1990–2015	Annual, Quarterly, Monthly
	Unit Labour Cost (2010 = 100)			Singapore	1992–2015	Annual, Quarterly, Monthly

Source: Compiled by Asia Competitiveness Institute.

Table 4.10: Control Variables — Sources and Definitions

Variable	Unit	Definition	Source
REER (+/–)	Index	REER is calculated from nominal effective exchange rate and a measure of the relative price or cost between the country under study and its trading partners.	Bruegel Institute
REER Volatility (+/–)	Standard Deviation	Monthly standard deviation of REER.	Bruegel Institute
FDI Stock (+)	US Dollars	"FDI is defined as an investment involving a long-term relationship and reflecting a lasting interest in and control by a resident entity in one economy of an enterprise resident in a different economy. FDI stock is the value of the share of their capital and reserves (including retained profits) attributable to the parent enterprise, plus the net indebtedness of affiliates to the parent enterprises."	UNCTAD
Real GDP per capita (+)	US Dollars (constant 2007 prices)	GDP per capita in constant 2007 US dollars.	Calculated from IMF and World Bank
Population (+)	Number of People	Total population is based on the *de facto* definition of population, which counts all residents regardless of legal status or citizenship — except for refugees not permanently settled in the country of asylum, who are generally considered part of the population of their country of origin. The values shown are midyear estimates.	World Bank
Inflation (–)	Percent Change	Inflation as measured by the consumer price index reflects the annual percent change in the cost to the average consumer of acquiring a basket of goods and services that may be fixed or changed at specified intervals, such as yearly.	World Bank
Trade Openness (+/–)	Percent of GDP	Trade openness is the sum of exports and imports of goods and services measured as a share of Gross Domestic Product (GDP).	World Bank
Length of Roads (+)	Kilometres	Total road network includes motorways, highways, and main or national roads, secondary or regional roads, and all other roads in a country.	Euromonitor Passport
Adult Literacy Rate (+)	Percent of Population	Adults are defined as persons aged 15 years and older. A person is literate who can, with understanding, both read and write a short simple statement on his or her everyday life.	Euromonitor Passport
M2 as Percentage of GDP (+)	Percent	Money and quasi-money comprise the sum of currency outside banks, demand deposits other than those of the central government, and the time, savings, and foreign currency deposits of resident sectors other than the central government.	World Bank
Foreign Exchange Reserves (+/–)	Average of Monthly Percent Change	Total foreign exchange reserves excluding gold	IMF International Financial Statistics

Notes: (+) denotes expectation for a positive association between FDI inflows and the variable *a priori*; (–) indicates negative association, while (+/–) means the prior is ambiguous.
Source: Asia Competitiveness Institute.

Table 4.11: Summary Statistics

Variable	Mean	Between Std. Dev.	Within Std. Dev.	Min	Max	Observations	Number of Economies
Growth Rate of FDI Inflows (percent)	89.76	157.63	725.32	−508.76	9,794.07	180	9
Lag of FDI Stock	63,036.40	97,580.94	92,378.79	59.01	869,857.80	180	9
Growth Rate of GDP per Capita (percent)	7.29	2.32	12.04	−56.38	45.01	180	9
Population Growth Rate (percent)	1.69	0.50	0.59	−1.47	5.47	180	9
Inflation (percent)	6.29	6.01	11.54	−2.32	128.42	180	9
Change in Trade Openness (percent)	1.20	2.08	12.25	−79.43	41.00	180	9
Ln(Length of Roads)	10.78	1.74	0.28	7.86	13.14	177	9
M2 as Percentage of GDP (percent)	72.42	38.54	15.64	7.70	140.06	172	9
Change in Adult Literacy Rate (percent)	0.42	0.25	0.51	−3.70	3.30	180	9
REER (Bruegel Monthly 138)	103.89	5.45	11.77	52.13	141.37	180	9
REER Volatility (Standard Deviation)	2.75	1.20	2.56	0.34	17.92	180	9
Change in Foreign Exchange Reserves (FXR) (percent)	1.15	0.44	1.48	−3.20	5.65	172	9

Source: Asia Competitiveness Institute.

4.5 Empirical Methodology

4.5.1 Baseline Model: Panel Fixed-effects Regression

As mentioned in the previous section, for our empirics we rely on FDI data from UNCTAD and Bruegel's REER Monthly 138 series, which is available from 1995 to 2014, to calculate annual average REER and REER volatility as the standard deviation of monthly REER. As Myanmar's data is only available from April 2012 onwards, the country is dropped from the sample.

To examine the impact of exchange rates on FDI, we construct a panel dataset of nine ASEAN economies for the period 1995–2014. We use a panel fixed-effects model to investigate the determinants of FDI inflows into ASEAN economies with a focus on the impacts of REER movements on FDI inflows. The model specifications are as follows:

$$gfdi_{it} = \alpha_0 + \delta Y_{it} + \beta_1 REER_{it} + \beta_2 Volatility_{it} + \gamma_i + e_t + \varepsilon_{it} \tag{4.1}$$

where, $gfdi_{it}$ refers to the annual growth rate of FDI inflows in year t into country i,
$REER_{it}$ is the annual average REER level in year t for country i,
$Volatility_{it}$ is the monthly standard deviation of REER in year t for country i,
Y_{it} is a vector of control variables other than $REER_{it}$,
γ_i represents country fixed effects,
e_t denotes time fixed effects and
ε_{it} it is the idiosyncratic error term.

Most panel data settings typically suffer from endogeneity issues arising due to omitted variable bias which can be reasonably addressed by introducing entity and time fixed effects in our estimation. We expect the estimates of the fixed-effects regression to remain robust when the potential source of endogeneity arises from the correlation between the time-invariant component of the error term and the regressor of interest, as a fixed-effects model resolves this problem by excluding the unobservable time-invariant effects through a time-demeaning of the data. Considering the applicability of fixed-effects model, we now discuss the empirical approach along with the priors within the underlying model.

Equation (4.1) investigates the relationship between annual growth of FDI inflows and macroeconomic, human capital, infrastructure development and financial development, variables which are all specified under the vector Y_{it}. Following related literature,[13] the vector Y_{it} includes the first lag of FDI stock, annual growth rate of population, annual growth rate of GDP per capita, annual inflation rate, change in trade openness, annual change in adult literacy rate, length of road specified in log form and M2 as percentage of GDP.

In terms of the priors, we expect annual growth rate of GDP per capita, human resource development captured by annual change in adult literacy rate, infrastructure development captured by length of road specified and financial sector development as proxied by M2 as percentage of GDP to have a positive impact on FDI, whereas inflation rate is expected to be negatively related; trade openness can have either a positive or negative impact on FDI. A brief explanation of the variables and their priors are provided in Table 4.12. Furthermore, in order to ensure that our model is free from multicollinearity issues we construct a correlation matrix of the variables (see Table 4.13).

4.5.2 Augmented Model

In order to capture the effects of a sustained expectation of appreciation, we augment the model with the average monthly percent change in foreign exchange reserves (FXR) and its interaction term where $REER_{it}$, $fxr_{it} * REER_{it}$. β_1 and β_2 are the key coefficients of interest. The augmented model is as follows:

$$gfdi_{it} = \alpha_0 + \delta Y_{it} + \beta_1 REER_{it} + \beta_2 Volatility_{it} + \beta_3 fxr_{it} + \beta_4 fxr_{it} * REER_{it} + \gamma_i + e_t + \varepsilon_{it} \quad (4.2)$$

[13] See Koojaroenprasit (2015), Hoang and Bui (2015), Xaypanya *et al.* (2015) as well as Nwosu *et al.* (2013).

Table 4.12: List of Variables and Priors

Variable	Expected Direction of Relationship	Prior
GDP per Capita	Positive	Reflects the different levels of development in the economies. Higher income level implies greater consumer demand, thus leading to profitable investment opportunities in the host country. Thus, we expect to see a positive relationship between GDP per Capita and FDI.
Total Population	Positive	Captures the market size. A larger market size reduces per unit cost of production (economies of scale), and attracts greater FDI flows. *A priori*, we expect to see a positive relationship between FDI and market size.
Inflation	Negative	Measured by the Consumer Price Index (CPI), it is expected to have a negative impact on FDI as high inflation would lead to increased investment risks thus making the investors reluctant to invest in turn discouraging FDI.
Trade Openness	Ambiguous	For export-oriented FDI, higher level of trade openness reduces transaction costs. For FDI in vertical MNCs, it facilitates ease of importing intermediate goods. In general, trade openness signals better growth prospects and larger market size of the host country in future: is expected to have an ambiguous effect on FDI. A liberal trade regime may encourage or discourage FDI.
Human Resource Development	Positive	Availability of skilled and educated workers in an economy is highly likely to have a positive relationship with FDI.
Infrastructure	Positive	It effects FDI inflows by improving utilisation of labour force. Thus, good infrastructure increases profits by reducing cost of production. *A priori*, we expect to see a positive impact of improved infrastructure on FDI flows.
Financial Sector Development	Positive	It captures the level of financial development in the state. A financially developed state would reduce investment risk, thereby attracting investors and FDI.

Source: Asia Competitiveness Institute.

where, $gfdi_{it}$ refers to the annual growth rate of FDI inflows into each ASEAN country i at time t, fxr_{it} is the average monthly percent change in foreign exchange reserves in year t for country i, $fxr_{it} * REER_{it}$ is the interaction term between fxr_{it} and $REER_{it}$. We also incorporate a vector of year dummies to control for the time fixed effects e_t.

The interaction term $fxr_{it} * REER_{it}$ is designed to proxy for market expectation of exchange rate movements. The building up of reserves in concurrence with exchange rate appreciation may indicate the central bank's intention to prevent its currency from appreciating through sustained reserve accumulation. Thus, a large interaction term may indicate market expectations of further appreciation and the coefficient β_4 reflects the effects of this expectation on the annual growth rate of FDI inflows $gfdi_{it}$.

Table 4.13: Correlation Matrix

	Growth Rate of FDI Inflows	FDI Stock	GDP Per Capita	Population	Inflation	Change in Trade Openness	Length of Roads	M2 as a Percentage of GDP	Change in Adult Literacy Rate	REER (Bruegel Monthly 138)	REER Volatility	Change in Foreign Exchange Reserves (FXR) (percent)
Growth Rate of FDI Inflows	1.00											
FDI Stock	0.00	1.00										
GDP Per Capita	0.25	−0.03	1.00									
Population	−0.06	0.12	−0.13	1.00								
Inflation	−0.03	−0.11	−0.15	−0.01	1.00							
Change in Trade Openness	−0.07	−0.13	−0.11	−0.10	0.09	1.00						
Length of Roads	0.02	−0.30	0.08	−0.39	0.08	−0.05	1.00					
M2 as a Percentage of GDP	0.04	0.45	−0.09	−0.08	−0.28	−0.06	−0.09	1.00				
Change in Adult Literacy Rate	−0.03	−0.11	0.11	0.08	0.32	0.15	−0.03	−0.24	1.00			
REER (Bruegel Monthly 138)	−0.06	0.28	0.16	0.12	−0.31	−0.12	−0.23	0.14	−0.11	1.00		
REER Volatility	−0.03	−0.14	−0.33	0.00	0.40	0.13	0.26	−0.09	0.13	−0.22	1.00	
Change in Foreign Exchange Reserves (FXR) (percent)	0.06	−0.16	0.20	0.00	−0.05	0.05	−0.02	−0.22	0.03	−0.03	−0.23	1.00

Source: Asia Competitiveness Institute.

In the next section, we discuss the results of the baseline and augmented model using fixed-effects regressions with robust standard errors for a panel of nine ASEAN economies over the period 1995–2014.

4.6 Empirical Results

First, as the baseline case, we estimate the model by taking growth rate of FDI as a function of macroeconomic, institutional and financial factors. In order to capture the key variable of interest (REER), the baseline model applies REER in levels and REER volatility to study the impact of exchange rates on FDI. The second part of our analysis is where we augment the baseline model with FXR and an interaction of FXR and REER.

Table 4.14 displays the main empirical findings. The first column shows the baseline model without REER and REER volatility. These two variables are added subsequently in the regressions in the second and third columns. Finally, the last column shows the augmented model which includes average monthly percent change in FXR and the interaction term between average monthly percent change in FXR and annual average REER.

Our findings reveal that annual average REER is negatively associated with the annual growth rate of FDI inflows and its coefficient is significant at the 5 percent level. The results imply that a 1 percentage point increase in REER will lead to a decline in FDI annual growth rate by approximately 5 percentage points. The sign and significance of REER is consistent across the second, third and fourth columns of Table 4.14. The negative relationship is suggestive of the fact that FDI inflows into ASEAN economies are export-oriented in nature, which is an interpretation consistent with the theoretical priors discussed in Section 4.4. This is also perhaps unsurprising as ASEAN economies have largely pursued a strategy of attracting MNCs to manufacture in their countries for exporting to serve the regional and global market. In line with the result for REER, REER volatility is also negatively associated with the annual growth rate of FDI inflows even though its coefficient is not statistically significant.

The signs of the coefficients on the lag of FDI stock, annual growth rate of GDP per capita, annual growth rate of population, inflation rate, annual change in trade openness, the log of length of roads, M2 as percentage of GDP and the annual change in adult literacy rate are consistent across all columns. Among these variables, growth rate of GDP per capita and M2 as percentage of GDP are consistently significant as both enter the regressions positively, which is in accordance with the priors discussed in the previous section. A high rate of GDP per capita growth implies strong economic performance and more profitable investment opportunities, which would attract more FDI. Greater financial market development facilitates capital inflows and repatriation of profits, thus encouraging greater FDI as well. As for the other variables which do not appear as statistically significant determinants, the signs of their coefficients are still mostly consistent with the priors.

Finally, the findings from the augmented model are shown in column 4 of Table 4.14. We observe that the coefficients of average monthly percent change in FXR and the interaction term between average monthly percent change in FXR and annual average REER are both statistically insignificant. One interpretation of these results is that market expectation of

Table 4.14: Empirical Findings on Determinants of FDI Inflows into ASEAN

Dependent Variable: Growth Rate of FDI Inflows (percent)	**Model 1a: Baseline**	**Model 1b: Augmented with REER**	**Model 1c: Augmented with REER Volatility (SD)**	**Model 1d: Augmented with FXR and FXR Interaction**
Lag of FDI Stock	7.27×10^{-5}	8.17×10^{-5}	8.18×10^{-5}	1.06×10^{-4}
	(9.21×10^{-5})	(8.83×10^{-5})	(8.68×10^{-5})	(9.90×10^{-5})
Growth Rate of GDP per Capita (percent)	4.872**	6.838**	6.837**	7.561**
	(1.924)	(2.507)	(2.508)	(2.326)
Population Growth Rate (percent)	−21.00	−25.97	−25.97	−26.28
	(13.29)	(15.22)	(15.09)	(14.49)
Inflation (percent)	−0.224	−1.399*	−1.397	−1.610
	(0.427)	(0.749)	(0.798)	(0.920)
Change in Trade Openness (percent)	0.341	0.358	0.360	0.638
	(0.879)	(0.990)	(1.030)	(1.118)
Ln (Length of Roads)	34.25	14.88	14.70	19.04
	(35.05)	(30.55)	(35.63)	(41.26)
M2 as Percentage of GDP (percent)	0.992*	1.617***	1.621***	1.938***
	(0.454)	(0.427)	(0.447)	(0.511)
Change in Adult Literacy Rate (percent)	−21.78	−23.99	−24.00	−22.16
	(21.25)	(21.45)	(21.73)	(20.57)
REER (Bruegel Monthly 138)		−5.357**	−5.361**	−6.054**
		(2.137)	(2.063)	(2.411)
REER Volatility (Standard Deviation)			−0.0822	−0.623
			(4.606)	(4.588)
Change in Foreign Exchange Reserves (FXR) (percent)				−42.19
				(52.31)
REER * FXR				0.351
				(0.423)
Constant	−370.0	387.4*	389.6	400.3
	(363.1)	(203.3)	(225.9)	(277.5)
Observations	168	168	168	164
R-squared	0.190	0.239	0.239	0.254

Notes: (i) Robust standard errors in parentheses; (ii) ***, ** and * denote significance at 1 percent, 5 percent and 10 percent, respectively; (iii) State fixed-effect and Time fixed-effect are incorporated.
Source: Asia Competitiveness Institute.

future exchange rate movements perhaps do not explain FDI inflows into ASEAN economies. However, the results may also point to a need for more suitable proxies for market expectations.

4.7 Robustness Checks

We check the robustness of our results using alternative specifications of FXR, definitions of REER and REER volatility. For the first robustness check, we use average monthly change in foreign exchange reserves levels in place of percent change. Next, we try using coefficient of variation rather than standard deviation of monthly REER to measure REER volatility. All robustness checks are conducted using the same sample as the original results, which spans 1995–2014 and covers all ASEAN economies except for Myanmar.

The results of the first robustness check, using average monthly change in FXR levels instead of percent change, are akin to our main findings given in Table 4.14. Table 4.15 shows that REER is negatively related to percent growth of FDI as it is statistically significant at 5 percent level of significance. The coefficient for volatility and the interaction term of REER and FXR remain negative and positive, respectively, though statistically insignificant. Furthermore, the signs and significance levels of the control variables are also in line with our main findings.

Next, we re-estimate the model using coefficient of variation as a measure of volatility instead of standard deviations (see Table 4.16). Results from this robustness exercise are also consistent with our main findings given in Table 4.14. REER continues to be significant and negatively correlated at the 5 percent level, while REER volatility remains insignificant and negative, and the interaction term is insignificant yet positive.

We also undertake additional robustness exercises by specifying REER as a change in annual averages instead of using annual averages (see Table 4.17). Finally, in Table 4.18 we use Bruegel's REER Monthly 41 series to calculate the REER (as annual average of REER series) and REER volatility (measured as standard deviation of monthly REER). Our findings remain robust and consistent with the main findings given in Table 4.14.

Table 4.19 summarises the robustness checks results for REER, REER volatility and the interaction term between FXR and REER. In general, our empirical findings as presented earlier are robust. The coefficient on the REER variable is consistently negative across all robustness checks. Meanwhile, the coefficient of REER volatility also remains negative and statistically insignificant in almost all instances. The only exception is when REER is specified as change in annual average REER (column 3). In this case, the coefficient on REER volatility becomes positive although it still remains statistically insignificant. Finally, the interaction term enters positively throughout except in column 4 where we use Bruegel's REER Monthly 41 data to calculate the REER and REER volatility. However, its coefficient is consistently insignificant in all cases.

Our findings for the control variables also remain robust. By and large, apart from REER, growth rate of GDP per capita and M2 as percentage of GDP are the other two significant determinants of growth rate of FDI inflows into ASEAN.

Table 4.15: Using Average Monthly Change in FXR

Dependent Variable: Growth Rate of FDI Inflows (percent)	**(1) Baseline**	**(2) Augmented with REER**	**(3) Augmented with REER Volatility (SD)**	**(4) Augmented with FXR and FXR Interaction**
Lag of FDI Stock	7.27×10^{-5}	8.17×10^{-5}	8.18×10^{-5}	9.03×10^{-5}
	(9.21×10^{-5})	(8.83×10^{-5})	(8.68×10^{-5})	(8.80×10^{-5})
Growth Rate of GDP per Capita (percent)	4.872**	6.838**	6.837**	7.688**
	(1.924)	(2.507)	(2.508)	(2.370)
Population Growth Rate (percent)	−21.00	−25.97	−25.97	−25.11
	(13.29)	(15.22)	(15.09)	(15.28)
Inflation (percent)	−0.224	−1.399*	−1.397	−1.363
	(0.427)	(0.749)	(0.798)	(0.800)
Change in Trade Openness (percent)	0.341	0.358	0.360	0.587
	(0.879)	(0.990)	(1.030)	(1.117)
Ln (Length of Roads)	34.25	14.88	14.70	21.79
	(35.05)	(30.55)	(35.63)	(42.80)
M2 as Percentage of GDP (percent)	0.992*	1.617***	1.621***	1.879***
	(0.454)	(0.427)	(0.447)	(0.488)
Change in Adult Literacy Rate (percent)	−21.78	−23.99	−24.00	−22.99
	(21.25)	(21.45)	(21.73)	(21.57)
REER (Bruegel Monthly 138)		−5.357**	−5.361**	−5.647**
		(2.137)	(2.063)	(2.134)
REER Volatility (Standard Deviation)			−0.0822	−0.500
			(4.606)	(4.815)
Change in Levels of Foreign Exchange Reserves (FXR)				-8.86×10^{-8}
				(1.49×10^{-7})
REER * FXR				7.83×10^{-10}
				(1.36×10^{-9})
Constant	−370.0	387.4*	389.6	314.6
	(363.1)	(203.3)	(225.9)	(277.9)
Observations	168	168	168	164
R-squared	0.190	0.239	0.239	0.252

Notes: (i) Robust standard errors in parentheses; (ii) ***, ** and * denote significance at 1 percent, 5 percent and 10 percent, respectively; (iii) State fixed-effect and Time fixed-effect are incorporated.
Source: Asia Competitiveness Institute.

Table 4.16: Using Coefficient of Variation as a Measure of Volatility

Dependent Variable: Growth Rate of FDI Inflows (percent)	**(1) Baseline**	**(2) Augmented with REER**	**(3) Augmented with REER Volatility (CV)**	**(4) Augmented with FXR and FXR Interaction**
Lag of FDI Stock	7.27×10^{-5}	8.17×10^{-5}	8.26×10^{-5}	0.000105
	(9.21×10^{-5})	(8.83×10^{-5})	(8.70×10^{-5})	(9.91×10^{-5})
Growth Rate of GDP per Capita (percent)	4.872**	6.838**	6.823**	7.560**
	(1.924)	(2.507)	(2.501)	(2.340)
Population Growth Rate (percent)	–21.00	–25.97	–26.05	–26.26
	(13.29)	(15.22)	(15.10)	(14.42)
Inflation (percent)	–0.224	–1.399*	–1.381	–1.615
	(0.427)	(0.749)	(0.792)	(0.972)
Change in Trade Openness (percent)	0.341	0.358	0.371	0.631
	(0.879)	(0.990)	(1.024)	(1.106)
Ln (Length of Roads)	34.25	14.88	13.87	19.94
	(35.05)	(30.55)	(33.21)	(40.12)
M2 as Percentage of GDP (percent)	0.992*	1.617***	1.647***	1.918***
	(0.454)	(0.427)	(0.440)	(0.482)
Change in Adult Literacy Rate (percent)	–21.78	–23.99	–24.09	–22.14
	(21.25)	(21.45)	(21.79)	(20.60)
REER (Bruegel Monthly 138)		–5.357**	–5.412**	–6.048**
		(2.137)	(2.032)	(2.312)
REER Volatility (Coefficient of Variation)			–0.504	–0.192
			(3.071)	(3.676)
Change in Foreign Exchange Reserves (FXR) (percent)				–42.25
				(56.25)
REER * FXR				0.352
				(0.457)
Constant	–370.0	387.4*	403.7*	390.2
	(363.1)	(203.3)	(207.5)	(261.7)
Observations	168	168	168	164
R-squared	0.190	0.239	0.240	0.254

Notes: (i) Robust standard errors in parentheses; (ii) ***, ** and * denote significance at 1 percent, 5 percent and 10 percent, respectively; (iii) State fixed-effect and Time fixed-effect are incorporated.
Source: Asia Competitiveness Institute.

Table 4.17: REER as a Change in Annual Averages

Dependent Variable: Growth Rate of FDI Inflows (percent)	**(1) Baseline**	**(2) Augmented with dREER**	**(3) Augmented with REER Volatility (SD)**	**(4) Augmented with FXR and FXR Interaction**
Lag of FDI Stock	7.27×10^{-5}	5.81×10^{-5}	5.62×10^{-5}	8.25×10^{-5}
	(9.21×10^{-5})	(8.48×10^{-5})	(8.34×10^{-5})	(9.41×10^{-5})
Growth Rate of GDP per Capita (percent)	4.872**	6.414	6.375	8.227
	(1.924)	(4.526)	(4.541)	(4.864)
Population Growth Rate (percent)	−21.00	−18.94	−18.81	−15.98
	(13.29)	(12.35)	(11.95)	(10.77)
Inflation (percent)	−0.224	−0.187	−0.242	−0.241
	(0.427)	(0.449)	(0.431)	(0.453)
Change in Trade Openness (percent)	0.341	0.264	0.247	0.389
	(0.879)	(0.908)	(0.941)	(1.026)
Ln (Length of Roads)	34.25	18.41	23.02	30.74
	(35.05)	(28.77)	(39.68)	(40.09)
M2 as Percentage of GDP (percent)	0.992*	0.946*	0.860	1.334**
	(0.454)	(0.444)	(0.490)	(0.544)
Change in Adult Literacy Rate (percent)	−21.78	−19.66	−19.79	−18.40
	(21.25)	(20.23)	(19.98)	(19.57)
dREER		−2.450	−2.298	−4.024
		(4.042)	(4.056)	(4.515)
REER Volatility (Standard Deviation)			1.817	0.0818
			(6.005)	(5.586)
Change in Foreign Exchange Reserves (FXR) (percent)				−2.368
				(10.40)
dREER * FXR				0.0578
				(0.700)
Constant	−370.0	−190.4	−236.4	−351.7
	(363.1)	(309.1)	(410.6)	(423.0)
Observations	168	162	162	158
R-squared	0.190	0.193	0.193	0.211

Notes: (i) Robust standard errors in parentheses; (ii) ***, ** and * denote significance at 1 percent, 5 percent and 10 percent, respectively; (iii) State fixed-effect and Time fixed-effect are incorporated.
Source: Asia Competitiveness Institute.

Table 4.18: Using Bruegel's REER Monthly 41 Series

Dependent Variable: Growth Rate of FDI Inflows (percent)	(1) Baseline	(2) Augmented with REER41	(3) Augmented with REER Volatility (SD)	(4) Augmented with FXR and FXR Interaction
Lag of FDI Stock	7.27×10^{-5}	5.86×10^{-5}	6.02×10^{-5}	7.10×10^{-5}
	(9.21×10^{-5})	(8.42×10^{-5})	(8.21×10^{-5})	(9.51×10^{-5})
Growth Rate of GDP per Capita (percent)	4.872**	6.533**	6.541**	7.356**
	(1.924)	(2.496)	(2.501)	(2.267)
Population Growth Rate (percent)	−21.00	−21.68	−21.68	−20.13
	(13.29)	(13.43)	(13.58)	(12.73)
Inflation (percent)	−0.224	−1.338	−1.312	−1.326
	(0.427)	(0.783)	(0.847)	(1.004)
Change in Trade Openness (percent)	0.341	0.307	0.329	0.519
	(0.879)	(0.917)	(0.991)	(1.093)
Ln (Length of Roads)	34.25	6.268	6.018	14.00
	(35.05)	(23.73)	(25.17)	(30.05)
M2 as Percentage of GDP (percent)	0.992*	1.722**	1.764**	2.101**
	(0.454)	(0.532)	(0.562)	(0.633)
Change in Adult Literacy Rate (percent)	−21.78	−23.76	−23.76	−23.73
	(21.25)	(20.60)	(20.65)	(20.30)
REER (Bruegel Monthly 41)		−4.836*	−4.870*	−4.827
		(2.357)	(2.325)	(2.944)
REER Volatility (Standard Deviation)			−0.962	−2.099
			(4.814)	(4.873)
Change in Foreign Exchange Reserves (FXR) (percent)				13.09
				(80.87)
dREER * FXR				−0.163
				(0.707)
Constant	−370.0	415.3**	421.1*	308.7
	(363.1)	(170.5)	(186.0)	(320.1)
Observations	168	168	168	164
R-squared	0.190	0.228	0.228	0.241

Notes: (i) Robust standard errors in parentheses; (ii) ***, ** and * denote significance at 1 percent, 5 percent and 10 percent, respectively; (iii) State fixed-effect and Time fixed-effect are incorporated.
Source: Asia Competitiveness Institute.

Table 4.19: Summary Table

Variables	Baseline (Bruegel Monthly 138)	Δ FXR Level	REER Volatility (CV)	Change in REER	Bruegel Monthly 41
REER	Negative & Significant	Negative & Significant	Negative & Significant	Negative & Insignificant	Negative & Insignificant
REER Volatility	Negative & Insignificant	Negative & Insignificant	Negative & Insignificant	Positive & Insignificant	Negative & Insignificant
Interaction Term (FXR*REER)	Positive & Insignificant	Positive & Insignificant	Positive & Insignificant	Positive & Insignificant	Negative & Insignificant

Source: Asia Competitiveness Institute.

4.8 Concluding Notes and Policy Implications

ASEAN has been a major player in attracting FDI inflows. The region has been among the major recipients of global FDI inflows, accounting for about 11 percent of world FDI inflows in 2014. While, factors attracting FDI inflows towards ASEAN are well-researched, there exists a lack of research on the impact of exchange rates on FDI, especially at a regional level. Most existing literature focuses on only a subset of ASEAN economies, mostly the more mature ASEAN-5 (Indonesia, Singapore, Malaysia, Philippines, and Thailand) as part of a larger panel of East Asian or developing economies.

In this chapter, we compile a panel dataset for the ASEAN economies covering the time period from 1995 to 2014 to examine the impact of exchange rate on FDI. We employ a panel fixed-effects model to explore the nexus between REER and FDI, controlling for a combination of macroeconomic, institutional and financial variables. We find that REER is negatively and significantly associated with the annual growth rate of FDI inflows suggesting that FDI inflows into ASEAN economies are export-oriented in nature. On the other hand, the impact of REER volatility on FDI inflows is negative but remains insignificant, implying that REER movements in levels tend to be more important determinants of FDI inflows to the ASEAN economies than REER volatility.

We observe that the signs of the coefficients on the lag of FDI stock, annual growth rate of GDP per capita, annual growth rate of population, inflation rate, annual change in trade openness, the log of length of roads, M2 as percentage of GDP and the annual change in adult literacy rate are consistent across all regressions. However, among these variables, only growth rate of GDP per capita and M2 as percentage of GDP consistently appear as statistically significant determinants of FDI inflows growth rate.

Our results have important policy implications especially on policies that would be fundamental in attracting more foreign investment. First, growth-enhancing economic policies would ensure continuous inflow of foreign investment into the region. Over the past decade following the AFC, most ASEAN member economies have recorded substantial GDP growth, and this was also the key to huge inflow of FDI into ASEAN.

Second, exchange rate stabilisation and inflation control should occupy important positions in the monetary policy agenda of the central banks in member economies. After the financial crisis, many investors are still sceptical of the investment climate in the region. Therefore, the pursuance of good stabilisation measures would help restore the confidence of foreign investors in the region.

Third, ASEAN economies should aim to enhance transparency and communication in exchange rate policies and eschew short-term beggar-thy-neighbour policies. While managing exchange rate volatility is somewhat less controversial, if too successful it might lead to moral hazard problems, i.e. agents may fail to take actions in covering individual risks, which hinders the development of financial markets and instruments to hedge against foreign exchange risks. Based on our research, rapid economic growth and better economic policies (coupled with political stability) would set ASEAN as the next best destination for foreign investment in the coming decades.

References

Alfaro, Laura, Areendam Chanda, Sebnem Kalemli-Ozcan, and Selin Sayek. 2004. "FDI and Economic Growth: The Role of Local Financial Markets". *Journal of International Economics* 64 (1): 89–112.

ASEAN Secretariat. 2008. *ASEAN Economic Community Blueprint*. Jakarta: ASEAN Secretariat.

Athukorala, Prema-chandra, and Hal Hill. 1998. "Foreign Investment in East Asia: A Survey". *Asia Pacific Economic Literature* 12 (2): 23–50.

Baek, In-Mee, and Tamami Okawa. 2001. "Foreign Exchange Rates and Japanese Foreign Direct Investment in Asia". *Journal of Economics and Business* 53: 69–84.

Barro, Robert J. 1997. "Determinants of Economic Growth: A Cross-Country Empirical Study". The MIT Press.

Bayoumi, Tamim, and Gabrielle Lipworth. 1997. "Japanese Foreign Direct Investment and Regional Trade." IMF Working Paper WP/97/103. Washington DC: International Monetary Fund.

Bénassy-Quéré, Agnès, Lionel Fontagné, and Amina Lahrèche-Révil. 2001. "Exchange Rate Strategies in the Competition for Attracting FDI". *Journal of the Japanese and International Economies* 15 (2): 178–198.

Blonigen, Bruce A. 1997. "Firm Specific Assets and the Link between Exchange Rates and Foreign Direct Investment". *American Economic Review* 87: 447–465.

Borensztein, Eduardo, Jose De Gregorio, and Jong-Wha Lee. 1998. "How does foreign direct investment affect economic growth?" *Journal of International Economics* 45: 115–135.

Bosworth, Barry P., Susan M. Collins, and Carmen M. Reinhart 1999. "Capital Flows to Developing Economies: Implications for Saving and Investment". *Brookings Papers on Economic Activity* 1: 143–169.

Byrne Joseph P, and Davis. E. Philip. 2003. "Panel Estimation of the Impact of Exchange Rate Uncertainty on Investment in the Major Industrial Countries", Discussion Paper No 208, National Institute of Economic and Social Research.

Carkovic, Maria, and Ross Levine. 2005. "Does foreign direct investment accelerate economic growth?" University of Minnesota Department of Finance Working Paper.

Chakrabarti, Rajesh, and Barry Scholnick. 2002. "Exchange Rate Expectations and Foreign Direct Investment Flows". *Review of World Economics* 138 (1): 1–21.

Cushman, David O. 1988. "Exchange Rate Uncertainty and Foreign Direct Investment in the United States". *Weltwirtschaftliches Archiv* 124 (2): 322–336.

Darby, Julia, Andrew Hughes Hallet, Jonathan Ireland, and Laura Piscitelli. 1999. "The Impact of Exchange Rate Uncertainty on the Level of Investment". *The Economic Journal* 109 (454): 55–67.

De Mènil, Georges, Stefan Gerlach, and Lucrezia Reichlin. 1999. "Real Capital Market Integration in the EU: How far has it gone? What will the Effect of the Euro be?" *Economic Policy*: 167–201.

Dhakal, Dharmendra, Raja Nag, Gyan Pradhan, and Kamal P. Upadhyaya. 2010. "Exchange Rate Volatility and Foreign Direct Investment: Evidence from East Asian Countries". *International Business and Economics Research* 9 (7): 121–128.

Foad, Hisham S. 2005. "Exchange Rate Volatility and Export Oriented FDI." Department of Economics, San Diego State University.

Froot, Kenneth A., and Jeremy C. Stein. 1991. "Exchange Rates and FDI: An Imperfect Capital Markets Approach". *Quarterly Journal of Economics* 427 (4): 1191–1127.

Goldberg, Linda S., and Michael Klein. 1998. "Foreign Direct Investment, Trade and Real Exchange Rate Linkages in Developing Countries." Proceedings, Federal Reserve Bank of San Francisco, 73–100.

Goldberg, Linda S., and Michael Klein. 1997. "Foreign Direct Investment, Trade and Real Exchange Rate Linkages in Southeast Asia and Latin America". NBER Working Paper 6344, National Bureau of Economic Research (NBER), Cambridge.

Goldberg, Linda.S. 2009. "Exchange Rates and Foreign Direct Investment." *The Princeton Encyclopedia of the World Economy*. Princeton: Princeton University Press

Gottschalk, Sylvia, and Stephen Hall. 2008. "Foreign Direct Investment and Exchange Rate Uncertainty in South-East Asia". *International Journal of Finance and Economics* 13 (4): 349–359.

Hattari, Rabin, Ramkishen S. Rajan and Shandre Thangavelu. 2008. "Understanding Intra-ASEAN FDI Inflows: Trends, Determinants and The Role of China and India." Unpublished paper.

Herzer, Dierk. 2012. "How Does Foreign Direct Investment Really Affect Developing Countries' Growth?" *Review of International Economics* 20 (2): 396–414.

Hoang, Hong Hiep, and Duc Hung Bui. 2015. "Determinants of foreign direct investment in ASEAN: A panel approach". *Management Science Letters* 5: 213–222.

Hobday, Mike. 2001. "The Electronics Industries of Pacific Asia: Exploiting International Production Networks for Economic Development". *Asia Pacific Economic Literature* 15: 13–29.

Hsieh, Wen-Jen, and Min-Ching Hong. 2005. "The determinants of foreign direct investment in Southeast Asian transition economies." In *Proceedings of the Eighth Conference on Cross-Strait Chinese Culture and Management*, Sichuan University, China.

Iamsiraroj, Sasi. 2016. "The Foreign Direct Investment-Economic Growth Nexus". *International Review of Economics and Finance* 42: 116–133.

Ismail, Normaz Wana. 2009. "The Determinant of Foreign Direct Investment in ASEAN: A Semi-Gravity Approach". *Transition Studies Review* 16 (3): 710–722.

Kaplinsky, Raphael. 2000. "Globalisation and Unequalisation: What Can Be Learned from Value Chain Analysis?" *Journal of Development Studies* 37 (2): 117–146.

Kiyota, Kozo, and Shujiro Urata. 2004. "Exchange Rate, Exchange Rate Volatility and Foreign Direct Investment". *World Economy* 27 (10): 1501–1536.

Koojaroenprasit, Sauwaluck. 2015. "Determinants of Foreign Direct Investment in AEC Countries". *International Journal of Economic Research* 12 (1): 113–120.

Lily, Jaratin, Mori Kogid, Dullah Mulok, and Rozilee Asid. 2014. "Exchange Rate Movement and Foreign Direct Investment in ASEAN Economies". *Economics Research International* 2014: 1–10.

Mencinger, Joze. 2003. "Does foreign direct investment always enhance economic growth?" *International Review for Social Sciences* 56 (4): 491–508.

Mehrens, Dorothy, Balasundram Maniam and James Bexley. 2002. "A Survey of Determinants of US Foreign Direct Investment in ASEAN-5 Countries". *Journal of Economics and Economic Education Research* 3 (1): 87.

Mody, Ashoka, and Antu Panini Murshid. 2005. "Growing Up with Capital Flows". *Journal of International Economics*: 249–266.

Ng, Francis, and Alexander Yeats. 2003. "Major Trade Trends in East Asia. What are their Implications for Regional Cooperation and Growth". Policy Research Working Paper: No. 3084. Washington DC: World Bank.

Nwosu, Emmanuel O., Anthony Orji, Nathaniel Urama, and Joseph Amuka. 2013. "Regional Integration and Foreign Investment: The Case of ASEAN Countries". *Asian Economic and Financial Review* 3 (12): 1670–1680.

Organisation for Economic Co-operation and Development (OECD). 2014. "Southeast Asia Investment Policy Perspectives". Paris: OECD.

Pain, Nigel, and Desirée Van Welsum. 2003. "Untying the Gordian Knot: The Multiple Links between Exchange Rates and Foreign Direct Investment". *Journal of Common Market Studies* 823–846.

Pham, Thi Hong Hanh, and Thinh Duc Nguyen. 2013. "Foreign Direct Investment, Exports and Real Exchange Rate Linkages in Vietnam: Evidence from a Co-Integration Approach." *Journal of Southeast Asian Economies* 30 (3): 250–262.

Razin, Assaf. 2004. "The Contribution of FDI Flows to Domestic Investment in Capacity, and Vice Versa." In *Growth and Productivity in East Asia, NBER-East Asia Seminar on Economics* (vol. 13), edited by Takatoshi Ito and Andrew K. Rose. Chicago: University of Chicago Press.

Sazanami, Y., S. Yoshimura, and Kozo Kiyota. 2003. "Japanese Foreign Direct Investment to East Asia and Exchange Rate Policies: Some Longer-Term Policy Implications after the Crisis". *Keio Economic Studies* 40 (1): 1–26.

Stokman, Alan C., and Peter J.G. Vlar. 1996. "Volatility, International Trade, and Capital Flows". *Risk Management in Volatile Financial Markets* 115–132.

Tan, Khee Giap, Sangiita Wei Cher Yoong, Sasidaran Gopalan, and Le Phuong Anh Nguyen. 2015. *2014 Annual Competitiveness Ranking and Simulation Study for ASEAN-10 and Development Strategies to Enhance Asia Economic Connectivity*. World Scientific, Singapore.

Udomkerdmongkol, Manop, Oliver Morrisey, and Holger Görg. 2009. "Exchange Rates and Outward Foreign Direct Investment: US FDI in Emerging Economies". *Review of Development Economics* 13 (4): 754–764.

Van Assche Ari, and Byron Gangnes. 2010. "Electronics Production Upgrading: Is China Exceptional?" *Applied Economics Letters* 17 (5): 477–482.

Xaypanya, Phonesavanh, Poomthan Rangkakulnuwat, and Sasiwimon Warunsiri Paweenawat. 2015. "The Determinants of Foreign Direct Investment in ASEAN: The First Differencing Panel Data Analysis". *International Journal of Social Economics*, 42, 3: 239–250.

Xing, Yuqing. and Guangua Wan. 2006. "Exchange Rates and Competition for FDI in Asia". *World Economy* 29 (4): 419–434.

Discussant Notes 4.1

Dr Darius Tirtosuharto

Economist, Economic and Monetary Policy Department, Macroeconomic Division, Central Bank of Indonesia

What is fascinating about the ASEAN economies is the fact that they remain a major recipient of FDI. ASEAN has received around 16 percent of the global FDI among developing countries. Since the 1998–1999 economic crisis, FDI has built up quite a remarkable success story in developing ASEAN countries. Globalisation has fueled the need for external financing, which in many cases has been the primary source of investments as well as a source of risk associated with exchange rate volatility and currency mis-match.

In determining the impact of the REER on FDI, the focus is in the transmission of currency appreciation or depreciation of trade and cost competitiveness. Both trade and cost competitiveness is considered as the primary factor that drives profits of private enterprises. An increase in REER (appreciation) implies that exports become more expensive and imports become cheaper, which may lower trade competitiveness for FDI that are export oriented and particularly with less dependency on import of raw materials. For this type of enterprise or investments, the key is whether lower cost of production translates to being more competitive. Nevertheless, appreciation of REER does not always result in a higher price of exported goods due to differences in the cost structure between countries.

Inflow of FDI could also target the domestic market particularly in a country such as Indonesia that has a large population and a growing middle class consumers. In this case, REER appreciation may actually build consumer confidence to spend, as import becomes cheaper, although income from export is potentially less. Hence, without a certain incentive structure, import substitution will not take place naturally. Thus, amidst currency appreciation, the impact on FDI with domestic orientation is also no less favorable, likewise in the case of FDI with export orientation. This becomes an issue when countries are determined to depreciate their currency to gain the most economic benefits including attracting FDI, but have not considered other factors in play such as REER volatility that is relatively common in emerging market economies.

The contribution of this paper is an effort to identify the impact of cost competitiveness using REER as a proxy towards FDI, which is also consistent with the impact of REER volatility. Whereas, in the case of ASEAN countries, the findings are consistent with the hypothesis in which FDI is deterred by REER appreciation and increasing REER volatility. The paper concluded that FDI inflow into ASEAN is mostly export oriented and therefore there are incentives for policy makers to maintain REER competitiveness.[14]

---

[14] All the five ASEAN countries, initially focused on import-substitution strategy before shifted to export-oriented industrialisation (Singapore 1960s; Malaysia, Philippines, Thailand 1970s; and Indonesia 1980s). Consequently, there are different strategies on managing exchange rate and also different motives of attracting FDI in ASEAN.

In the case of Indonesia, the study shows that REER appreciation has a negative impact on FDI. Hence, volatility of the exchange rate seems to have a positive correlation with FDI. Despite this surprising result, another study also came to the same conclusion.[15] Among other factors, including one argued in the paper where FDI inflow in Indonesia is more and more toward export-oriented, there are a number of factors that should be considered related to the finding that is specific to the Indonesian case. First, is whether the consideration of foreign investors is merely on output growth? Thus, some degree of exchange rate volatility can still be tolerated as long as there is stability over expected growth. In other word, this is the phenomenon of risk-averse investors.

Other study highlights the importance to address the possible misperception by foreign investors. The panel data on East Asia countries (China, Indonesia, Malaysia, Philippines, South Korea and Thailand) indicates that exchange rate volatility tends to induce FDI.[16] This finding is perceived as the possible misconception over REER volatility that is assumed to lean toward depreciation and therefore, it provides an incentive to invest.

In sum, macroeconomic stability still holds the key to maintain sustainability of output growth, which is considered as the most important factor in attracting FDI. Macroeconomic stability shall be also directed to guide investors' perception towards measurable risks and opportunities. Central Bank as the monetary authority is responsible to manage exchange rate volatility with the balancing over optimum exchange rate based on the economic fundamental (inflation target) and investment promotions that will generate new jobs and sustain growth. While foreign investors are assumed to be able to measure the risks associated with macroeconomic stability, market expectation, and also costs competitiveness in which REER is the key indicator.[17]

References

Crowley, Patrick, and Jim Lee. 2003. "Exchange Rate Volatility and Foreign Investment: International Evidence" *The International Trade Journal* 17(3): 227–252.

Dhakal, Dharmendra, Raja Nag, Pradhan Gyan, and K.P. Upadhyaya. 2010. "Exchange Rate Volatility and Foreign Direct Investment: Evidence from East Asian Countries," *International Business & Economics Research Journal* 9(7): 121–128.

[15] See Crowley and Lee (2003) as well as Dhakal *et al.* (2010).

[16] See Dhakal *et al.* (2010).

[17] Forex reserve management or hedging is necessary to guard againts possible currency mis-match in emerging market economies.

Discussant Notes 4.2

Professor Sin Chor-Yiu

Department of Economics,
College of Technology Management,
National Tsing Hua University, Taiwan, Republic of China (ROC)

1. Introduction

Foreign direct investment (henceforth FDI) inflows to developing economies have been a hot topic for quite a period of time. Among many reasons, this may be due to the fact that FDI arguably plays a significant role to play in supplementing not only domestic capital, but also technology, skills as well as regional value chains. Consequently, it is important to understand how FDI inflows accelerate economic growth quantitatively.

FDI inflows is different from portfolio investments and typically it is a type of capital flow which is more stable. It is documented that Asian economies, which are well-known of rapid growth in the last half-a-century or so, have been receiving FDI inflows from 25 percent of world FDI to Asia in 1995 to 40 percent in 2014.

A number of crucial determinants on FDI have been considered in the literature. For instance, there are concerns the movement of exchange rates both in terms of their levels and volatility. This is because for developing or emerging economies, cost-competitiveness is crucial to attract global FDI inflows.

More concretely, this chapter considers the impact or impacts of real effective exchange rates (henceforth REERs) on the FDI inflows. REER is used as a proxy for cost-competitiveness. The research question is how the level and volatility of the REER affect FDI inflows.

Four panel data sets are considered in this chapter. They are:

a. The Association of Southeast Asian Nations countries excluding Indonesia (henceforth ASEAN-9);
b. The sub-national economies of Mainland China;
c. The sub-national economies of India; and
d. The sub-national economies of Indonesia.

Sub-national data are used so that heterogeneity within a country can be accounted for. Annual data are used which time span, due to the availability of data, varies with different data sets. More precisely, for ASEAN-9 and Mainland China, the time span is 1995–2014. For India, it is 2000–2013. And for Indonesia: 2000–2014.

2. Methodology and Results — A Summary

This section gives short summaries of the methodology and empirical results of the chapter. Methodologically, in the baseline model, while FDI inflows is the explained variable (for different countries/states/federal territories i and different year t),

- Apart from REER, there are a whole bunch of explanatory variables, various across the four panel data models, as controls;
- Country/state/federal territory-specific dummy;
- Time dummy.

In the augmented model, there are two more explanatory variables, namely, foreign exchange reserves (FXR), and an interaction term between FXR and REER. These two variables aim to capture the impact of the sustained appreciation (to a lesser extent, of the sustained depreciation). These major empirical findings include:

- The level of REER is significantly negative for all four panel data models.
- The volatility of REER, which is measured by its standard deviation, renders various results. More specifically, for ASEAN-9, it is insignificant. For Mainland China and Indonesia, it is significantly negative. And for India, it is significantly positive.
- The interaction term between FXR and REER is insignificant for all four panel data models.

3. Comments

Having offered an overview of the chapter, this section will focus on some specific comments, concerns and suggestions about the methodology, empirical results and some others.

In most, if not all, of the developing or emerging countries/sub-national economies, FDI is constrained by the host countries/economies. This certainly affects the demand side of direct investment. One of the authors responded that the constraints are some macroeconomic variables, which possibly affect the FDI across countries/economies.

For the supply side, if the total supply is the only concerned, this kind of regulatory constraints may not be substantial. The idea of this paper is how the costs of production (or the profitability) affect the amounts of FDI. The related policy implication(s) is also discussed in this chapter. It is unclear why the REER is the major factor in determining the costs. Professor Saikat Sinha Roy commented that other factors may involve many infrastructure variables and the authors may want to take the principal components of them.

For the demand side, the factors affecting the costs may include (i) wage in terms of the host currency (or the home currency). Unfortunately, the authors do not consider any variable "wage" for ASEAN-9. For the sub-national economies, only the minimum wage is used; (ii) other costs of production; (iii) tax holiday; (iv) nominal exchange rate between the host country and the home country, and those between the competitive country and the home country; and (v) the uncertainty of the nominal exchange rate or the nominal exchange rates.

All in all, the REER used in this chapter may be more relevant to trade, rather than FDI. For the FDI, the (nominal or real) exchange rate (or several choices of exchange rates) between the host economy and the home economy may be more relevant. One of the authors responded that REER is a commonly used variable in international finance.

To investigate the uncertainty of the nominal exchange rate(s), apart from the standard deviation, some other factors may be considered. They include (i) various exchange rate regimes (one of the authors responded that these can be captured in the time-specific dummies); (ii) the foreign exchange reserves, which is unfortunately only considered in the augmented model. Further, the authors may want to use the spread between the forex futures and the forex spot instead of the standard deviation of the REER.

On the other hand, for the regulatory constraints in the demand side, one may consider variables such as the competitiveness of the domestic firms, and the political power of those firms. All in all, while panel data model is used and the number of observations increases, the general principle applies: heterogeneity among the countries/economies needs to be taken care. In particular, it is unclear whether fixed-effect dummies capture all the heterogeneity. More precisely, both country/economy-specific effects and time-specific effects should be carefully accounted for. The time-specific effects seem particularly important since, just name a few pieces of fact:

- "FDI to the region has also risen in terms of its share in ASEAN's GDP which increased from 3.49 percent in 1990 to 5.39 percent in 2014."
- "FDI inflows averaged around 1.5 percent of GDP between 1990 and 1997. FDI inflows were in the negative from 1998 to 2003 following AFC. Its share has remained modest post-AFC, peaking at 2.9 percent in 2005, and hovering just under three percent in 2014."
- "Mainland China — Peaks in 1995, recovers after the AFC and significant turns around since 2000 up until the GFC and then picks up again."
- "India — Steady and gradual increase since 1990s, but marked turnaround since 2001 up until GFC and then a slow down before picking up again since 2012, reaching pre-GFC levels."

Thus, if resources permit, the authors may want to consider some other disaggregate data.

In the existing literature, the impact of the REER and that of the standard deviation are diverse. That said, the authors may want to elaborate how the current research may potentially have certain new contributions. The inclusion of the interaction term between FXR and REER is new. Unfortunately, it is insignificant for all four panel data models. One of the authors responded that there may be a better choice of variables.

The major empirical findings are not easy to interpret. The authors may want to elaborate why the impact of the standard deviation are different in the four panel data models.

Based on the empirical findings, the authors jump to a number of policy implications. On various pages of the presentation slides, the following recommendations are made:

- "ASEAN and Mainland China tend to be more export-oriented in nature." "As India positions itself as a platform for more export-oriented FDI, policy makers need to be more concerned about exchange rate competitiveness and managing REER appreciation." Judging from the empirical findings, will ASEAN and Mainland China deserve the same policy recommendation?

- "To maintain cost competitiveness, policymakers might be better off focusing on controlling domestic unit business costs." Is this a conclusion out of the empirical findings? Or is it a general comment?
- For India, "Impact of REER (levels) being weakly significant is suggestive of FDI inflows into India being relatively more domestic-oriented in nature." the results for ASEAN and Mainland China seem to be more strongly significant, though qualitatively the same. Will ASEAN and Mainland China deserve a similar policy recommendation?
- "Maintaining cost competitiveness through an exchange rate regime centred on inflation targeting, supported by disciplined fiscal policy likely to be more durable than trying to manage the currency per se" This is another strong policy recommendation. Will ASEAN and Mainland China deserve a similar policy recommendation?
- "For ASEAN countries and Mainland China: countries should aim to enhance transparency and communication in exchange rate policies and eschew short-term beggar-thy-neighbour policies." Is this a conclusion out of the empirical findings? Or is it a general comment?
- "For all countries: While managing exchange rate volatility (by the so-called "leaning against the wind") is somewhat less controversial, if too successful, might lead to moral hazard problems, i.e. agents fail to take actions in covering individual risks, which hinders the development of financial markets and instruments to hedge against FX risks." Is this recommendation also applied to ASEAN — 9 and India, when the impact of the standard deviation is insignificant for the former, and it is significantly positive for the latter?

Last but not least, we would like to make the following editorial comments:

- All the references are missing.
- For a general readership, some special terms such as gross state domestic products (GSDP and gross region domestic products (GRDP) should be defined at the outset.
- "weight the FDI inflows" should read "weigh the FDI inflows".
- Why Java provinces make a difference? One of the authors responded that this is to avoid the "Java effect" whose DGP accounts for 80 percent of the Indonesian GDP.
- Why change in foreign exchange reserves (FXR) is omitted.

The summaries and comments above notwithstanding, this chapter makes an important contribution to the interesting topic of the impacts of real effective exchange rates on foreign direct investment inflows.

Discussant Notes 4.3

Dr Wang Lee-Rong

Research Fellow, International Division, Chung-Hua Institution for Economic Research, Taiwan, Republic of China (ROC)

Distinguished guest, ladies and gentlemen, Good Afternoon!

US President Elect Donald Trump is likely to accuse some of the ASEAN to manipulate the exchange rate. Traditionally, the Central Bank has several jobs to do, one of which is financial stability, and the other is probably to stimulate industrial development or macroeconomics and so on.

For the manipulation of exchange rate, the focus is probably on the part of trade. Today, your focus is on the impact of exchange rate on FDI. I guess this is very informative and you provide a lot of insight for those entrepreneurs who may be interested to invest in the ASEAN countries, maybe in the sub-regional consideration. I think this is the main contribution of this paper. And also, it will be very helpful for Taiwan, when we are promoting the new South Bound policy. I will bring this back for reference to my colleagues and government officials. Thank you for that.

Second, I pointed out how the contribution of this paper is from the view of economics and entrepreneurs. This paper comprehensively sorts out literature, including theoretical and empirical studies. The paper also takes into account regional factors, for which the literature review is very abundant. So academically it is very useful. Practically, as I mentioned, it is useful for those entrepreneurs whose interest lies in FDI activity in this area.

There are several questions I would like to raise however. One is the confusion of the theory explanation raised in this paper. My suggestion is that when you mention the domestic market oriented FDI, it should be properly classified as export oriented and domestic oriented. It would be clearer. The domestic market oriented FDI, as you mentioned, can be explained by the wealth effects and cost competitiveness effects.

My major comment is that I would suggest to you to combine the effect of trade liberalisation. The reason is for instance in China, there are several so called free trade areas. Like Shanghai free trade area, Guangdong and so on. If you brought in these kind of factors in the research, I guess you can make it more informative.

Here I would like to remind you that the definition of the controlled variable, trade openness, is the sum of exports and imports of goods and services measured as a share of regional domestic product. This is what you call trade openness. However, trade openness is usually mentioned in relation to trade liberalisation, which is also a very important factor to include in FDI inflows. I provide you several literature that has been done in the past. For instance, the one done by Thangavelu and Findlay (2011). This paper indicates whether membership of bilateral or regional trade agreements has a differential impact on FDI Inflows in the Asia Pacific region. As

Figure 1: FDI Inflows into ASEAN, 1990–2014

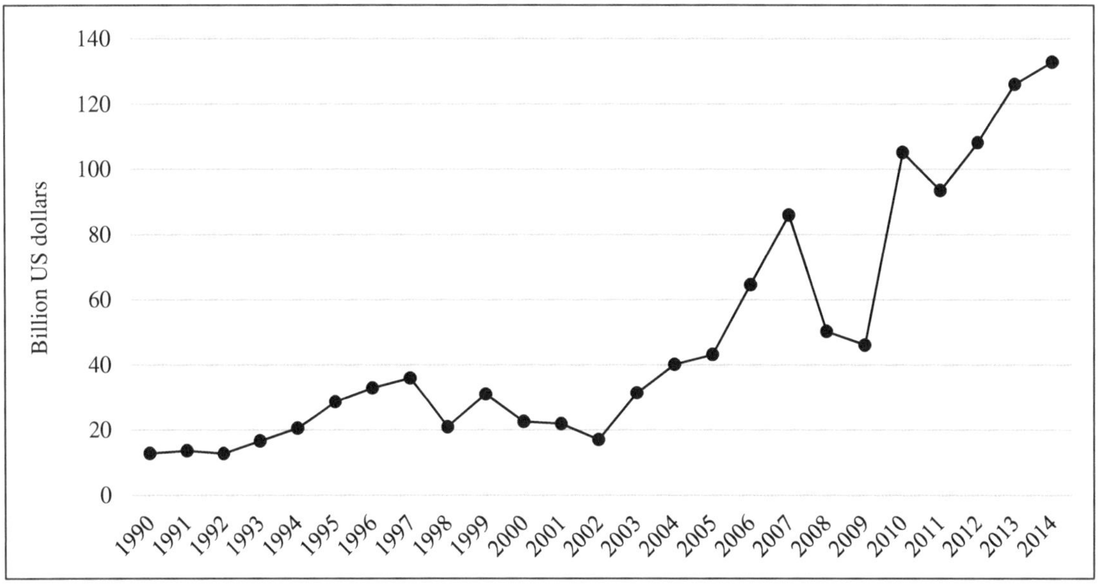

Source: UNCTAD.

Figure 2: Relation between FTA and FDI Inflows — the Cases of Taiwan's Financial FDI to Viet Nam

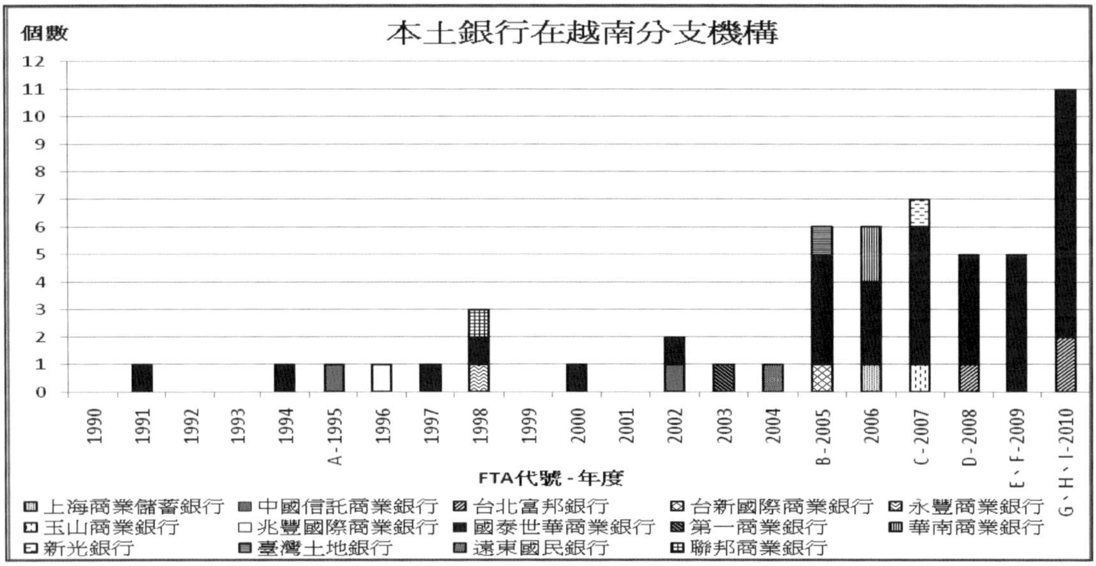

Source: Wang, Lee-Rong *et al.*, "The Impact of Asia Pacific Regional Integration on the Development of Financial Service Industry", Research Project Entrusted by Financial Supervisory Commission R.O.C. (Taiwan), November 2011.

Figure 3: FDI Expressed as Share of Fixed Asset Investment (FAI)

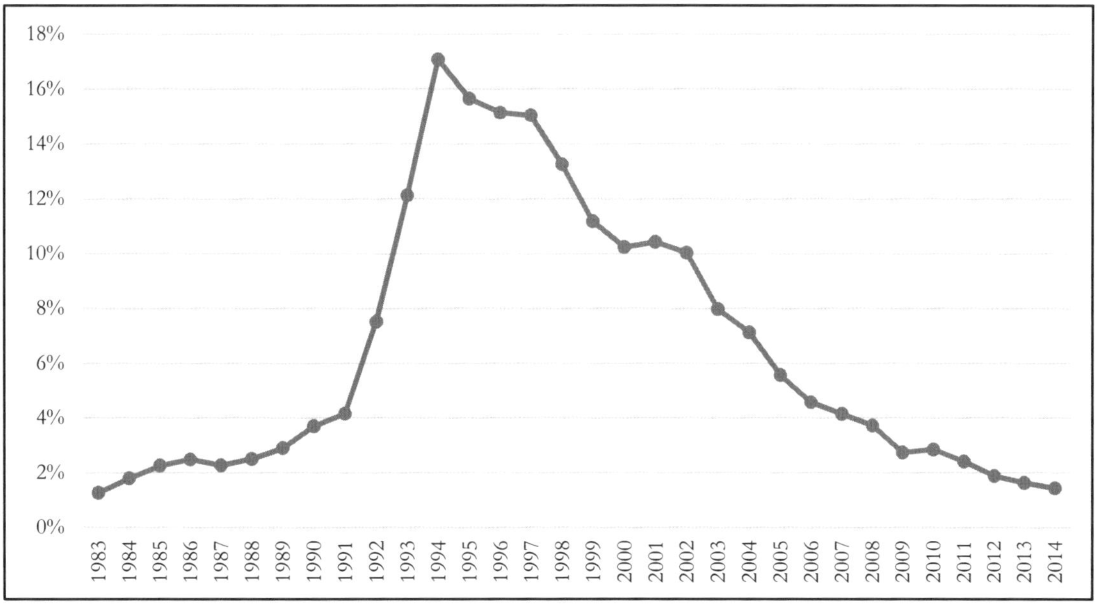

Note: Fixed Asset Investment data are collected from National Bureau of Statistics of China and are expressed in current local currency unit, namely Chinese Yuan or Renminbi. We transfer the data into the current USD using the annual exchange rates provided by the World Bank.
Source: Asia Competitiveness Institute based on National Bureau of Statistics of China.

I just mentioned, in the ASEAN area there are a lot of free trade which took effect in different years. For instance, ASEAN China Free Trade Agreement (FTA) took effect in 2005. Especially in 2010, three ASEAN related FTA took effect, between ASEAN — Australia, New Zealand, ASEAN — India and the third being ASEAN — Korea. So the impact brought by these FTA can be observed from Figure 1, which was most significant in year 2010.

In the work I have done before, I conducted a project related to Taiwan's financial FDI to Vietnam. You see in Figure 2 (especially in 2010, which I mentioned had at least three ASEAN related FTAs), the horizontal axis is the time period and the vertical axis represents the number of branches which were established by Taiwan's bank in Vietnam. You can see it is very clear from 2005 until 2010, the FDI related to Taiwan's bank in Vietnam significantly increased. So, that's for your reference.

The last one I will mention is about the Asian Financial Crisis. In the picture below you can see, the impacts of Asian financial crisis on FDI seem big and last for long in the case of China. The Asian financial crisis took place in the year 1997, which was not covered. However the global financial crisis will be covered by your data. You can cover it and see what impact it will have.

These are my comments, thank you.

Chapter 5

One Belt One Road Initiative: Global and Geo-economic Perspectives

5.1 Introductory Notes

The origin of the One Belt One Road (OBOR) initiative can be traced back to the speech by President Xi Jinping when the idea of building an economic belt along the ancient Silk Route was proposed during his state visit to Kazakhstan in September 2013. The idea was reiterated a month later when President Xi visited Indonesia and put forward another initiative of 21st Century Maritime Silk Road.[1] The proposal which was officially termed OBOR or the Belt and Road Initiative (BRI) took off rapidly with concrete steps being taken subsequently. The commitment of the Chinese government in promoting the initiative is also reflected in the enshrinement of the initiative in the party's constitution during the 19th National Congress of the Chinese Communist Party.[2]

Inspired by the ancient Silk Route which connected the East and the West and allowed the exchange of goods, culture and knowledge, OBOR will be covering the continents of Africa, Asia and Europe, which account for more than 60 percent of world population and 30 percent of world GDP.[3] It took almost two years since President Xi's 2013 speech for an action plan detailing the structure and mechanism of OBOR to be announced at the Boao Forum in March 2015. The multilateral cooperation which laid out five cooperation priorities, namely (i) Policy coordination; (ii) Facilities connectivity; (iii) Unimpeded trade; (iv) Financial integration; and (v) People-to-people bonds,[4] aim to go beyond building economic synergy and incorporates the importance of sharing mutual social, political and cultural interests. These are to be achieved through connectivity enhancement.

The main feature of OBOR which envisions a common prosperity future augmented by an efficient and integrated network of land, sea and air connectivity has distinguished the initiative from other forms of multilateral cooperation. While some sceptics view this as China's move to exert its influence on the international scene, the formulation of OBOR is well received as illustrated in the establishment of Asian Infrastructure Investment Bank (AIIB), an initiative in line with OBOR which has received endorsement from 57 founding members.[5] Indeed, OBOR has come in a timely manner amid great infrastructure investment needs in Asia. For instance, the Asian Development Bank Institute (ADBI) has estimated that the overall infrastructure financing

[1] See Ploberger (2017) and President Xi's keynote speech given at the opening ceremony of the Belt and Road Forum for International Cooperation.

[2] See Goh and Ruwitch (2017).

[3] See Huang (2016).

[4] See Tian (2015).

[5] See the full list of members on the official website, https://www.aiib.org.

need for Asia from 2010 to 2020 amount to approximately 8 trillion US dollars, or an average of 730 million US dollars annually.[6]

While the Association of Southeast Asian Nations (ASEAN), particularly the less developed economies, namely Cambodia, Laos, Myanmar and Vietnam (CLMV), have achieved notable economic progress in the recent decades, inadequate infrastructure remains the bottleneck for the economies to forge ahead.[7] In particular, shortfalls in funding for infrastructure development among these developing economies has resulted in deadlock and hampered their growth potentials. Being part of the OBOR as well as founding members of the AIIB, ASEAN economies should leverage on its firstcomer advantage by taking active roles in formulating the policy direction and channelling the infrastructure funding mechanism towards fostering intra- and inter-ASEAN connectivity.

As OBOR gathers pace, more needs to be done to ensure its feasibility and sustainability as an emerging key growth engine. Given the potential ripple effects of OBOR on the global economy, it is relevant in today's context to achieve a deeper understanding of the initiative. The following sections continue with speeches on the OBOR from Mr K Shanmugam, who is Singapore's Minister for Home Affairs and Minister for Law, and Professor Liew Mun Leong, who is Chairman of Surbana Jurong and Changi Airport Group as well as Provost Chair and Professor of National University of Singapore. These two luminaries offer new lenses to look at OBOR from the global and geo-economy perspectives.

5.2 One Belt One Road Initiative: A Global Perspective[8]

INTRODUCTION

I thank the World Bank, and ACI for organising this forum, and for inviting me. Khee Giap asked me in June, and I agreed.

Now let me give my personal views on possible implications/ impact of OBOR:

(1) First, in the context of larger geopolitical trends — one of the consequences of which was indeed the OBOR;
(2) Second: The historical antecedents for OBOR, and the implications of that history today; and
(3) Third: Some aspects of the current international situation, which may, in my view, accelerate the impact of OBOR, and the larger geopolitical trends.

I will then set out what I think are the likely implications of OBOR in terms of: (1) the world economy; (2) security architecture; and (3) geopolitics.

[6] See Chapter 5 in Asian Development Bank Institute (2009).

[7] See Chapter 4 of Tan *et al.* (2017) for more discussion on development progress of CLMV.

[8] This section is a reprint with permission of the opening remarks by Minister K Shanmugam, Minister for Home Affairs and Minister for Law of Singapore, at the 2017 Asia Economic Forum organised by the Asia Competitiveness Institute (ACI), Lee Kuan Yew School of Public Policy (LKYSPP), National University of Singapore (NUS) on 28 August 2017. The speech is also available at https://www.mha.gov.sg/newsroom/speeches/Pages/Asia-Economic-Forum-on-The-One-Belt-One-Road-Initiative-Impact-and-Implications.aspx (accessed on 15 March 2018).

CONTEXT: (1) GEOPOLITICAL TRENDS

First, let's look at the larger geopolitical trends. Why do we need to look at them? Because OBOR is a result of these trends, and it will in turn shape these trends. What are the trends? The larger geopolitical trends are well known, can be put simply.

First: The rise of China. It is likely to be the largest world economy in absolute terms, though not in per capita terms. This is likely to happen sooner rather than later. Technologically, militarily — China will become a more significant player over the next 20–30 years. China aims to be a superpower — understandably. When you consider the combined metrics of economy, technology, population: You will conclude that China's aim to be a superpower is realistic.

Second: There will inevitably be a change of relative power between America and China. I am not suggesting that America is in decline. I want to make that clear. It will be a brave person who bets against the US or suggests that it is in actual decline. It is more a question of relativity. The relativities have already changed and will continue to change. In absolute terms, it will be some time yet before China or any other country can match the US, let alone surpass it, militarily. The US has a significant lead today. Its capabilities are huge, and its ability to project its power around the world impressive — indeed, unprecedented in world history.

Nevertheless, over time, the US will have less and less scope for unilateral action, especially in areas of the globe where China has strong interests. And China will not be able to ignore US interests either, even as its power increases. They will have to find a new Modus Vivendi. I don't see any of these as particularly controversial conclusions. I will share, in this context, what I had said in Washington in 2012, when I was Foreign Minister (see below).

"It is quite untenable to speak in terms of the "containment" of China. **China with a population of 1.3 billion people is** determined to progress in all fields and take its rightful place in the community of nations. **It will succeed in that. Its people are bright and technologically savvy.** The country and its people are not going to be contained.

From Singapore's perspective, the relationship between the US and China is not a zero-sum game. **The rise of China does not imply the decline of the US.** Competition between both countries can take place within a stable framework, with both countries playing a constructive role in world and regional affairs."

– Speech at The Center for Strategic and International Studies Singapore Conference, 8 February 2012

At that time, the US pivot to Asia was a big topic. I was quite blunt. I said: Some view the US engagement of Asia as a means to contain China. Such rhetoric was a mistake on many levels.

Any attempt by the US to contain China will not work, and it will not be supported by almost all countries in the region.

What is the situation today? Fast forward five years — China is fast drawing level with the most advanced countries, in many fields, and surging ahead in some. Its infrastructure, technology, education system, are now better than world class. Despite all the criticisms it receives, China has lifted 700 million people out of poverty within 30 years (see below). This is a feat unparalleled in history.

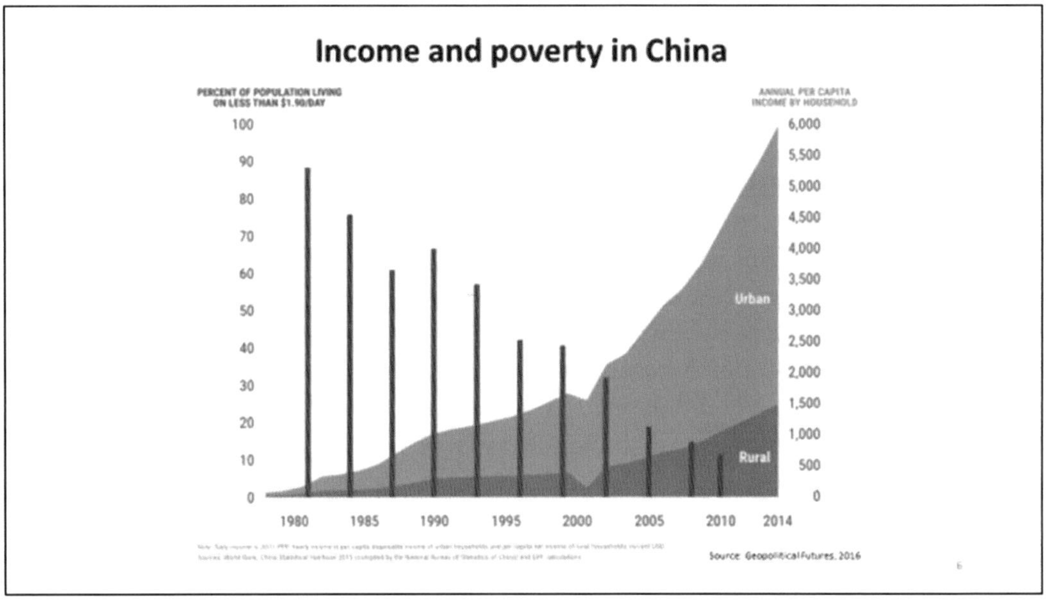

This was a country which, in our lifetimes, in the 80s was poor and backward. China's human rights critics will do well to bear this in mind. 700 million people's lives improved substantially; compared with the points they make. Let's look at some data.

(1) GDP

China and the US make up about 40 percent of the global economy in nominal GDP terms (see below). Today: US — is at about 25 percent, China — at 15 percent. If you go back to 1980: the US — was at about 26 percent, China — was at 2.7 percent. China's progress has been exponential; the US has more or less maintained its position.

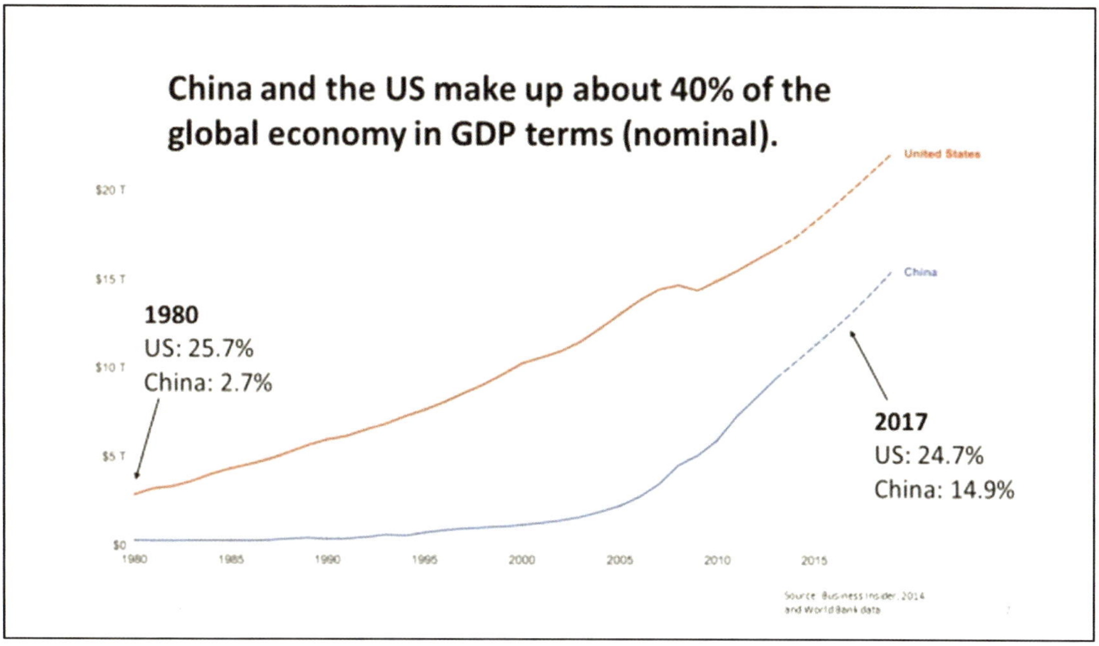
China and the US make up about 40% of the global economy in GDP terms (nominal).
United States
China
$20 T
$15 T
$10 T
$5 T
$0
1980
1985
1990
1995
2000
2005
2010
2015
1980
US: 25.7%
China: 2.7%
2017
US: 24.7%
China: 14.9%
Source: Business Insider, 2014
and World Bank data

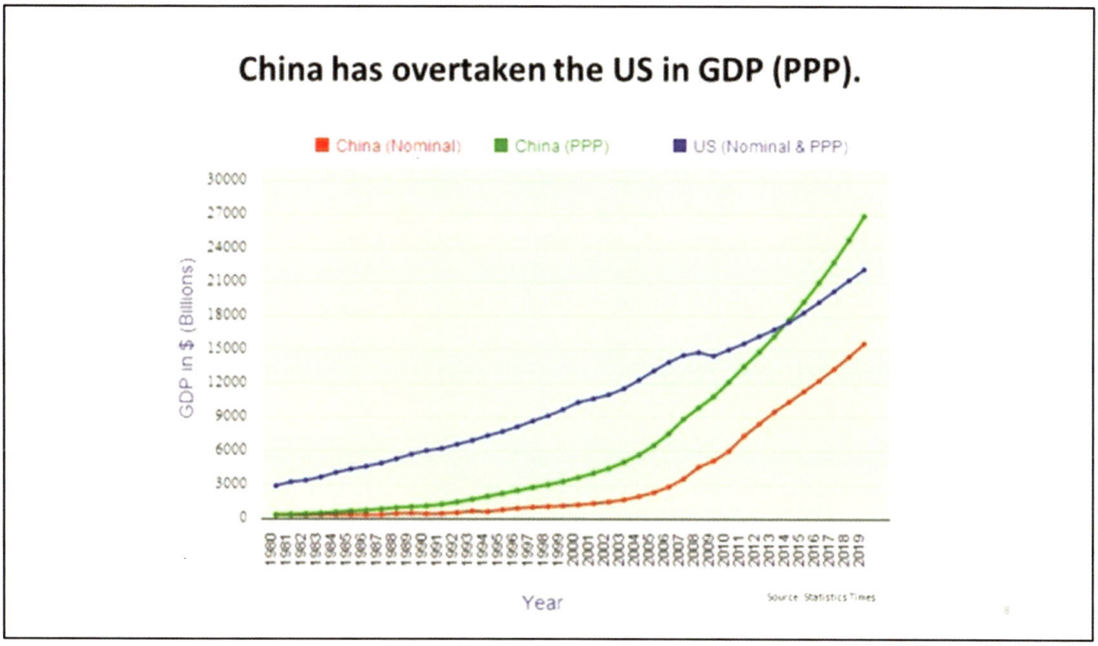
China has overtaken the US in GDP (PPP).
China (Nominal)
China (PPP)
US (Nominal & PPP)
GDP in $ (Billions)
30000
27000
24000
21000
18000
15000
12000
9000
6000
3000
0
1980 1981 1982 1983 1984 1985 1986 1987 1988 1989 1990 1991 1992 1993 1994 1995 1996 1997 1998 1999 2000 2001 2002 2003 2004 2005 2006 2007 2008 2009 2010 2011 2012 2013 2014 2015 2016 2017 2018 2019
Year
Source: Statistics Times

And China's share of world GDP will continue to grow (see above). Its GDP has already overtaken the US's GDP in PPP terms. Though, it is quite some way behind in per capita terms — and will probably remain so for some time to come. China's rate of growth now is roughly double that of the US (see below).

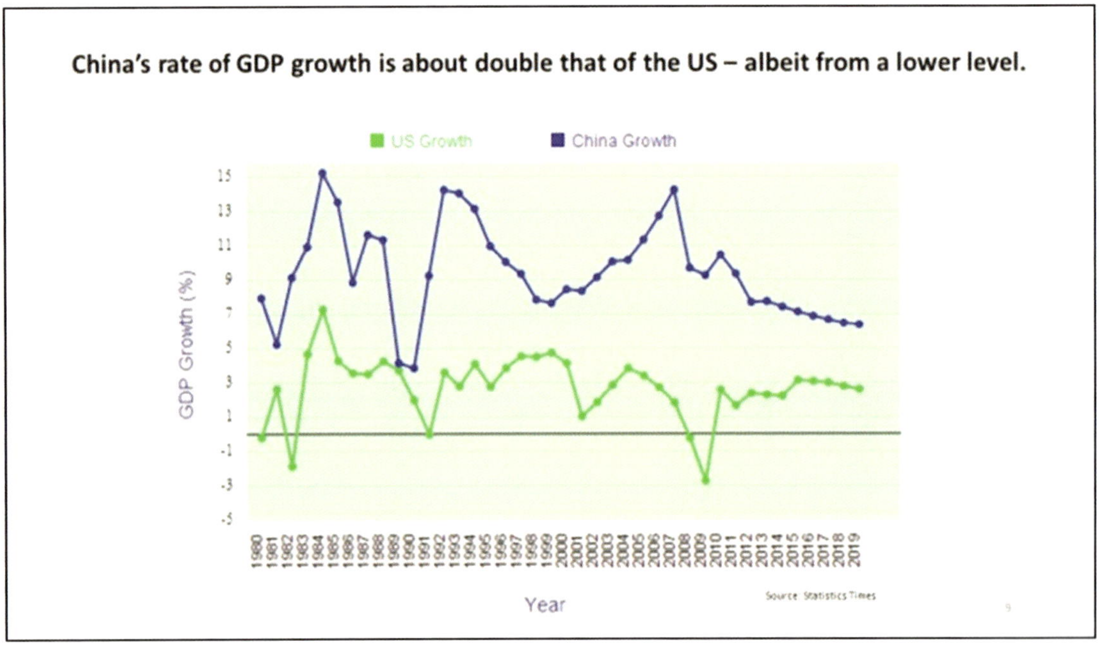

(2) <u>Population</u>

If you go to population, China's population is four times that of the US (see below). It is also interesting to look at the breakdown by age groups over population.

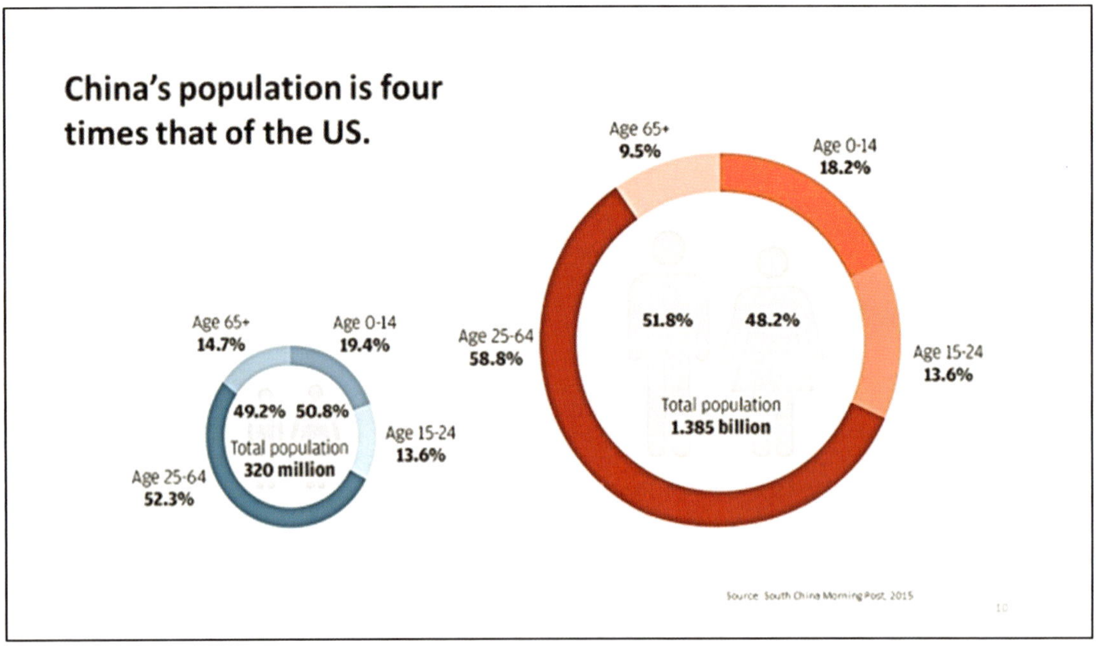

(3) Trade

If you look at trade, it is now the world's largest trading nation (see below).

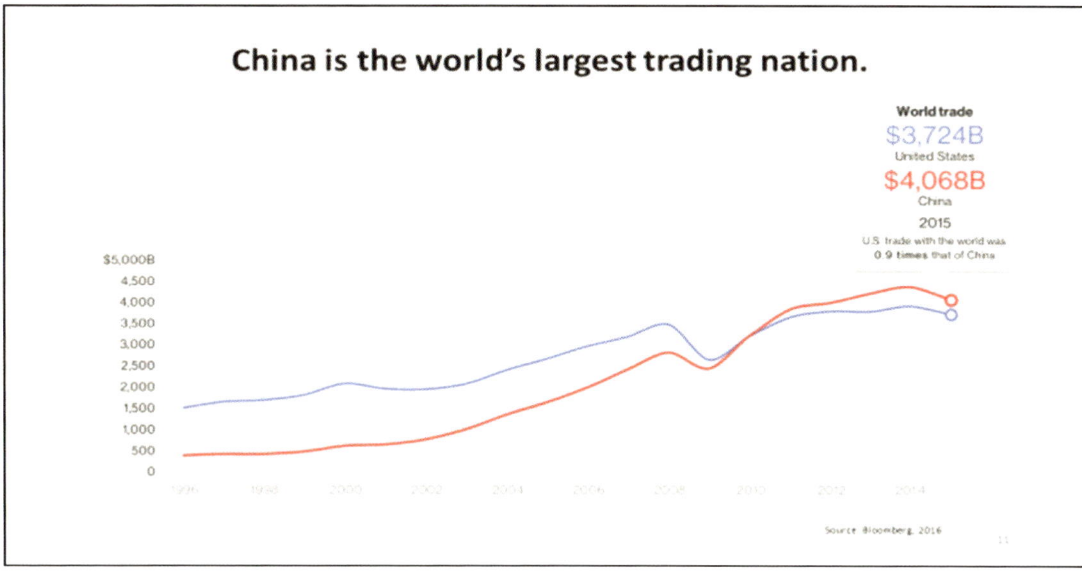

And the largest trading partner for most countries (see below).

These trends are irreversible. Any attempt to reverse or stem them will fail. I'll give you one illustration: The US Congress put up roadblocks to giving China its rightful role in the World Bank. But how is it possible to shut out a country with such a strong economy, such massive foreign reserves? China simply set up its own international Bank — the AIIB. And many countries, including Western countries, made haste to support the AIIB. So with or without OBOR — these underlying trends are inexorable. The OBOR is both a result of these trends and may well accelerate them. We'll come back to this later.

CONTEXT: (2) HISTORY

Let me now deal with the second of the three contextual points I wanted to make, which is history.

[A] <u>The History Taught in Schools</u>

The history that we are taught in schools, particularly in the colonies covered the early civilisations — Mesopotamia, Egypt, the Indus valley, Greece, China, but usually as a prelude to the rise of the West. China, India, the birth of Islam, the Jewish Diaspora — would get guest appearances, but it was generally a very Western-centred world view: the history of western empires, the great voyages of western exploration, and the western conquests.

[B] <u>Another Aspect of History: The Silk Route</u>

However, there is another perspective, which is quite important. Before you had Columbus, Magellan, Vasco da Gama, you had the Silk Route. And again, the slide (see below) speaks for itself in terms of the share of world trade throughout most of the last 2000 years, except for the last 300 years.

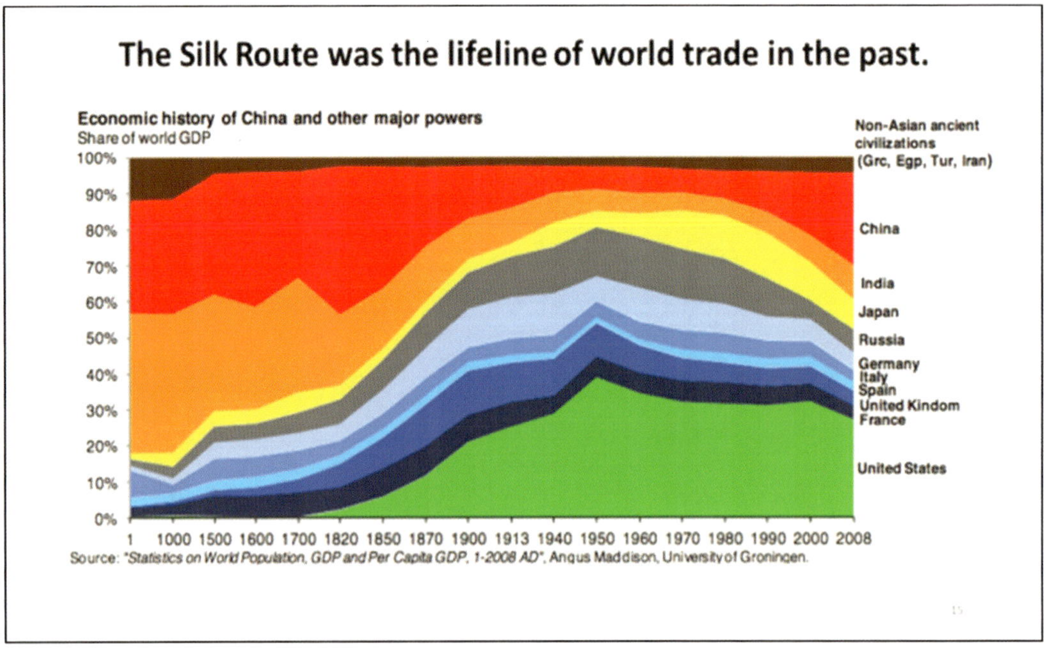

The history of trade shows that the global economic centre of gravity for much of human history was in China and India. And the Silk Route was the spine of world trade. It played a key role in world trade. Great cities of the past — Samarkand, Bukhara, Merv, prospered from their locations on this Silk Route.

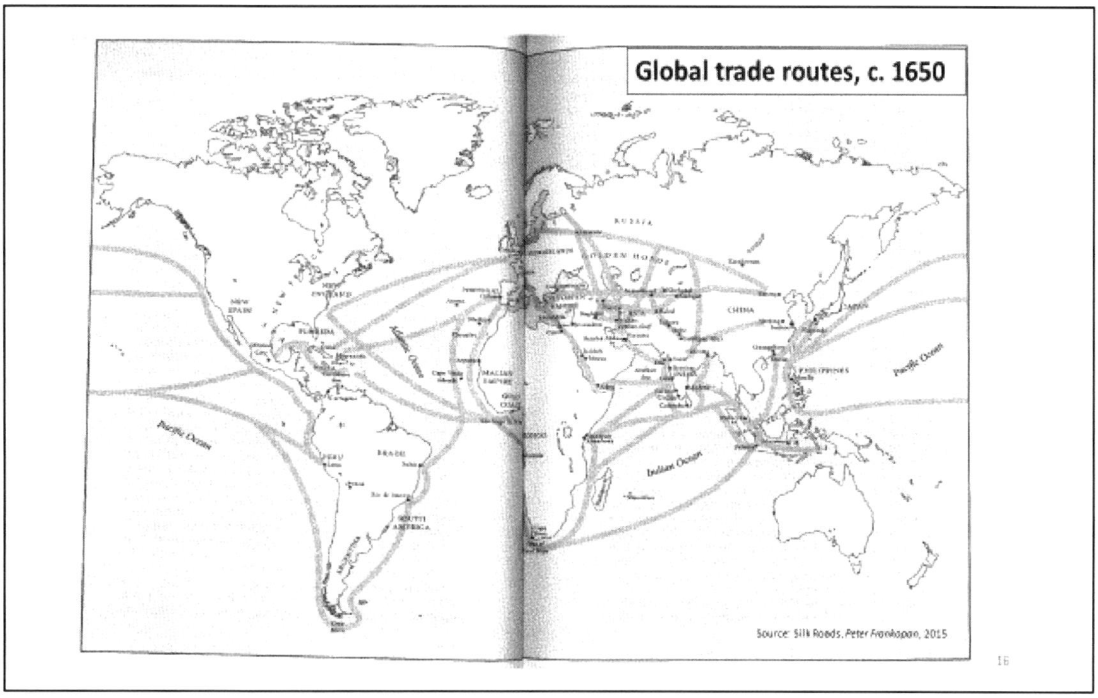

The Silk Route brought great wealth to China, and to the cities along the Route.

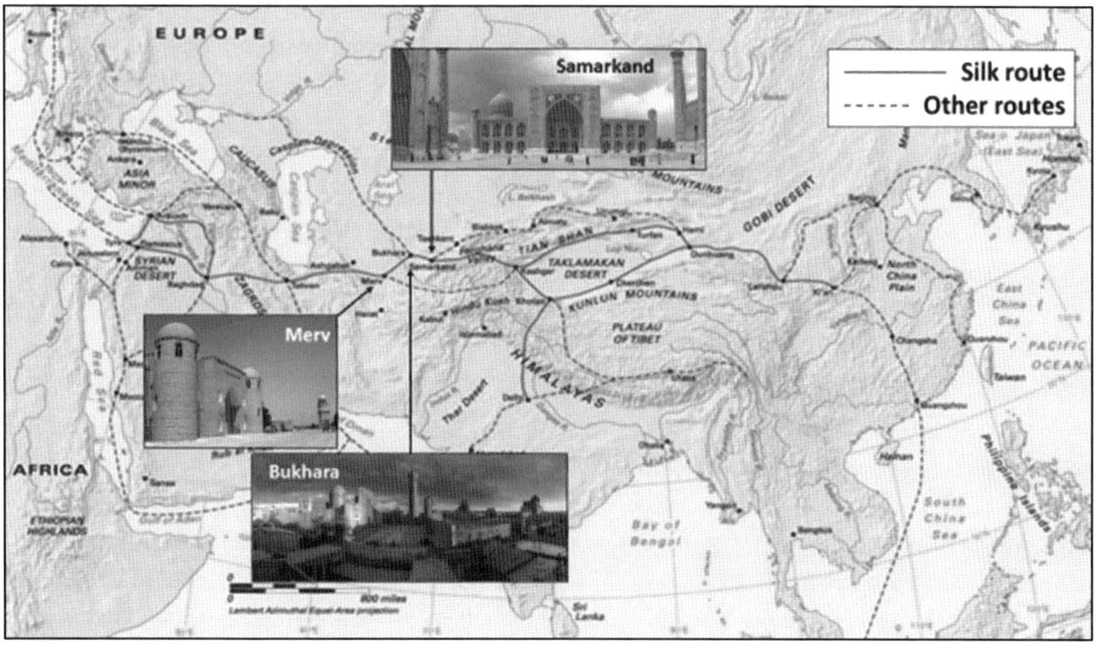

Ideas too spread along Silk Route. Buddhism began in India, spread to Afghanistan, on to China. Samarkand and Bukhara were centres of trade, scholarship, religion, culture. Asia was the centre of civilisation. And Asia, Central Asia was the centre of civilisation, centre of technology, centre of the world. With the OBOR, China tries to recreate this history. It is bold, it is imaginative, it is ambitious. It exemplifies the vision of a country that is today the world leader in many aspects of infrastructure technology (see below).

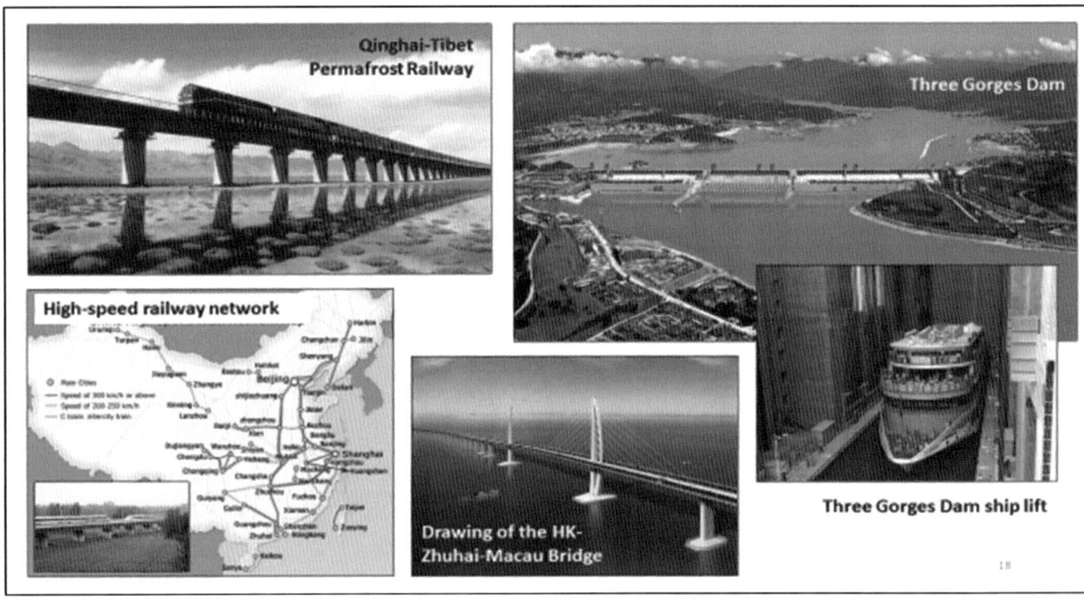

Take Permafrost railway for example: it presents multiple engineering challenges. Permafrost melts with slight changes in temperature — heat from trains can also cause melting. Permafrost thaws, ground becomes muddy, affecting integrity of entire system. For fragile sections, Chinese engineers built elevated tracks with pile-driven foundations sunk deep into the ground. And China has built an impressive rail network on Permafrost — quickly as well.

If you look at China's high-speed rail network — largest network in the world; 19,000 km of high-speed rail lines. 80 million passengers annually. China's First Emperor Shi Huang Di's feats of construction inspired the idiom "shave off mountain peaks and fill valleys" (*qian shan yin gu*). It is a country which centuries ago built a wall, which today can still be seen from space. The Chinese understand infrastructure.

CONTEXT: (3) CURRENT INTERNATIONAL SITUATION

Let me now deal with the third of my three points: the current international situation. The current international situation will, in my view, tend to accelerate the larger geopolitical trends which I spoke about. And I will list three developments that will impact these trends.

[A] China's Strategic Economic Engagement

China has been very strategic in the way it has been investing, linking up with countries, building relationships. If you see what is happening across the world — Asia, Africa, even South America.

China's companies have spread out (see below). They have invested billions. They are prepared to take risks, invest in large infrastructure projects.

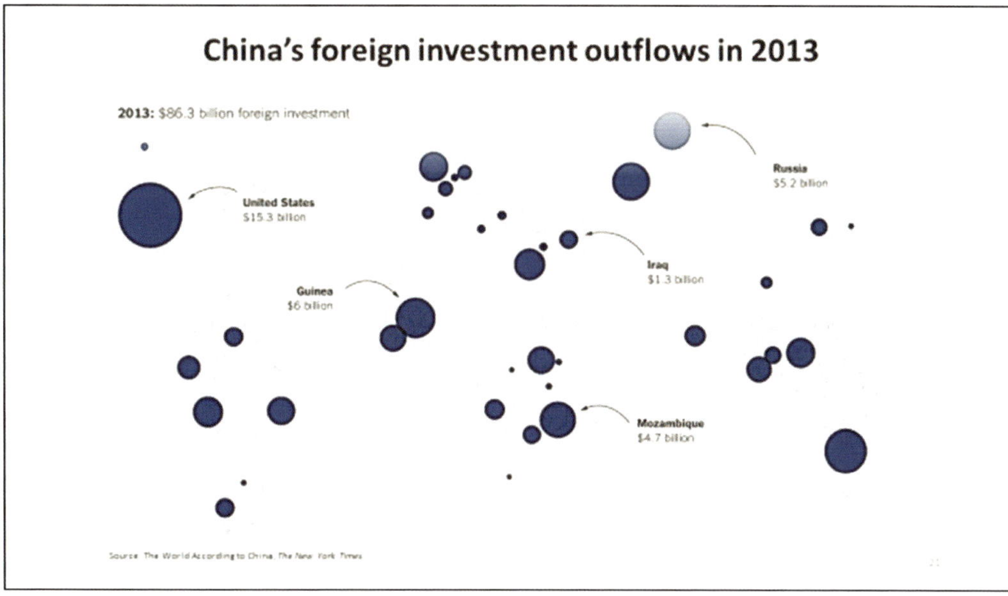

China identifies regions of interest, and then focuses on them relentlessly. Neither the US nor Europe can do the same. Their political + economic systems are different. Their leaders cannot make the same type of long-term commitments. For example, in Africa: China-Africa trade (see below) — was 10 billion dollars in 2000, it's 220 billion dollars in 2014. Chinese companies purchase stakes in mining operations in Africa, in return for loans to finance large-scale infrastructure projects — roads, railways, ports.

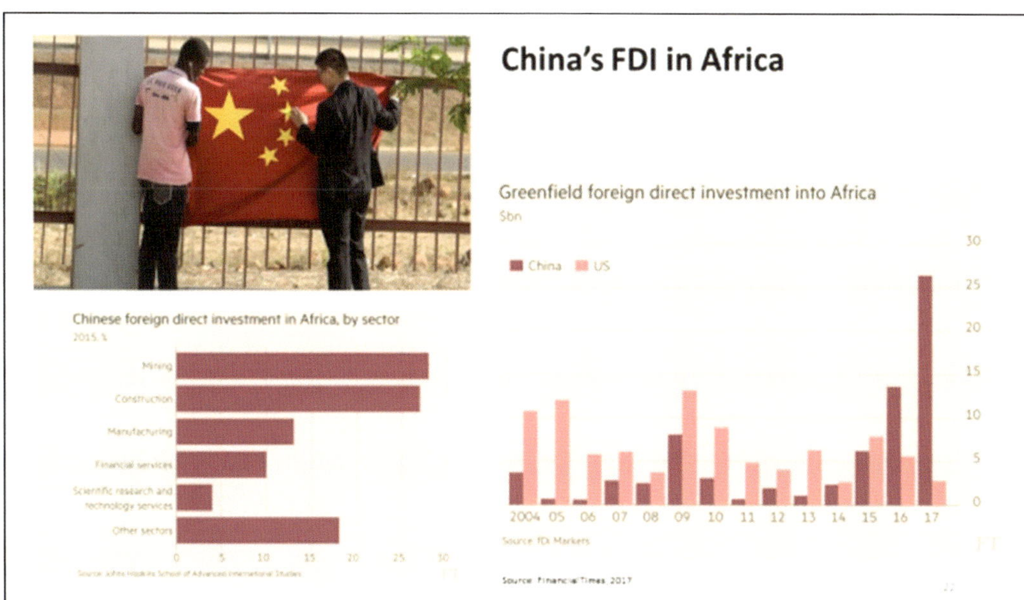

These investments create strong relationships. Of course, they have not been without some backlash. But on the whole, they predispose many countries towards BRI. Mainland Southeast Asia (SEA) has also seen very substantial Chinese investments. In addition, China offers a large market. And we are still only in the early stage of this trend. As the Chinese economy grows, this trend will accelerate.

[B] <u>China's Ability to Bring Together Its Resources and Focus Relentlessly on the Desired Outcome</u>

China's centralised system allows it to bring together the necessary resources and focus intensely, relentlessly, on the outcome that it wants. This is not to say that everything about the Chinese system is good or works well. China does have some serious issues, as China itself acknowledges — for instance, corruption is a serious issue and is being actively dealt with by President Xi and his team (see below).

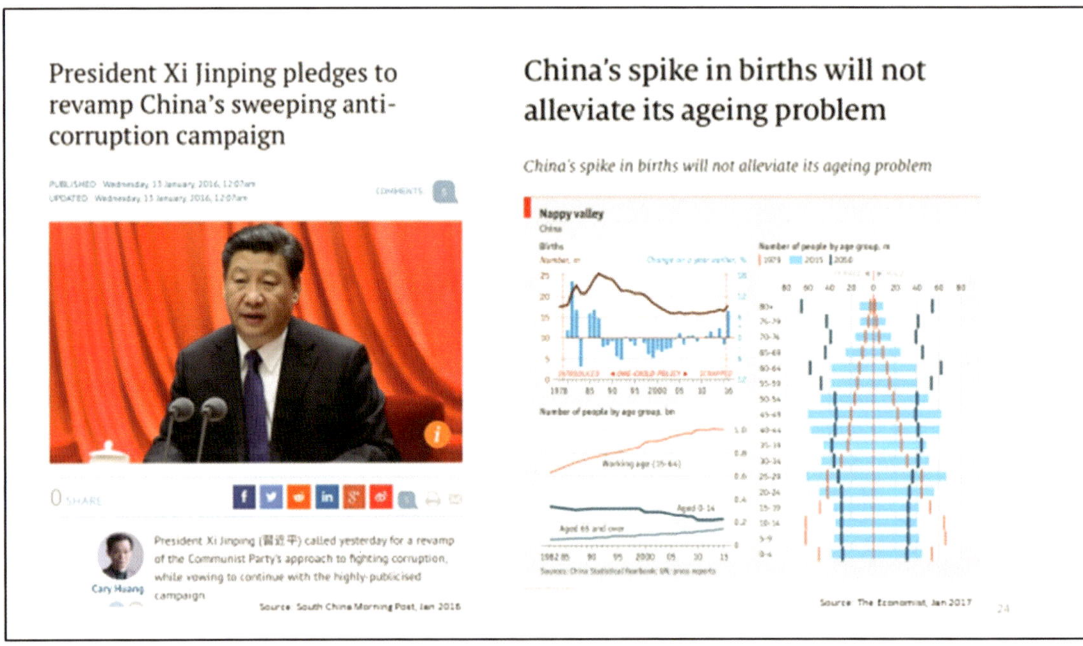

And over time China will have to deal with other social issues and political issues as well. These are pretty significant issues-

(a) Aging, for example. The Chinese will need to invest heavily in social infrastructure. (China, some say, will grow old, before it grows rich.)
(b) And the demands of a younger, better educated population.

Just to mention a few of the challenges. But objectively, one must acknowledge that over the last 35 years, China has achieved results for its people, on a scale that no other country in history has — both in terms of the speed with which the country has progressed and the sheer number of people who have made the leap from poverty to prosperity. Thus, while there can be many criticisms levelled at China and its political system, nevertheless, they are often skewed, or a little unbalanced. For example, you will often hear this: Chinese political system does not allow innovation, and so China cannot compete at the frontiers of modern science and technology. Therefore, it will not ultimately succeed. These and other variants of this arguments — including relating to the dominance of the Communist Party — are quite prevalent.

China has been showing its detractors are getting it wrong. Just take one field: Science and technology. China has shown it can move up the tech-value chain quickly. I have spoken earlier about China's infrastructure technology. Take another example: telecoms. Huawei is now a world leader in info technology. They make world-leading hardware, and also make world leading software as well. UK has been buying latest tech from them. Look at this quote (see below). 30 percent increase in UK revenue in 2016, to more than 900 million pounds.

Another illustration: quantum satellites (see next page). China is moving ahead on space-to-ground quantum key distribution technology — It is a way to send data over long distances which is very difficult, if not impossible, to hack. Any attempt to eavesdrop on the quantum channel introduces detectable disturbances. Once intercepted or measured, the quantum state of the key changes, and the information being intercepted will self-destruct. This technology was actually developed in Europe. But China put in the necessary resources to take it further.

China is confident of its position. It has the population, resources, money. It is able to make long term commitments on investments, economic relationships. It can think long-term — where the country should go — and implement the strategy.

[C] American Foreign Policy

Now let me touch on the third of the three points — in the context of American foreign policy. America's long held position post-World War II, was that the maintenance of global peace and order was in itself, in America's interests. Now it has been suggested that America should define its interests more narrowly, an "America First" approach. This shift in thinking was for example articulated by General McMaster (see below), who is highly respected for his military and strategic thinking.

"America First signals the restoration of American leadership and our government's traditional role overseas – to use the diplomatic, economic and military resources of the US to enhance American security, promote American prosperity, and extend American influence around the world."

– General McMaster, US National Security Advisor

General McMaster was careful to say America First, does not mean America Alone. But it does signal a shift from the previous American position on how America engages the world. Every country acts in what it considers to be its best interests. When that country is America, and there is a change in how it perceives its interests, then that affects the rest of the world.

The current American Administration's reassessment of its position is driven by the need to answer to its electorate and is understandable. In the same vein, America has wondered aloud on positions which were once considered fundamental. For example: Its commitment to the North Atlantic Treaty Organisation (NATO), stability in the relationship with China, Free Trade, and so on. Some of this led to the German Chancellor saying in May this year (see below): "The times when we could completely count on others, they are over to a certain extent... We Europeans must really take our fate into our own hands…".

> "The times when we could completely count on others, they are over to a certain extent. **I have experienced this in the last few days.**
>
> **And that is why I can only say that** we Europeans must really take our fate into our own hands, **of course in friendship with the United States, in friendship with Great Britain and as good neighbours wherever that is possible, also with other countries, even with Russia.**
>
> **But we have to know that** we must fight for our future on our own, for our destiny as Europeans, **and that's what I want to do together with you."**
>
> ***– Angela Merkel, German Chancellor***

To be fair, some of the questions being raised by America are understandable. The US, for example, has been pointing out since the 1980s, that it bears a disproportionate share of the cost of NATO. The current Administration is not wrong to point this out and insists that something be done about it. American weariness, after years of the cold war — M–E engagements, bearing the burden primarily by itself; its demand that others share equitably in the costs of security engagements — are all quite understandable. In fact, the current situation is probably politically unsustainable for the US. Thus, in a way, if Europe, led by Germany, can take more of the burden of global leadership, particularly in the security of Europe, that could lead to a more balanced and sustainable global structure.

The Administration has decided to raise issues which it thinks need the attention of other countries. What will be the consequences, how the Administration will follow through on these questions — is less clear. I think it will take some time for us to understand how these issues will play out. For example — despite raising the questions it has, this Administration has shown the readiness to act, when it sees the need to act.

Beyond this Administration, America's engagement of East Asia has been largely consistent post-World War II, despite the ups-and-downs across administrations. This Administration has continued this tradition. For example, it has continued to put pressure on North Korea, while holding out the possibility of negotiations. The US has major security and economic interests in Asia, which it cannot afford to neglect. How it handles them — we have to wait and see. When the Administration's policies become clearer, and if there continues to be a perception that the US is withdrawing or reducing its global footprint, that may then accelerate the larger geopolitical trends that I spoke about. And, if the US continues with anti-trade rhetoric, removes itself from trade agreements, targets countries with economic sanctions, and there are tariff wars, then more countries may find the BRI to be more attractive. With this context, let me now look at the OBOR initiative.

ONE BELT ONE ROAD INITIATIVE

[A] <u>The Most Ambitious Infrastructure Project in History</u>

The OBOR is arguably the most ambitious infrastructure project in history. Trillions of dollars in infrastructure spending expected, in over 60 countries. Nearly 50 billion US dollars has already been invested in economies along the Belt and Road. The Asian Infrastructure Investment Bank, Silk Road Fund and New Development Bank together have a total registered capital of 240 billion US dollars. The BRI seeks to capture the imagination of partner countries. Many would-be partners believe that when the routes are laid, wealth will flow as it once did. It has the potential to bring Eurasia, China and Southeast Asia even closer together. If it succeeds, future trade routes could look like this — on land, and over sea (see below).

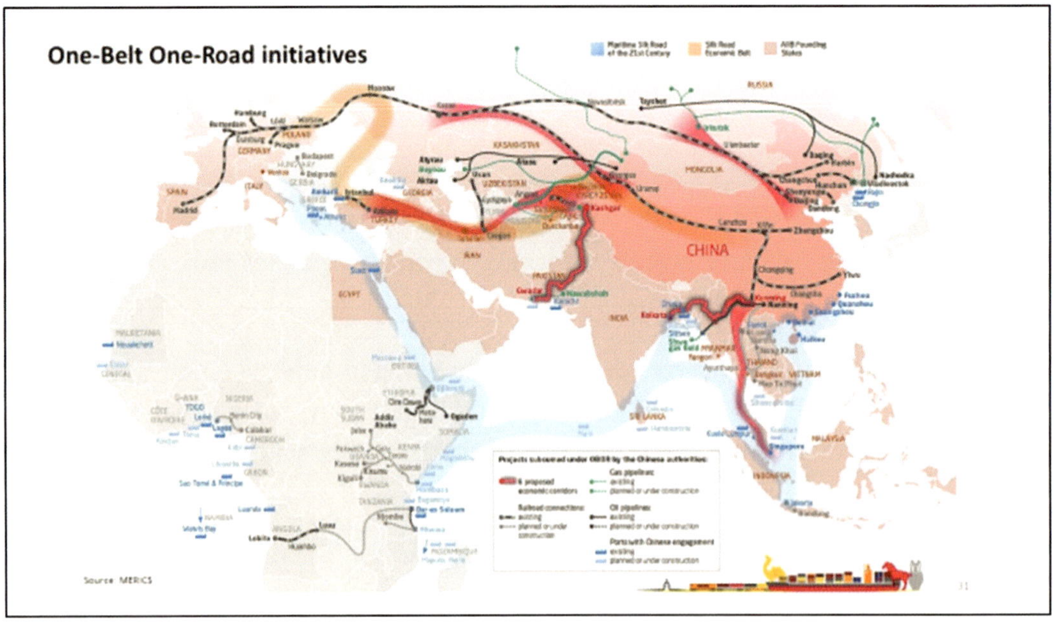

[B] <u>A Note of Caution</u>

But let me strike a note of caution as well. Names like Samarkand, Bukhara, Merv — they evoke a sense of romance, a glorious past. Nevertheless, the Chinese are not romantics with their heads in the clouds. They are practical, hard-headed. And they know that the Silk Route has historically been beset with conflict and violence. The risks are not insignificant.

Let us consider Central Asia. For centuries, conquerors have swept through the area. Ghenghis Khan, Tamerlane, Nader Shah, many others. It is a hostile environment, difficult to enforce law and order. Take Afghanistan. Russia, Britain, US — all had difficulties. Afghanistan has been called the "Graveyard of empires" for good reason. There is a poem by Kipling, "The Young British Soldier", on fighting in Afghanistan. Mr Lee Kuan Yew gave a copy of the poem to President Obama. It is worth reading (see below).

Rudyard Kipling – The Young British Soldier (extract)

If your officer's dead and the sergeants look white,
Remember it's ruin to run from a fight:
So take open order, lie down, and sit tight,
    And wait for supports like a soldier.
        Wait, wait, wait like a soldier...

When you're wounded and left on Afghanistan's plains,
And the women come out to cut up what remains,
Jest roll to your rifle and blow out your brains
    An' go to your Gawd like a soldier.
        Go, go, go like a soldier...

32

These are some pretty tough areas. Amongst the toughest in the world. And they continue to see some serious instability. Roads and Belts enable trade. But they can also enhance connectivity between extremists, and Jihadist influences. Works both ways. Thus, success of the OBOR in these areas is not a given.

There are other associated risks as well. First, the institutions in Central Asian countries are still developing. Much still depends on a leader, or a small group of leaders. If there is a change in leadership, then there could be changes in policy. Second, Russia has very substantial interests in the region. It is not a given that Russian and Chinese interests will align on BRI, necessarily. Russia has the ability to impose its will, if it believes that its own interests are affected. The Central Asian states are unlikely to want to choose between China and Russia. Third, India also has key interests in the Central Asian region, and the will to seek to protect, and advance those interests. Fourth, other countries, like Turkey, Iran also have their interests, and the will to push for those interests. China will have to try and work with these different interests and align them. That is not going to be easy. In many ways, building the infrastructure is the easier part. Beyond the specific difficulties of Central Asia, China also has to try and engage countries which have been less than enthusiastic about OBOR, for example, India, Japan.

China, being so big and successful has to take the steps to assure, engage, recognise that its actions will have a lot of impact, because of its size, heft, and impact. It is good for China to be respected, liked and trusted. Because the starting point is that actions of a very big country will be analysed very closely by others. If there is a deficit in trust we then might see regional counter blocs forming, for example: India, Japan, perhaps with powers outside Asia. History has many examples of such dynamics developing. And the possible US influence, impact should not be underestimated. US will continue to be a superpower, with tremendous economic, military and technological strength. Bismarck is reported to have said: "There is a Providence that protects fools, drunkards, children and the United States of America". So never write off the US.

If such blocs / counter-blocs are formed, that is not optimal. For China, or for anyone else, or for BRI. No country, not even China, can go it alone in the modern world. How it can align these conflicting interests, assuage other powers, are tricky issues. I have not dwelt too much on them, but that is not to understate their importance. It's in China's interest — and ours too — that its rise to great power status, superpower status, is peaceful, and is seen to be peaceful.

Fifth and quite fundamentally: BRI is not a substitute for the current international order. The current order is built on free trade. If the world turns protectionist, that will affect OBOR. If there is a trade war between US and China, that will affect the OBOR. The US has become energy independent. With a lowered cost of energy, it is trying to now onshore industries. That could also have an impact. Let me explain it this way: Infrastructure facilitates trade. But infrastructure does not by itself often create trade. Trade flows ultimately depend on supply and demand. In a globalised world, countries trade with many partners. And for many Asian countries, while China is the biggest trading partner, the ultimate consumer of most of the finished products is still the US. The products go as intermediate products to China; they get finished there, and then the finished products go from China to the US. This will likely remain so for some time.

So, for OBOR to succeed to its full capacity you need world trade and globalisation to carry on as it has been, and for the globalised economy to function. This means there must be no trade wars between China and the US; there must be continued growth, peace and stability — all of this and more will be necessary. But if China plays this right and successfully conveys that it has benign intentions, through the OBOR and other regional initiatives (including the Regional Comprehensive Economic Partnership (RCEP)), it has got the potential to build a new economic architecture that can uplift economic growth in this hemisphere.

The OBOR is a bold vision. China can overcome the challenges and turn the vision into reality. If anyone can, China can do it. It will be easier for China to achieve that if China is able to work harmoniously with countries which have weight, influence in the world economy; and receives the cooperation of countries with weight and influence along the Silk Route. China will be aware of this.

We in Singapore are too small to influence or be involved in these sorts of combinations and counter-combinations. We are an observer, often a price-taker. So we observe, we say things clearly, when our own interests are affected, and hope that there will be wisdom, peace and stability.

[C] SEA

China is likely to find SEA easier in the context of BRI. The connectivity — roads, rails, ports, airports — will be of great benefit. And the potential to create a vibrant economic zone, including the maritime states as well, is huge.

[D] Some Key Institutions Which Might Help OBOR

China has set up some key institutions, both before and after the BRI idea, which will, I think, help the BRI initiative.

(1) AIIB

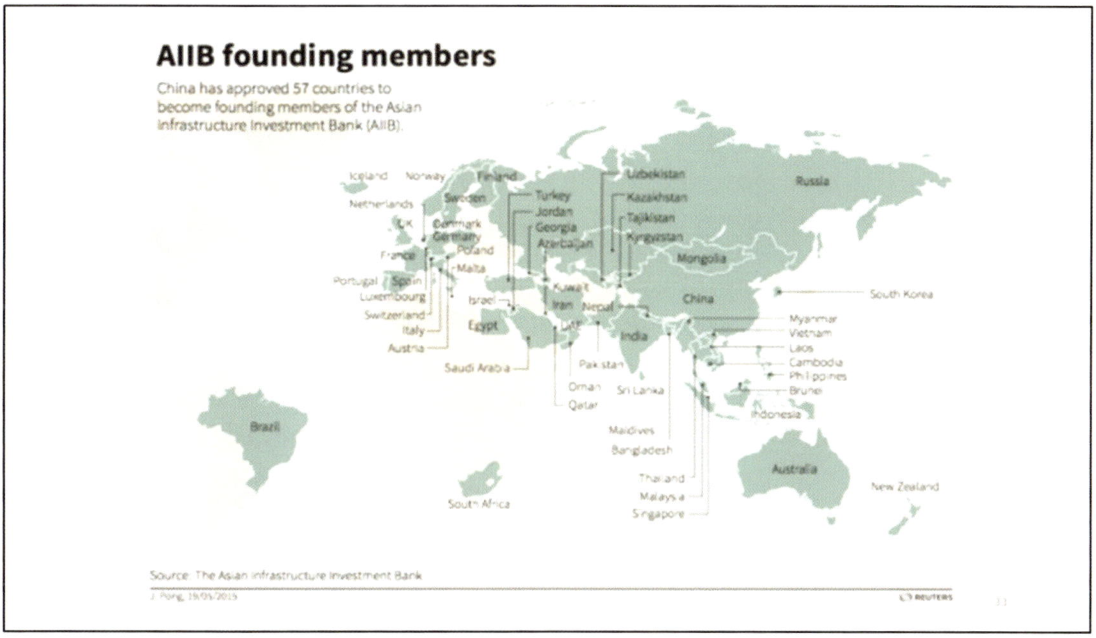

One: AIIB: it will finance the infrastructure projects along the Belt and Road, together with other international institutions — World Bank, for example, who is supporting this conference, is actively involved.

(2) Shanghai Cooperation Organisation

Two: Shanghai Cooperation Organisation (SCO): it is a political, economic and security organisation that will cover Eurasia. India and Pakistan were full members from June this year. And SCO represents half of humanity; a quarter of the world's GDP.

The BRI will therefore improve infrastructure, physical connectivity greatly, across the region. And has the potential to be a game-changer. Now let me move, to set out what I see as the impact, implications of BRI on the world economy, security architecture, geopolitics.

IMPLICATIONS, IMPACT

Fairly obvious what my conclusions on these are, given what I have already said. And I can therefore state them quite summarily.

[A] Economics

BRI, if successfully executed, will reshape global trade.

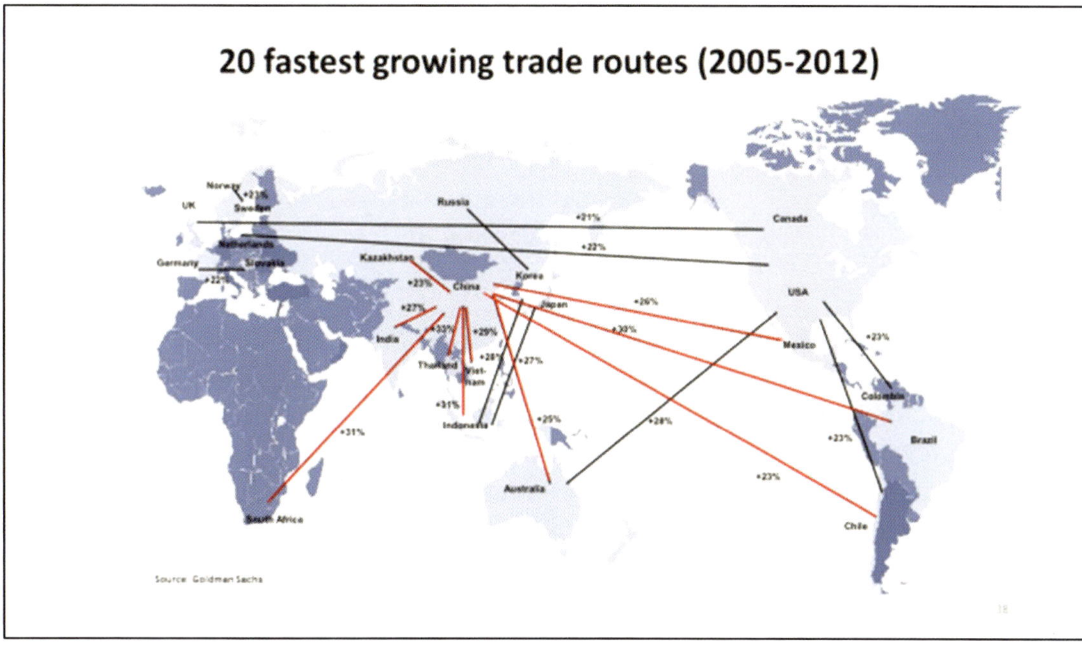

Already — as I said earlier, China, India, Japan are in the top 10 economies in the world in terms of GDP (see below). ASEAN, as a single economic unit — also in the top 10. BRI will anchor the world's centre of economic gravity in Asia. And China will be the centre of that centre. Not all roads will lead to Beijing, but many roads will.

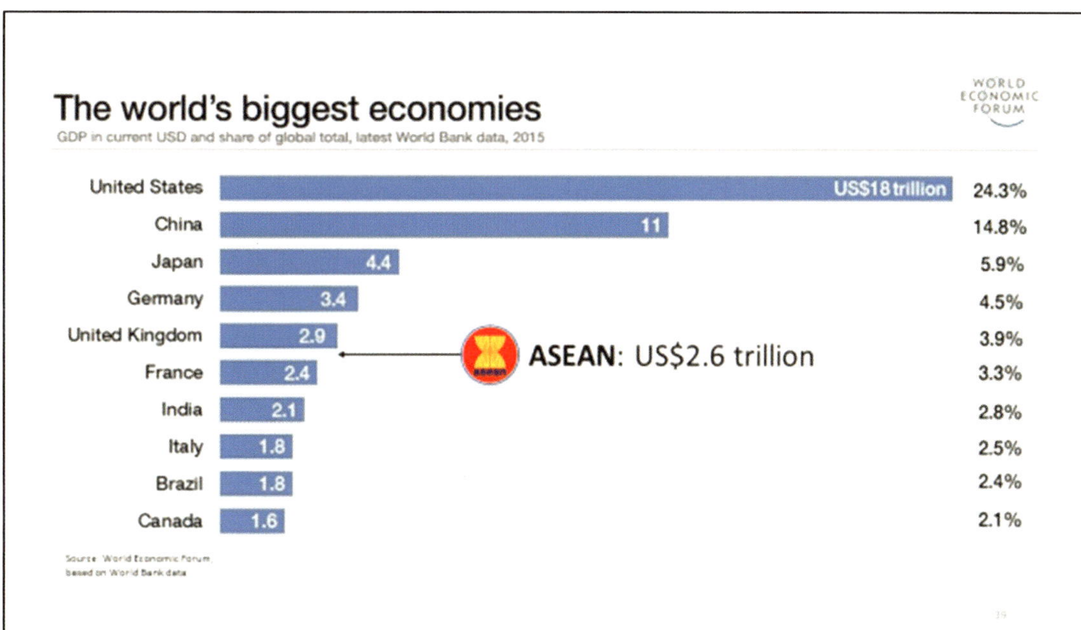

This is on the assumption that the major economies of Asia work together, there is no trade war, and no alliances which face off against each other.

[B] <u>Security Architecture</u>

Security usually follows economics. As its trade routes expand, China will probably seek to protect those routes. Both the land and the maritime routes. So you may well see more Chinese military bases, security arrangements, along the new Silk Routes.

[C] <u>Geopolitical Impact</u>

We are likely to see a more multi polar world. US, Europe, India, Japan, Australia, other countries, are not going to disappear from the geopolitical equation — in Asia or elsewhere. As I said earlier, it is likely that the US ability to decide unilaterally, will be reduced, from what it has been in the last 25 years.

At the same time, it is difficult to see any one country — including China — taking over the US's role of global leadership. And in several parts of the world, the US is likely to remain the predominant power. How stable such a multi-polar world will be is difficult to predict, but it will be in US's, China's and other countries' interests to ensure and work for stability.

SINGAPORE

Finally, Singapore — what does all this mean for us? Singapore recognised very early the potential for China's growth, from the early 1980s, and was an active proponent of that growth.

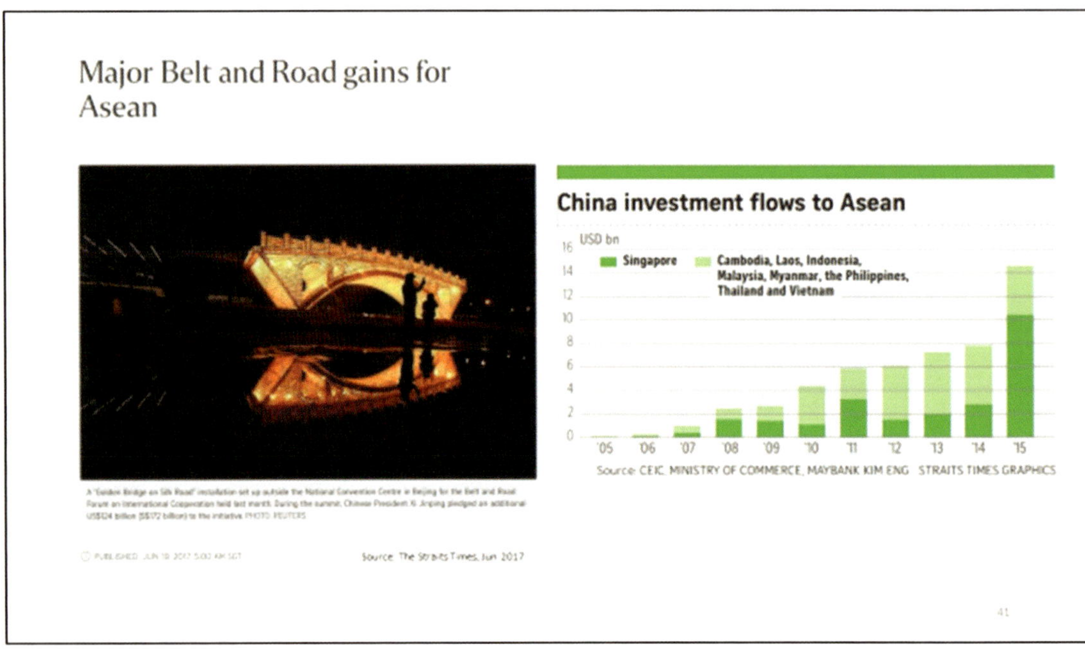

We supported BRI since its early years of inception. Recognised that it would benefit Asia and ASEAN (see above), and lead to greater regional economic integration. We were among the first few countries to support the AIIB, because we recognised its importance for the OBOR. There are lots of opportunities in Asia. From OBOR, and China's growth, to India's growth. And ASEAN's own growth is high: By 2020, combined GDP is expected to be close to 4 trillion.

As a small country, that is well governed, with rule of law, a highly educated population, we should be able to benefit from all of this economic growth. And OBOR in itself: offers tremendous economic opportunities — exciting. If connectivity improves, people travel, investment flows increase, then we can benefit — if we are ready and smart. An FT article in May this year noted that "among BRI countries, the leading investment destination in 2016 was Singapore, a high-income country with well-developed infrastructure". The figures show that we are already benefitting significantly from the opportunities offered by the BRI: China's investments in Singapore alone amount to about 1/3 of its total investments in "Belt and Road" countries. Singapore's investments in China accounted for 85 percent of total inbound investments from "Belt and Road" countries. With the new opportunities we can, should be able to find ways of being economically relevant.

In this unfolding multi-polar world, even more important for us to have as many good relationships as possible. Small states must continually earn their relevance on the international stage. China, the US, India — will be there a hundred years from now. For us: Nothing is guaranteed. The world can pass us by in an instant. The forgotten cities of the Silk Route are a salutary warning to us. Need to keep improving, reinventing the way we operate. Finding new ways to be of value to others. We will continue to support initiatives like the OBOR, because it benefits us, and the region. We will also continue to maintain good relationships with our neighbours, with China, and with our Western counterparts in Europe, and the US. This is how we have prioritised our nation's needs over the years, and we will continue to do so.

Can Singapore remain relevant in the future? We can. If we are smart.

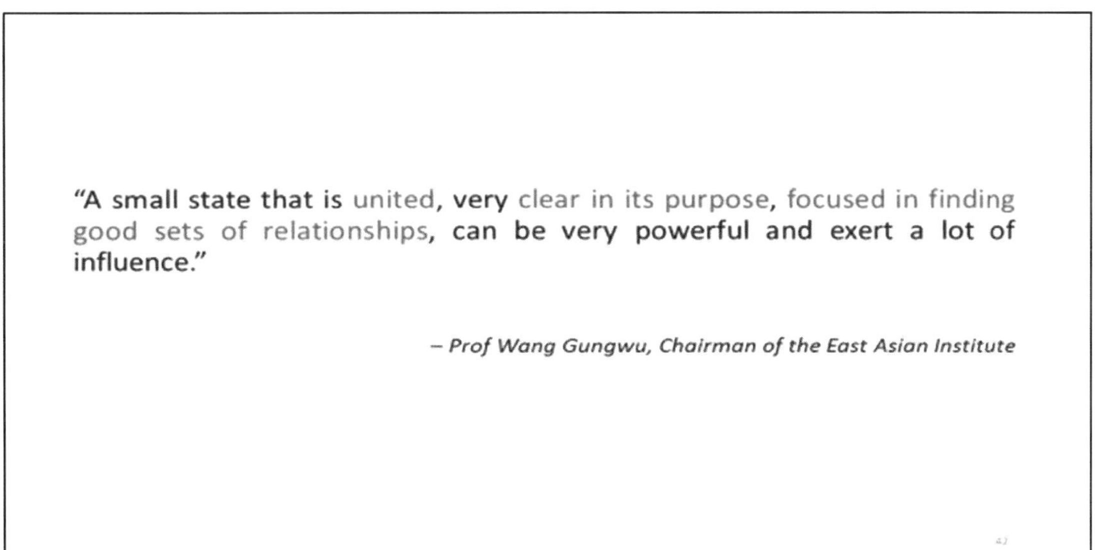

It is useful to note what Prof Wang Gungwu says (see above): "A small state that is united, very clear in its purpose, focused in finding good sets of relationships, can be very powerful and exert a lot of influence." We should try to punch above our weight, rather than just to be seen as a 700 km^2 rock in the Southern tip of Peninsular Malaysia. And we have good reasons to be optimistic. We pack quite a punch (see below).

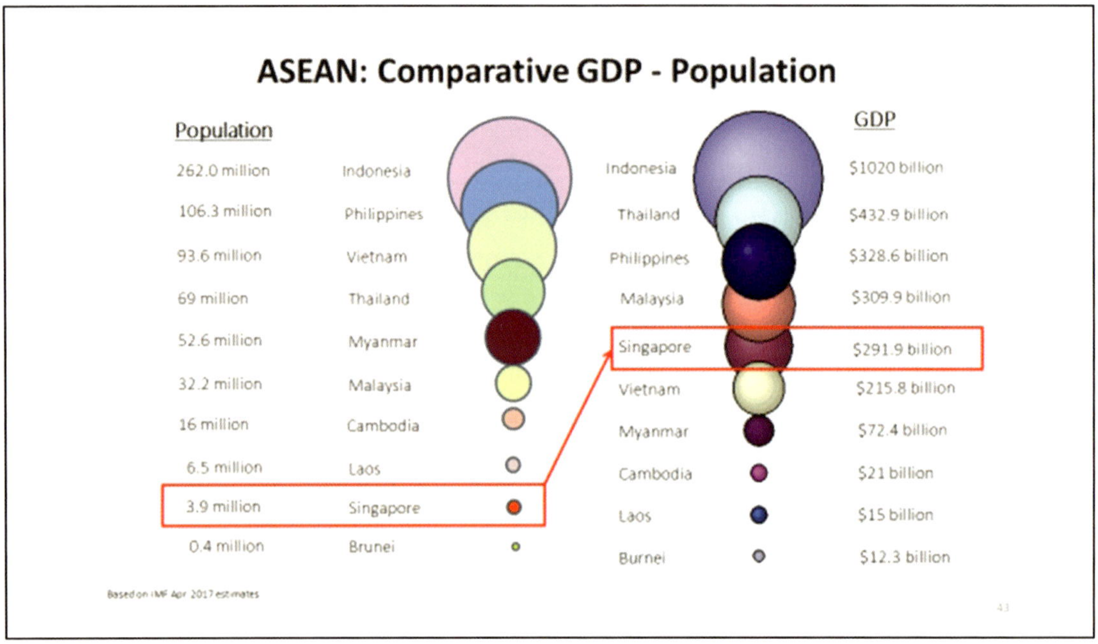

Note what Prof Tommy Koh said earlier this month: While we may be small in terms of territory or population size, we are not so small when you consider other yardsticks: GDP per capita, size of our foreign reserves, our connectivity with others, ease of doing business — to name just a few factors.

There will be fierce competition, certainly. We must expect, anticipate that our neighbours will, for example, want to build big ports, challenge our port, as they have every right to do so. And we must be nimble, quickly adapt — modernise, expand our own container port; have the foresight to make the necessary changes today for a better tomorrow, as we have done in the past. If we do so, we can secure our future, and ensure we remain a key port of call in SEA. And don't be easily rattled. As the ST article (see below) points out, it is not so easy to displace our port.

We can't be complacent; we must take competitors very seriously; we should be paranoid; but don't be spooked by social media disinformation campaigns that claim we are about to be surrounded and cut off.

And let me end by saying this: we achieved what we have by thinking bold, and thinking big. We didn't allow anyone to bully us, or subject ourselves to the demands of other countries. Many have tried. We resisted. International relations, it is not unlike a jungle. And small states are at risk. Small states that are intimidated or cajoled by bigger states into allowing their identity and interests to be defined by bigger states are not going to remain sovereign states for very long. They may retain a flag, a national anthem and a vote in the United Nations (UN), but that is about all. They will lose the autonomy to be themselves. The issue is existential.

If we allow ourselves to be bullied or seduced by bigger powers, that can break or severely stress our own domestic social-political compact, on which modern Singapore rests. Once broken, it will be difficult, if not impossible, to put together this compact again. If our founding fathers had conceded that Singapore should behave like a small state — "adeks" — we would not be having this conversation today. We would not be speaking in English, certainly; and there would be no Lee Kuan Yew School of Public Policy. But thankfully, our founding fathers thought boldly so we have a vibrant, confident modern state.

Again, thank — World Bank and ACI for inviting me. Heard ACI was ranked 13th globally, 2nd in Asia and 1st in Singapore amongst 90 think-tanks worldwide by U-Penn. Glad to hear the ACI is doing well. Look forward to more of your good work. And look forward to discussing these issues further with you at the Q&A. Thank you.

5.3 Belt and Road Initiative (BRI) from a Geo-economic Perspective[9]

Let me start with a note about the crucial role that urbanisation and infrastructure development in the world economy. Economics Nobel Prize winner Professor Joseph Stiglitz postulated a theory that the world's economic growth in the 21st Century will depend on two key drivers — (1) Digital Technology and (2) Urbanisation & Infrastructure. I read that these two drivers are often quoted by China's Premier Li Keqiang and his officials as China's key strategies for economic growth.

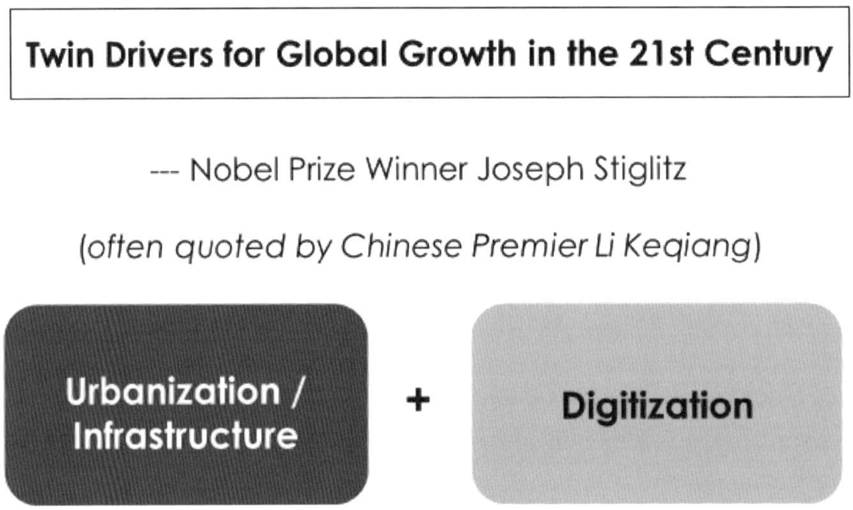

Proposed by China in 2013, "One Belt One Road", now renamed the "Belt and Road Initiative" is a global master plan to promote world trade and economic growth with infrastructure connections. It will connect 65 countries across Asia, Central Asia, the Middle East to Europe by land along the historic Silk Route and another by maritime route, down the Pacific and Indian Ocean and up the Mediterranean Sea. Fully implemented, the land route could connect the world's biggest landmass from Vladivostok in Russia to Portugal, the westernmost country in Europe.

[9] This section is a reprint with permission of the keynote speech by Professor Liew Mun Leong, Chairman of Changi Airport Group and Surbana Jurong, as well as Provost Chair and Professor of National University of Singapore delivered at 2017 Asia Economic Forum at Lee Kuan Yew School of Public Policy, National University of Singapore on 28 August 2017. The speech is also included in Liew (2017).

DRIVING ECONOMIC GROWTH THROUGH INFRASTRUCTURE DEVELOPMENT

Professor Joseph Stiglitz's economic development theory that urbanisation and infrastructure are fundamental drivers of growth has been proven in many countries. Good infrastructures will attract foreign direct investments, help promote trade, improves national productivity and create jobs. There is an old Chinese saying "If you want to be rich, build road". We now say "Build it and they will come".

Japan rapidly accelerated her economic growth with extensive infrastructure investments, after World War II. China leapfrogged and reformed her economy with the same strategy in the 90s and so did other Asian countries like South Korea, Taiwan, Australia and Hong Kong.

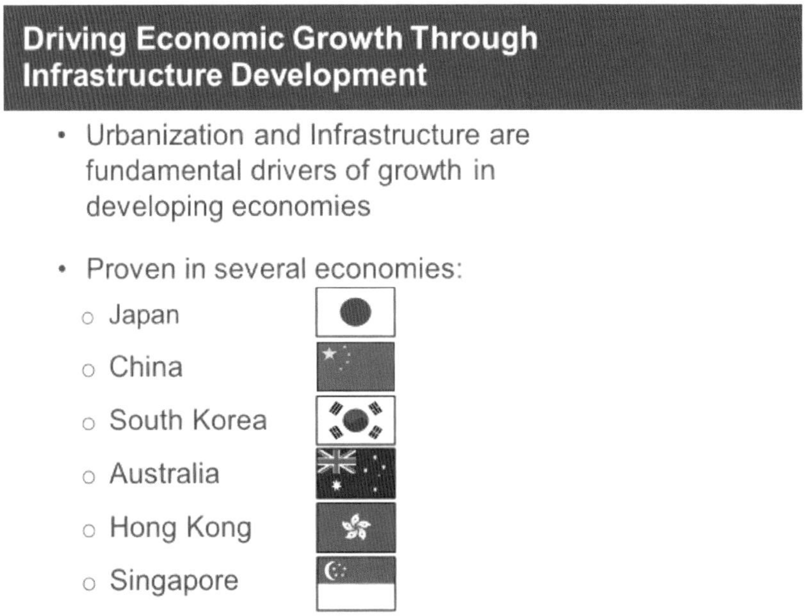

Singapore is another showcase story of how we transformed a fishing village with no natural resources, from the third world to a first world city, through infrastructure investments. We built up our economy with world class infrastructures including housing, airports, seaports, power, water, telecommunication, Information Technology (IT) and transportation.

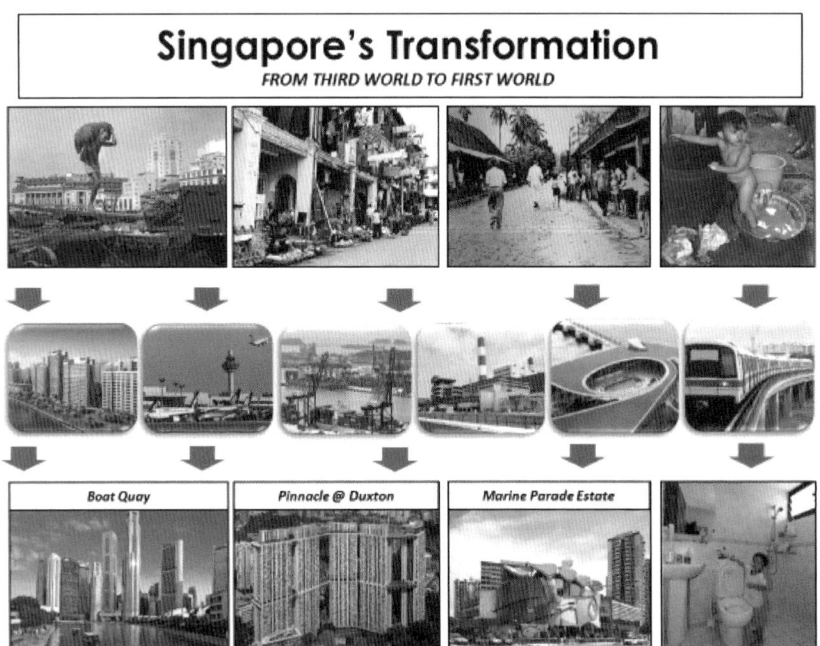

UNDERSTANDING THE BRI

Due to its massive scale and vast geography, there is presently inadequate understanding of what BRI really embraces. But it is still early days. I was privileged to be invited to the "Belt & Road Forum" held in Beijing in May this year. I wanted to personally assess the vibe and spirit at the forum and to listen to the responses from participating countries on BRI. More than 1,500 guests from 130 countries attended the forum. This included 29 state and government leaders, as well as the heads of major world organisations like the UN, World Bank, IMF, International Finance Corporation (IFC), European Commission, WTO, International Labour Organisation (ILO) and several other economic agencies.

Belt and Road Forum for International Cooperation
Beijing, China (14 – 15 May 2017)

1500 Participants from 130 Countries
29 State / Government Leaders including Heads of UN, World Bank, IMF, WEF, WTO, ILO

At the forum, China's President Xi Jinping assured world leaders of China's commitment in BRI's infrastructure investments. He pushed for globalisation, connectivity with other countries, win-win projects, inclusive development, and emphasised China's intention for peaceful economical collaboration. The mood was visibly positive and encouraging.

In a nutshell, BRI aims to connect 65 countries with about 65 percent of the world's population through a network of infrastructure projects. Today, BRI countries contribute 33 percent of the world's GDP, 40 percent of global trade and 25 percent of global goods and services moved. It is also endowed with 75 percent of the world's energy resources. By its sheer size and geographic spread, BRI is currently the most ambitious economic project of the 21st Century, and possibly in history.

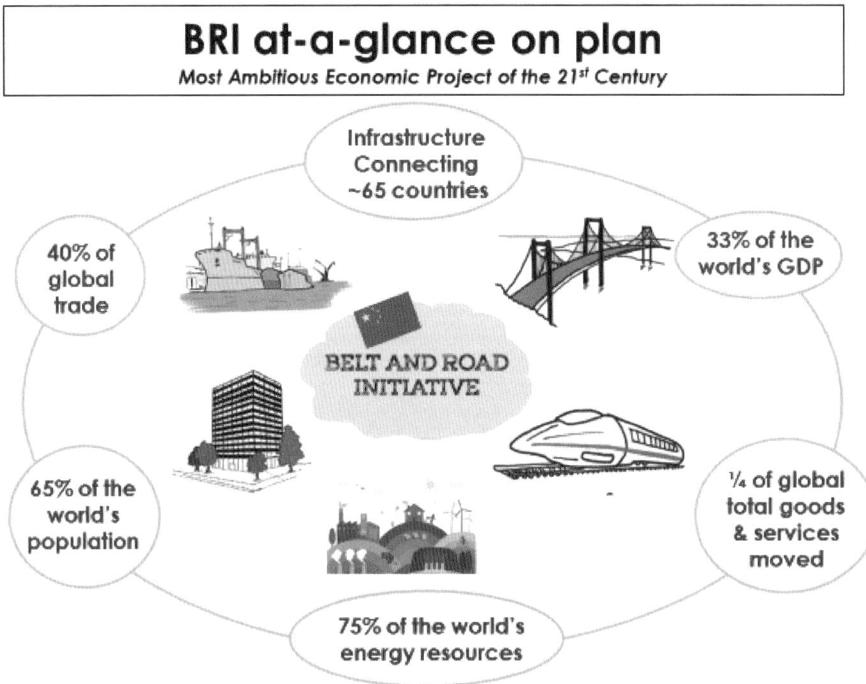

Some economists estimate that the BRI is at least 12 times that of the US's Marshall Plan which rebuilt Western Europe at what is the equivalent of 130 billion US dollars in today's value. If all parties concerned do go on board and work with China in this global plan, BRI will dramatically transform the world economic landscape for the better.

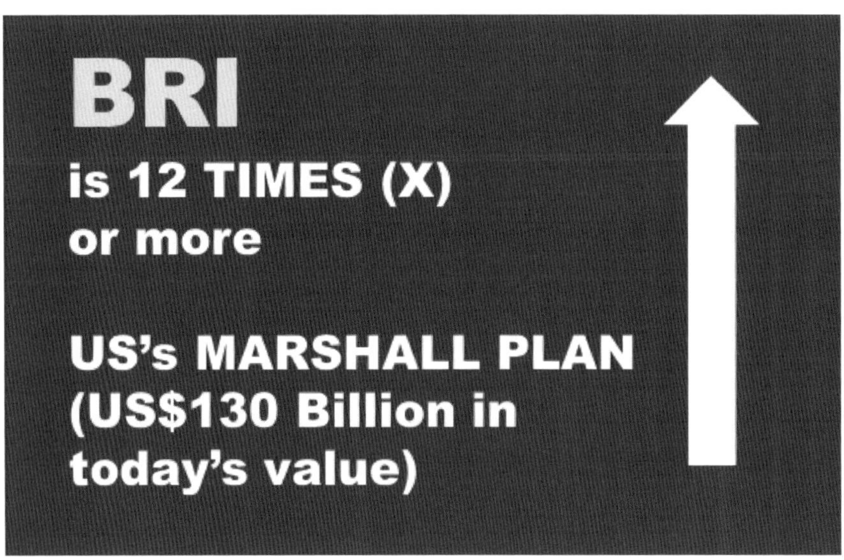

ECONOMIC SCALE OF BRI AND FUNDING

Asia-Pacific is presently severely deficient in infrastructure investments. It is estimated that Asia-Pacific will need 26 trillion US dollars for infrastructure investments from now to 2030.

Asia Pacific Infrastructure Needs

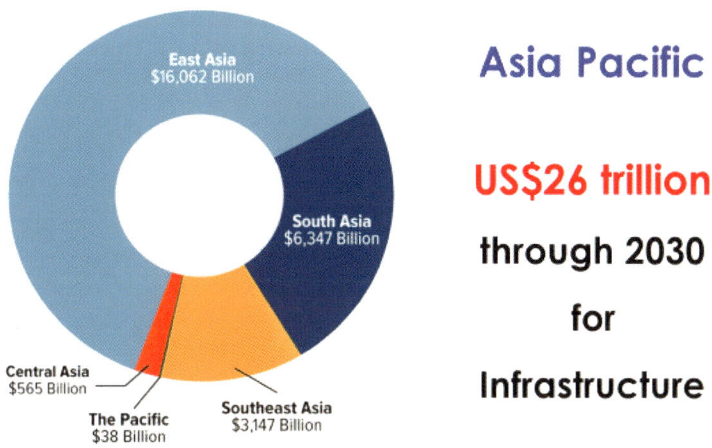

Source: Asian Development Bank, Bloomberg, U.S. Global Investors

Asia alone will need 1.7 trillion US dollars in infrastructure investments every year over the next 10 years.

Asia's Infrastructure Needs

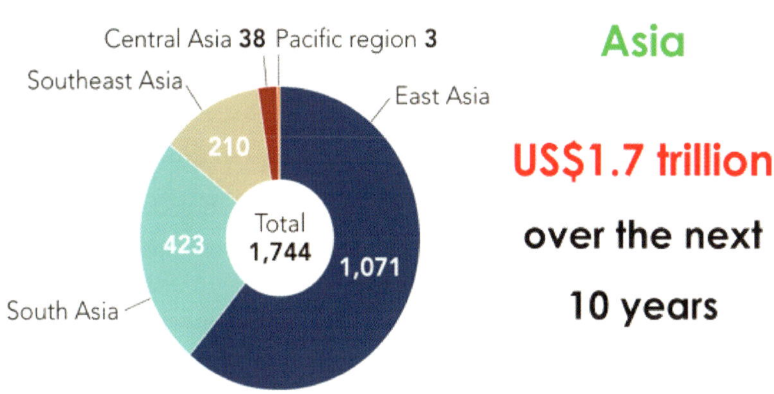

Source: Asian Development Bank

One estimate is that the BRI's cumulative investments may chalk up to 8 trillion US dollars. China has now taken the lead to initiate and kick start the BRI investment programme. Since 2013, China has poured in 60 billion US dollars in BRI countries. It recently announced its plans of total outbound investments of up to 130 billion US dollars per year over the next five years, giving it a total of 600 billion US dollars.

China has initiated three innovative multi-lateral development funds to assist in financing BRI investments. These are the AIIB with 100 billion US dollars, the New Development Bank with another 100 billion US dollars and the Silk Road Fund with 40 billion US dollars. China has also directed its major national banks to support funding of BRI projects. But these are nowhere near the estimated total funding requirements. This is evidently clear and China knows that it will need financial partnership support from international and multi-lateral financial institutions as well.

DOES CHINA HAVE THE CAPABILITY AND CAPACITY TO IMPLEMENT THE BRI?

Over the last few decades, we have witnessed China's demonstrated capability to transform its own economy implementing many mega world class infrastructure projects. This includes transforming paddy fields in Shanghai's Pudong District into one of the world's most vibrant districts, the Three Gorges Dam, more than 20,000 km of high speed railway, the Hong Kong-Zhuhai-Macau 50 km Bridge and the Beijing Capital Airport which was then the largest building project in the world, just to mention a few. As a professional engineer, I have learned not to doubt their engineering and construction prowess and their determination to undertake and complete technically challenging projects.

We should, of course, bear in mind that cross border BRI projects, will pose additional and different challenges.

Mega projects of such scale will face multi-faceted and complex issues ranging from financial and funding, technical, political, environmental, social, to G to G collaboration issues. These are a "given" in global infrastructure businesses, whether it is promoted by China or by any other economic powerhouse. Execution risks in emerging countries in particular are always higher, and a host country's internal issues such as political instability, local vested interests, mismanagement, and the recent anti-globalisation movements may inevitably come into play.

Implementation Issues
Global Infrastructure Challenges & Obstacles

1. **Funding & Project "Bankability"**
2. **Technical Challenges**
3. **Host Country's Internal Issues & Associated Risks**
4. **Completed Infrastructure Performance**

Notwithstanding this and based on her past track records, I do not doubt China's capabilities and capacity to implement the BRI programme. China has started to make positive headways in her plans. At the Beijing forum in May, President Xi Jinping as China's top leader, made a firm commitment to world leaders that China would spare no efforts to undertake the BRI plan. However, China knows that the BRI must be open and inclusive of all interested parties to succeed, and that she will need the cooperation and support of the host countries and other developed countries to succeed. Therein lies huge opportunities for the rest of the world.

BRI needs Global Trade & Collaboration

INTERNATIONAL COLLABORATIONS

Many countries and business leaders have also pledged their efforts to support and collaborate on the BRI projects at the Beijing meeting. The business community in the West has commercially acted fast too.

The Economist recently reported that many Western MNCs have seen quantum increase in their sales of construction equipment, technology and professional services to Chinese firms. These include GE, Caterpillar, Honeywell, ABB, Schneider Electric and BASF. DHL and Maersk have also found that their business with BRI countries have increased significantly. Deutsche Bank has secured several trade deals and entered into collaboration agreements with the China Development Bank to fund BRI projects. Western companies are now capitalising on BRI opportunities quickly. Shorn of geopolitical arguments, they are actively jumping onto the BRI wagon with their more technologically advanced products and services.

CAN SINGAPORE BENEFIT FROM THE BRI?

In my view Singapore is uniquely qualified to work in BRI projects. In a relatively much smaller scale we have done it before.

I recall that 25 years ago in 1993, our founding Prime Minister and then Senior Minister Lee Kuan Yew proposed a regionalisation plan called the "Second Wing" to further expand Singapore's economy. The visionary idea was to use our infrastructure experience and expertise in both the public and private sectors to assist neighbouring countries in ASEAN, China and India in their infrastructure development programmes.

At that time, I was leading a government linked development company called Pidemco Land (which later became CapitaLand) to undertake several projects in ASEAN, China and India. We successfully built modern hotels in Yangon, Hanoi and Suzhou and residential projects in Kuala Lumpur, as well as an IT Industrial Park in Bangalore. We were also a partner in the development of Suzhou Industrial Park, now a showcase of our successful G to G collaboration with China in the early 90s.

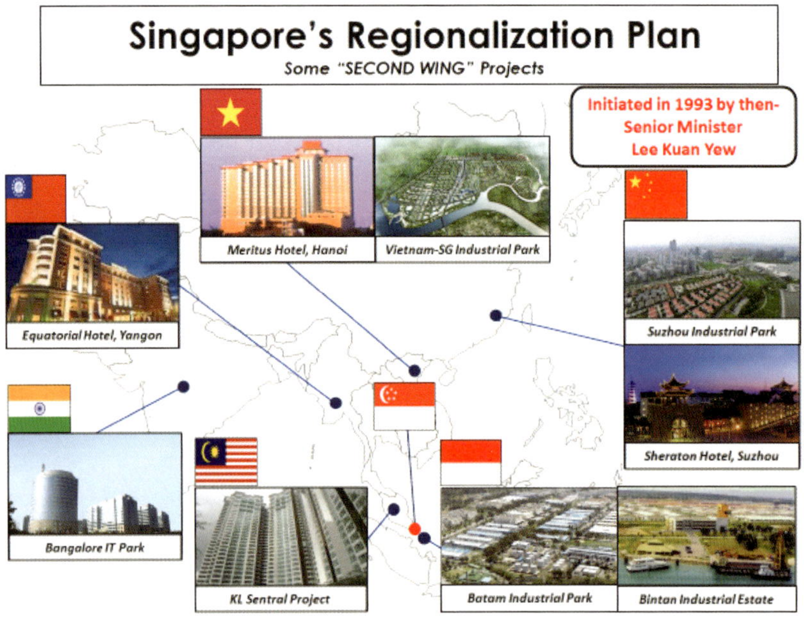

With the experiences gained from the "Second Wing" regionalisation programme, CapitaLand was able to evolve and export its overseas expertise to undertake real estate projects in more than 110 cities in 20 countries across Asia Pacific and Europe. With Singapore's successful track records in infrastructure projects and our trusted reputation, our companies and institutions should well capitalise on our experiences, expertise and track records to seek opportunities in BRI projects.

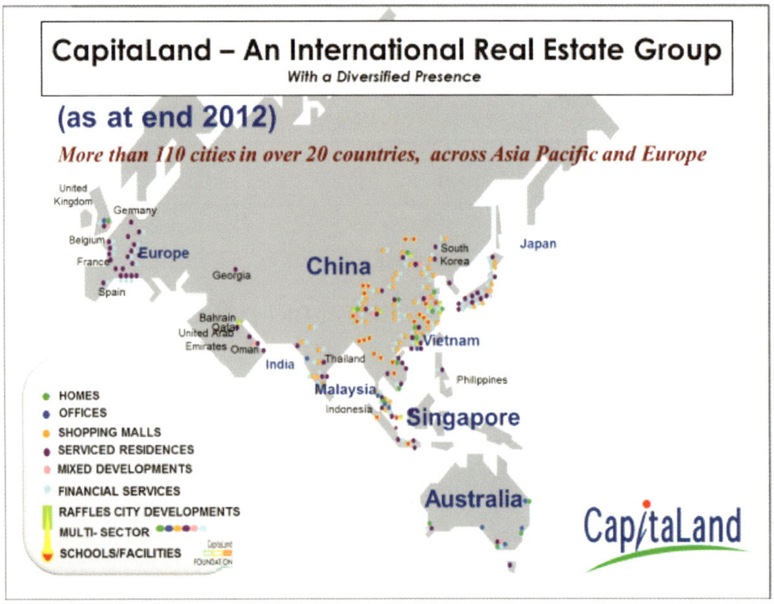

I am pleased to share that the 2 companies that I currently chair, Surbana Jurong Group and the Changi Airport Group, are already actively involved in BRI countries. Surbana Jurong Group, one of Asia's largest urbanisation and infrastructure consultancy groups, is currently planning, designing and project managing 17 mega infrastructure projects in 12 BRI countries. Changi Airports International, a subsidiary of Changi Airport Group, is collaborating on several airport projects in China, Central Asia, Russia and the Middle East too. These airport projects help improve aviation connectivity from the world to many BRI countries.

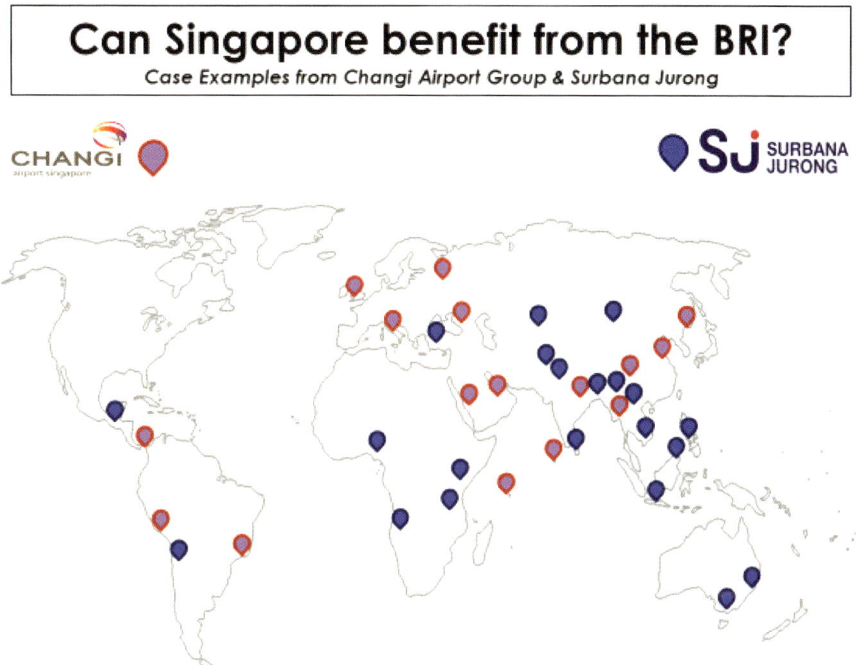

Besides infrastructure and development expertise, the BRI will also generate demand for other ancillary professional services in the whole value-added chain of the service industry, ranging from development consultancy services, project management, IT and e-commerce, legal and corporate services, financial and other related business services etc.

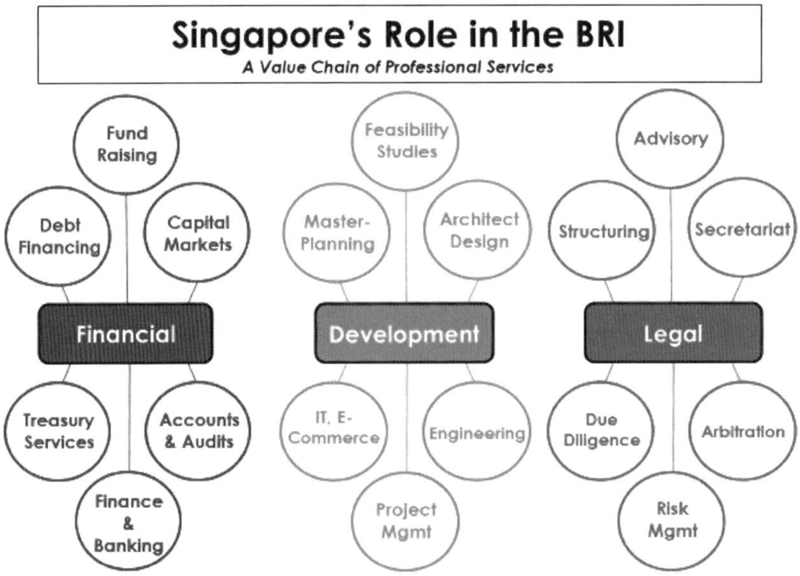

I was told that Singapore financial institutions currently handle 85 percent of the investments by BRI countries into China and almost 1/3 of the investments by China into the BRI countries. There is a unique opportunity for Singapore as the world's third leading financial centre to provide financial services for BRI businesses including raising funds for infrastructure investment, debt financing, treasury services and handling RMB denominated transactions. Businesses must be alert for such a wide range of opportunities in the BRI countries and be ready to be the first movers in the market.

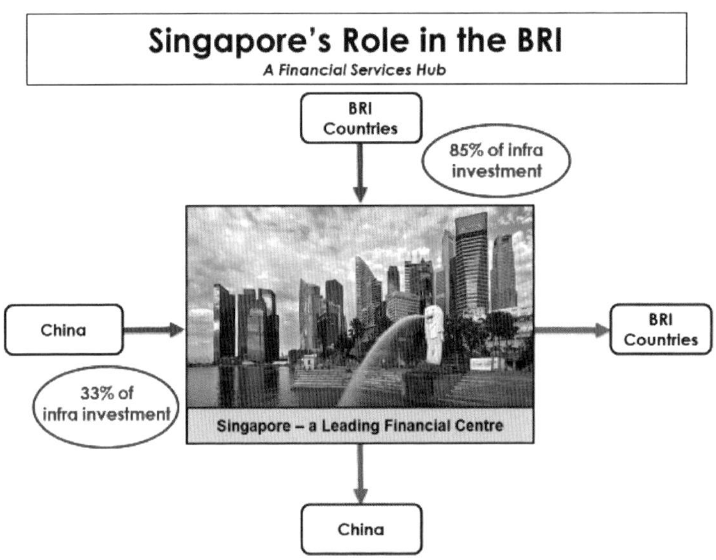

Our people, particularly our youth, must be ready to get out of their comfort zones to venture into less cushy working environment in BRI countries. Young Singaporeans need to learn from the Chinese in ancient times, who undertook long and arduous journeys to carve out the Silk Route to expand trade, with far less technological and modern logistical support. There is a Chinese saying, "You have to read 10,000 books and travel 10,000 li to grow your mind. The distance between Beijing to London is only 8,000 km."

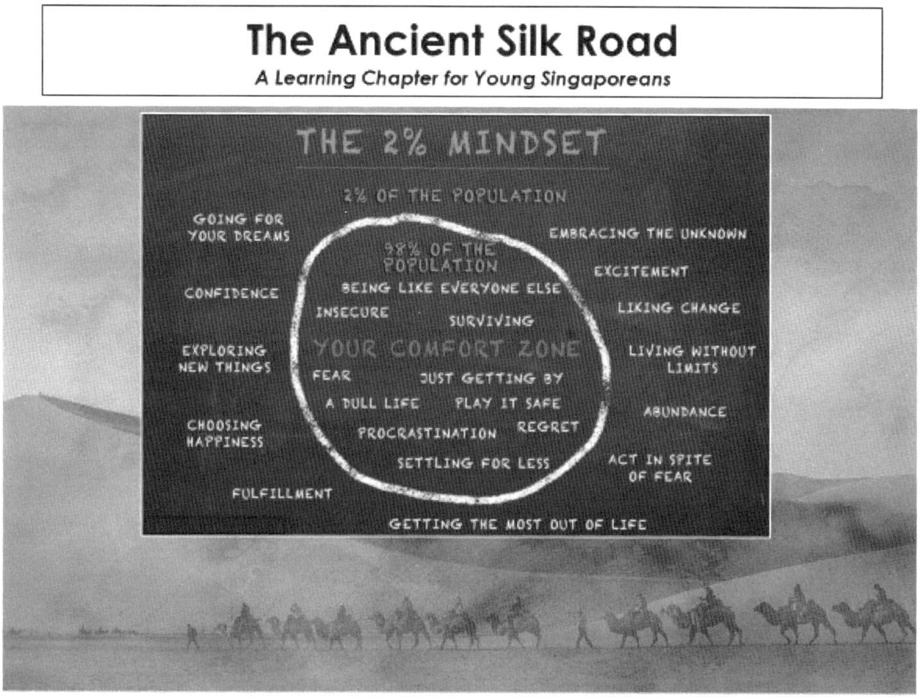

Conclusion

In conclusion, let me sum up three points.

First, two years ago, when the world's economy was slowing down there were two potential locomotives that could resuscitate global growth — the TPP and BRI. Now that the TPP has been aborted at least for the time being, BRI is the only major geo-economics locomotive to fuel growth. China has signalled at the highest political level her readiness to take a leadership role in BRI to promote growth in the world economy.

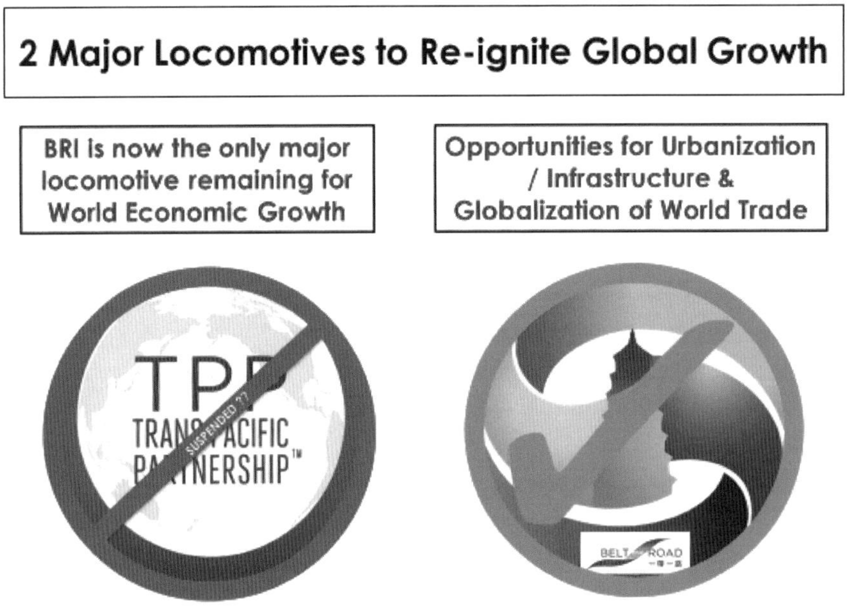

The sooner we realise and accept this and work on it, the better for us. Whatever may be the sentiments about China's potential dominance on the world stage, the BRI is a real and cogent strategy for world economic growth.

Second, the implementation of the BRI, by itself, will generate high levels of economic activities in the BRI countries. By its sheer size, China will not be able to undertake the BRI programme entirely on her own. She will need capital partners and those with advanced technologies and expertise to collaborate on BRI.

Lastly, Singapore businesses and businesses from other developing or developed countries should take full advantage of the opportunities from the BRI programme. We will all need capital, technology, specialist skills, especially engineering expertise, experience and local knowledge to secure and undertake projects in BRI countries. We must be prepared to enter into international collaborations with interested parties to address the BRI market demand.

Singapore firms can also form consortiums for collective strengths and small and medium enterprises (SMEs) should find the right opportunities to participate in these consortiums. Singapore can also provide a wide range of professional services for BRI projects. We have done it before some twenty years' ago with our Second Wing Regionalisation programme.

Singapore's first-class infrastructure projects showcase our ability to deliver high quality infrastructure projects. With our local knowledge in the Asia Pacific, Singapore should position ourselves as a trusted and preferred partner to parties involved in BRI projects. We should act fast to secure a first mover advantage in the BRI market place. We must not let our expertise and experience in infrastructure development go to waste. Thank you.

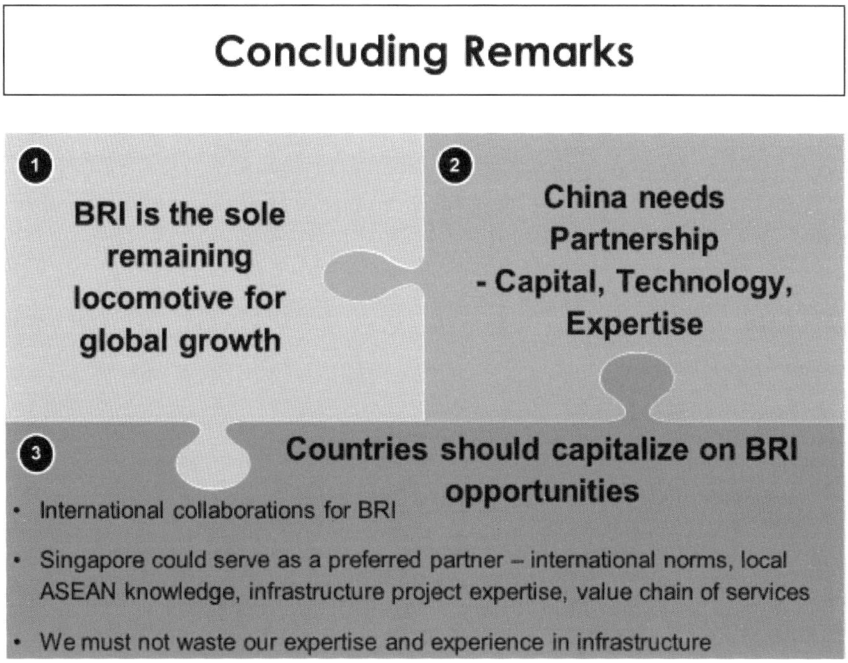

References

Asian Development Bank Institute. 2009. *Infrastructure for a Seamless Asia*. Manila: ADB.

Asian Development Bank Institute. 2009. *Infrastructure for a Seamless Asia*. Tokyo: Asian Development Bank Institute.

Goh, Brenda and John Ruwitch. 2017. "Pressure on as Xi's 'Belt and Road' Enshrined in Chinese Party Charter". *Reuters*, 24 October, available at: https://www.reuters.com/article/us-china-congress-silkroad/pressure-on-as-xis-belt-and-road-enshrined-in-chinese-party-charter-idUSKBN1CT1IW (accessed on 20 November 2017).

Huang, Yiping. 2016. "Understanding China's Belt & Road Initiative: Motivation, Framework and Assessment". *China Economic Review* 40: 314–321.

Liew, Mun Leong. 2017. "To View 'One Belt One Road' from a Geo-Economy Perspective". In *Seminar 1: Competitiveness, Trade, Liveability and Productivity in ASEAN Economies*, edited by Khee Giap Tan, Tao Oei Lim, Tracy Jiao Cai and Xin Yi Yap. Lee Kuan Yew School of Public Policy, National University of Singapore: Asia Competitiveness Institute.

Ploberger, Christian. 2017. "One Belt, One Road — China's New Grand Strategy". *Journal of Chinese Economic and Business Studies* 15 (3): 289–305.

Shanmugam, K. 2017. "The One-Belt One-Road Initiative: Impact and Implications". Speech at the 2017 Asia Economic Forum on Singapore, 28 August. Available at https://www.mha.gov.sg/newsroom/speeches/Pages/Asia-Economic-Forum-on-The-One-Belt-One-Road-Initiative-Impact-and-Implications.aspx (accessed on 2 November 2017).

Tan, Khee Giap, Nguyen Le Phuong Anh, and Luu Nguyen Trieu Duong. 2017. *2016 Annual Competitiveness Analysis and Growth Slowdown Analysis for ASEAN-10*. Singapore: World Scientific.

Tian, Shaohui. 2015. "Full Text: Vision and actions on jointly building Belt and Road". *Xinhua*, 28th March, available at: http://news.xinhuanet.com/english/china/2015-03/28/c_ 134105858.htm (accessed on 15 October 2017).

Xi, Jinping. 2017. Speech at the opening ceremony of the Belt and Road Forum for International Cooperation on "Work Together to Build the Silk Road Economic Belt and The 21st Century Maritime Silk Road." China, 14 May. Available at: http://news.xinhuanet.com/english/2017-05/14/c_136282982. htm (accessed on 15 October 2017).

Chapter 6

Concluding Remarks and Future Research Agenda

6.1 Summary of Key Findings

With this compendium on *2017 Annual Competitiveness Analysis and Impact of Exchange Rates on Foreign Direct Investment Inflows to ASEAN Economies*, the Asia Competitiveness Institute (ACI) at the Lee Kuan Yew School of Public Policy (LKYSPP), National University of Singapore (NUS) presents not only our latest competitiveness ranking and simulation analysis for the 10 member states of the Association of Southeast Asian Nations (ASEAN) but also studies of various economic issues, with a view of contributing to policy formulation in the region for continued prosperity and balanced development. The year 2017 marked a momentous milestone as the bloc commemorated its golden jubilee. This was preceded by the official launch of the ASEAN Community in 2015, another cause for celebration.

Chapter 1 recounts ASEAN's development experience since its founding with the signing of the Bangkok Declaration in 1967. At the time, few would expect that ASEAN would have endured and thrived given the tumultuous backdrop of regional territorial disputes, heightened Cold War tension, and rising communist insurgencies into which the organisation was born. Furthermore, fundamental diversity in terms of culture, language, religion and political system adds another layer of complex challenges to regional integration in Southeast Asia. Against all odds, ASEAN has played an instrumental role in promoting peace and stability, cooperation and cohesion among its members over the past 50 years. The organisation has grown to encompass 10 Southeast Asian countries. In addition, ASEAN has proven to be effective at fostering economic development. Rapid growth facilitated by deepening economic integration has transformed the 10-member bloc into the seventh largest economy in the world, with potentials to become the fourth largest by 2030.

Nevertheless, ASEAN leaders cannot afford to be complacent. Section 1.3 of Chapter 1 reflects on long-term issues and mega-trends which will affect the development trajectory of ASEAN over the next few decades. The foremost concern is the persistent development divide between member countries which have undermined the regional integration effort and created the risk of a two-tier ASEAN whereby the frontrunners, ASEAN-6 (Brunei, Indonesia, Malaysia, Philippines, Singapore and Thailand), will surge too far head of the late developers Cambodia, Laos, Myanmar and Vietnam (CLMV) in terms of socio-economic development. The rise of protectionist sentiments also threatens to derail economic growth in ASEAN. At the same time, ASEAN countries need to be mindful of fundamental shifts in demographic trends. Countries which are expected to experience a youth bulge need to implement appropriate policies to make the most of the future demographic dividends while avoiding a demographic bomb of high youth unemployment. Meanwhile, those whose population will soon age at rapid rates

(Singapore, Thailand and Vietnam) must grapple with new strategies to sustain growth in the face of tightening fiscal constraints, diminishing labour force and productive resources as well as rising dependencies in the economy. Besides demographic transition, rapid technological advancements in the Fourth Industrial Revolution will prove to be another disruptive megatrend for all ASEAN economies. To forge ahead as a community amid an increasingly challenging environment, it is imperative that ASEAN members address gaps in their integration agenda by strengthening the bloc's institutional mechanism, promoting inclusive and sustainable development and fostering an "ASEAN identity".

Having assessed opportunities and challenges confronting ASEAN economies, Chapter 1 proceeds to outline ACI's development vision for ASEAN-10. ACI's vision encompasses five elements with specific actionable policy recommendations for ASEAN to transform into the fourth largest economy in the world by 2030. First, we envisage that ASEAN will benefit from the southward shift of foreign direct investment (FDI) from China to become a highly integrated manufacturing hub and single market connected by high-quality infrastructure networks. Second, we propose that in tandem with fast-paced industrialisation, ASEAN leverages on its comparative advantages in agricultural production to become a productive food basket of Asia and the world. To this end, enhancing agricultural productivity and promoting technological innovations to improve the resilience of the agriculture sector against climate change are paramount. Third, we call on ASEAN leaders to work towards making ASEAN an innovative and future-ready growth centre, with a clear strategy to build digital capacity for individuals and businesses. Fourth, we seek to enhance existing programmes to narrow the development gap in ASEAN under the current Initiative for ASEAN Integration (IAI) and foster small and medium enterprises (SMEs) as means to achieve equitable and inclusive development in Southeast Asia. Finally, we emphasise ASEAN as a major force for regional and global economic integration. We seek for the 10-member bloc to strengthen its internal unity, maintain its centrality in the regional economic and security architecture, and play a key role in deepening economic integration through multilateral platforms including the ASEAN Economic Community (AEC), the Regional Comprehensive Economic Partnership (RCEP), the Comprehensive and Progressive Trans-Pacific Partnership (CPTPP), the Free Trade Area of the Asia-Pacific (FTAAP) and the One Belt One Road (OBOR) initiative.

At this juncture when ASEAN celebrates its success over the past five decades while contemplating the course for its future development, it is timely that Chapter 2 presents a thoughtful reflection on the ASEAN Charter and more generally the institutional arrangements of ASEAN by Professor Tommy Koh, Ambassador-at-Large at the Ministry of Foreign Affairs of Singapore and a key insider who was actively involved in the drafting of the ASEAN Charter. Throughout ASEAN's existence, the "ASEAN Way" which emphasises consensus-based decision making, informality and consultation, as well as non-interference in domestic affairs has served as the fundamental principle underpinning the organisation. However, over time, ASEAN leaders recognised that informal institutional framework and a lack of legal personality would not always serve the common interests of ASEAN as an organisation as well as its members. As a result, the 10th ASEAN Summit in 2004 set out the commitment to work towards the development of an ASEAN Charter which was originally proposed by General Carlos P. Romulo at the seventh

ASEAN Foreign Ministers Meeting in 1974. Momentum for the Charter gathered throughout 2005–2007, leading to its adoption in 2007 and its coming-into-force in December 2008.

In his analysis, Professor Koh considered the ASEAN Charter a revolutionary document for eight reasons. First, the Charter seeks to bring about a paradigm shift to ASEAN's nature, strengthening the ASEAN Way with greater reliance on institutions. Second, given the reality of political diversity in Southeast Asia, it is commendable that member states have committed to the principles of "democracy, the rule of law and good governance" as well as "constitutional government" Third, even though only four out 10 ASEAN countries had national commissions of human rights before the promulgation of the Charter, the bloc has set up two regional bodies dealing with human rights issues, namely the ASEAN Intergovernmental Commission on Human Rights (AICHR) and the Commission on the Rights of Woman and Child. Fourth, the Charter commits ASEAN members to sustainable development, in particular the protection of the environment. Fifth, the Charter affirms ASEAN's respect for international law and the peaceful settlement of disputes. Sixth, the Charter sets out dispute settlement mechanisms for ASEAN countries, thus addressing a major weakness of the bloc since its founding. Seventh, the Charter has tried to rationalise and streamline ASEAN's institutional structure and to empower the Secretary-General and the Secretariat. Finally, the Charter emphasises that ASEAN should be a people-oriented and people-centred organisation.

Going forward, while ASEAN will continue to evolve, Professor Koh believed that the organisation should resist the temptation to depart from the principles of non-interference, consensus-based decision making or to adopt suspension of membership or expulsion as harsh sanctions for non-compliance. This is because ASEAN unity is paramount. Professor Koh's suggestions to strengthen ASEAN include (i) ensuring ASEAN to be a people-oriented organisation through fostering SMEs and cultivating youths; (ii) improving communication between ASEAN leaders and civil society; and (iii) promoting cooperation on specific issues in the field of human rights in which there is consensus, such as human trafficking.

Next, Chapter 3 provides a comprehensive and rigorous methodological framework not only to produce in-depth assessment of annual competitiveness ranking for ASEAN individual member states but also to offer constructive country-specific policy roadmaps for growth and development. We construct a competitiveness index by making use of a holistic set of 121 indicators spanning four different dimensions encompassing (i) Macroeconomic Stability, (ii) Government and Institutional Setting, (iii) Financial, Businesses and Manpower Conditions, and (iv) Quality of Life and Infrastructure Development, which carry equal weight. This allows us to measure the multidimensional aspects of economic competitiveness in each ASEAN member state. Furthermore, in this year edition, we relax the assumption of equal weights and instead make use of "Shapley values" to construct alternative weights for our competitiveness index as a robustness check. Shapley values enable us to measure the marginal contribution of a particular indicator we use in our analysis and are embedded in solid mathematical foundations. By introducing such objectivity to our methodological computations, we add a significant layer of robustness to our research findings. Finally, we delve further into the competitiveness studies of the 10 members of ASEAN through a policy simulation analysis which depicts the impacts of addressing the bottom 20 percent weakest indicators for individual ASEAN country.

In general, the Overall Competitiveness rankings of ASEAN-10 were relatively stable over the study period 2000–2014. The most significant change was that Brunei overtook Thailand as the third-ranked economy for the first time in 2014. The significant divide in terms of economic development level is well reflected in our annual ranking as the top four economies were the same for 15 consecutive years (Singapore, Malaysia, Brunei and Thailand). Meanwhile, Vietnam, Cambodia, Laos and Myanmar were consistently the bottom four. Indonesia has decidedly surpassed the Philippines at fifth despite having a similar standardised score level to the latter in 2000. These results are robust under the Shapley weightage methodology.

Moreover, as pointed out in Chapter 3, competitiveness ranking in itself is a mere beauty contest which offers little insights on policy to improve economic competitiveness. In this respect, the identification of the top 20 percent strongest and weakest indicators, and the *What-if* simulation analysis that we conduct offers a constructive policy roadmap for domestic reforms to address economic malaises in each ASEAN member states. The post-simulation results for the transitional CLMV are particularly worth noting. *Ceteris paribus*, if each economy improved on its top 20 percent weaknesses to catch up with the regional average, Laos and Vietnam would climb one place in the overall ranking, from ninth to eighth and seventh to sixth, respectively, while Myanmar would jump from 10th to eighth. Furthermore, while Cambodia's post-simulation ranking would remain at eighth, the gap between its standardised score and that of other ASEAN members would narrow considerably.

Given the importance of FDI in propelling growth in ASEAN and more generally East Asian economies, Chapter 4 investigates the determinants of FDI inflows to ASEAN, specifically the impacts of fluctuations in exchange rate levels and exchange rate volatility on FDI. As we have established in great detail in Chapter 4, FDI flows have evolved over the last two decades to become an important source of external financing for ASEAN, relative to other types of capital flows such as portfolio investments, financial derivatives and other investments. One of the often-noted trends relate to the highly asymmetric distribution of FDI inflows among ASEAN countries, which has resulted in significant concentration of FDI in specific economies including Singapore, Indonesia, Thailand, Malaysia and Vietnam. Among other factors, the distribution of FDI reflect the ease of doing business and economic growth potentials of ASEAN economies.

Keeping this heterogeneity in mind, we have examined the empirical importance of cost competitiveness resulting from exchange rate in driving FDI inflows in ASEAN. With a specific focus on real effective exchange rates (REER) and REER volatility, we have empirically investigated how movements in REER (both in levels and volatility) affect the growth of FDI inflows to ASEAN countries. Interestingly, we find that fluctuations in REER levels are negatively and significantly associated with the annual growth rate of FDI inflows. On the other hand, REER volatility is also negatively associated, but the relationship is statistically insignificant. As explained in Chapter 4, these results provide indicative evidence that FDI inflows into ASEAN countries are export-oriented in nature and that REER movements in levels tend to be a more important determinant of FDI than REER volatility. Other variables found to be statistically significant determinants of FDI include the growth of Gross Domestic Product (GDP) per capita and the stock of M2 (as percentage of GDP) to indicate the level of financial development. These findings give rise to important policy implications discussed in more detail in Section 6.2.2.

With concerns about rising protectionist sentiments in the West and deglobalisation weighing down the global economy, emerging market economies in Asia have their task cut out for them to achieve high-quality economic growth by wading through the challenges stemming from a relatively less favourable and open international trading and financial system. Against this backdrop, the OBOR initiative spearheaded by China presents a timely opportunity to enhance greater global economic cooperation through bolstering and deepening trade and investment linkages as well as greater connectivity within and outside the region as a means to sustain the economic growth momentum.

In this context, Chapter 5 centres on the analyses of OBOR by two luminaries: Mr K. Shanmugam, Minister for Home Affairs and Minister for Law of Singapore, and Professor Liew Mun Leong, Chairman of Surbana Jurong and Changi Airport Group as well as Provost Chair and Professor of NUS. Minister Shanmugam delivered an in-depth historical narrative on the economic, political and geostrategic significance of the OBOR. His insightful and thought-provoking speech provided an account of the changing geopolitical trends defined by the economic rise of China and the change of relative power between China and the United States (US). He recollected how the grand vision of the OBOR today was an attempt to recreate and revive the historical importance of the ancient Silk Route that remained the epicentre of global trade for a long time in history. However, he also cautioned that China has to be mindful of the notable institutional challenges in several countries in the Central Asian region as well as aligning the potentially conflicting interests between China and fast-growing emerging markets like Russia and India. Finally, Minister Shanmugam noted that Singapore has always been supportive of initiatives such as the OBOR and the Asian Infrastructure Investment Bank (AIIB) and must continue to innovate and tap into newer opportunities that arise from such efforts in order to stay relevant in the multipolar world order.

The Minister's discourse was followed by Professor Liew Mun Leong's discussion which placed the relevance and importance of the OBOR in the context of the pivotal role assumed by urbanisation and infrastructure development in driving global economic growth in the 21st century. He noted that despite China's capabilities to pull off such a mammoth initiative, cross-border infrastructure projects of such enormous proportions tend to be marred by execution risks. Such risks offer substantive opportunities for international collaboration, including that with Singapore which would prove vital for the initiative to succeed. In particular, Professor Liew highlighted the unique role of Singapore as one of the leading global financial centres which placed the country in a special position to contribute to the success of OBOR, also vindicated by the fact that 85 percent of investments made by countries part of OBOR into China and 33 percent of the investment by China into OBOR countries are handled by Singapore's financial institutions. In closing, Professor Liew reiterated the salience of the OBOR as a major engine of growth in the region, and how its implementation can generate a variety of positive spillovers in those countries which take part in this massive economic initiative. He wound up by emphasising how businesses from Singapore and abroad must make a concerted effort to exploit the opportunities offered by OBOR.

6.2 Policy Implications

6.2.1 Positioning ASEAN in the One Belt One Road Initiative

By the sheer size of intended investment and geographical coverage, OBOR is indeed the most ambitious economic project of the 21st century. It is gathering pace as the global economic gravity is shifting from the West to the East. Embracing export-led industrialisation and a state capitalism paradigm where the government plays a major role in establishing new growth industries and addressing infrastructure, financing and production bottlenecks, Japan, China, South Korea and, to a smaller extent, Taiwan, Hong Kong, Singapore, Indonesia, Malaysia and Thailand have achieved remarkable economic development over the past half a century. In particular, the meteoric rise of China with average GDP growth rate exceeding 9 percent per annum since 1979 has lifted tens of millions out of poverty. Going forward, India as the other large emerging economy with billion-plus population may become the next phenomenal development success. The country has demonstrated great potentials, being the second fastest growing major economy in the world with an average annual GDP growth rate of 7.1 percent in real terms over the 2000–2016 period.[1] Indeed, if Asian economies can sustain the current growth momentums, the total GDP of Asia will once again surpass the West in 2030 after a hiatus of 160 years.[2]

At the same time, the success story of Asia is due in no small part to robust growth among ASEAN economies. Following the success of Singapore, Indonesia, Malaysia and Thailand, the late developers CLMV have adopted the export-led industrialisation model and achieved rapid socio-economic development. Concurrently, economic linkages between ASEAN and other Asian economies, particularly China, have strengthened over the past two to three decades. ASEAN countries have become increasingly integrated into China-centric regional production networks since the 1990s, positioning themselves as exporters of commodities and intermediate goods to China, and benefiting from China's transformation into an exporting behemoth of finished goods. Indeed, China has already become ASEAN's largest trading partner since 2009.

Growing economic interdependencies between ASEAN and China can be demonstrated through ACI's Structural Vector Autoregressive (SVAR) model for eight ASEAN economies and three control economies over the period 2001–2013.[3] By examining the five-year multiplier effects for the periods before and after the introduction of the Masterplan for ASEAN Connectivity (MPAC) in 2010, it is found that although the OECD is still the dominant engine of growth for the eight ASEAN economies, China's growth effect on ASEAN has increased considerably, particularly for Cambodia, Malaysia, Philippines, Singapore and Thailand. In addition, China's growth multipliers on ASEAN countries are drawing near to the OECD's levels (see Tables 6.1–6.3).[4]

---

[1] Based on data from World Bank World Development Indicators.

[2] The forecast is based on an update of the ground-breaking work by Maddison (2007). See Tan *et al.* (2015) for more details.

[3] The eight ASEAN economies in the SVAR model are Brunei (BRN), Cambodia (KHM), Indonesia (IDN), Malaysia (MYS), Philippines (PHL), Singapore (SGP), Thailand (THA) and Vietnam (VTN), and the three control economies are China (CHN), India (IND) and the Organisation for Economic Co-operation and Development (OECD), which includes trading partners Australia, South Korea, Japan, European Union (EU) and US.

[4] Notable values greater than 0.20 are in bold for the result tables.

Table 6.1: Five-year Multiplier Effects of a 1 Percent Point Positive Growth Shock on Each of the 11 Economies (Pre-2010)

	Engines of Growth										
	Eight ASEAN Economies								**Control Economies**		
	BRN	KHM	IDN	MYS	PHL	SGP	THA	VTN	CHN	IND	OECD
BRN	0.751	0.003	0.186	0.128	0.042	0.137	0.073	0.100	**0.409**	0.090	**2.703**
KHM	0.002	1.162	0.114	**0.206**	0.060	**0.241**	0.111	0.193	**0.670**	0.112	**4.406**
IDN	0.001	0.001	0.762	0.042	0.012	0.047	0.021	0.024	0.116	0.022	**0.631**
MYS	0.007	0.013	**0.221**	1.271	0.101	**0.455**	0.207	**0.233**	**0.989**	0.183	**5.376**
PHL	0.003	0.006	0.118	**0.232**	0.836	**0.238**	0.119	0.135	**0.661**	0.101	**3.611**
SGP	0.011	0.019	**0.426**	**0.709**	0.158	1.266	0.294	**0.380**	**1.443**	**0.265**	**7.531**
THA	0.005	0.033	**0.234**	**0.421**	0.122	**0.418**	0.894	**0.304**	**1.135**	0.192	**6.195**
VTN	0.000	0.005	0.021	0.038	0.012	0.041	0.019	1.952	0.117	0.018	**0.686**
CHN	0.002	0.004	0.065	0.114	0.032	0.123	0.063	0.080	1.207	0.066	**2.338**
IND	0.001	0.002	0.039	0.068	0.020	0.080	0.037	0.049	0.214	0.632	**1.209**
OECD	0.001	0.005	0.096	0.175	0.053	0.185	0.096	0.114	0.612	0.100	4.162

Note: Notable values greater than 0.20 are in bold for the result table.
Source: Tan *et al.* (2015).

Table 6.2: Five-year Multiplier Effects of a 1 Percent Point Positive Growth Shock on Each of the 11 Economies (Post-2010)

	Engine of Growth										
	Eight ASEAN Economies								**Control Economies**		
	BRN	KHM	IDN	MYS	PHL	SGP	THA	VTN	CHN	IND	OECD
BRN	0.753	0.009	0.163	**0.203**	0.048	0.180	0.122	**0.266**	**0.745**	0.131	**3.266**
KHM	0.006	1.169	0.184	**0.263**	0.070	**0.318**	0.166	**0.282**	**1.078**	0.151	**4.533**
IDN	0.001	0.003	0.770	0.048	0.013	0.053	0.027	0.040	0.177	0.031	**0.665**
MYS	0.012	0.023	**0.281**	1.278	0.104	**0.451**	**0.238**	**0.358**	**1.426**	**0.221**	**5.243**
PHL	0.006	0.013	0.177	**0.244**	0.844	**0.288**	0.162	**0.241**	**1.035**	0.141	**3.971**
SGP	0.019	0.036	**0.511**	**0.711**	0.154	1.277	**0.328**	**0.552**	**2.014**	**0.309**	**7.333**
THA	0.010	0.057	**0.319**	**0.438**	0.128	**0.425**	**0.929**	**0.448**	**1.636**	**0.239**	**6.131**
VTN	0.000	0.007	0.030	0.042	0.012	0.041	0.025	1.970	0.178	0.024	**0.706**
CHN	0.003	0.009	0.092	0.127	0.038	0.135	0.083	0.136	1.397	0.088	**2.398**
IND	0.003	0.004	0.056	0.072	0.019	0.083	0.041	0.076	**0.297**	**0.642**	**1.188**
OECD	0.005	0.013	0.157	**0.215**	0.065	**0.232**	0.139	**0.224**	**1.048**	0.147	4.747

Note: Notable values greater than 0.20 are in bold for the result table.
Source: Tan *et al.* (2015).

Table 6.3: Differences in Multiplier Effects for the Pre-2010 and Post-2010 Tables

	Engine of Growth										
	Eight ASEAN Economies								**Control Economies**		
	BRN	KHM	IDN	MYS	PHL	SGP	THA	VTN	CHN	IND	OECD
BRN	0.002	0.006	–0.023	0.075	0.006	0.043	0.049	0.166	0.336	0.041	0.563
KHM	0.004	0.007	0.070	0.057	0.010	0.077	0.055	0.089	0.408	0.039	0.127
IDN	0.000	0.002	0.008	0.006	0.001	0.006	0.006	0.016	0.061	0.009	0.034
MYS	0.005	0.010	0.060	0.007	0.003	–0.004	0.031	0.125	0.437	0.038	–0.133
PHL	0.003	0.007	0.059	0.012	0.008	0.050	0.043	0.106	0.374	0.040	0.360
SGP	0.008	0.017	0.085	0.002	–0.004	0.011	0.034	0.172	0.571	0.044	–0.198
THA	0.005	0.024	0.085	0.017	0.006	0.007	0.035	0.144	0.501	0.047	–0.064
VTN	0.000	0.002	0.009	0.004	0.000	0.000	0.006	0.018	0.061	0.006	0.020
CHN	0.001	0.005	0.027	0.013	0.006	0.012	0.020	0.056	0.190	0.022	0.060
IND	0.002	0.002	0.017	0.004	–0.001	0.003	0.004	0.027	0.083	0.010	–0.021
OECD	0.004	0.008	0.061	0.040	0.012	0.047	0.043	0.110	0.436	0.047	0.585

Source: Tan *et al.* (2015).

Growing economic ties between China and ASEAN as demonstrated through the analysis above will facilitate ASEAN's participation in OBOR, which in turn will help to strengthen Sino-ASEAN linkages in a symbiotic relationship. OBOR will prove to be beneficial for all ASEAN economies first and foremost as a means to plug the infrastructure financing gap in the region. The McKinsey Global Institute has estimated that ASEAN requires seven trillion US dollars in real terms (constant 2013 prices) for infrastructure, housing and commercial space from 2014 to 2030.[5] Meanwhile, the Asian Development Bank Institute (ADBI) has noted that the infrastructure investment needs for connectivity of the 32 developing member countries in Asia and the Pacific might reach at least 8.22 trillion US dollars in real terms (constant 2008 prices) between 2010 and 2020. Specifically, 5.47 trillion US dollars, or 67 percent of the total estimate, will be needed for East and Southeast Asia (see Table 6.4). The critical nature of infrastructure investment at this stage of Asian economic growth is well-acknowledged, having been reiterated on multiple occasions by scholars, policy-makers, representatives of the World Bank group and members of the intelligentsia across Asia.[6] Considerable financial resources committed by China to realise OBOR through the AIIB, the Silk Road Fund and the New Development Bank shall go a long way in meeting this need. Moreover, China's proactive role may spur more competition from Japan through the Asian Development Bank (ADB) and perhaps even the US

[5] See McKinsey Global Institute (2014).

[6] At the 2014 ACI Annual Conference, speakers presented their findings on the infrastructure needs of Asia, the AIIB and infrastructure cooperation between emerging powers; see Gopalan (2014), Mandri-Perrott (2014) and Wuryanto (2014).

Table 6.4: Infrastructure Investment Needs in Asia, 2010–2020: Sub-region and Sector (in 2008 Constant Prices Billion US Dollars)

Sector/Sub-sector	East and Southeast Asia	South Asia	Central Asia	The Pacific	Total
Electricity	3,182.46	653.67	167.16	—	4,003.29
Transportation	1,593.87	1,196.12	104.48	4.41	2,898.87
Airports	57.73	5.07	1.41	0.10	64.31
Ports	215.20	36.08	5.38	—	256.65
Rails	16.14	12.78	6.03	0.00	34.95
Roads	1,304.80	1,142.20	91.65	4.31	2,542.97
Telecommunications	524.75	435.62	78.62	1.11	1,040.10
Telephones	142.91	6.46	4.45	0.05	153.87
Mobiles	339.05	415.87	71.97	0.95	827.84
Broadband	42.78	13.29	2.21	0.11	58.39
Water and Sanitation	171.25	85.09	23.40	0.51	280.24
Water	58.37	46.12	8.60	0.14	113.22
Sanitation	112.88	38.97	14.80	0.36	167.02
Total	5,472.33	2,370.50	373.66	6.02	8,222.50

Source: Bhattacharyay (2010).

to augment financial and technical assistance for regional infrastructure development in Asia. Therefore, ASEAN stands to gain from participating in the OBOR.

Besides direct benefits accrued from infrastructure investment, there are other potential synergies between OBOR and ASEAN economies' development strategies which can be exploited to achieve growth take-off. The 21st Century Maritime Silk Road is complementary to President Joko Widodo's vision for Indonesia to become a global maritime axis with enhanced inter-island connectivity and upgraded port infrastructure. Meanwhile, as pointed out by Professor Liew Mun Leong in Chapter 5, Singapore can leverage on its experience and track records in engineering, consultancy and legal services to benefit from OBOR. In particular, OBOR offers a unique opportunity for Singapore as the world's third-most important financial centre and the regional gateway for renminbi to provide financial services for OBOR-related businesses and investments. Finally, the implementation of OBOR will generate high levels of economic activities in OBOR-participating countries. Chinese firms will need partners in providing capital, expertise, technologies and, above all, local knowledge to undertake OBOR projects. Thus, OBOR will create positive spillovers which help to catalyse growth and employment creation in local economies.

For ASEAN countries to reap the most benefits from OBOR, there must be greater efforts to raise awareness, build popular support and prepare for the initiative. Businesses in ASEAN, both big and small, must be alert for potential opportunities arising from OBOR investment in order to grasp the first-mover advantage. In addition, due to the ambitious reach of OBOR to connect

Africa, Asia and Europe, ASEAN young professionals must adopt a global outlook and be ready to venture to OBOR countries in search of opportunities. At the governmental level, Indonesia as the largest economy in ASEAN, supported by Vietnam as the frontrunner of CLMV, should take a lead in fostering closer G to G economic cooperation between ASEAN and China under the OBOR umbrella and ensuring that OBOR projects serve the interest of the ASEAN people.

Insofar as infrastructure development is concerned, ASEAN countries should leverage on their status as founding members of the AIIB to shape the governance structure, operational guidelines and agendas of the institution. They must seek to ensure that the funding mechanisms of the AIIB serve as complementary and supplementary efforts to bolster MPAC through people-centric and sustainable cooperation programmes. Key projects include the ASEAN Highway, the Singapore–Kunming Railway Link, the ASEAN Integrated Inland Waterway Network, and the ASEAN Maritime Transport System, which help to create an integrated seamless multimodal ASEAN transport system. Additionally, ICT infrastructure and services for an e-highway are a given if the bloc is to achieve 21st century connectivity. Above all, electricity is the main crux to powering modern economic activities, so investing in energy infrastructure projects to resolve the energy shortage in many ASEAN countries is also a top priority.

A potential snag for effective Sino-ASEAN cooperation through OBOR is the ongoing territorial disputes between China and some ASEAN states in the South China Sea. Muddying the water, both literally and figuratively, is the larger tussle between China and US for regional influence in the Asia-Pacific. In this context, it is imperative that negotiations on the Code of Conduct on the South China Sea are expedited while all parties to the dispute ensure the implementation of the 2002 Declaration of Conduct of Parties in the South China Sea and pledge to peacefully resolve their disagreements. Furthermore, the maintenance of ASEAN unity is more pressing than ever as ASEAN risks "devolving into a house divided against itself"[7] if member states are to choose sides between the two powers. Member states must strengthen trust among themselves and be active in identifying fault lines which may weaken the bloc's cohesion. In addition, participation in OBOR must be driven by a balance of diverse national interests and the regional agenda anchored by MPAC. This is to minimise the likelihood of overlapping projects in different countries cannibalising one another, thus reducing the efficacy of investments and creating frictions between ASEAN member states.

In the long run, ASEAN should seek to capitalise on its involvement in OBOR, RCEP, APEC and other multilateral cooperation platforms to bring Asian economies together in an Asia Economic Connectivity Vision 2030 (AECV 2030). Proposed by ACI in 2015,[8] AECV2030 has set its sights on becoming a new regional master plan which takes stock of the current prevailing willingness to explore closer Asian inter-sovereign cooperation. AECV2030 pushes for a new wave of people-centric market integration, under an Asian mode of globalisation with full participation from all major Asian economies especially China, Japan, Indonesia and India. Furthermore, the AECV2030 seeks to ensure ASEAN-centrality in the dynamic development of

---

[7] See Mahbubani (2015).

[8] See Tan *et al.* (2015).

Asia and draws on Asians' capabilities, foresight and wisdom to forge new relations and innovative institutions for a collective good.

6.2.2 Stimulating Foreign Direct Investment

As touched on in Chapter 4, there is a large extant literature which emphasises the growth-enhancing nature of FDI, especially in developing economies. The influx of capital through FDI increases capital accumulation in the host economy. Furthermore, given appropriate policies, FDI may also promote technological transfer and diffusion, in addition to augmenting local managerial expertise. While there are a number of factors that could affect FDI, countries are keenly aware of the need to remain cost competitive if they want to continue to attract FDI inflows.

In particular, swings in currencies matter. The FED's ultra-loose policy stance through quantitative easing (QE) in the aftermath of the Global Financial Crisis has resulted in currency appreciations in Asia due to massive capital flows to the region. Meanwhile, the tapering of the same has generated corresponding capital outflows which led to rapid currency depreciations and rising uncertainties, as witnessed during the "taper tantrum" episode of 2013. Although the severity of the impact was felt most keenly by fragile economies with weak fundamentals, ebbs and flows of international capital which are sensitive to US monetary policy adjustments have given rise to a variety of policy challenges concerning exchange rate management in Asia.

Clearly, exchange rate stabilisation and inflation control are important policy priorities for central banks in ASEAN economies. The pursuance of stabilisation measures would help to build foreign investors' confidence in the region, thus helping to attract FDI. In addition, ASEAN economies should aim to enhance transparency and communication in exchange rate policies and eschew short-term beggar-thy-neighbour policies. Financial development, especially enhancing the availability of instruments to hedge against exchange rate risks, should also be encouraged.

In addition to the importance of exchange rate management, our empirical analysis in Chapter 4 found that growth of GDP per capita is positively associated with growth of FDI inflows. This indicates that pro-growth policies are important levers which help ASEAN economies attract FDI. The transformation of the AEC into a "single market and production base" in the truest sense of the phrase will go a long way in enhancing the attractiveness of ASEAN as a whole to foreign investors. To this end, member states must redouble their efforts to fulfil outstanding items under the AEC blueprint.

Moreover, from the experiences of the East Asian economies', especially China, special economic zones (SEZs) — geographic areas with special regulations, policy incentives and priority infrastructure development — are important engines for trade and investments. Properly implemented, SEZs promise to offer spillover of economic activities without being detrimental to the environment for the purposes of employment creation; improvement of local budgetary position through tax revenue collection; productivity enhancement; localisation of management expertise and human resource improvement with social harmony and stability. As a result, setting up SEZs is a cornerstone of the strategy to attract FDI by many ASEAN economies. Vietnam, for instance, is looking to establish three new special administrative–economic zones which offer investors greater incentives and more conducive business environment than existing economic areas designated for preferential policy treatment.

Nevertheless, a comprehensive strategy based on evidence-based research is required for the successful execution of the SEZ model. In light of this, the ACI proposes the formulation of an SEZ Index which assesses the viability, operations and outcomes of SEZs in ASEAN economies, be they existing or under planning. The SEZ index will serve as a basis for detailed analysis to identify strategies to prioritise the development of SEZs so that they may achieve a good level of competition and complementarity with one another at both the national and regional levels. The index will also enable nationwide and cross-border comparison of SEZs across ASEAN economies, thus facilitating cross-country learning and promoting best practices in planning, managing and attracting investment to SEZs. In addition, the proposed index shall help to map and inform the international business community on various investment potentials and opportunities in ASEAN. Details on the ACI's SEZ index may be gleaned from Vu *et al.* (2018, forthcoming).

Finally, for ASEAN countries to move up the industrial ladder, FDI inflows from developed economies must be accompanied by appropriate technological capabilities and human resource for ensuring effective transfer of technology- and knowledge-intensive manufacturing activities from multinational corporations (MNCs) rather than mere employment creation in low value-added processes. Therefore, there must be proactive policies to incentivise technological transfer and the integration of domestic enterprises into MNCs' supply chains. At the same time, strengthening human capital and nurturing best-performing SMEs are crucial if ASEAN economies are to enhance their capabilities to attract and absorb FDI in high value-added activities.

6.3 Future Research Agenda: Impacts of Exchange Rate Movements and Volatility on Exports in the Global Value Chain Context in ASEAN

Together with FDI, trade is a factor which has significant effects on economic growth. Literature such as those by Keesing (1967), Heller and Porter (1978), Balassa (1978), Feder (1983), and Marin (1992) have posited that an increase in exports, in particular, would spur economic growth — a phenomenon more widely-known as "export-led growth". Growth is propelled through the positive externalities exports generate on non-exporters, as well the resulting technological spillovers, optimal reallocation of resources to high productivity export sectors and economies of scale that arise from greater specialisation.

As a region, ASEAN has pushed for a more integrated economy through the establishment of the AEC. A strong external sector remains important to the overall economic performances of the 10-member ASEAN. As illustrated in Chapter 1, the average share of exports of goods and services in GDP for ASEAN-10 has consistently been higher than that for many other regions as well as the world average. Over the period 1995–2015, ASEAN-10's average share of exports in GDP was more than 65 percent.

The nature in which trade is conducted, however, has evolved over the years. Due to advancements in transportation and communication technologies, firms have found it increasingly profitable to split previously integrated production procedures into two or more components located in different countries in a phenomenon known as "production fragmentation".[9] This process has accelerated since the early 1990s, creating sequential production chains or complex production networks that stretch across multiple economies and regions.[10] Such mechanisms are commonly referred to as the global value chains (GVCs). In East and Southeast Asia, global production chains have played an essential role in the expansion of trade.[11] In particular, Athukorala (2005) found that East and Southeast Asian economies are more dependent on production networks than their counterparts in North America and Europe.

The rise of GVCs means that exports are seldom produced in their entirety within a single country using only domestic inputs. On the contrary, exports are likely to contain foreign value-added components. For instance, almost 30 percent of the value content of ASEAN economies' gross exports are generated overseas. Because of the prevalence of GVCs, economies across the globe have become increasingly interconnected and interdependent. As a result, protectionist tendencies are especially dangerous in the current context, as the undoing of the intricate linkages between regional and global production centres will not only unleash great damage on the protectionist country's direct trade partners but will also be an act of self-harm and generate negative ripple effects further down the supply chain.

Furthermore, the rise of GVCs has led to calls to re-evaluate our understanding of trade, especially in the ways it is measured as well as its determinants.[12] One of the crucial factors affecting trade and export performance is movements of exchange rates in terms of their levels and volatility. Recent research has recognised the role of GVC participation on the responses of exports to exchange rate adjustments,[13] but studies on the nexus between GVCs and exchange rates remain relatively few. In addition, current research in this vein has largely focused on the exchange rate elasticity of exports instead of volatility.

The ACI shall attempt to fill this gap. We aim to contribute to the literature by empirically examining the effects of exchange rate movements and volatility on exports of goods and services among ASEAN economies in the GVC context. Moreover, we believe that our proposed ASEAN-centric study will provide ASEAN-specific insights and policy implications for policymakers in the region, thus playing a part in helping ASEAN navigate the increasingly challenging global environment to achieve robust, sustainable and equitable economic development.

References

Amador, João, and Sónia Cabral. 2016. "Global Value Chains: A Survey of Drivers and Measures." *Journal of Economic Surveys* 30(2): 278–301.

Ando, Mitsuyo. 2006. "Fragmentation and Vertical Intra-Industry Trade in East Asia." *North American Journal of Economics and Finance* 17(3): 257–281.

[9] See Jones and Kierzkowski (2001).

[10] See Deardorff (2001), World Trade Organisation (2008), Timmer *et al.* (2014) as well as Amador and Cabral (2016).

[11] See Ng and Yeats (2001), Wakasugi (2007), Ando (2006) as well as Yamano *et al.* (2011).

[12] See Amador and Cabral (2016).

[13] See, for instance, Bems and Johnson (2012).

Athukorala, Prema-Chandra. 2005. "Product Fragmentation and Trade Patterns in East Asia." *Asian Economic Papers* 4(3): 1–27.

Balassa, Bela. 1978. "Exports and Economic Growth: Further Evidence." *Journal of Development Economics* 5(2): 181–189.

Bhattacharyay, Biswa Nath. 2010. "Estimating Demand for Infrastructure in Energy, Transport, Telecommunications, Water and Sanitation in Asia and the Pacific: 2010–2020." ADBI Working Paper Series No. 248, Japan: Asian Development Bank Institute (ADBI).

Bems, Rudolfs, and Robert C. Johnson. 2012. "Value-Added Exchange Rates." NBER Working Paper No. 18498. National Bureau of Economic Research (NBER): Massachusetts.

Deardorff, Alan V. 2001. "Fragmentation in Simple Trade Models." *The North American Journal of Economics and Finance* 12(2): 121–137.

Feder, Gershon. 1983. "On Exports and Economic Growth." *Journal of Development Economics* 12(1–2): 59–73.

Gopalan, Sasidaran. 2014. "A Win-Win China-India Infrastructure Cooperation: Opportunities and Challenges." Presentation at the *2014 Annual Asia Competitiveness Institute Conference on Competitiveness Analysis of 112 Asian Economies, Asia Economic Connectivity, Liveable Cities Index for 100 Greater China Cities and Cost of Living Index for Expatriates and Ordinary Residents.* Singapore, November 26–27.

Heller, Peter S., and Richard C. Porter. 1978. "Exports and Growth: An Empirical Re-Investigation." *Journal of Development Economics* 5(2): 191–193.

Jones, Ronald W., and Henryk Kierzkowski. 2001. "A Framework for Fragmentation." In *Fragmentation: New Production Patterns in the World Economy*, edited by Sven Arndt and Henryk Kierzkowski. Oxford: Oxford University Press.

Keesing, Donald B. 1967. "Outward-Looking Policies and Economic Development." *The Economic Journal* 77(306): 303–320.

Maddison, Angus. 2007. *Contours of the World Economy, 1–2030 AD: Essays in Macroeconomic History.* Oxford: Oxford University Press.

Mahbubani, Kishore. 2015. "ASEAN as a Living, Breathing Modern Miracle." *CIRSD Horizons (2)*: 136–148.

Mandri-Perrott, Cledan. 2014. "Public–Private Partnerships (PPP) and Infrastructure Financing." Presentation at the *2014 Annual Asia Competitiveness Institute Conference on Competitiveness Analysis of 112 Asian Economies, Asia Economic Connectivity, Liveable Cities Index for 100 Greater China Cities and Cost of Living Index for Expatriates and Ordinary Residents*. Singapore, November 26–27.

Marin, Dalia. 1992. "Is the Export-Led Growth Hypothesis Valid for Industrialized Countries?" *The Review of Economics and Statistics* 74(4): 678–688.

McKinsey Global Institute. 2014. *Southeast Asia at the crossroads: Three paths to prosperity*, available at: http://www.mckinsey.com/insights/energy_resources_materials/three_paths_to_sustained_economic_growth_in_southeast_asia (accessed on 20 March, 2015).

Ng, Francis, and Alexander Yeats. 2001. "Production Sharing in East Asia: Who Does What for Whom and Why?" In *Global Production and Trade in East Asia*, edited by Leon and K. Cheng and Henryk Kierzkouski, 63–109. Boston, MA: Springer US.

Tan, Khee Giap, Sangiita Wei Cher Yoong, Sasidaran Gopalan, and Le Phuong Anh Nguyen. 2015. *2014 Annual Competitiveness Ranking and Simulation Study for ASEAN-10 and Development Strategies to Enhance Asia Economic Connectivity*. Singapore: World Scientific.

Timmer, Marcel P., Abdul Azeez Erumban, Bart Los, Robert Stehrer, and Gaaitzen J. de Vries. 2014. "Slicing Up Global Value Chains." *The Journal of Economic Perspectives* 28(2): 99–118.

Vu, Tien Loc, Khee Giap Tan, Nguyen Trieu Duong Luu, and Duy Nguyen. 2018 (forthcoming). *Balanced, Sustainable and Competitiveness Enhancement Study for Vietnam: A Critical Evaluation with Development Potentials*. Singapore: Asia Competitiveness Institute.

Wakasugi, Ryuhei. 2007. "Vertical Intra-Industry Trade and Economic Integration in East Asia." *Asian Economic Papers* 6(1): 26–45.

Wuryanto, Luky Eko. 2014. "Accelerating Infrastructure Development Programs and Expected Roles of AIIB." Presentation at the *2014 Annual Asia Competitiveness Institute Conference on Competitiveness Analysis of 112 Asian Economies, Asia Economic Connectivity, Liveable Cities Index for 100 Greater China Cities and Cost of Living Index for Expatriates and Ordinary Residents*. Singapore, November 26–27.

World Trade Organisation. 2008. "Trade, the Location of Production and the Industrial Organization of Firms." In *Trade in a Globalizing World*, 81–122. World Trade Report 2008. Geneva: World Trade Organisation.

Yamano, Norihiko, Meng Bo, and Kiichiro Fukasaku. 2011. "Fragmentation and Changes in the Asian Trade Network." *ERIA Policy Brief*. Jakarta: Economic Research Institute for ASEAN and East Asia (ERIA).

Appendix 1

Competitiveness Analysis of ASEAN-10 Economies, 2000–2014

List of Indicators

No.	Indicator	Unit	Reversed Indicator*
1	**Macroeconomic Stability**		
1.1	**Economic Vibrancy**		
1.1.01	Gross Domestic Product	US Dollars, Constant 2000 Prices	
1.1.02	Real GDP Growth	Percentage Change Per Annum	
1.1.03	GDP Per Capita	US Dollars, Constant 2000 Prices	
1.1.04	Output Agriculture (Value Added)	US Dollars, Constant 2005 Prices	
1.1.05	Output Industry (Value Added)	US Dollars, Constant 2005 Prices	
1.1.06	Output Services (Value Added)	US Dollars, Constant 2005 Prices	
1.1.07	Gross Domestic Savings	Percentage of GDP	
1.1.08	Gross Fixed Capital Formation	Percentage of GDP	
1.1.09	Inflation	Percentage Change Per Annum	R
1.1.10	Money Supply Growth (M2)	Percentage Change Per Annum	R
1.2	**Openness to Trade and Services**		
1.2.01	Current Account Balance	Percentage of GDP	
1.2.02	Exports of Goods and Services	US Dollars, Current Market Prices	
1.2.03	Imports of Goods and Services	US Dollars, Current Market Prices	
1.2.04	Openness to Trade	Ratio	
1.2.05	International Tourism Receipts	US Dollars, Current Market Prices	
1.3	**Attractiveness to Foreign Investors**		
1.3.01	Foreign Direct Investment Inflows	US Dollars, Current Market Prices	
1.3.02	Foreign Owned Companies	Survey Data	
1.3.03	Corporate Income Tax	Percentage of Profit	R
1.3.04	Lack of Discrimination Against Investors	Survey Data	
1.3.05	Levelness of Playing Field	Survey Data	
1.3.06	Transparency of Processes for Investors	Survey Data	
1.3.07	Business Impact of Rules on FDI	Survey Data	

(Continued)

(*Continued*)

No.	Indicator	Unit	Reversed Indicator*
2	**Government and Institutional Setting**		
2.1	**Government Policies and Fiscal Sustainability**		
2.1.01	Government Revenue (Including Grants)	US Dollars, 2000 Constant Prices	
2.1.02	Tax Revenue	US Dollars, 2000 Constant Prices	
2.1.03	Tax Revenue/Government Revenue	Percentage	
2.1.04	Government Consumption Expenditure	Percentage of GDP	
2.1.05	External Debt	US Dollars, Current Market Prices	R
2.1.06	International Reserves	US Dollars, Current Market Prices	
2.1.07	Net Foreign Assets	US Dollars, Current Market Prices	
2.1.08	International Monetary Fund Credit	US Dollars, Current Market Prices	R
2.1.09	Budget Balance	Percentage of GDP	
2.1.10	Tax Burden	Percentage of GDP	R
2.1.11	Money Supply (M2)	Percentage of GDP	
2.1.12	Deposit Interest Rate	Percentage	
2.1.13	Lending Rate	Percentage	R
2.1.14	Interest Rate Spread	Percentage	R
2.1.15	Exchange Rate Appreciation	Annual Average Percentage Change (Local Currency Unit per US Dollar)	R
2.2	**Institutions, Governance and Leadership**		
2.2.01	Quality of Government Policies	Survey Data	
2.2.02	Government Effectiveness	Survey Data	
2.2.03	Government Environmental Protection Policies	Percentage of Total Territorial Area	
2.2.04	Quality of Central Bank/Monetary Authority	Survey Data	
2.2.05	Government Stability	Survey Data	
2.2.06	Government Responsiveness	Survey Data	
2.2.07	Quality of Political Leadership	Survey Data	R
2.2.08	Political System Risk	Survey Data	R
2.2.09	Legislature/Parliament (Functioning of Government System)	Survey Data	
2.2.10	Strength of Auditing and Reporting Standards	Survey Data	
2.2.11	Institutional Sophistication	Survey Data	
2.2.12	Bureaucracy/Red Tape	Survey Data	
2.2.13	Lack of Corruption	Survey Data	
2.2.14	Lack of Cronyism	Survey Data	
2.2.15	Lack of Market Distortion due to State-Ownership	Survey Data	

(*Continued*)

(*Continued*)

No.	Indicator	Unit	Reversed Indicator*
2.3	**Competition, Regulatory Standards and Rule of Law**		
2.3.01	Corporate Governance	Survey Data	
2.3.02	Quality of Regulatory Environment	Survey Data	
2.3.03	Transparency of Government	Survey Data	
2.3.04	Monopolies and Cartel	Survey Data	
2.3.05	Policy Towards Private Enterprise Rating	Survey Data	
2.3.06	Ease of Starting Business	Number	R
2.3.07	Barriers to Trade	Survey Data	
2.3.08	Intellectual Property Rights Protection	Survey Data	
2.3.09	Regional Competitiveness	Survey Data	
2.3.10	Quality of Judiciary	Survey Data	
2.3.11	Effectiveness of Legal System	Survey Data	
2.3.12	Integrity of Legal System	Survey Data	
2.3.13	Quality of Police	Survey Data	
2.3.14	Political Change	Survey Data	
3	**Financial, Businesses and Manpower Conditions**		
3.1	**Financial Deepening and Business Efficiency**		
3.1.01	Claims on Private Sector	Annual Growth as Percentage of Broad Money	
3.1.02	Domestic Credit to Private Sector	Percentage of GDP	
3.1.03	Quality of Banking and Financial System	Survey Data	
3.1.04	Domestic Credit Provided by the Financial Sector	Percentage of GDP	
3.1.05	Listed Domestic Companies	Number	
3.1.06	Market Capitalisation	US Dollars, Current Market Prices	
3.1.07	Total Value of Stocks Traded	Percentage of GDP	
3.1.08	Sovereign Debt Risk	Number	R
3.1.09	Quality of Stock Market Regulatory Authority	Survey Data	
3.2	**Labour Market Flexibility**		
3.2.01	Labour Force	Number	
3.2.02	Unemployment Rate	Percentage	R
3.2.03	Cost of Production Labour	US Dollars, Current Market Prices	R
3.2.04	Availability of Scientists and Engineers	Survey Data	
3.2.05	Cost of Management Staff	US Dollars, Current Market Prices	R
3.2.06	High-quality Management Staff	Survey Data	

(*Continued*)

(*Continued*)

No.	Indicator	Unit	Reversed Indicator*
3.2.07	Extent of Staff Training	Survey Data	
3.2.08	Labour Market Rating	Survey Data	
3.3	**Productivity Performance**		
3.3.01	Agriculture, Value Added Per Worker	US Dollars, 2005 Constant Prices	
3.3.02	Industry, Value Added Per Worker	US Dollars, 2005 Constant Prices	
3.3.03	Services, Value Added Per Worker	US Dollars, 2005 Constant Prices	
4	**Quality of Life and Infrastructure Development**		
4.1	**Physical Infrastructure**		
4.1.01	Population	Number	
4.1.02	Local Road System	Survey Data	
4.1.03	Rail Facilities	Survey Data	
4.1.04	Airport Facilities	Survey Data	
4.1.05	Port Facilities	Survey Data	
4.1.06	Electric Power	Survey Data	
4.1.07	Access to Water	Percentage of Population	
4.1.08	Access to Sanitation	Percentage of Population	
4.2	**Technological Infrastructure**		
4.2.01	Telecommunications System	Percentage of GDP	
4.2.02	Telephone Main Lines	Number Per 100 Persons	
4.2.03	Internet Subscribers	Number Per 100 Persons	
4.2.04	Cellular Mobile Telephone Subscribers	Number Per 100 Persons	
4.2.05	Networked Readiness Index	Survey Data	
4.2.06	Personal Computers	Number Per 100 Persons	
4.2.07	Information and Communication Technology (ICT) Expenditure	Percentage of GDP	
4.3	**Standard of Living, Education and Social Stability**		
4.3.01	Literacy Rate	Percentage	
4.3.02	Primary Schooling	Percentage	
4.3.03	Secondary Schooling	Percentage	
4.3.04	University and Post-Graduate Education	Percentage	
4.3.05	Human Development Index	Composite Statistic	
4.3.06	Health Expenditure	Percentage of GDP	
4.3.07	Urban Population	Percentage of Total Population	
4.3.08	Urban Population Growth	Percentage Per Annum	
4.3.09	Public Security and Safety	Survey Data	

(*Continued*)

(*Continued*)

No.	Indicator	Unit	Reversed Indicator*
4.3.10	Freedom of Press	Survey Data	R
4.3.11	Freedom of Speech	Survey Data	
4.3.12	Access to Print Media	Number	
4.3.13	Freedom of Religion	Survey Data	
4.3.14	Religious Unrest	Survey Data	
4.3.15	Labour Unrest	Survey Data	
4.3.16	Social Unrest	Survey Data	
4.3.17	Labour Activism	Survey Data	R
4.3.18	Daily Organic Water Pollutant Emissions	Kilogram Per 100 Persons	R
4.3.19	Air Quality	Micrograms Per Cubic Metre	R
4.3.20	Traffic Congestion	Number of Vehicles Per Kilometre of Road	R

Note: * R indicates that the indicator is a reversed indicator.
Source: Asia Competitiveness Institute.

Appendix 2
Competitiveness Analysis — The Algorithm

A step-by-step description of the ranking process is described below for N economies, M practical indicators and C environments, with each environment comprising S sub-environments.

(1) Compute the mean value of practical indicator j ($j = 1, \ldots, M$),

$$\bar{X}_j = \frac{1}{N}\sum_{i=1}^{N} X_{ij}$$

where X_{ij} represents the value that economy i ($i = 1, \ldots, N$) takes for practical indicator j.

(2) For each practical indicator j ($j = 1, \ldots, M$), calculate its standard deviation (SD),

$$SD_j = \sqrt{\frac{1}{N}\sum_{i=1}^{N}\left(X_{ij} - \bar{X}_j\right)^2}$$

(3) Compute the standardised value of indicator (SVI) that each economy i ($i = 1, \ldots, N$) takes under each of the practical indicators j ($j = 1, \ldots, M$),

$$SVI_{ij} = \frac{X_{ij} - \bar{X}_j}{SD_j}$$

(4) Compute the "ranked" standardised value of indicator (RSVI) that each economy i ($i = 1, \ldots, N$) takes under each of the practical indicators j ($j = 1, \ldots, M$),

$$RSVI_{ij} = \begin{cases} SVI_{ij}, & \text{if a higher value is better} \\ -SVI_{ij}, & \text{if a lower value is better} \end{cases}$$

(5) For each of the practical indicators j ($j = 1, \ldots, M$), a ranking can be obtained for economies: economies with a higher value of RSVI for indicator j are ranked ahead of those with a lower value.

(6) For each economy i ($i = 1, \ldots, N$), calculate the RSVI for each sub-environment k ($k = 1, \ldots, S$) belonging to environment l ($l = 1, \ldots, C$),

$$Raw\_RSVI_{i,lk} = \frac{1}{y_{lk}}\sum_{p=1}^{y_{lk}} RSVI_{i,j_{lk,p}}$$

$$Mean\_RSVI_{lk} = \frac{1}{N}\sum_{i=1}^{N} Raw\_RSVI_{i,lk}$$

$$SD\_RSVI_{lk} = \sqrt{\frac{1}{N}\sum_{i=1}^{N}\left(Raw\_RSVI_{i,lk} - Mean\_RSVI_{lk}\right)^2}$$

$$RSVI_{i,lk} = \frac{Raw\_RSVI_{i,lk} - Mean\_RSVI_{lk}}{SD\_RSVI_{lk}}$$

where y_{lk} is the total number of practical indicators under sub-environment k of environment l and $(RSVI_{i,jlk,1}, \ldots, RSVI_{i,jlk,ylk})$ are the RSVIs for economy i that make up sub-environment k of environment l.

(7) For each economy i ($i = 1, \ldots, N$), calculate the RSVI for each environment l ($l = 1, \ldots, C$),

$$Raw\_RSVI_{i,l} = \frac{1}{S_l}\sum_{k=1}^{S_l} RSVI_{i,lk}$$

$$Mean\_RSVI_{l} = \frac{1}{N}\sum_{i=1}^{N} Raw\_RSVI_{i,l}$$

$$SD\_RSVI_{l} = \sqrt{\frac{1}{N}\sum_{i=1}^{N}\left(Raw\_RSVI_{i,l} - Mean\_RSVI_{l}\right)^2}$$

$$RSVI_{i,l} = \frac{Raw\_RSVI_{i,l} - Mean\_RSVI_{l}}{SD\_RSVI_{l}}$$

where $(RSV_{li,l1}, \ldots, RSV_{li,lS})$ are the RSVIs for the S sub-environments under each environment l.

(8) Overall score of economy i ($i = 1, \ldots, N$) is

$$Raw\_R_{i} = \frac{1}{C}\sum_{l=1}^{C} RSVI_{i,l}$$

$$Mean\_R = \frac{1}{N}\sum_{i=1}^{N} Raw\_R_{i}$$

$$SD\_R = \sqrt{\frac{1}{N}\sum_{i=1}^{N}\left(Raw\_R_{i} - Mean\_R\right)^2}$$

$$R_{i} = \frac{Raw\_R_{i} - Mean\_R}{SD\_R}$$

Economies with a higher R_i are ranked ahead of those with lower value of R_i, and the economy with the highest R_i is the most competitive economy.

Step (5) provides the ranking of each economy for each individual practical indicator. To achieve this ranking, Step (4) adjusts the value of the SVIs so that a higher value will lead to a better ranking in terms of "competitiveness". Depending on the nature of the indicator in question, a higher or lower value may reflect a more "competitive" economy. Take, for instance, the practical sub-indicators "Gross Domestic Product (GDP)" and "Unemployment Rate". A higher GDP but a lower "unemployment rate" suggests better economic performance, which makes an economy more "competitive". In most cases where a higher value is better (e.g. GDP), the SVIs of regions are considered, and those with a higher SVI value will have a better ranking. However, for indicators where the inverse is true (e.g. Unemployment Rate), the "negative SVI" values are compared between economies and a lower SVI value will lead to a better ranking. Step (4) thus seeks to make all standardised values of all practical indicators consistent for ranking purposes.

Step (6) determines the sub-environment rankings of each economy. The average RSVI of all the indicators in the sub-environment are calculated, restandardised across all the economies and compared to other economies. Economies with a higher average RSVI rank better in the sub-environment.

To arrive at the ranking for each environment, the RSVIs of the sub-environments are averaged and restandardised across all economies as detailed in Step (7). Finally, Step (8) requires the RSVI values of each environment to be averaged and restandardised across all economies to determine the overall ranking of the economy. Economies with a higher RSVI are ranked ahead of those with a lower RSVI.

Although the number of sub-environments and indicators may vary for each environment, the aggregate score for each environment is given an equal weight, which is 25% of the ASEAN-10 Overall Competitiveness Index. This method is repeated and applied consistently across all economies to ensure precision of the ranking. Mathematically, this can be illustrated as follows:

ASEAN-10 Overall Competitiveness Index:
= 25% × (Macroeconomic Stability)
+25% × (Government and Institutional Setting)
+25% × (Financial, Businesses and Manpower Conditions)
+25% × (Quality of Life and Infrastructure Development)

Appendix 3
The Shapley Value Methodology

Shapley value is widely applied in cooperative game theory, and it measures the marginal contribution of an agent. In our context, the agent could be indicators, sub-environments and environments. The formula for Shapley value is as follows:

$$\Phi(v) = \sum_{S \subseteq N \setminus \{i\}} \frac{|S|!(N - |S| - 1)!}{N!} (v(S \cup i) - v(S))$$

With different marginal contribution to the overall competitiveness ranking, different weights can be assigned to indicators, sub-environments and environments. We propose an objective weighting method based on Shapley value — the "Bottom-Up" approach as a robustness check to the equal weightage methodology of the competitiveness framework by the Asia Competitiveness Institute (ACI).

Formally, let v^I be the characteristic function of the indicators, where $v^I: 2^I \to \mathbb{R}$. Then for each indicator $i \in I$, $v^I(i): \mathbb{R}^E \to \mathbb{R}$, which reflects that the value of indicator i is derived from X_{ei} for all $e \in E$. As we involve a large number of indicators in our case studies, for the ease of numerical computation, we simply define

$$v^I(i) = \sum_{e=1}^{E} |SV_{ei}|$$

We further assume the Additivity of the characteristic function v^I, i.e. $v^I(i \cup j) = v^I(i) + v^I(j)$ for any indicator $i, j \in I$.

With all these defined, we are able to proceed with the computation of the Shapley value Φ_i^I of indicator $i \in I$:

$$\Phi_i^I = \sum_{\mathbb{I} \subseteq I \setminus \{i\}} \frac{|\mathbb{I}|!(I - |\mathbb{I}| - 1)!}{I!} (v^I(\mathbb{I} \cup i) - v^I(\mathbb{I})) \quad \text{for all } i \in I$$

$$= \sum_{\mathbb{I} \subseteq I \setminus \{i\}} \frac{|\mathbb{I}|!(I - |\mathbb{I}| - 1)!}{I!} (v^I(\mathbb{I} \cup i) - v^I(\mathbb{I})) = \sum_{\mathbb{I} \subseteq I \setminus \{i\}} \frac{|\mathbb{I}|!(I - |\mathbb{I}| - 1)!}{I!} v^I(i) = v^I(i) \cdot$$

Then the indicator weight w_i^I based on Shapley value is simply

$$w_i^I = \frac{\Phi_i^I}{\sum_{j=1}^{I} \Phi_j^I} = \frac{v^I(i)}{\sum_{j=1}^{I} v^I(j)}$$

To operationalise this framework, we pursue the following "Bottom-Up" approach to calculate ACI's competitiveness index based on Shapley weights. First, we start from the lowest level of analysis (indicators) and identify the inequality of the units being measured (economies and sub-national economies). This is called the "Shapley value", which is computed from the standardised score of each indicator. Subsequently, the Shapley value is used to calculate Shapley weight, where more weights are assigned to those indicators with higher Shapley values. Next, the weights of sub-environments are computed in "bottom-up" manner according to both **standardised scores** and **Shapley weights** of indicators under that particular sub-environment. Finally, the weights of Environments and Overall Index are computed in a similar way.

Asia Competitiveness Institute - World Scientific Series

(Continued from page vi)

2016 Growth Slowdown Analysis by Income Thresholds and Annual Update of Competitiveness Analysis for 34 Greater China Economies
by Tan Khee Giap, Wang Peng & Xie Teleixi (Lee Kuan Yew School of Public Policy, NUS, Singapore)

Inaugural 2016 Ease of Doing Business Index on Attractiveness to Investors, Business Friendliness and Competitive Policies (EDB Index ABC) for 21 Sub-National Economies of India
by Tan Khee Giap, Sasidaran Gopalan, Jigyasa Sharma & Tan Kong Yam (Lee Kuan Yew School of Public Policy, NUS, Singapore)

2016 Annual Competitiveness and Growth Slowdown Analysis for Sub-National Economies of India
by Tan Khee Giap, Sasidaran Gopalan, Anuja Tandon & Tan Kong Yam (Lee Kuan Yew School of Public Policy, NUS, Singapore)

2016 Growth Slowdown Analysis, Ease of Doing Business Index, and Annual Competitiveness Studies of Indonesia's Sub-National Economies
by Tan Khee Giap, Mulya Amri, Nursyahida Ahmad & Tan Kong Yam (Lee Kuan Yew School of Public Policy, NUS, Singapore)

2016 Annual Competitiveness Analysis and Development Strategies for Indonesian Provinces
by Tan Khee Giap, Mulya Amri & Nursyahida Ahmad (Lee Kuan Yew School of Public Policy, NUS, Singapore)

2015

2015 Annual Competitiveness Analysis, Agricultural Productivity and Development Vision for ASEAN-10
by Tan Khee Giap, Nguyen Le Phuong Anh, Sasidaran Gopalan & Luu Nguyen Trieu Duong (Lee Kuan Yew School of Public Policy, NUS, Singapore)

2015 Estimation of Agricultural Productivity and Annual Update of Competitiveness Analysis for Greater China: Optimising Agricultural Productivity and Promoting Innovation Driven Growth
by Tan Khee Giap, Yuan Randong & Xie Teleixi (Lee Kuan Yew School of Public Policy, NUS, Singapore)

2015 Agricultural Total Factor Productivity and Competitiveness Analysis for States and Federal Territories and Five Regions of India: Annual Competitiveness Update and Evidence on the Agricultural Development Models for Selected Indian States
by Tan Khee Giap, Sasidaran Gopalan & Anuja Tandon (Lee Kuan Yew School of Public Policy, NUS, Singapore)

2015 Agricultural Productivity, Decentralisation, and Competitiveness Analysis for Provinces and Regions of Indonesia
by Tan Khee Giap, Nurina Merdikawati, Mulya Amri & Tan Kong Yam (Lee Kuan Yew School of Public Policy, NUS, Singapore)

2015 Annual Competitiveness Analysis and Development Strategies for Indonesian Provinces
by Tan Khee Giap, Mulya Amri, Nurina Merdikawati & Nursyahida Ahmad (Lee Kuan Yew School of Public Policy, NUS, Singapore)

2014

2014 Annual Competitiveness Ranking and Simulation Study for ASEAN-10 and Development Strategies to Enhance Asia Economic Connectivity
by Tan Khee Giap, Sangiita Yoong Wei Cher, Sasidaran Gopalan & Nguyen Le Phuong Anh (Lee Kuan Yew School of Public Policy, NUS, Singapore)

2014 Annual Provincial and Regional Competitiveness Analysis for Greater China Economies: Development Strategies under the New Normal
by Tan Khee Giap, Yuan Randong & Sangiita Yoong Wei Cher (Lee Kuan Yew School of Public Policy, NUS, Singapore)

2014 Regional Competitiveness Analysis and a Master Plan on Regional Development Strategies for India: Annual Competitiveness Update and Evidence on Economic Development Model for Selected States of India
by Tan Khee Giap, Linda Low, Kartik Rao & Tan Kong Yam (Lee Kuan Yew School of Public Policy, NUS, Singapore)

2014 Provincial and Inaugural Regional Competitiveness Analysis: Safeguarding Indonesia's Growth Momentum
by Tan Khee Giap, Nurina Merdikawati, Mulya Amri & Tan Kong Yam (Lee Kuan Yew School of Public Policy, NUS, Singapore)

2014 Annual Competitiveness Analysis and Development Strategies for Indonesian Provinces
by Tan Khee Giap, Nurina Merdikawati, Mulya Amri & Blake Harley Berger (Lee Kuan Yew School of Public Policy, NUS, Singapore)

2013

Annual Analysis of Competitiveness, Simulation Studies and Development Perspective for 34 Greater China Economies: 2000–2010
by Tan Khee Giap, Yuan Randong, Sangiita Yoong Wei Cher & Yang Mu (Lee Kuan Yew School of Public Policy, NUS, Singapore)

Annual Analysis of Competitiveness, Simulation Studies and Development Perspective for 35 States and Federal Territories of India: 2000–2010
by Tan Khee Giap, Linda Low, Tan Kong Yam & Kartik Rao (Lee Kuan Yew School of Public Policy, NUS, Singapore)

Competitiveness Analysis and Development Strategies for 33 Indonesian Provinces
by Tan Khee Giap, Mulya Amri, Linda Low & Tan Kong Yam (Lee Kuan Yew School of Public Policy, NUS, Singapore)